FLYING
7 CONTINENTS
SOLO

FLYING
7 CONTINENTS
SOLO

HARRY R. ANDERSON, Ph.D., P.E.
Bainbridge Island, WA USA

Copyright © 2015 by Harry R. Anderson

All rights reserved. No part of this publication may be reproduced, distributed, or transmitted in any form or by any means, including photocopying, recording, or other electronic or mechanical methods, without the prior written permission of the publisher, except in the case of brief quotations embodied in critical reviews and certain other noncommercial uses permitted by copyright law. For permission requests, write to the publisher, addressed "Attention: Permissions Coordinator," at the address below.

PHYwave, Inc.
250 Eagle Place NE
Bainbridge Island, WA 98110
www.phywave.com/publishing

Email: publishing@phywave.com

Printed in the United States of America

First Edition

ISBN 978-0-9967450-1-7

Cover photo by Harry R. Anderson

Contents

Chapter 1	Christmas Island	1
Chapter 2	Flight Preparations	8
Chapter 3	Crossing the United States	20
Chapter 4	Crossing the Atlantic	32
Chapter 5	England	45
Chapter 6	England to Greece	52
Chapter 7	Greece to Dubai	65
Chapter 8	Dubai to Thailand	77
Chapter 9	Thailand to Australia	94
Chapter 10	Crossing Australia	106
Chapter 11	Australia to Hawaii	114
Chapter 12	Hawaii to California – The Longest Flight	132
Chapter 13	Heading Home – the Final Flights	141
Chapter 14	Preparations for Antarctica	146
Chapter 15	Oregon to Florida	154
Chapter 16	Crossing the Caribbean	165
Chapter 17	On to Brazil	177
Chapter 18	Southbound Through Argentina	195
Chapter 19	Waiting in Punta Arenas	207
Chapter 20	Giving Up and Going North	222
Chapter 21	Chile and Easter Island	233
Chapter 22	Peru and Machu Picchu	244
Chapter 23	North to the USA	254
Chapter 24	Westward and Home	264
Chapter 25	Re-Thinking Antartica	272
Chapter 26	Santiago Southward	277
Chapter 27	King George Island, Antarctica	284
Epilogue		295

Appendices

Appendix A	Aviation Terminology	297
Appendix B	Resources and Websites	305
Appendix C	N788W Weight and Balance	313
Appendix D	Flight Plan Routes	315
Appendix E	Entry Procedures for Australia and Brazil	321
Appendix F	Self-Handling at Brazilian Airports	325
Appendix G	Antarctica Permit Documents	334

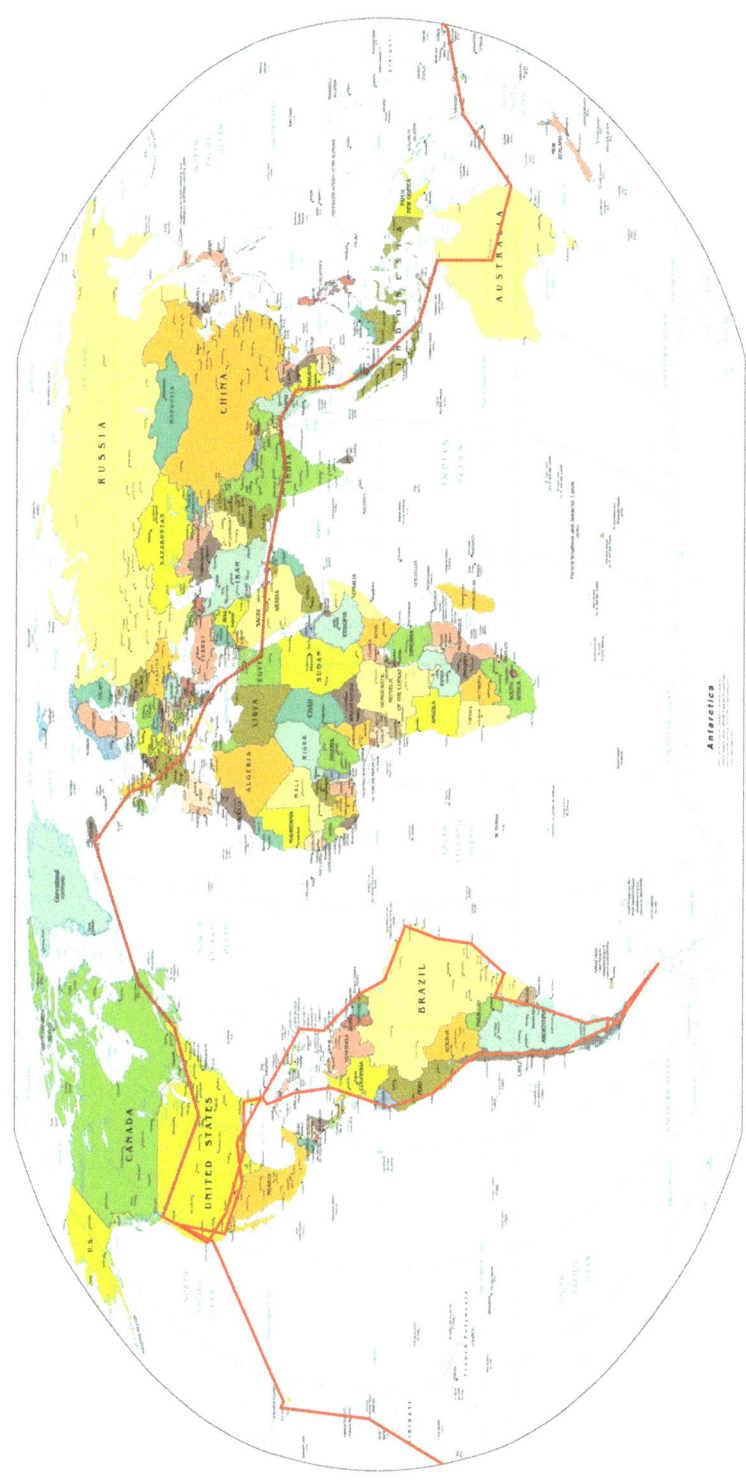

1

Christmas Island

I could set my watch by when the sun rose and set. Near the equator, sunrise and sunset vary only a few minutes either way, so I was unlikely to arrive late for anything I might want to do, but schedules don't matter much here anyway. I remember in Kenya they used to call it "Swahili time." Zero hour was when the sun rose. Many bus schedules in Eastern Africa were given in Swahili time – it was easy to miss the bus if you didn't know that.

I didn't wake up with the sunrise on Christmas Island. I was already lying awake listening to a rat nibble away at something in the wall of the one-story, concrete-block Captain Cook Hotel, one of two quasi-hotels on this coral atoll 1200 miles south of Hawaii, very near the equator. The name was appropriate. Captain Cook christened this island, at the time uninhabited, when he came across it on Christmas Eve in 1777 on one of his repeated far-flung explorations around the Pacific Ocean. Although Cook named it, there is evidence that a Spanish explorer claimed to be the first European to sight it in the 16th century. It is now part of the Pacific island country of Kiribati and officially known as Kiritimati, an approximation of "Christmas" in the Kiribati language where "ti" is pronounced as "s". Really.

None of that history mattered to me. More recent history, that the British and Americans had both used Christmas Island for airborne tests of nuclear weapons in the late 1950s and early 1960s, without even relocating the inhabitants, gave me pause. Would I see giant mutant coconut crabs climbing the palm trees? Maybe it was a bad idea to dig my toes too deeply into the sand and risk encountering a layer that was still radioactive? I knew nothing, so I was resigned to being a little wary of the most common things.

The rat already had breakfast, so I pulled on my shorts, T-shirt, and sandals and wandered outside in the direction of the dining room where I found a flurry of activity already under way. The main reason anyone visits Christmas Island is to fish, in particular, to fish for bonefish. This island is the bonefishing capital of the world, so the dozen or so fisherman tourists from all over the world staying at the hotel were already awake making sandwiches at a makeshift sandwich bar the hotel's cook had set up. They piled the sandwiches high and packed them away for lunch later. A chalkboard in the dining room was filled with columns of guest names scrawled under the names of fishing guides – the group assignments for the day. I sat down with a cup of coffee and watched the low-key logistical spectacle of these fishermen assembling gear, sandwiches, ridiculously huge sun hats, fishing vests, etc., tossing everything into the back of their guide's 4x4 truck, and heading off down a sand/dirt track to a remote lagoon somewhere on the island. By the time I felt like having the cook fry me some eggs, the fishermen were gone.

Captain Cook Hotel, Christmas Island

I've very occasionally fished in rivers back home in the Pacific Northwest, when friends dragged me along, but I am definitely not a fisherman. I couldn't appreciate the excitement of these fishermen about going to shallow lagoons to hook bonefish that, once hooked, apparently take off at 25 mph across the water, dragging line off the reel so rapidly you have to dip it in the water to cool off the friction heat. They would come back in the evening bragging of three-figure days, actually hooking and catching over a hundred fish of all types in one day. I was too blurry-eyed that morning from the party last night to do the math, which figures to averaging one catch every five minutes or so.

Technically, I crashed the party last night, although the good-natured Australians throwing the party were happy to invite me once I was already on the beach drinking their beer. The Australians were part of a construction crew on the island to fix up the runway at the airport. Two of them were rotating back home for a break from Kiritimati on the Fijian Air flight arriving the following day. A going-away party, a coming-to-the-island party: they didn't need much excuse for a party. This one seemed to be a special event, an elaborate grand banquet with a pig roast and the local (world-renowned!) Kiritimati dance troupe performing after dinner. The charming young girls in their wraparound lava-lavas faithfully went through their routines, no doubt conveying some old island history or maybe aspects of daily life, but it was lost on me. It was sometimes slow and peaceful, sometimes mournful, sometimes full of energy. I liked it all; I didn't need to understand it.

Captain Cook Hotel, Christmas Island

I had only arrived on Christmas Island myself late that afternoon, so the evening's event was a total surprise. I've never been very successful at keeping up with Australians when it comes to drinking beer so I made my excuses early and headed off to bed while the hard-core group continued to have fun on the beach late into the night.

I'm not a fisherman and I don't build runways, so what was I doing here? On the chalkboard where they kept track of what hotel guests were doing, they had written "ferry pilot" instead of my name. I smiled at that. I was not the first of my type to arrive here and I would be gone as soon as possible, so there was no point to learning my name.

There were at least two answers to the question of why I was there. Maybe I could contrive a third by strolling down the beach, collecting seashells and anything else that washed ashore to become an itinerate beachcomber in the enduring South Sea tradition. The easy, obvious, straightforward answer starts with an airplane. I am a pilot. I am flying my little single-engine airplane around the world. Christmas Island is the logical intermediate place to stop and refuel when flying from Pago Pago in American Samoa to Hawaii. Airplanes being re-located (ferried) between the United States and Australia or other South Sea destinations routinely stop at Christmas Island, provided there is fuel for their planes, which is not always the case. It is usually easier to relocate a plane by flying it somewhere rather than taking the wings off, putting it

Christmas Island airport terminal

in a crate, and shipping it. Ferry pilots charge a lot of money to fly these ferry flights, in no small part because of the risk associated with flying over long stretches of open ocean where an engine failure will certainly put you in the water far from shipping lanes and any chance of a speedy rescue, assuming you survived the crash landing, euphemistically known among pilots as an "off airport" water landing. Ha! This was the business of ferry pilots; it was about the money, not seashells or bonefish.

Last night, between the first beer I bought at the little hotel bar and the beach party, I had pulled out my satellite phone, sat outside at a rickety picnic table under a palm tree, and stared at the phone's LCD screen as it booted up and searched the twilight sky for a useable signal. I needed to call Hawaii, not because I knew anybody in Hawaii - I didn't - but they had weather forecasters whose uncomfortably ambiguous pronouncements nevertheless impacted whether I could expect flying to be a dangerous, turbulent misery or a blue sky

Christmas Island beaches

dawdle. Most of these forecasters speak monotone weather-speak, so I felt lucky to talk to a surprisingly articulate young woman who, after giving me the required chapter and verse of what the 36–hour forecast showed, concluded with something simple and actionable. "Wait a day," she said.

Having just flown 1100 nautical miles north from Pago Pago to Christmas Island, I now had to address the weather between Christmas Island and Hawaii, where the dreaded Inter-Tropical Convergence Zone (ITCZ) was currently positioned. This zone is where the weather systems of the northern and southern hemispheres crash into each other. They are usually not happy about the encounter and throw fits full of angry thunderstorms, sometimes even hurricanes, that can turn little planes into twisted metal pretzels that ultimately hit the ocean surface and disappear without a trace. The forecast showed a break in the conga line of convergence zone thunderstorms along my track for the day after tomorrow. Wait a day, she said. OK, I can do that.

My layover day was mostly empty, except I returned to the airport to have the plane refueled rather than wait for the day of departure. K-OIL, the company that handles fueling here, showed up with two of the rustiest barrels I had ever seen. "It's a new shipment" they explained, which I knew to be true since not that many weeks before they'd had no aviation gas. These barrels had obviously been sitting around outside in a fuel depot somewhere for quite a while. But they were sealed, and the fuel guys poured a sample into a bucket for me to check. Like at many of the more remote places I've stopped, this was Green 130–octane full lead aviation gas, not the Blue 100LL (low lead) found in the US, Europe and other places. The stuff in the bucket was green, smelled like gas, and was clean. Their hand crank pump included a filter. Beyond that, there really was nothing else for me to check, so I told them to pump it into my plane. I was reassured knowing that many ferry pilots stop here and get refueled with the same pump setup from the same kind of rusty barrels. I hadn't heard of anyone getting a bad batch of aviation gas from Christmas Island…but then I don't hear everything. With no aviation gas a pilot could be stuck here.

In the afternoon I sought shade near the hotel, occasionally interrupted by a quick dip in the ocean. It really was a quaint and beautiful place, a mostly tranquil sea with light breakers hitting the beach, reflecting a blue sky with a few harmless white puffs of clouds lingering overhead, scenes that deserved consideration for the *Islands* calendar I sometimes have hanging on my wall at home.

So why was I here? Unlike ferry pilots, I was not in the business of flying airplanes from one faraway place to another. I was here because I was flying my plane around the world, nearing the end of a trip I'd begun months before, explaining that I was doing it "for the adventure." Well, when I tell people that they nod with approval, pat me on the back, wish me luck, and lament that they don't have the time, money, or mental energy for a similar leap of lifestyle. Of course, my explanation is mostly a fiction, and "for the adventure" sounds like what you put in the blank space on a form where it asks "Reason for trip?" and can't think of an honest answer, or are unwilling to write one down. Telling people I'm flying my plane from place to place around the

My plane, N788W, parked at Christmas Island

world, erratically bouncing between earth and sky in some endless pinball purgatory because I had nothing better to do, intrigued in some ways by the thought of crashing into the ocean because the shocking reality of it would be refreshing, fortified knowing that at some point the best anyone could hope for was death with at least some adventurous nobility – that answer would not make anybody happy.

Many pilots I know had been determined to learn to fly and became pilots at an early age. They will tell you they love flying. I started flying later in life. I got my private pilot certificate when I was 47, at a time when I was on a campaign to learn at least one new skill every year. I learned snowboarding the year before I learned to fly. For me, flying a plane was an interesting thing to know how to do, a skill that could open the door to some new experiences. But I don't "love" flying; flying is often a routine, tedious pain in the ass, not an act with an emotional connection.

I have a few good friends who are pilots, but I don't routinely hang out with pilots nor belong to pilot organizations. I rarely go to aviation shows and only then when I'm shopping for something specific for the plane. In the community of pilots, I am an outsider. Yet I am a skilled and experienced pilot with commercial, instrument, multi-engine, and seaplane ratings who, prior to beginning this long round-the-world flight, had flown across the United States several times, including flights over the ocean to the Cayman Islands, the Bahamas, and Alaska.

What follows is an account of my flying adventures to all seven continents and many things that happened at the places I visited, places that are fascinating, mysterious, beautiful, isolated, ancient, modern, opulent, desolate, sexy, sad, and broken.

2

Flight Preparations

Bainbridge Island is situated about five miles due west of downtown Seattle across Puget Sound, a 35-minute ferry ride, an arms-length relationship that makes the fun and interesting activities in Seattle readily accessible without colliding with the big city traffic mess and crowds. The house I built on Bainbridge Island faces south and east over the Sound across the ferry route and the shipping lanes, with a steady parade of container ships arriving from, or en-route to, distant ports around the globe. On a clear day Mt. Rainier defines the horizon. Rising to over 14,000 feet, it gives depth and dimension and scale to the view.

A beautiful view is useful because I can just stare out the window at all this and call it "enjoying the view," like I'm actually doing something instead of doing nothing. I'd been spending too much time "enjoying the view" and needed some ambitious project I could sink my teeth into, get me off my ass, and get me moving. The container ships and long-distance flights I could see leaving Sea-Tac Airport and turning west for Asia were nagging reminders of the interesting, curious, and stimulating places and people I had experienced on my international travels. It wasn't enough, though, to jump on a commercial flight and go somewhere. Anybody could do that. I wasn't looking for ordinary. My small single-engine airplane was the answer. By flying my own plane, the international journey itself would be the adventure – the destinations along the way were almost secondary.

When I returned from a cruise to Antarctica in March 2011, I was finally sufficiently invigorated to get serious about setting off. I got my head into pilot mode and starting contemplating what I could do that had some challenge to it. After prowling around the internet awhile, flying across the Atlantic Ocean to Europe became my project.

I had a great plane for long-distance flights. Most small planes have a comfortable range of maybe 500 or 600 nautical miles (nm). My plane, a 2001 Lancair Columbia 300, with a nominal range of about 1200 nm using the 98 gallons of useable fuel in the wing tanks, was much better suited to this kind of flight to Europe than most small planes. I had also upgraded the avionics shortly after purchasing it the previous June, so it was able to perform all navigation and other operations using the onboard GPS connected to the autopilot. "Avionics" is the general term used to describe all the radios and navigation electronics on a plane, like the GPS. An entire flight plan could be programmed into the GPS and the plane would fly it on its own – I could just sit there and watch the world go by.

The company Lancair was known for making kit planes, planes that pilots with a lot of time and construction acumen could put together themselves. This really wasn't the best way to build a plane, though it did allow some customization, which in turn earned the somewhat dubious registration categorization as an "experimental" or "homebuilt" plane. Those descriptions on a registration definitely lead to problems when trying to fly to some places in the world like Singapore and Japan. One of the main factors that led a number of companies to offer kit planes, and others to go out of business entirely, was the cost of liability in a crash. Until a change in the law, liability for a crash that could be blamed on the manufacturer of the plane had no time limit. By selling a kit, not a finished plane, the liability fell to whomever finished building the kit into an "experimental" plane. Though the law has now changed to limit a manufacturer's liability, kit planes are still an important segment of the new plane market.

With the change in the law, Lancair launched a production model called Columbia which they began building in 2001 at their factory in Bend, OR. Mine is serial number 22, manufactured at a time when a small group of people were still custom-building each plane. For that reason it was pretty high quality with pieces individually tailored to fit together. Lancair ran into trouble when they tried to ramp up production in later years with more mechanized construction techniques. An unexpected, out-of-season hailstorm that clobbered several newly finished planes parked outside contributed to the company ultimately going bankrupt and selling off their designs, patents, and other assets to Cessna, the world's largest manufacturer of small planes.

Destination Europe. I'd been there many times over the years, almost every other year when I think about it, usually visiting France. I had traveled to essentially every country there. I had lived in Bristol, England, and in both Paris (briefly) and Montpellier, France. It was familiar territory to me as a tourist and as a short-term resident. Having a plane to get around would be a novel way to see it compared to riding trains, ferries, and taking commercial flights as I'd done in the past.

From my internet research, it appeared there were two common routes to cross the North Atlantic for planes without the range to make it in one hop. The most commonly used route begins in Goose Bay, Canada, with fuel stops in Narsarsuaq, Greenland, then on to one of two airports in Reykjavik, Iceland, and finally on to Wick or elsewhere in Scotland. The longest flight leg on this route is 676 nm. Alternately, it is possible to depart from Iqualuit, Canada, and make refueling stops in Sondre Stromfjord or Nuuk on the west coast of Greenland, then Kulusuk on the east coast of Greenland, then Reykjavik, then the Faroe Islands, then finally Scotland. Using this route, the longest leg is only 487 nm. Note that throughout this book when talking about the distance between airports I am referring to the great circle (shortest) distance, not the actual flying distance along common flight routes shown on the aeronautical charts, called "airways." Generally an efficient route along airways will be only a few percent longer than the great circle distance.

An event in April 2011, however, changed my perspective on a preferred route. A volcano erupted in Iceland throwing ash and gases into the air and disrupting commercial air travel for a time. Although this eruption did not have the multi-week impact of other eruptions, it made me realize there is some uncertainty associated with flying by way of Iceland. I started looking at alternative routes. The next best alternative is a much more southern route departing from St. John's in Canada followed by a long flight leg to Santa Maria in the Azores and then on to Lisbon, Portugal. The flight leg from St. John's to Santa Maria is 1374 nm, beyond the range of my plane, N788W, with wing tanks only. To ensure I could complete the flight to Europe, volcanoes or not, I decided to install an additional fuel tank in the cabin of N788W. That decision led me down the interesting path (some would say rabbit hole) of ferry fuel tanks and FAA Special Flight Permits.

A ferry tank is an extra fuel tank temporarily installed in a plane to give it more range so it can be flown or "ferried" to a distant location beyond the plane's normal range with its built-in fuel tanks. In small planes this is usually accomplished by taking out the seats and installing an aluminum fuel tank in their place. The plane's fuel system is also temporarily modified to connect the fuel lines from the ferry tank to the plane's fuel system through the use of various valves the pilot manually controls. Once the plane reaches its intended destination, the ferry tank is removed, the seats replaced, and the plane restored to its original configuration. All these temporary modifications require FAA inspection and approval. With the extra fuel on board, the plane usually weighs more than its authorized Maximum Takeoff Weight, so flying it in such an overweight condition also requires FAA approval.

The decision to install a ferry tank would extend the range of the plane to more than 2300 nm. That enhanced capability led to inevitable "mission creep" because long flight legs with no fuel stops across the open ocean would now be possible. With the ferry tank, flying around the world was now feasible. Looking at the length of flight legs involved in flying around the world using routes similar to what others had used before me, I saw they all could be comfortably flown with that range, except perhaps the longest leg from Hawaii back to the US mainland, which was around 2100 nm. A second ferry tank could be installed in Hawaii for extra fuel reserve on this leg. With ferry tanks now incorporated in my planning process, I made the decision to change my mission from just flying to Europe and back, to flying around the world.

Auxiliary (Ferry) Fuel Tank

Unlike other small planes like Cessnas, Pipers, and Bonanzas, my Columbia 300 is not a common plane. I spent some time trying to track down a place that had put ferry tanks on a Columbia before. A call to RDD Enterprises in Redmond, OR, a company that has done custom modifications on Columbia aircraft before, gave me two interesting pieces of information. First, they gave me the name of Fred Sorenson, who put ferry tanks in a Columbia 400 that flew around the world in 2007. Fred, an airline pilot and mechanic with Inspection Authorization, a high-level FAA qualification, told me he could do the installation in either Las Vegas at his shop or in Merced, CA at a company called TDL Aero which he often uses to do such installations. I chose

Merced because it was closer. We set a time to get it done. It was a major step in getting the plane ready for this trip.

RDD also told me that Erik Lindbergh, grandson of Charles Lindbergh, flew a Columbia 300 in replicating the famous flight of his grandfather from New York to Paris (3160 nm) on its 75th anniversary. The Columbia 300 he flew was built specifically for the flight with additional fuel tanks in the wings as well as ferry tanks in the cabin in place of the seats as I planned to do. That flight was completed successfully; the plane now sits in a museum in St. Louis.

As it happens, Erik Lindbergh, now primarily an artist, also lives on Bainbridge Island near me. Though I never met him, I did trade emails with him. He gave me some helpful tips on the performance and handling of a Columbia 300 under grossly overloaded conditions.

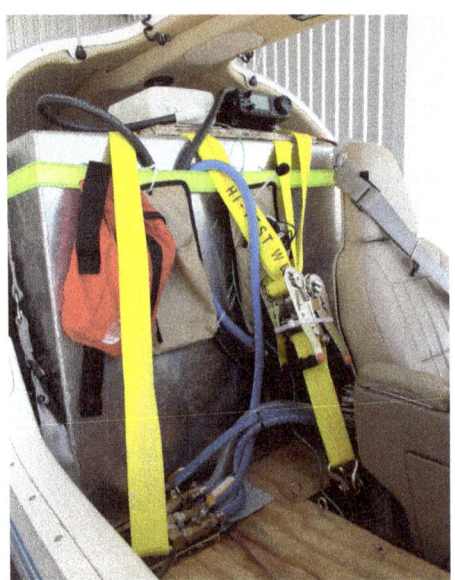

Ferry tank installation with HF radio on top

The ferry tank and HF radio installation took place in mid-June at TDL Aero in Merced. They took out the back seats and the co-pilot seat, installed a ¾" plywood "floor," placed the 78-gallon ferry tank on the plywood, and HF radio on top of the tank. Two-inch tie-down straps were hooked to ⅛" steel cable loops attached to the seat-belt connection points. The seatbelt connection points are the strongest attachment points inside the cabin.

As I mentioned, installation of a ferry tank requires a Special Airworthiness Certificate as part of a Special Flight Permit that allows flight operation at greater than the normal Maximum Takeoff Weight of 3400 pounds for the Columbia 300. My Special Flight Permit allowed for a Maximum Takeoff Weight of 3989 pounds and covers the modifications to the fuel system since the ferry tank is plumbed into the regular fuel system. TDL Aero had done many ferry tank installations in a variety of aircraft, which resulted in a good working relationship with a local FAA Flight Standards District Office (FSDO) in nearby Fresno. FAA personnel at that office are the ones who inspect the installation and issue the approved Special Flight Permit paperwork.

The ferry tank installation included a valve manifold that allowed switching from the right wing tank to the ferry tank. The fuel return goes back to the right wing tank so that as fuel is drawn from the ferry tank, some of it goes to the engine and is burned and some of it is returned to the right wing tank. Thus the fuel quantity shown for the right wing tank actually goes up when the ferry tank is in use. When the right tank is once again full, I switch off the ferry tank and switch the right wing tank back on. This back-and-forth switching continues until the fuel in the ferry tank is down to about 5–10 gallons. The amount of fuel remaining in the ferry tank must thus be calculated by subtracting the amount that went into the engine (given by the fuel flow meter in the aircraft) and the amount that went back into the right wing tank as indicted by the right wing fuel gauge. The left wing tank works in a conventional way and is not involved in the ferry tank switching operation. All this meant I would have to be on my toes monitoring fuel flows and switching tanks at the appropriate time.

Anticipating that I would install a second ferry tank in Hawaii to have sufficient reserve fuel for the long Hawaii-to-California flight leg, the valve manifold we installed at TDL Aero had a second connection to attach the second ferry tank when the time came. Adding that tank would involve getting a new Special Flight Permit from the FAA to cover that future installation.

Communications

In addition to the normal VHF aviation radios in the airplane's control panel, I also carried an HF (shortwave) radio for communications over the ocean when I would be out of the range of VHF radio facilities. This radio is actually a ham radio rig – an ICOM IC-760MKIIG – which I modified to transmit in the aviation shortwave bands. It is connected to a standard ICOM AH-4 automatic antenna tuner to tune the wire antenna strung beneath the fuselage out to the tail and back. In addition, I carried a satellite phone, an Iridium 9555 which can be purchased or rented from several places on the internet.

Emergency Equipment

I carried emergency equipment for this flight that I normally wouldn't carry, including a life raft and an immersion suit. The life raft is a covered Winslow

Ultra-Light model 46FAUL which weighs 35 pounds –actually a lot – but the package contains some survival gear and signaling devices in addition to the raft itself.

The cold-water immersion suit I took is an inexpensive Stearns foam "gumby suit" – one size fits all. These immersion suits are very cumbersome and very hot to wear. It's impossible to put them on in the cramped cockpit of a small plane. Consequently, the prevailing theory is to put it on before climbing in the plane and wear it for the entire flight. This is very uncomfortable because it's so hot. The suit also greatly restricts movement so that if I were forced down in the water, trying to exit the plane wearing this thing would be a challenge, especially if I were injured.

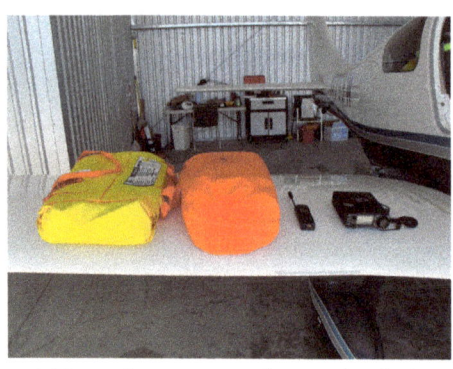

Additional equipment taken on this flight

My dubious alternate theory is to carry the suit on the plane and put it on to warm up once I was out of the plane and in the life raft. Getting in the life raft is also easier without the suit on. If I can't get in the life raft, I'm pretty much dead anyway. Even wearing the suit and bobbing around in open water, there isn't much chance of survival when rescue may be many hours or even days away. Using either approach, the chances of survival are still slim if forced down in the ocean far from any ship or opportunity for helicopter rescue. Of course, closer to shore or nearer to shipping lanes certainly improves those odds, so carrying this emergency gear still has worthwhile benefits.

In addition, there is emergency gear I always carry in a dry bag on the plane: an ICOM A4 handheld aviation VHF radio, a cheap handheld Garmin GPS, an ACR PLB-350C Aqualink View personal locator beacon with GPS, flares, a signal mirror and whistle, a basic pre-packaged survival kit, and spare batteries. I also always carry an inflatable suspender-type life jacket since I routinely fly over Puget Sound and other bodies of waters in the Pacific Northwest.

Insurance

Unlike others I've read about who had serious problems getting insurance for flights outside the US, especially over the North Atlantic, I didn't have any real difficulty getting insurance, although it was expensive. This may in part be due to my pilot-in-command flight hours and additional pilot ratings. My regular insurance carrier didn't offer insurance for international operations. Instead I started shopping around and finally obtained a policy through CS&A in Kennesaw, Georgia. The insurance company was StarNet, a Berkley Company. This annual policy provided worldwide coverage and the approximately US$5 million liability coverage required in Europe. It also provided US$50,000 for search and rescue (SAR), which Iceland sometimes checks for (though they didn't for my flight), and covered operation outside the parameters of the normal airworthiness certificate (i.e. with a ferry tank installed and overweight). The annual premium was about 2.5 times what I had previously paid for a US-only policy. I've since found less expensive insurance with AIG Aerospace, although through the same broker company – CS&A in Georgia. Now that I have successfully completed long international flights over the ocean, I think I have "street cred," which lowered my insurance premiums.

Document e-copies

I scanned all the important documents I might need to show various government officials and others during this flight. That included documents for the plane (airworthiness, registration, maintenance logs, insurance policy, etc.) and personal documents (passport, pilot and medical certificate, etc.) It was useful to have all these as pdf files on my laptop in case I needed to print more copies or email them to someone.

Aeronautical Charts

Aeronautical charts can be thought of as maps of the sky that show pilots where they can safely fly. The primary charts used for flying between airports are called "enroute charts." They are crisscrossed with numbered "airways," equivalent to highways on a road map. Planes usually fly along these airways, although for some types of flying they can fly almost anywhere. The charts show mountains, airports, radio frequencies for talking to air traffic control (ATC), and many other types of information for pilots. Certain other charts are called "approach charts" or "approach plates." They are very detailed, large-scale maps for the area around an airport, which show the very precise courses and altitudes a pilot must fly, using his instruments, to successfully land on a specific runway even when there are low, overcast clouds that obscure that runway from the pilot's view until just before he lands. That's called an instrument landing. It's an essential part of flying to have and use both types of charts, no way around it. To fly around the world I would need these charts for everywhere along my route and for every airport where I intended to land.

Traditionally, enroute charts were printed on large folded pieces of paper like most maps, or bound into books in the case of approach plates. The charts are updated frequently, every few months. Keeping paper charts current was a nightmare of subscription services and piles of out-of-date paper cluttering the plane and the hangar.

As I was preparing for my flight there was a revolution under way in how aeronautical charts were made available to pilots. Paper charts were in the process of being replaced with digital versions of these same charts, largely enabled by the availability of small, easy-to-use display devices like notebook computers and tablets. Updating the charts to keep them current became as straightforward as downloading an update for an app. In addition, by connecting the tablet to a GPS device, the tablet screen can show the position of the plane directly on the chart, something that's impossible with paper charts.

While the transition to digital charts was largely complete for charts in the US at the time of my flight, for other countries it was still in process. For my international flight legs I initially bought paper charts; the number of charts and approach plate books was staggering, easily filling a duffle bag in the plane. I tried to minimize the chart burden by only taking the ones relevant to my planned flight route but it was still a massive amount of heavy paper. Upon reaching England I realized my flight route would change, perhaps several times, so some of the paper charts I had onboard were already useless. During a break to return home I abandoned the idea of using paper charts, bought an iPad 2, and invested in digital charts and the software to display it. This turned out to be a much better way to handle charts; in fact, the only practical way for a round-the-world flight like this. More detailed information about charts and display devices can be found in Appendix B.

Navdata

The charts provide a graphic picture used to plan a flight. A version of the essential information from the charts can also be loaded into the GPS in the plane using a memory card, like the one used in a digital camera, for example. The data on the memory card that plugs into the GPS is called "navdata."

N788W ready to go

With the navdata in the GPS you can simply dial in the destination airport code, or waypoint name, and the GPS will show you direction and distance to destination airport or waypoint. It's much more convenient that calculating them from a paper chart. Once you are flying, the navdata in the GPS will also use the speed of the airplane to calculate how long it will take to get there. With the GPS connected to the autopilot, the plane will automatically fly to the destination airport (or any of the other thousands of waypoints in the navdata database) without intervention by the pilot. My plane N788W is equipped with such a GPS, a Garmin GNS530W, connected to the autopilot, thus eliminating most of the manual flying I had to do on this trip.

Some waypoints over the open ocean at latitude/longitude intersections (like N60W50) are not identified by name in the navdata database. In such cases it's possible to manually program these points into the GPS as user-defined waypoints with an appropriately chosen five-letter name, like ATL01, ATL02, etc. for waypoints I defined over the North Atlantic.

Weight and Balance

Any plane can become difficult or impossible to control if it is loaded with too much weight or that weight is distributed inside the plane such that the plane is out of balance. Many accidents have been caused in small planes, and in large commercial planes, because they were incorrectly loaded and the pilot lost control.

With my plane overloaded by extra fuel and emergency equipment, a careful and detailed calculation of the weight and balance was definitely needed. Typically the information in the Pilot Operating Handbook, required on every small plane, provides information on how to calculate the weight and balance for the load on the plane, along with charts showing whether the weight and balance are within the plane's acceptable design limits. The information in the Pilot Operating Handbook is relatively crude for my purposes, so I had to create some new, more precise definitions of where things were loaded to get a detailed assessment of the weight and balance. The table in Appendix C shows the weight and balance spreadsheet calculation for N788W in its most loaded configuration with two ferry tanks for the flight leg from Hawaii to California.

Electronics

I normally carry my cellphone, notebook computer, and Canon G12 camera when I travel, along with a case of power adapters and cables to keep it all charged and connected. The G12 is a small, rugged, but very capable point-and-shoot camera that I can operate with one hand while still operating the plane's controls with the other hand. I can't do that with larger, heavier, poorly balanced DSLR cameras. I also carry an iPad with aeronautical charts and reading material. After moving to electronic charts on the iPad, I eventually used two iPads with identical information, one kept in the plane and the other carried with me so I could work up flight plans and routes in the hotel.

Special Training

Other pilots making long flights over the water in small planes have taken training in a water tank that simulates what it's like to end up in a plane in the water, both right side up and upside down. It provides a chance to practice detaching the seatbelt, pushing open the cabin door, and exiting the aircraft under those circumstances. Survival Systems, Inc. in Groton, Connecticut is one place that offers such training. I didn't bother taking this training. All things considered, crashing into the ocean is a pretty unlikely event. Having some experience with getting out a plane if it does happen certainly raises survival prospects, but how much? Two percent? Ten percent? Certainly not 50 percent. I felt the improvement in survival chances from this training was not sufficient to warrant the time and effort the training would take. There are other, more significant risk factors where I chose to focus my attention.

Budget

I didn't make a budget for this trip. My high-tech businesses had been very successful over the years so the cost really didn't matter. Nor did I keep careful track of expenses during all my flights, something I wish I had done because many people have asked what it costs for flying adventures like mine. As this story reveals, I certainly made a few mistakes along the way that raised the cost, money that could have been saved if I had been a little smarter about what I was doing. In retrospect, though, I've been able to estimate costs for such a trip based on average aviation gas prices around the world (US$10–US$12/gallon), three months in good-quality hotels (average US$150/night), permits, handlers, ferry tank installation, e-charts, emergency gear, etc. Considering all these expense categories together I now tell people to budget US$50,000 and three months to make an around-the-world flight in a small plane. The flights to South America and Antarctica are an additional cost which can be estimated in the same way.

Money

Credit cards work everywhere for hotels and restaurants but not for fuel or for handlers. Handlers are explained in Appendix B. I carried a substantial amount of US currency to pay for these things. Most of it was in $100 bills. Old $100 bills with the small head of Ben Franklin (Small Head Bens) generally were not accepted, so it's best to bring very recently printed currency. Also, fuel people and handlers rarely have any change, so $10 and $20 bills are also useful to avoid overpaying when they can't or won't offer change.

3

Crossing the United States

The ferry tank installation only took three days, but an additional week was needed to finally get the FAA Flight Standards District Office guys to turn up, inspect it, and sign off on the Special Flight Permit and Operating Limitations. The Special Flight Permit gave me 90 days to get to the specified ferry flight destination of Honolulu, by the specified route the long way around. In Honolulu I planned to add the second ferry tank and get another Special Flight Permit for the flight back to California. The Operating Limitations was a five-page document that set forth a number of operating limits ranging from things like not to use the autopilot when the plane is overweight to my exact routing from Merced to Honolulu, a routing I eventually had to change.

When the installation and paperwork were completed, I flew back to my home base in Bremerton which gave me a chance to test the ferry tank operation and the HF radio along the way. After returning from the ferry tank installation, I spent a week at home organizing charts and other things I would need for the flight, as well as taking care of the more mundane tasks needed to keep my household running while I was away on what would be an extended vacation.

Flying a Small Plane

So what's the big deal here? Small planes are much less complicated, much less sophisticated machines than your average automobile. They are designed to be simple and reliable. Like a car, they have standard controls like a throttle and brakes. They differ from cars in that they have "control surfaces" (aileron, rudder, and an elevator) on the wings and tail that will make a plane climb, descend, or turn while in flight. Hand controls and pedals in the cockpit are connected to these surfaces via cables or rods so the pilot can move them. Learning to move these hand controls and pedals so they make the plane do what you want is a matter of understanding what they do, followed by repetitive practice, like swinging a golf club or learning to sail. Anyone with the modest discipline to learn a task can learn to fly.

Small planes have internal combustion engines like the ones in almost all cars. A mixture of gas and air is ignited by a spark that makes an explosion in a cylinder, which causes a piston to push a crankshaft around. In a car the crankshaft is connected to a transmission, which in turn is connected to the wheels. In a plane there is no transmission; the crankshaft is connected directly to the propeller. The airplane throttle controls the revolutions per minute (RPM) of the engine, which are usually limited to the range of 500 to 2700 RPM. The propeller is therefore also limited to a range of 500 to 2700 RPM. Control of the fuel-air mixture is done manually by the pilot rather than by a computer chip typical of modern cars. More direct control, less chance of failure. Some engines have carburetors but faster, higher-powered airplanes like mine use fuel injection similar to most modern automobiles. Airplane engines are air-cooled; there is no radiator. Like the plane itself, aircraft engines are designed for simplicity and reliability. But in their fundamental operation, they really don't differ from the engines in most cars.

If the engine is running, the propeller is spinning and the plane is being pulled through the air. If it's being pulled fast enough, the winds flowing over the wings will create enough lift and the plane will fly. Once it's flying, the pilot can make it climb and descend using more or less power (via the throttle) and by moving the elevator in the tail up or down. The pilot can make it turn using the rudder in the tail (like on a boat) and the ailerons, which are moving panels along the trailing edges of the wings. That's pretty much it: that's how you fly a plane.

If the engine stops running, the plane becomes a glider and starts to descend. But all the control surfaces still function, so the pilot still has a lot of control. Depending on the plane's design and its altitude when the engine failed, it can glide for several miles. If the failure occurred within gliding range of an airport, it's possible to glide the plane in for a safe landing. During training, every pilot practices such "power off" landings. If no airport is within gliding range, the pilot will be forced to make an "off airport" landing in an open field, on a road, on a lake or any other place where it might be possible to land and still survive while minimizing damage to the aircraft.

When I want to go flying, I drive to the airport, open the hangar, and use a tow bar attached to the front wheel of the plane to pull it out of the hangar. Once it's outside, I do a cursory inspection by walking around the plane to make sure nothing important like the control surfaces, airspeed sensor, or radio antennas are stuck or broken. I then check the engine oil level using a dipstick just like the one in a car's engine. With those things done, I climb in the plane and start the engine by turning a key, just as you would in a car.

The door on the plane is opened with a simple key, often the same key as the ignition key. Some small planes don't even require a key to start them; the engine is started by pushing a button. Small planes do not have even the modest security or anti-theft protection you would find on low-priced cars.

Once the engine is running, I let it warm up while I check various engine gauges (oil temperature and pressure, for example). I also check the current weather conditions by listening to a special airport broadcast on the plane's radio. Depending on the flight I may also program the code for my destination airport into the GPS so I know what direction I'm going to fly after I take off. With the engine warmed up, I apply some power by moving the throttle forward. The propeller spins faster and the plane starts to move. I taxi at a slow speed, maybe 10–15 mph, along a taxiway to get to the end of the runway. Most runways have a place to park before taking off (a so-called run-up area) where you can bring the engine up to about 30–40% power to make sure everything is running okay at higher RPM.

With those final checks completed, I'm ready to take off. I first check to see no other planes are coming in to land, make a call on the radio that I'm about to take off, giving the runway number I'm going to use, then taxi onto the runway and apply full power by pushing the throttle knob all the way in. The plane accelerates rapidly. Although it varies greatly from plane to plane, when my plane reaches about 70 knots (80 mph) it is going fast enough to fly. I pull back on the control stick a little, which operates the elevator causing the nose of the plane to rise. A few seconds later the main wheels leave the runway and the plane is flying. From there on it's a matter of adjusting power and using the control surfaces – operated via the control stick and rudder pedals – to climb, descend, and turn the plane.

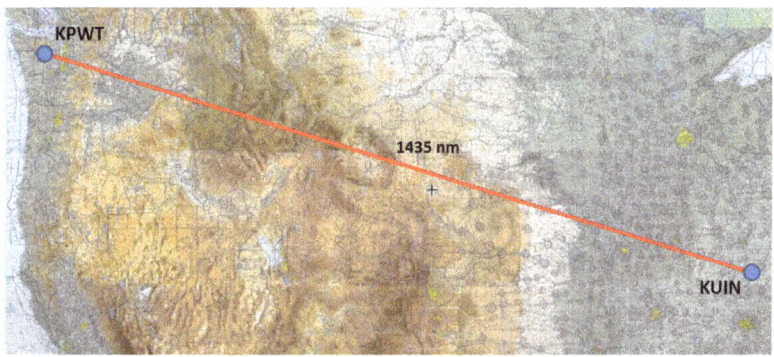

Flight from Bremerton to Quincy

For landing, the power is substantially reduced to slow the plane down so it will descend to the runway elevation while at the same time using the control surfaces to keep the nose of the plane lined up with the runway. When the plane is a few feet above the runway and flying at its landing speed (about 70–75 knots in my plane), the nose can be raised a little so the main wheels touch down first, the nose wheel after. With all three wheels on the runway and power reduced to minimum, the plane will gradually slow down with the help of foot brakes until it is coasting slow enough to turn off the runway, onto the taxiway, and finally to a parking place or back to the hangar.

Flying to Quincy, Illinois

My flight to Quincy was almost delayed when I discovered a strong gasoline smell coming from the ferry tank inside the cabin the day before my intended departure day. One of the hose clamps on the hose connecting the ferry tank to the fuel system was not tight. At least I hoped that was the problem. I tightened the clamp. When I returned the next day the leak and smell were gone.

Using exactly the takeoff procedure described above, I left Bremerton, WA (airport code KPWT), early on the morning of June 27, 2011 on a VFR flight to Quincy, IL (airport code KUIN), a little over 1435 nm away. I wanted to fully test the ferry tank operation, tank switching, fuel flow, and fuel quantity indicators on a long flight over land before attempting to use the tank over the ocean. All went well. I had sunny weather most of the way but it was bumpy (light turbulence) over Wyoming in the hot summer afternoon, as usual. The altitudes I used varied from 9,000 to 12,000 feet.

"VFR" means flying using Visual Flight Rules. Using these rules I must stay away from the clouds and look out for other aircraft myself to avoid a

Mount St. Helens, Washington State

collision. In the US it is not necessary to file a flight plan for a VFR flight. The alternative is to fly IFR (using Instrument Flight Rules). For an IFR flight, a flight plan must be filed with ATC but I am allowed to fly in the clouds. It is ATC's responsibility to keep me clear of other aircraft because I can't see them if I happen to be inside a cloud.

During this flight I also figured out how I wanted to set up economy cruise – how to get the most flying distance out of a gallon of fuel. For power settings less than 65%, the manufacturer of the engine in my plane, TCM, says you can run the engine at so-called lean-of-peak settings. Using the performance charts in the aircraft's Pilot Operating Handbook, I could set the fuel flow at around 11.5 gallons per hour, and get about 165 knots true airspeed. These settings resulted in cylinder head temperatures in the mid-300s (except #6 which routinely runs hotter) and no engine roughness. Depending on cruising altitude, these became fairly standard engine settings for my flight around the world.

My flight from Bremerton to Quincy took 9.1 hours, so it was also a test for me as the human element sitting in the pilot's seat. I almost always use the autopilot to fly the plane once I'm at my cruising altitude. That means there really isn't much for me to do except switch fuel tanks every hour or so and watch the gauges for any abnormal readings. If there are storm clouds or cloud buildups in front of me I may alter course to drive around them and avoid the turbulence they certainly contain. Otherwise, I just sit back and watch the world go by and maybe take a photo if I see something interesting. In the US, I can also listen to XM radio but otherwise I'm left with the catalog of music stored on my iPod.

There are no toilets in little planes so relief comes by peeing in a small plastic jug designed for this purpose. Fortunately for me, male plumbing is better suited to this process than female plumbing, although there are attachments for the pee bottle that supposedly make them usable by women. I have no direct experience with that.

Quincy

Great River Aviation is the "FBO" in Quincy. FBO stands for Fixed Base Operator but those words don't really explain what FBOs are. An FBO can be one of a wide variety of businesses that provide aircraft services, maintenance, supplies, etc., located at an airport. Most commonly it refers to the airport business where small general-aviation planes can park and the pilot can do such things as buy fuel, rent a car, check weather on computer terminals, use the restroom, or just hang out and wait for bad weather to pass. Passengers can also be picked up and dropped off. FBOs can be very sophisticated facilities that mainly serve corporate jets and provide a wide range of support services, even on-site conference rooms and catering. Because of all these services, an FBO can be thought of as a general-aviation terminal compared to the regular commercial-aviation terminal that most passengers use.

I had stopped at Great River Aviation several times before and always gotten good service. This time I made careful note of the amount of fuel they put in each wing tank and in the ferry tank, and compared those amounts with the written log of fuel usage I had maintained during the flight from Bremerton. The numbers compared pretty well. It was important that I had a calibrated understanding of real fuel consumption as the flight legs became longer and more demanding.

Quincy carries a lot of memories for me. The Antique Inn was a little-known hideaway bar in Quincy when I lived there in the early 1980s. On most nights a duo consisting of an old man on drums and a fat black woman on organ would play a mixture of jazz and torch song favorites. The old man's mouth would hang open as he played a repetitive, uninspired rhythm with an occasional snare fill and cymbal crash. But the woman could, at times, truly sing a gritty, heartfelt rendition of some songs – usually little-known jazz numbers. On Friday and Saturday nights, she would wear a sequined dress, cut low in front to reveal her ample cleavage.

Even at its busiest, the Antique Inn never seemed to be much more than half full. It really wasn't a common meeting place or singles pickup bar like a few others in Quincy. Built into what was once a two-story ramshackle home, its tables were mismatched and nondescript, the secondhand store artwork and posters on the walls conveyed no particular theme or intent, except maybe to cover holes in walls or flaws in the paint, a lost cause with flakes peeling away everywhere. The oak bar was interesting, though, having been rescued before being engulfed in flames from a stern-wheeler that had caught fire on the Mississippi River and burned to the waterline. The zinc-topped oak bar was rare – the only one in the city, it showed the nicks and scratches from the idle tapping of thousands of customers hunched over it. Looking at the bar, it was easy to imagine a classic movie fistfight erupting over some trivial slight. Bottles broken, chairs thrown at the mirror, maybe it was all Hollywood invention. But at least such bars were real, like the Antique Inn.

Sign on the closed Antique Inn

I stayed two nights in Quincy and, of course, had to stop by the Antique Inn to see what had become of it. It certainly had seen better days. The paint had almost disappeared and the building's entire roof was several years past needing replacement. Weeds growing through cracks in the sidewalk and the drawn-shut window blinds made it obvious it was no longer open. The slightly crooked martini-glass neon sign was dark and the door locked tight. A "For Sale" sign was attached to the side of the building but even that looked like it had been there awhile.

I lived in the Quincy countryside for three years in a small A-frame house on 13 acres surrounded by large corn and soybean farms. My place was located about 12 miles east of Quincy, where I initially was employed at Harris Corporation, Broadcast Products Division, and later was on my own as an engineering consultant, which ultimately evolved into my career as a high-tech entrepreneur. I drove by my old house – the trees I planted were surprisingly tall. I also visited old restaurants (like the Abbey) and drove by the houses of friends and girlfriends I remembered, though all had moved away long ago.

A huge windstorm had blown through ahead of me in the early morning hours of the day I arrived, knocking down a number of trees and creating power outages in half the town. Dozens of power crews were in town during my stay repairing the electrical grid. I was lucky to have booked a room at the Holiday Inn, now relocated to the east side of town from downtown, since the power crews had taken every available hotel room.

Bridges over the Mississippi River at Quincy

My current favorite restaurant in Quincy is The Pier, a relatively new restaurant on the Quincy waterfront that had been built at the top of a 30-foot steel cylinder that promised to protect it from the next 100-year flood. The long flight of stairs from the parking lot leads to a door opening onto a large octagon-shaped two-level dining room, every table situated to take best advantage of the view of the river through large windows facing every direction.

A subdued jazz trio started into their second set as I sat down. It was a glowing, spacious evening on the river. Dinner came and went almost invisibly as I took in the passing scene outside. The new bridge built alongside the old one crossed the river at a different angle to the old one, and led to the Missouri side which had been protected by a levee. The levee had saturated and sagged before the 1996 flood finally breeched it.

I was surprised to see a multi-page wine list; I picked a bottle from the Gigondas appellation in France, something I recognized from many visits to Provence. Was Quincy actually growing up and out? The thick red wine swirled in the glass and filtered the sunset over the river, overshadowing the food, and I drank it all.

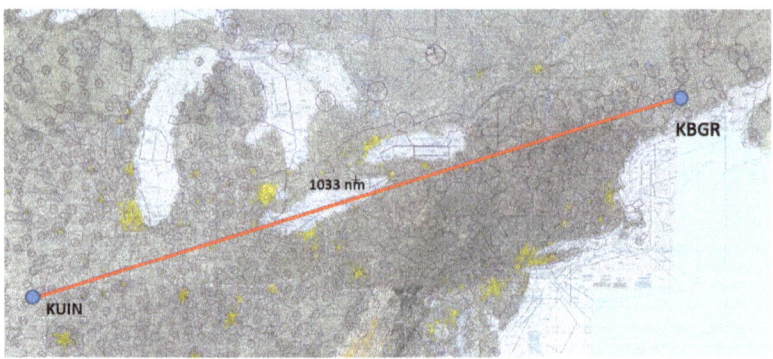

Flight from Quincy to Bangor

    I left the Pier and wandered around a bit before sitting on a bench in a small nearby park just above the river, near an off-ramp for the new bridge. The sun was gone, a late evening in mid-summer. The quiet of the flowing twilight shadows was interrupted by the last of the weekend speedboats returning to their marinas on Quinsippi Island. The boats would roar down the river at high speed from the north, make a tight turn just south of the bridge tower footing, and almost instantly drop their speed to 5 mph as they crossed under it. It was an intermittent, disorganized summer parade that got thinner and lonelier as the sky grew darker. The red and green and white of their running lights reflected off the shifting river water and the bow wakes that marked their passage.

    Along the railing that protected the park's promenade from the steep drop to the water, a hundred feet from me, a couple embraced in the fading light. Hand in hand, they turned toward the river and leaned against the railing. The steady muffled throb of a throttled-back ski boat was suddenly interrupted by a man's voice from the railing, loudly announcing to the river "I just asked her to marry me!" The voice, the announcement, so out of place, went unanswered. "I just asked her to marry me!" Louder, this time, and now the boaters understood. I saw the enthusiastic thumbs up and heard the applause from the people on the boat; another boat blew its horn and flashed its running lights.

    And so for the next boat too, and the river and Missouri and the bridge traffic and the ski boats would know this news. The darkness deepened and merged the couple's outline into a single shape. For them at that moment the future was clear.

    From the riverfront I walked up the street to Washington Park, a grassy patch in the middle of old downtown Quincy with an imposing bandstand built of local river cliff limestone. The park was crisscrossed with sidewalks that had small twists and buckles from repeated winter freezes and spring thaws. Few nearby streetlights and no storefront lights penetrated the darkness as I strolled through the park. Fireflies danced in clusters and a tugboat horn sounded far down on the river as I absorbed the effortless silence of the empty downtown. I lingered there, quietly appreciating this unpretentious small town in America.

Over the years I've stopped in Quincy many times on my cross-country flights. I never tire of the green fields, the thriving farms, the rumbling thunderstorms (as long as I'm not flying), the simple heartland feel of the place.

Bangor, Maine

My next stop after Quincy was Bangor, Maine (airport code KBGR), the commonly used exit point from the United States for small planes crossing the North Atlantic to Europe. The weather was a little uncertain along the route, so I filed an IFR (Instrument Flight Rules) flight plan at 9,000 feet from Quincy to Bangor, a great circle distance of approximately 1033 nm. The IFR flight plan had over a dozen waypoints along airways following a long list of VOR (VHF Omnidirectional Radio Range) navigation stations whose density in the eastern US is much greater than in the western US. Fortunately, once I was airborne and maybe 75 nm along the route, air traffic control gave me direct routing using my GPS to a VOR station in New York some 700 nm away. Instead of flying a complex route defined by all those waypoints, I could simply set the GPS for the distant point and let the autopilot fly the plane there. The efficiency of direct GPS routing was really paying off on this flight leg. I requested a changed routing again once I was near Maine to avoid thunderstorm buildups over mountains in the western part of the state. Finally arriving at Bangor I was confronted with an overcast cloud deck of 1000 feet above ground level which meant I had to fly the instrument (ILS) approach to land on runway 15. An ILS approach uses radio beacons from transmitters on the ground that are received by a navigation radio in the cockpit where a display device called a course deviation indicator (CDI) shows where the plane is in relation to the runway centerline and the correct descent path to the beginning of the runway. By keeping the two needles on the CDI centered, the pilot can accurately and reliably fly the plane exactly to the beginning of the runway to land even if the runway isn't visible due to clouds, rain, smoke, or other things that limit visibility.

I had visited Maine in 2004 in my first plane, a 1979 Archer II, N3048T, on a flying mission I dreamed up that required I go to the airports that were the farthest north, south, east, and west in the continental United States. The eastern-most airport is at Eastport, Maine (airport code KEPM). Eastport is a small town located on Moose Island, which is connected to the mainland by a causeway. It has very little industry (a mustard factory), some fishing and tourism, but is struggling with a shrinking population. When I visited in 2004, I had planned to stay for a couple of nights at a nicely restored Victorian bed and breakfast. However, after walking around the whole town during the afternoon I arrived and eating dinner at the best restaurant, situated on the waterfront, there was really nothing else to do, so I left after one night. I made an excuse for my early departure, telling the owners of the B&B I needed to get out ahead of approaching bad weather. I didn't want to offend them by saying the place was boring since they probably were hoping for two nights rent – other than me, their B&B was empty and dead, like the rest of the town.

Acadia National Park in Maine

Flying over the coast of Maine in 2004 I was reminded of how much it looks like the Pacific Northwest, especially the San Juan Island group in Washington with its mix of water, rock, and fir trees spread across hundreds of small islands, inlets, and sheltered coves.

On this trip I stayed six nights in the Bangor area, getting a few things reorganized for the flight across the ocean, buying a few items I had forgotten, and touring the Maine coast and Acadia National Park in a rental car. I stayed one night at the lakeside cabin of my Bainbridge friend Kathy Maher near Camden, Maine, where she was enjoying a family reunion with many East Coast relatives. We indulged in a fresh-caught lobster dinner with corn on the cob, an iconic part of any visit to Maine.

While in Maine I was also checking the weather patterns along my route over the North Atlantic between Goose Bay, Canada, and Reykjavik, Iceland. The weather fronts pretty consistently move from west to east, so looking at what was moving across Canada today was a good indicator of what would be on my route in a few days. Based on what I saw, I decided to delay my departure for Goose Bay a few days as a front moved through and off to the east. It was easier and more comfortable to wait out weather in Bangor with a rental car than in Goose Bay, where I had heard there wasn't much going on. I finally took off from Bangor for Goose Bay on July 5.

Exploiting the extended range of the plane with the ferry tank, I realized I had crossed the US from coast to coast in two pretty easy flight legs, a task that I had planned and labored over with my Archer II not too many years before. I was appreciating the benefits of having a fast, long-range aircraft. For now the long flights were still more interesting than tedious; the passing tapestry of farm fields, mountains, rivers, and towns out my window provided some entertaining scenery. I wondered whether it would become tedious and boring when there was nothing to look at but water over the North Atlantic.

Lobster dinner with friends in Camden, Maine

4

Crossing the Atlantic

I left Bangor on July 5, 2011, headed for Goose Bay, Labrador (airport code CYYR), in Canada, the most commonly used departure point for small planes flying across the North Atlantic to Greenland and Iceland. The weather was forecast as cloudy with a possible low ceiling at Goose Bay so I filed an IFR flight plan for this 620 nm leg.

I set the autopilot for the climb-out as usual, but a few minutes in, it disengaged by itself and the elevator trim position for climbing was way off from where I normally set it. I reset the elevator trim positon and re-engaged the autopilot, but 30 seconds later it happened again. I concluded I had a problem with the autopilot or trim of some sort so I called air traffic control and told them I needed to return to Bangor. They gave me a VFR clearance back to Bangor; thankfully I hadn't flown too far north. Once on the ground I had a chance to look over the situation and the problem became clear – and it was totally stupid. I had placed my duffle bag with clothes and personal stuff on top of the life raft in the co-pilot seat position. The duffle bag had shifted such that it was pushing on the electronic trim control on the side stick on that side of the plane. Pressing on the trim control automatically disengages the autopilot. I pushed the duffle bag back into place and strapped it down so it wouldn't happen again.

It only took a few minutes to resolve the autopilot/trim issue but as expected, once I had abandoned my flight to Goose Bay and turned around, my flight plan clearance to Goose Bay was canceled. I had to file a new flight plan to Goose Bay, which meant getting back on the phone with ATC. I didn't bother to inform Canadian Customs that my arrival time at Goose Bay had changed since I had left some flexibility in my initially notified arrival time. I also didn't re-file my eAPIS notification since I was still departing within about an hour of my originally notified time.

The eAPIS notification system was put in place after the terrorist attacks on the US on September 11, 2001. It requires all planes, large or small, to file a flight manifest when leaving or entering the United States. The manifest must not only specify the details of the flight route and departure/arrival times but also information about the flight crew and passengers including addresses, nationalities, and passport numbers. Arriving in the US without filing a proper eAPIS is a serious mistake.

Goose Bay

After crossing the US-Canada border and flying some distance into Canada, Canadian ATC gave me a direct routing to Goose Bay

En-route to Goose Bay

that shortened my flight somewhat. I was flying in and out of mixed clouds along the way but it was clear enough at Goose Bay when I arrived for a visual app-roach and landing.

I parked at Woodward Aviation, the general-aviation terminal at the airport where most private aircraft park. Given their role as a launching point for flights across the North Atlantic, I expected them to have great weather websites and associated information well organized for these crossings. I was disappointed when I learned they had fewer resources set up on their in-house computer than I had on my laptop. On the morning of departure, though, the line guy did give me a printout of the most recent weather information for my route. I appreciated the effort, though it was information I already knew from my own research online earlier that morning.

Before leaving Bangor, I had called the Canadian Customs line to notify them of my flight to Goose Bay and the arrival time. I also answered their usual questions about who and what I had on board. Based on a few other

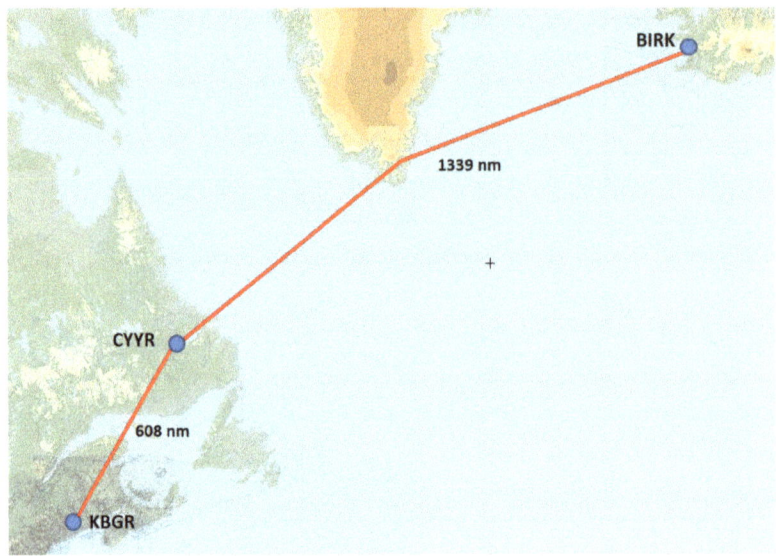

Flight legs from Bangor to Reykjavik

flights I've made into Canada, and what I've heard from other pilots, usually upon arrival in Canada you can call Customs again so they can give you an authorization number and then release you to enter Canada. This time, however, I was met on the ramp by two Canadian Customs guys who asked a lot of questions and searched my luggage. After they were satisfied nothing was amiss and left, I asked the Woodward Aviation people if they had singled me out for some reason. They said Customs had started this thorough search process for most general-aviation planes coming from the United States. I don't know what they may have been looking for, but searching my luggage was pretty useless in any event. If I were going to hide something, I would hide it on the plane. They didn't search the plane.

I stayed two nights in Goose Bay at the Hotel North Two waiting for weather along my route to improve. I knew I was in Canada because there were Vienna sausages in the snack basket in the hotel room. The front I had seen pass through Goose Bay a few days before was stalled over Greenland, making it problematic to get into Narsarsuaq (airport code BGBW), near the southern tip of Greenland, to re-fuel. I wanted to see the front move on. I was bored the second day, so I rented a car and drove around a bit. There isn't much to see in the immediate area and the available roads really don't go very far. There was a mixture of small general-aviation planes passing through

Goose Bay Airport destined for other airports in Canada, including some floatplanes headed for fishing camps located on lakes in the distant woods.

I spent much of my time in Goose Bay assessing the weather conditions across the North Atlantic because there wasn't much else to do. I wanted to stop in Narsarsuaq, but it seemed

Trapper's Cabin restaurant in Goose Bay

unlikely I'd get a combination of good weather there and at my destination in Reykjavik any time soon. The weather front was still stalled over Greenland, so the weather in Narsarsuaq was not good. While the weather was still OK in Goose Bay, a front was approaching from the west and promised to make things much worse by the afternoon. The forecast for Reykjavik was for sunny skies, so I made that my deciding factor. I elected to go directly to Reykjavik (airport code BIRK) and skip Narsarsuaq. I hated to miss landing in Narsarsuaq; it had been an important fueling stop during WWII for American bombers being ferried to the European war from the United States. As always, though, opting for the best weather situation was my first priority. It's a direct consequence of taking long flights like

Climbing out of Goose Bay into the dawn

these that the requirements for reasonable weather expand considerably over a larger geographically area. For shorter flights, it's easier to find a window of suitable weather since there is limit to how variable the weather can be over a smaller geographical area.

When flying above 5,500 feet over the North Atlantic, an IFR flight plan is required. I filed an IFR flight for a cruising altitude of 10,000 feet, with the routing shown in Appendix D. The flight plan route included three waypoints I had to manually program into the GPS by their latitude and longitude since they weren't included in the navdata database.

I departed Goose Bay as the sun was coming up. When I'd arrived in Goose Bay I'd filled both wing tanks and the ferry tank full for the first time. With all the extra weight I was prepared for the takeoff to be a little different, but it was relatively normal, although it took longer to reach takeoff speed. Accelerating to about 80 knots, greater than my normal takeoff speed, I just eased the nose wheel up and let the plane fly off the runway. With normal weight in the aircraft I would climb at a rate of 1000–1500 feet per minute (fpm). However, for this very overweight climb-out, I throttled back and accepted a lower climb rate of about 300–400 fpm while monitoring the engine temperature to make sure it wasn't getting too hot. Climbing with the airplane overloaded like this can definitely overheat the engine if the climb rate is too high.

Ice floes approaching Greenland

I levelled off at 10,000 feet and adjusted the power, propeller, and fuel mixture controls for the economy cruise settings discussed before. As I passed the waypoint called LOACH over the ocean, I was handed off to Gander Radio on 127.9 MHz. At that point they assigned me two shortwave (HF) frequencies: primary (8891 kHz) and secondary (5616 kHz). I also asked them for their phone number as a backup in case I couldn't get through to them on the HF. They asked for the number for my satellite phone (satphone). HF radio is used for communicating with air traffic control over the ocean by all aircraft because the normal aviation frequencies in the VHF band (118 to 136 MHz) don't have sufficient range when far from land, depending on the plane's altitude. HF radio is much less consistent and reliable compared to VHF radio. If the HF radio connection to air traffic control is not working, it's possible to simply call them using a satphone if you have the right number. This HF/satphone issue became a real predicament on my flight from Hawaii back to California.

At the first position reporting point (first waypoint) I was required to contact air traffic control and let them know I had arrived at the waypoint and give them an estimate for the time I would arrive at the next waypoint. There is no radar coverage over the ocean, so the only way ATC knew where I was, or where any other plane was for that matter, was based on what I told

The eastern coast of Greenland after passing through the weather front

them at these reporting points. I tried to call in on the HF but got no response; in fact, I heard massive interference in my VHF radios and interference in the autopilot which caused it to execute a slow left turn when I keyed the HF microphone. However, I could hear ATC trying to call me. I finally gave up on using the HF, plugged the headset into the satphone, and called them with that. It worked perfectly. I gave them my position report and told them I'd use the satphone from then on when I was outside of VHF radio range.

Approaching Greenland, the expected weather front loomed in front of me. There was no way under, around, or over it so I flew straight into it; I was in solid clouds (instrument meteorological conditions) for the next 90 minutes. Instrument meteorological conditions means weather conditions that require flight by instruments rather than by visual reference to the horizon outside the window. When I am inside clouds I can't see any visual reference to keep the wings level. It is like flying with the airplane completely wrapped in cotton: a little unnerving when first experienced. It takes substantial training to learn to fly an airplane by just looking at the plane's instruments and not out the window.

I was in the clouds and still flying at my assigned altitude of 10,000 feet. But the temperature now had dropped to -5° Celsius (C). Clouds are visible moisture; i.e., water vapor. At that temperature I was not surprised to start picking up rime ice on the wings. It first manifested as an airspeed drop as the plane pitched up to maintain altitude. I could see the ice on the landing light lens and the leading edge of the wing.

Ice is a killer when you're flying a small plane. It not only adds weight and drag to the plane, but more significantly, the buildup of ice changes the shape of the wings and tail so they no longer provide the expected lift and control. Within a matter of a few minutes or less, depending on the icing conditions, ice buildup can render a plane beyond control and lead to a crash. It has happened many times; it still happens today. The buildup of ice requires the pilot take immediate action to deal with the situation.

At that point I was not talking to ATC over Greenland, even though I had tried to make contact using the VHF frequency they gave me. Continued ice buildup would definitely become a serious problem. I decided the best option was a blind descent to warmer temperatures. Normally I would only do a descent like this with the permission of ATC. For a blind descent over Greenland's high terrain, I made use of the colored terrain elevation display on the GPS moving map display in my cockpit to avoid colliding with mountains I couldn't see. The display shows a red color for terrain that is higher than my flying altitude, yellow for terrain at about my altitude, and green for terrain which is safely below me. As I descended I watched these colors, steering away from the red and yellow areas and over to the green areas. It was a procedure I had never done before and certainly not something anyone would recommend or train pilots to do, but given the ice buildup I really had no choice. That said, though, it seemed like a reasonable solution to the problem. Upon reaching an altitude of 6,000 feet, the temperature had warmed up to +2°C (just above freezing) and the ice on the plane began to melt.

Base leg into Reykjavik (BIRK)

Passing the east coast of Greenland I left the weather front behind and was once again over the ocean, which is reliably at an elevation of zero: the GPS map shows it colored black. The clouds cleared, the temperature warmed up further, and I climbed back up to my assigned altitude of 10,000 feet. The rest of the flight into Reykjavik was uneventful. I switched to Iceland Radio on the VHF frequency 127.85 MHz and made contact with them before reaching the waypoint named EMBLA.

Regarding communications, when out of VHF radio range a useful technique is to ask planes flying at higher altitudes to relay messages to ATC. At higher altitudes, a plane has greater range on VHF frequencies. For this purpose I keep my #2 VHF radio tuned to a frequency of 123.45 MHz which is used to talk between one plane and another. To experiment with this, on this flight leg I tried to call other aircraft a few times on 123.45 MHz so they could relay a position report for me instead of using the satphone. I never got a response, nor did I hear any other radio chatter on the frequency while over Greenland. However, this relay method would become useful on subsequent flight legs.

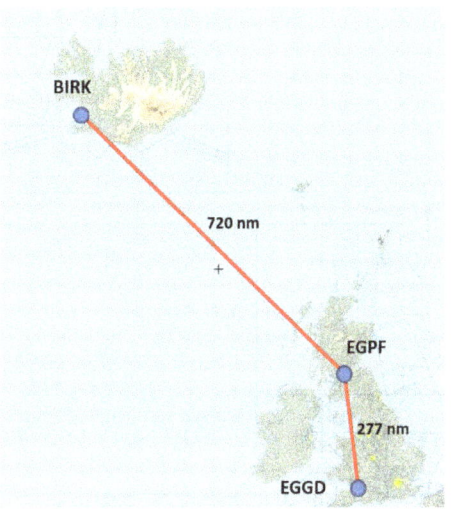

Flight legs from Reykjavik to Bristol

I elected to land at the Reykjavik city airport (airport code BIRK) rather than the big international airport at Keflavik (airport code BIKF) 50 km from town. After landing and parking the plane, the general-aviation terminal got me a taxi to the Holt hotel downtown.

After a long day of flying – more than eight hours in the cockpit – and dealing with a potentially dangerous icing situation, I was ready to relax and have a beer. From the hotel I wandered around the downtown looking for restaurant. It never really gets dark in Iceland in mid-summer. It was warm and sunny with the outdoor cafes full of people late into the night. The long hours of sunlight do make it a little harder to sleep. Reykjavik and Iceland are great places to visit. I committed to going back for a return visit when I had more free time and was not pursuing a demanding flying mission.

Sitting in a cafe enjoying the sunshine, I had a chance to reflect on how far I had come and savor the reality that one of the more difficult flights on this trip was behind me. Crossing the North Atlantic was certainly the longest ocean crossing I had ever done, and from a weather perspective, turned out to be one of the more challenging flights on this trip. From here, until I was faced with flying across the Pacific Ocean from Australia, my flight legs would generally be over land or over smaller bodies of water with a greater abundance of alternate airports in case I encountered problems. It was a great feeling to have gotten here.

Glasgow

I delayed a day in Reykjavik waiting for thunderstorms to clear over Scotland, my next destination. The British Open golf tournament was under way, the foul weather and flooding causing havoc with the final rounds. I wanted to avoid icing issues if possible, so I sought a lower altitude route to the England. To get to Bristol in the UK, my first major milestone, I would need to fly at Flight Level (FL) 100 (FL100 is about 10,000 feet) which would put me back in the forecast ice zone. I found a routing to Glasgow (airport code EGFP) at FL070 that I thought would work and filed a flight plan for that along the route shown in Appendix D. The waypoint named RATSU was a little off a more direct routing but kept me out of the Stanwick Flight Information Region where I was told they insist on using HF radio. My HF radio wasn't really working, so I wanted to avoid the Stanwick region. RATSU is the transition waypoint from Iceland Radio to Scottish Radio, so I could still use the satphone if needed.

I tried filing a flight plan with this routing online from my hotel room, but when I got to the general-aviation terminal at the airport they said I had to file it with them, which they were happy to do. I don't think they filed exactly what I wanted. While this was happening, Immigration drove over and stamped my passport on the wing of my plane as I was supervising refueling. Very efficient. I filled the wing tanks and put 120 liters in the ferry tank. Even though I wouldn't need the ferry tank for this 720 nm flight to Glasgow, it's always good to have a lot more fuel than you think you'll need. The same old adage that applies to boats also applies to airplanes: "The only time you have too much fuel is when you're on fire."

After taking off from Reykjavik, ATC told me they could only give me a clearance at FL100, so my low-altitude plan to fly at FL070 out of the ice zone got squashed. Initially, the weather was OK, and I was still in contact with Iceland radio at RATSU so things were going well. The cloud tops got higher, however, and I was soon flying in clouds again with temperatures below freezing, resulting in ice building up again on the plane. With ATC's clearance, I descended to 8,500 feet to find warmer temperatures. I was over the water now so there were no issues with mountainous terrain like I had when trying to avoid the ice over Greenland.

Following my normal fuel tank switching procedure, I tried switching to the ferry tank and almost killed the engine before quickly switching back to a wing tank. Since I didn't need the fuel in the ferry tank for this relatively short flight, I wasn't overly concerned, but I still wanted to know why the engine wouldn't run with fuel from the ferry tank. The ferry tank has an exterior air vent through a ram jet nozzle on the belly of the plane and a backup air vent inside. A fuel tank vent serves two purposes. It supplies air to replace the volume of fuel that exits the tank as it's pumped out. It also provides some (limited) air pressure that helps push the fuel out of the tank into the engine to assist the fuel pump. A closed or blocked vent could inhibit fuel from exiting the tank and cause the engine to stop because it's starved for fuel. I opened the backup vent inside the cabin and tried switching to the ferry tank again. The engine ran OK using the backup vent. I suspect the exterior tank vent nozzle may have gotten iced over while I was still at 10,000 feet. It was an issue I resolved to explore further to see whether that was the correct explanation. For the moment I was glad the interior backup vent was there and working.

I picked up Scottish Radio some distance north of Scotland so I never had to use the satphone for communications on this flight leg. The remainder of the flight into Glasgow was typical instrument flying – in and out of clouds. Having climbed the highest point in the UK – Ben Nevis, at about 4,500 feet – back in 1994, I knew the Scottish terrain was not very high so I requested and was assigned an even lower altitude. The clouds cleared at Glasgow so I had an easy visual approach to the airport with a 10–12 knot wind blowing across the runway on landing (a crosswind) that requires a pilot to use particular techniques to keep the plane flying straight down the runway.

Over the English countryside en-route to Bristol

I parked at the general-aviation terminal, a company called Signature. There wasn't a single other small plane in sight. The people at Signature were helpful. They don't get many general-aviation planes, they said, and sell relatively little fuel for planes like mine. I'd been to Glasgow before so I really wasn't interested in tourism. The airport is inconveniently located some distance from town anyway. I'd booked the Holiday Inn at the airport for the night and planned to fly to Bristol the next day. Overall it was an expensive stop for fuel, ground handling, and landing fees – even the Holiday Inn was expensive. Glasgow is not an airport I'd visit again.

The weather was not great when I left Glasgow Sunday morning with overcast ceilings at about 1,500 feet, but the forecast showed better weather further south and at Bristol (airport code EGGD). I was anxious to get to Bristol and hang out with old friends, so I filed an IFR flight plan to Bristol at FL070, with the routing shown in Appendix D.

When calling for my flight clearance at Glasgow, the tower gave me the Dean Cross Standard Instrument Departure (SID), which didn't look too complicated. A Standard Instrument Departure is a written procedure consisting of specific courses and altitudes a pilot must fly after takeoff. They are used so that the flow of planes leaving an airport for particular destinations are following the same route and not flying all over the sky. It makes managing the airplane traffic easier for air traffic controllers and safer for the planes.

Even though they had assigned me to fly a Standard Instrument Departure, after takeoff Glasgow Radar (what we would call Approach or Departure in the US) gave me a direct routing to the WAL waypoint so I was quickly out of Glasgow airspace and on my way to Bristol. Again, I had typical IFR conditions flying in and out of clouds accompanied by a little turbulence at times. I was surprised to hear several commercial flights asking for diversions to avoid bad weather. I don't know what they were seeing; they must have been well north of me. A pilot will sometimes ask for a diversion from their assigned routing to avoid bad weather so the ride is more comfortable for the passengers.

The cloud layers limited my views of some places I really wanted to see from the air, like the Lake District, but there was nothing for it but to fly my assigned route and get to Bristol. On this flight there were numerous radio handoffs from one air traffic controller to another. There were also changes in transponder squawk codes, something that is unusual in the US. A squawk is a unique 4-digit number, for example 4716, assigned to each aircraft for each flight. The code is dialed into the transponder onboard each plane. When the ATC radar beam scan passes the aircraft, the transponder detects it and sends its own signal back to the radar receiver. The return signal gives the transponder squawk code and other information such as the location, altitude, speed, and direction of the plane. All this information shows up on the ATC controller's radar screen to help identify which plane is which so the controller can manage their positions.

Along with changes in radio frequencies and squawk codes, I was also being told that I was entering or leaving controlled airspace, with a corresponding change in radar services. I had been forewarned that UK air traffic control handles IFR flights differently than ATC in the US. I was told it's possible for your flight plan to be canceled upon exiting controlled airspace and you then have to re-negotiate a new flight plan where you enter a new controlled airspace. Because of these warnings, accurate or not, every time I was told I was exiting controlled airspace, I asked them if my flight plan to Bristol was still intact. It was. I have to say I never really understood all these airspace transitions vis-a-vis ATC. I did what they told me and I got where I was going without any screw-ups that I'm aware of. It does seem to me (and many others) that the UK system is unnecessarily complicated compared to the US system which handles a much higher volume of planes with a much simpler ATC protocol.

Once in contact with Bristol Radar, everything played the way I was used to. They gave me vectors to the approach course for landing on runway 27. Because the weather was good (scattered clouds at 3000 feet), I really didn't need to use the instrument approach. I flew the vectored course procedure anyway just for practice.

I parked at the Bristol Air Centre, the only general-aviation terminal on the field. I was gratified finally to see some small planes. They have a flight school here that uses Piper Cherokee-type planes, a plane that is very familiar to me since I have flown about 1100 hours in this family of planes, including Warriors, Archers, Arrows, and Seminoles.

I paid pretty high fees at Bristol for parking, fuel, landing, and ground handling, although no plane handling was involved. I had been told that Europe was expensive for general aviation so I wasn't really surprised, but the

N788W on the ramp at Bristol (EGGD)

contrast in costs when compared to a US airport of similar size was dramatic. In the US I would expect to pay only for parking and maybe a small parking or access fee at the general-aviation terminal if I didn't buy fuel. They waive the access fee and often the parking fee with the fuel purchase.

Bristol was my first significant milestone on this trip. I was now in Europe, in a city I had lived in for more than two years. I intended to take some time off from flying, more than the few days I had taken off waiting for weather at other stops. I could forget about flying for a while, enjoy the company of old friends, and indulge in some great memories of the time I'd lived in England.

5

England

Bristol

She hesitantly walked up to the window and pulled back the lace curtain a few inches so she could watch what was happening on the broad sidewalk below the first floor of their home in Clifton. Her husband had just arrived in a taxi escorting a beautiful young woman, Evie Elliot, who was a partner with her sister Beatrice in an upstart haute couture fashion enterprise called the House of Elliot. Her husband dared not touch Evie in public, but their body language, their extended conversation, their touching but not touching in the flickering light of the gas streetlamps, confirmed in her mind what she had already suspected. Her husband was having an affair with this young woman and she had no idea how to respond.

The sidewalk in front on my flat at 6 Victoria Square in Clifton

The director called, "Cut. One more," and everyone relaxed and busied themselves to re-shoot the scene. The film crew for the BBC production of the *House of Elliot* had paid me 50 pounds to use the flat I was renting on Victoria Square in the Clifton neighborhood of Bristol as a set. The building itself was a perfect Victorian-era row house: the huge crystal chandelier hanging in the drawing room and the 10-foot-tall windows of my flat resonated with the carved stone exterior that faced the street.

Brunel's bridge over Clifton Gorge

While the building itself and my flat were definitely period pieces, the cars routinely parked on the streets forming the perimeter of Victoria Square, and the small park it contained, were not. Having modern cars appear in the exterior shots for a story set in 1920's England would not do. Consequently, several weeks in advance of the days when they would be filming, they had placed flyers on the windshields of the cars alerting them to be parked out of sight on other streets on the designated days. While most had been moved, a few remained and had to be lifted by hand using a small crew onto what were essentially large roller skates under each wheel so that they could be pushed out of sight without damage. They took pains to mark the location of each car so they could return it to the same location. Reports to the police of stolen cars that appeared to be missing or stolen would not help a production schedule that was already a few days behind. Other modern features like parking meters or signposts had to be concealed or disguised with plants.

It was 1993 and I was living in Bristol while pursuing my Ph.D. in electrical engineering (wireless communications) at the University of Bristol. I watched the TV production with curiosity and amusement. I actually would have paid them 50 pounds for the entertainment value of it. *The House of Elliot* was a short-lived mini-series created and produced by the same team that had developed the wildly successful BBC series *Upstairs, Downstairs* which ran for years on PBS stations in the United States. The *House of Elliot* lasted only three seasons. I never got an explanation as to why the BBC terminated it. Apparently, it was a surprise to the producers as well. Season three ended with several unresolved story lines.

For old time's sake I bought a DVD set of the *House of Elliot* that now sits on the shelf in the media room of my Bainbridge Island home. I've never watched any of it, but one day I might, with curious friends who never had a chance to see it on PBS.

I was *very* happy to be back in Bristol – the first major milestone for my flight, and about 25% of the way along my route around the world. I spent the next 10 days in Bristol at the Marriott Royal Hotel on College Green, with some side trips and a short flight out and back to nearby Dunkeswell. I visited with old friends and, of course, walked by my old flat at 6 Victoria Square in Clifton. Many of my favorite restaurants, and one particular pizza place, Pizza Provencal where I used to hang out, were still in business. I enjoy walking around a foreign city I know so well that I don't need a map. Paris is another city that falls in that category.

I also spent time re-calibrating and re-planning my trip. As I mentioned, I had originally planned to fly just to Europe and back, but the intermittent volcanic activity in Iceland motivated me to install the ferry tank so that I could take the southern route via the Azores to Europe if necessary. The ferry tank also gave me enough range to hop between the islands of the Pacific completing a flight around the world if I chose to. That was the plan that was approved by the FAA on the Special Flight Permit when the tank was installed in Merced.

Dunkeswell aerodrome in the English countryside

The first part of the trip to this point had gone smoothly enough that I finally made the commitment to fly around the world. But in crossing the Atlantic to Europe in early July – perfect for going just to Europe – I had not considered the weather I would encounter further along the route. In particular, I hadn't considered the monsoon inundates India during the summer months and doesn't really start to subside until late September or early October. Because of these weather/timing issues I was in Europe too early. I needed to delay a couple of months, at least, to arrive in India during better weather. Certainly I could cross India now, but it would be harder flying on instruments and not really the pleasure trip, with aerial sightseeing, that I had in mind. I really didn't have a schedule or deadline to finish this trip so the delay really wouldn't matter, or so I thought.

I finally decided I would park the plane for a few months, return to the US, and get electronic charts and other things reorganized for the longer flight around the world. I planned my return to England for the first week of October when I would pick up the plane and carry on from there.

I started asking around for possible hangar options where I could park the plane and finally found Skypark in Gloucester Airport, not far from Bristol, where Steve Williams had room for my Columbia 300. I'd fly N788W up to Gloucester and park it in his hangar when I was done with my stay in Bristol.

Dunkeswell

Dunkeswell (airport code EGTU) is a tiny village about 45 miles southwest of Bristol. During WWII, there was an American airbase at Dunkeswell where my dad was stationed as the radioman on a B-24 bomber crew. As part of Navy Fleet Air Wing 7 (FAW-7), they flew missions against German submarine bases along the French coast and submarines operating in the English Channel.

Today at Dunkeswell a 3200-foot section of the original runway remains, providing an airfield for small planes like mine. I visited this place by car some 19 years

**My Dad's B-24 crew.
He's standing on the far right**

Sailors waiting to use a phone box in Dunkeswell

That iconic phone box is now a designated historical place

earlier when I lived in Bristol, but I wanted the experience of flying in to the place and getting a sense of what it was like to cross the verdant fields of England to a home airbase at Dunkeswell, as my father had done.

The airfield had changed a lot since I had visited before – it was much more active, with a flight school and more hangars. An expanded military museum of WWII FAW-7 activity was just across the road from the small terminal building, which now has a pleasant little restaurant. For English pilots it was the perfect "100-dollar hamburger" lunchtime flying destination, as we'd call it in the US. I had a good time strolling the lanes of this little English village on a sunny afternoon.

This was my first flight in England using visual flight rules (VFR). The airspace between Bristol and Dunkeswell is simple. They gave me a departure out of Bristol airspace with an altitude limit of 2000 feet and an exit point from Bristol airspace at a Visual Reporting Point (VPR) called Cheddar, which is apparently a reservoir of some kind. There is a string of Visual Reporting Points along the perimeter of the Bristol controlled airspace (and I suppose others in England) like towers along a castle wall. I really had no idea where Cheddar was – I doubted I could identify it anyway – but I presumed it was somewhere on the way to Dunkeswell, so basically I flew directly to Dunkeswell.

Returning to Bristol, it was the same deal: enter Bristol controlled airspace at Cheddar. However, this time I was armed with a 1:500,000 aeronautical chart of southern England that I bought at Dunkeswell for 18 pounds. It showed the Cheddar Visual Reporting Point so I knew where to go, and a good thing I did. ATC told me to remain outside Bristol airspace for about five minutes so I flew lazy circles over the beautiful countryside south of Cheddar. I learned later that specific details, including coordinates, are published for these Visual Reporting Points. If I flew in and out of Bristol often, I would program them into the GPS as user waypoints.

Gloucester

I moved my plane N788W from Bristol to Skypark at the Gloucester Airport (airport code EGBJ) on July 19, a short 35 nm flight. Skypark is a new hangar facility owned by Steve Williams. Steve is also a pilot and flies a Meridian. In addition to hangars and other businesses, Steve has a flight school at Gloucester where his wife is a flight instructor. Steve arranged for an oil change for my plane while I was away. The oil change would be done by a mechanic (in the UK they call them engineers) who actually had taken Lancair factory training when Lancair envisioned a European dealer network, before it got into financial trouble. Steve is a nice guy who was helpful to me.

After parking the plane in the hangar at the Gloucester airport, I spent the night in nearby Cheltenham. The next morning I took the train to London where I spent another night. The following day, July 21, I boarded a non-stop flight back to Seattle.

6

England to Greece

Paperwork

I flew back to London and took the train to Cheltenham on October 4. As I mentioned in earlier chapters, for this round-the-world flight I needed an FAA Special Flight Permit covering the installation and use of the extra fuel tanks and allowing aircraft operation at greater than the Maximum Certificated Takeoff Weight. This Special Flight Permit was issued in June by the FAA FSDO in Fresno for 90 days, so during my 10-week hiatus back in the US it had expired. I naively assumed it would be easy to get the expiration date extended but no such luck. I spoke directly to the guy at the Fresno FSDO who issued the original Special Flight Permit. He came back with FAA-speak: "It is the position of this office..." They were not helpful. Frankly, I think they declined to renew it because they were annoyed I didn't fulfill the terms of their original Special Flight Permit and complete my flight to Honolulu in the allotted 90 days. There was no good technical reason for them to deny the renewal since the installation had not changed.

Without their pro forma renewal, I had to get an entirely new permit. Getting a new permit required a new inspection process, and since the aircraft was now in Europe, the FAA's International Field Office in Munich had jurisdiction to sign off on the permit. What ensued was three days of chasing around an English inspector (an FAA Designated Airworthiness

Representative or DAR) who had the authority to inspect the plane and issue the proper documents. I didn't get the new Special Flight Permit in hand until 10:30 Friday night, October 7. This put me two days behind my original schedule. Since they knew my flight objective, the FAA people at the Munich International Field Office were particularly helpful in getting this permit processed in a timely fashion, so my hat's off to them.

I will also add the inspector (DAR) I used in England (whom I won't name) was profoundly incompetent, as if he really didn't understand why the Special Flight Permit was being issued. The first set of Operating Limitations he prepared had an allowed maximum weight for my plane that was *less* than the normal certificated weight of 3400 pounds! Ridiculous! The whole point of the permit was to *raise* the allowed weight for the extra fuel. All he really needed to do was copy the Operating Limitations that the Fresno FSDO had prepared and update the routing and dates for the onward flight to Honolulu – simple. He also asked many foolish questions. It was only through the help of the FAA guy in Munich, who pushed this inspector onto the right track, that I was finally able to get a viable Special Flight Permit. The inspector was also expensive – around 2,000 pounds for his services. If he had done an excellent and quick job I wouldn't really complain about the cost. I view this episode as one of the times I could have avoided a big expense with a better master plan and timing for the round-the-world trip.

While in Gloucester waiting for paperwork to be sorted out I did have a chance to meet with some new friends, Patrick Elliot and Linda Walker, who had completed a yearlong flight around the world the preceding month in a homebuilt Long EZ aircraft. It is a plane of novel design that has shorter range than mine and, as a homebuilt plane, is limited to daytime flight with visual flight rules (VFR). Taking shorter hops between airports, they ended up seeing a lot more places along the way than I would. Their route paralleled mine through the Middle East and Southeast Asia, so they had become a great source of recent information on what I might encounter.

Anxious to be on my way after getting the Special Flight Permit on Friday night, I left Gloucester for Cannes, France (airport code LFMD), the next morning, October 8, at 9:00 am. The people I dealt with at Gloucester where very helpful and friendly, particularly Steve Williams, the owner of the hangar where I parked my plane, and his wife Kathryn who is the chief flight instructor at the Staverton Flying School. I can also say that Gloucester is a great general-aviation-friendly airport with relatively low fees and businesses on the field that cater to small aircraft. An example is RGV Aviation – an FAA-certified repair station that had several US-manufactured Cirrus aircraft in their shop. They also were able to fill my portable oxygen bottle, something the general-aviation terminal in Bristol couldn't do. I had N788W's oil changed by Aerotech, another good resource based near Gloucester. Overall, if you're flying into UK and want a place to leave your plane for a while, Gloucester is a good choice. With good hotels in Cheltenham and a reasonable two-hour train ride to London, it is a convenient base to explore the southern parts of the England.

Gloucester to Cannes

I had originally planned to fly to Avignon (airport code LFMV) and spend three days in Provence in Southern France. However, Avignon is not a normal Airport of Entry so the Customs and Immigration people are generally not there. They do handle a few international flights a week, so they will process a private flight if given 24 hours' notice of arrival. Getting my FAA flight permit paperwork completed was so uncertain that it was not possible to predict 24 hours ahead of time when I would arrive. Consequently, I had to forego Avignon and instead fly to Cannes (airport code LFMD) which does have Customs and Immigration available throughout the day, every day. Though England is part of Europe in some respects, it is not part of the Schengen Area (basically countries in the EU) so passing through Customs and Immigration is necessary when traveling from England to France in a plane. This usually doesn't happen when traveling by conventional means: commercial flight, boat, or train.

Filing flight plans in Europe is not as straightforward as it is in the US. I used an online service available at the time called EuroFPL to file the IFR flight plan to Cannes. EuroFPL basically sends the flight plan to EuroControl for approval. If it is not approved, it will be necessary to file it again, perhaps with a different routing, which EuroFPL can suggest. Eventually, you'll get an approved plan. At this writing in 2015, there are now other online services such as RocketRoute that also perform optimum route selection and flight plan filing services for flying in Europe. Having a service to find and file approved flight plans is essential. In the US, you can file any reasonable routing to your destination and the flight plan will be accepted. If the requested routing doesn't work, ATC will simply change it once you first contact them before departure or modify it while you are en-route.

After taking off from Gloucester I was vectored a bit around Heathrow Airport but once over the English Channel, I was back on the flight plan route. Unfortunately, I was above or in the clouds so didn't see any of the channel below me. French ATC was efficient, giving me direct routing shortcuts to waypoints farther down my route, which saved time.

Over France I ran into ice again in the clouds at FL090. I asked for and got assigned a lower altitude, FL070, but after the descent the temperature didn't rise at all. In my experience temperature gradients with altitude in real weather are rarely the normal lapse rate of 2°C per 1000 feet they teach to pilots. So I lived with 0° at FL070 expecting it to warm up as I got further south, which it did.

The weather cleared south of the waypoint named ABDIL. I had briefed myself on flying the ABDIL 1V Standard Arrival Route, an instrument arrival procedure into Cannes. This was Nice airspace, though, so I started getting vectored around to avoid other planes arriving at these airports, finally being given a descent over the ocean south of Cannes for a visual approach to the airport. The visual approach to runway 17 at Cannes is precise and a bit bizarre, designed to control noise in this French Riviera town. There is an apartment building on the coast you must fly over while headed toward a bare patch on the mountainside north of town, before making a sweeping left turn back to the airport. They even have a "mandatory" written brief about it on the Cannes Airport website. You must download and read the brief – a completion certificate is awarded after

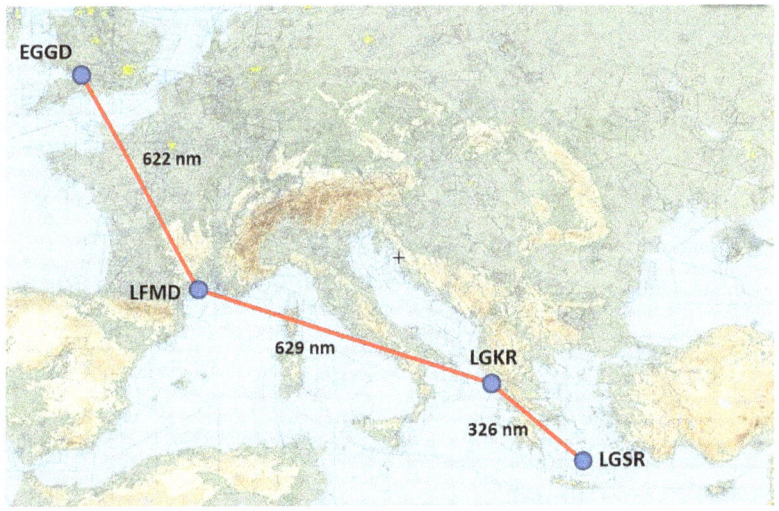

Flight legs from Bristol to Santorini

Approach to runway 17 at Cannes

doing it! I read the online brief, got my certificate, and was prepared to fly the procedure – I even had printed the photos showing the apartment building and bare patch – when the tower gave me a "short circuit" (short approach) to runway 17. That meant I could skip the roundabout approach in the online procedure and zip right into the airport.

Cannes is a convenient airport with limited commercial traffic, so I saw many small planes and private jets parked there. But security was still tight. I parked the plane in parking area G on the grass and left the airport through the Customs office. The Customs guy didn't even look at my passport; he just waived me through because he was too busy chatting to a cute stewardess with a great figure.

I checked into a small hotel 100 meters from the terminal: not a great place but very convenient. I then decided I should go back to the airport and fuel the plane. It took the help of a friendly guy at the local Aeroclub (Aeroclubs are a big part of GA flying in France) with limited English to show me how to get back on the ramp without passing through passenger security in the terminal. Access was through a locked gate with a guard where I had to show my pilot license for the first time. Once on the ramp refueling was no problem, but the hassle of returning to the airport taught me a valuable lesson: when arriving at an airport, the first thing to do is get ready to leave – i.e. refuel the plane to avoid departure delays (there was a line at the gas pump). The point is to minimize the number of times going through security to get back on the ramp.

That night I had to consider my options. There was a major weather system parked over Greece. Low clouds, rain, and high winds were prevailing at Kerkyra (Corfu), my next stop, and Santorini, and probably would be for the next few days. Given that, I decided to do what I had come to do in the first place: spend some time in Provence instead of trying to pick up the time I lost due to the FAA paperwork delay in Gloucester. So rather than fly the next day into poor weather I decided to rent a car and hang out for a few days in the south of France where it was warm and the sun was shining brilliantly.

Provence

Provence is one of my favorite places in the world. I first drove through the Luberon Valley in February or March 1976, many years before Peter Mayle turned life there into a cliché with the publication of *A Year in Provence*. Back then I was driving a beige VW Beetle I bought for US$500 in Paris. Parked along the curb of Rue Scribe outside the American Express office were a number of "traveler" cars for sale. In those days the American Express office was the place everybody visited to cash traveler's checks and even collect mail at a "General Delivery" window they had at the time. I bought the VW from an Israeli guy for cash, with the transaction recorded in one hand-written paragraph on a sheet of note paper. It was added to a stack of a dozen or so other such transactions, hand-written in a variety of languages. The car and title had not changed hands properly for years. It had old German export license plates instead of current French plates, and no insurance, and I never did get any. Insurance was very expensive and probably would have required a proper title.

It was great fun to have this car in France to visit many out-of-the-way places that were impossible to see using public transport. I even drove it to Amsterdam to visit a woman I had met in Salisbury, Rhodesia (now Zimbabwe), while hitchhiking around Africa a few months earlier.

I lived in the French town of Montpellier for several months, ostensibly as a student studying French but really just hanging out having a good time with the many college students that were spending the year abroad at the famous universities there. My car would be loaded with people as we went to clubs at night and excursions around the countryside on weekends. Those were some of the best times I've ever had.

When I left France that following spring, I sold the car for $500 to an American student in Montpellier. We used the same kind of hand-written transaction note to add to the others. I still had the key fob from that car at my country home in Oregon. It is the only car I've owned that I would be interested to know what happened to it. No doubt it could tell fascinating stories about the people who had owned it; some of those stories would be mine.

My memories of Montpellier are still vivid, made more so by a visit there in 2006 with the woman who had been my girlfriend back in 1976, while living in Montpellier. I lived in Montpellier for six months, in a room at the tennis club on Rue de la Roqueturiere, then on the edge of town. My walk to the university was along gravel lanes with low stone walls and vineyards on either side. Idyllic. My girlfriend Helen lived in centre ville on Rue Lallemand in a 500-year-old building. The stone steps leading to her third-floor room were worn with deep scoops from a million footsteps treading there over the centuries. Place de la Comedie was under construction – chaos we never saw finished but it was clear France had big plans for Montpellier as a business/industry/commercial center. We would hang out at various bars around town but one in particular, "Le Ranch," near the university. We'd play cards with the French geezers who sometimes would tell WW2 stories. One guy I remember had this dramatic way of turning over cards; in a low, serious voice he'd say, "Le neuf de coeur" ("The nine of hearts…") like a grand announcement. I've never been a smoker but something about a French bar makes me want to light up a Gauloise and let the acrid smoke drift up and sting my eyes while I bitterly reflect on my life. Oh well, too much Sartre.

Windmill in Provence

When we went back to Montpellier in 2006, the city had become the sprawling metropolis they had planned. We struggled to find the tennis club and my room there but eventually did, now buried in the city. The vineyards were long gone, replaced by stucco housing developments that could have been transported directly from Southern California. Helen's place was still there in the center of town but the door was repainted so we didn't recognize exactly which building right away. I remember taking a photo of her with her roommates in 1976 standing outside on the little iron balcony, like Juliet, so I took another one from the same courtyard perspective with my phone. When I got home I compared the two. The railing and wall details matched so we did have the right building. France! An important place in my life: endless, many stories, many adventures.

The village of Joucas

Back to current reality from my night of reminiscing, I rented a car at the Cannes Airport. Even though it was Sunday and the Europcar counter is normally closed, with two hours' notice from an online booking they came out, opened the counter, and gave me a car. Soon I was headed west on the A8, turned north at Aix-en-Provence, then west again to Loumarin where I stopped for lunch at Cafe Gaby in the center of this little town. From there I drove over the crest of the Luberon Mountains through Bonnieux, Goult, and finally to the hotel I had booked in Joucas, stopping for photos along the way and even finding an old windmill I remembered from a visit here nine years before.

Vineyards in the south of France

I have been back to the Luberon every few years for the last 15, usually renting a large house for a few weeks and inviting friends to join me. I know the area pretty well – it's nice to be able to drive around without using a map. I've eaten at the great restaurant at Le Mas des Herbes Blanches several times – a gastronomic feast – but had never stayed in the hotel until this trip. It's really a wonderful spot outside the tiny village of Joucas, maybe 8 km east of better-known Gordes and 6 km north of Roussillon. It was so pleasant I wanted to stay longer than one night. It motivated me to want to return here the following October and rent a house for an extended stay, but unfortunately, other things got in the way.

On Monday the 10th I took a leisurely, roundabout drive from Joucas back to Cannes by way of the Avignon Airport where I stopped to visit the Aeroclub and look around at what I had only seen on charts to that point. I finally returned to Cannes via the autoroute to spend the night at the same convenient hotel by the airport. I chose to do that rather than stay longer in Joucas because I wanted a very early start for my flight from Cannes to Kerkyra, Greece, on the island of Corfu. I was planning to fly two legs on the 11th, the first to Kerkyra (airport code LGKR) for a fuel stop and because it is an Airport of Entry for Greece, a stop required by Greece Civil Aviation Authority. From Kerkyra I would continue on to Santorini (airport code LGSR) and pick up a lost day. The forecast weather was excellent in Kerkyra, and not great but

Mount Vesuvius in Italy

acceptable in Santorini, so the two-flight setup looked plausible enough. Unfortunately, I didn't count on a work slowdown by Greek air traffic control.

I took off from Cannes at about 8:00 am. It was a beautiful, clear morning. I questioned again why I was leaving at all but the larger mission called, and I could always come back to this sunny weather once again. I filed the IFR flight route shown in Appendix D. I was given the SODRI 9K Standard Instrument Departure procedure at an altitude of 2000 feet, but once handed to Nice Control I was cleared directly to the waypoint called SODRI at an altitude of FL090. The weather along the way was about the best I'd had on this trip, with fantastic views of Italy, the villages clinging to the coastline and the islands offshore. I flew directly past Mt. Vesuvius and across the boot of Italy, now cruising at FL110, before starting a descent into Kekyra where I was given a shortcut to a visual approach for runway 35.

I used a handler at Kerkyra for the first time on this trip – Goldair Handling which operates throughout Greece. They offered a 50% discount to US pilots, so the handling charge was 30 euros total: very inexpensive

Final approach at Kerkyra

in the world of handlers. What I got for that was someone who met me on arrival, arranged for the fuel truck (though fuel is supplied by a separate company), and filed the next flight plan with the tower. The fuel truck was in demand that day, so it was worthwhile to have Goldair make sure I got my turn to be fueled based on my arrival time.

I had neglected to file an onward flight plan to Santorini from Kerkyra, thinking I would do it at the airport. That turned out to be a big mistake. While fueling we did file a flight plan to depart immediately, but when I called the tower for permission to start my engine, a step you must do outside the US, they told me my departure time slot would be some three hours later. With that departure time I would have arrived in Santorini well after dark in weather that was forecast to be somewhat dicey. On the original schedule, before the Gloucester paperwork delay, I had planned to spend the night in Kerkyra. Now it looked like Greek ATC was inadvertently going to make that happen. I gave up on flying to Santorini that night and booked a room in town. It meant having to file some paperwork (a General Declaration, or GENDEC for short) to exit the airport and re-enter the next morning. Goldair took care of that for me. I was pretty annoyed that I would miss one night in Santorini where I had a nice hotel lined up, but Kerkyra is also a great town with Mediterranean architecture, so I made the best of it, taking pleasure in wandering around the streets and harbor quays before and after dinner.

I suspected if I had filed a flight plan earlier, before leaving Cannes, my departure time wouldn't have gotten bumped so badly. So once at the hotel, I filed a flight plan for departure at 9:00 the next morning, hoping for the best. The Goldair guy also explained that delayed departure slots affected everybody, even scheduled commercial flights. There was a work slowdown by the Greek ATC people in an effort to get the government to pay attention to their economic woes. Apparently, they hadn't been getting paid what they should have been paid, so maybe they couldn't be blamed for a work slowdown to protest.

Though I filed for a 9:00 am departure from Kerkyra, once again I got bumped to a time slot at 10:27 am, which eventually they moved up to 10:16 am. I really don't understand this, since I fly too low to compete with air carriers on the enroute airspace, but maybe Santorini has more incoming flights than I imagined. Anyway, I waited it out sitting in the plane, although I did call the tower to report "Ready" in the event an earlier slot opened up, which it didn't. Reporting "Ready" may have been a waste of time, but it certainly was a waste of battery power since I had to sit there with the avionics and radios turned on in case the tower called me back. After 15 minutes of this, I got smart and shut off the avionics and used my backup ICOM handheld VHF radio to monitor the tower frequency in case they called me.

I was finally released for takeoff at the promised time on an IFR flight plan to Santorini. Before long, while passing the waypoint named MALED, I was asked for position reports about every 25 nm, a good indication they probably don't have radar coverage in that area to track the locations of planes.

That may also partly explain the departure slot problem. After I passed the TRL VOR navigation station, they told me I was in radar contact so I was back in their screen.

It was a pretty nice flight overall but my views were initially obscured by a thin cloud layer at 5000 feet over the water coming up to Santorini. Once I descended, it was clear flying. I set up for an instrument approach for runway 34R but it was not necessary. I asked the Santorini tower if I could fly a visual approach coming in from over the Aegean Sea, a request they granted.

Santorini

It might have been the same bar I remember from decades earlier, but there were so many bars like this I couldn't be sure. It had booze and music, sort of a nightclub in a way, with an odd assortment of tables and chairs arranged inside and out, but mostly it had people who wanted to hook up.

It was a warm night in Thira, Santorini's main town. I sat at a corner table of the bar watching as some hot young Greek guys chatted with two American college-aged girls in short summer dresses and sandals, their lightened hair and subtle golden tans from the Mediterranean sun. The Greek guys were skilled at picking up foreign women, and the girls were just as willing to be seduced by the men, their accents, and the romantic setting on a Greek island. Eventually, one of the girls agreed to ride off with one of the guys on the back of his motorbike. As they walked out I overheard him describing a remote beach that was perfect for a midnight swim in the moonlight. He had a blanket on the back of his motorbike ready for a beach liaison. I'm sure they were headed for a fun and adventurous night on the beach.

Whitewashed houses in Santorini

Many years before I was the guy with a motorbike and the blanket on the back. In a bar I invited three Australian women in their thirties to join me in a bottle of chilled white wine that turned into two, that led to ouzo. I connected with one of the women in particular, a blonde with green eyes and freckles, an intense Aussie accent, and a wry sense of humor. I've always had a weakness for that. Eventually, we decided to head off and see the beach ourselves and so said, "See ya later" to her friends, and got on my rented motorbike. In the darkness at the beach we made the most of the blanket. During intermission we took a naked dip in the surf. A few other couples had arrived and staked out places on the beach discreetly away from our blanket. In the half-moonlight and darkness we could see their outlined shapes moving with passionate rhythm.

When I lived in England, having a fantasy fling with a handsome stranger in Greece or some other sun-drenched place was a persistent theme for women in travel magazines, the perfect remedy to the short daylight and wintertime gloom of northern Europe. I seem to remember there was even a TV mini-series about a middle-aged woman, just divorced, who goes on holiday in Greece to find the erotic adventure she had been wanting.

Replaying my beach memories as I approached Santorini made for a pretty distracted landing! I used Goldair Handling once again as the handler here. They did a nice job marshaling me to a parking place, then waited with a bus while I unloaded my baggage and covered the plane. The bus ride was maybe 300 meters to the terminal. There were no other small planes in sight, just air carrier jets and turboprops. Refueling was not on the agenda because there was no aviation gas available in Santorini at the time, just fuel for jets and turboprops.

Magical sunset at Santorini

I had booked a room at the Astra Suites Hotel, which is perched on the cliff edge in Imerovigli just north of Thira. On the drive there, however, I saw that the island was actually worse, more over-built, than my relatively low expectations. It really is tourist-trashed out, with car rentals, scooter rentals, and every imaginable shop and walk-in restaurant that caters to tourists lining the streets. The narrow streets were jammed with people off several large cruise ships anchored in the old port inside the caldera. I counted six cruise ships as I flew in.

When I first visited Santorini 35 years ago in the off season, the place was almost quaint, with no cruise ships stopping. Arriving on a broken-down old ferry called the Kyclades, as I recall, a handful of backpackers from various countries, me included, were about the only tourists in town. We had a good time hanging out together. The handful of restaurants were small establishments with no printed menus. A meal was ordered by strolling into the kitchen, opening the lid of each pot on the stove, and pointing at the ones you wanted to eat. Very practical. It did rain often but that was typical of March. Of course, the island could never have stayed that way, but what I see now tells me there is really not much reason to return. I suppose I had to see for myself, sadly. Still, looking beyond the tourist hordes and what happens to an island that relies on that industry for its livelihood, the natural beauty still remains. The sunsets were as spectacular as I remember, with the whitewashed villages precariously clinging to the cliffs as if mother nature could shrug them off with the flick of an earthquake and put things back the way they once were.

I did take a tour on a small boat out to the volcanic cones in the center of the caldera. I hadn't done this tour before, so it was a new experience that provided a view of Thira and villages from a different perspective. It was a sunny, enjoyable day away from flying, providing a little exercise climbing around on the trails and up to the summit on these island cones. I wasn't getting any exercise sitting in the plane all day. I used my two nights on Santorini to enjoy dinner at some restaurants with spectacular views that perfectly complemented the excellent food and wine.

I had been originally bothered when the ATC delay on Corfu caused me to lose a night on Santorini. But given how overrun it now was with tourists, I felt the time I had there was enough to enjoy what I wanted and be reminded of some compelling adventures from my past. I was OK with the short stay – I was ready to leave.

7

Greece to Dubai

It was a beautiful morning to fly over the Aegean Sea. I flew from Santorini to Heraklion (airport code LGIR) on the island of Crete, a short flight of only 66 nm at an altitude of 4,500 feet, about 20 minutes in N788W. I didn't have any aeronautical charts for Greece, so I relied on the GPS navdata to show me the appropriate reporting point for entering the Heraklion-controlled airspace.

Once on the ground at Heraklion, the main business was refueling, again with the assistance of Goldair Handling. When I opened the door, however, they had bad news. I was informed my departure slot was three hours hence, two hours later than the time I had requested. Again, they said it was due to the work slowdown/strike by air traffic controllers. This delay would put me into Luxor after dark, which I generally wanted to avoid if I could. Luxor is renowned for being dusty and hazy, so a night landing would almost certainly be by instruments. Besides, this trip was meant to be a sightseeing flight, at least on one level, so flying over the Sahara desert at night when I couldn't see anything would defeat that purpose.

Someone at Goldair suggested I file for a VFR departure so I could depart right away, but I still needed an IFR flight plan to get into Egypt, so I finally decided to file a hybrid VFR/IFR flight plan. I climbed up four flights of a spiral staircase to the Heraklion tower where three controllers were working ground, tower, and approach frequencies. They were quite helpful, showing me to a desk and a pad of flight plan forms. Once I had filled out the hybrid

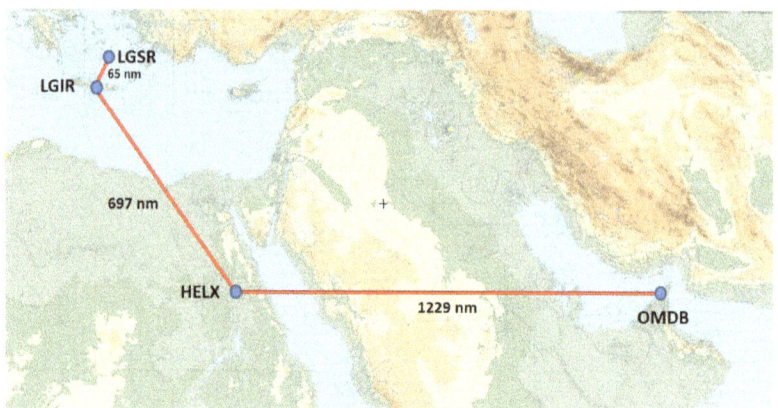

Flight legs from Santorini to Dubai

flight plan, they filed it for me, waited for its acceptance, and I was good to go. I finally got airborne only 40 minutes after my originally scheduled time. The slot delays were not affecting just private flights like mine, which are generally considered expendable, but also scheduled commercial flights which were being delayed to the point where passengers were demanding to be taken back to the terminal after hours sitting in a hot plane on the ramp.

Compared to the ATC delays, refueling went smoothly here. It was completed well before my departure release time. That gave me a chance to relax a bit and eat lunch on the ground instead of in the plane. The final successful flight plan routing that I filed with its initial VFR component is shown in Appendix D.

South of Crete, once again over the water, radio contact with Cairo Radar (what they call their ATC service) was a problem. I employed a relay for the first time on this trip through a commercial flight high overhead. They informed me that Cairo had me on radar but communications were not yet established. I used a relay again over the Egyptian desert in a similar situation. My relatively low altitude of about 9,000 feet is the main reason I couldn't hear them or be heard. When checking in with a new

Flying over the Sahara Desert

controller, it's a good strategy to ask what the next frequency will be after him. That way, if you fly out of range of the guy you're talking to, you've got the next frequency down the line where you can eventually make contact.

I had variable winds along the way, some tailwinds and some headwinds; overall it turned out to be a five-hour flight of 820 nm from Heraklion to Luxor (airport code HELX). Almost 400 nm of it was along the western/central desert of Egypt with curious smoothed stone formations that look like the bottom of the sea or a river bed, which it probably was once. There were very few signs of human activity. The most notable were remarkably isolated small settlements of concrete block buildings and what looked like clusters of tents through my binoculars. Occasionally, the almost featureless landscape would yield to some colorful escarpments.

Turning east toward Luxor, the haze thickened so I almost needed the guidance of the instrument approach to find the airport. The place was all but deserted, a huge modern terminal with no passengers and no commercial jets parked outside. On the ramp, I parked alongside a small twin-engine aircraft and a King Air turboprop. I had arranged for a handler here too, who marshaled me to a parking place but was most valuable for walking me though Immigration and Customs – it only took 15 minutes – and then gave me a ride to my hotel right on the River Nile. This was their "VIP service" which ended up costing quite a lot. I wasn't clever enough at this point about handlers to negotiate their fees prior to my arrival.

Overall it was a long day, but with some triumphs. I finally felt like I'd flown off the conventional grid of America and Europe to a place where there were some real cultural differences. Having spent several years of my adult life in Europe, I'd seen the differences between the US and Europe fade away to the point where languages

Columns at Karnak Temple

and maybe cuisine were the remaining distinctions. Europe had become a comfortable, unchallenging place. From Egypt on, the unusual would become more commonplace – I looked forward to it. I had also flown to my third continent, although at the time I wasn't counting since the goal of flying to all seven continents had not yet occurred to me.

From Crete onward I was now using Skyplan, the company in Calgary I had hired to obtain landing and overflight permits for this portion of my trip through to Australia. I had provided them with a spreadsheet of my intended schedule and they were in the process of obtaining the permits for all the countries down the line. Skyplan is a full-service flight support company which can also arrange handlers (as they did in Luxor), hotels, fuel, ground transportation, and anything else a flight crew might need. Although they cost somewhat more than companies that are only in the business of obtaining permits, I found that having a company which could help me in the variety of ways provided flexibility that simplified my task as I traveled to places that were not accustomed to dealing with small general-aviation aircraft.

Stone carvings at Luxor

Luxor

I had never been to Luxor before or even spent significant time in Egypt. I had allocated three nights here, so I had two full days for touring the famous sights like the Karnak Temple and the Valley of the Kings. I'd spent some time choosing a good hotel with a room overlooking the river. Like I had during my time in the south of France, I wanted to forget flying for a little while at least and look around. On the first night the setting sun, glowing through the haze, created a memorable sunset as Arab dhows with the ancient rigging style sailed along the river. It had been decades before during a hitchhiking trip through Kenya that I'd first encountered these (to me) oddly rigged sailboats.

The first night I had a pleasant dinner at the hotel restaurant on the terrace overlooking the Nile, which at the time was still serving alcoholic drinks. That was to change some months later as the Muslim Brotherhood gained power in Egypt and through overt intimidation, practices such as serving alcohol were stopped even in tourist hotels that mostly cater

Statues at Karnak

to foreigners. I had also switched to my "third world" eating restrictions –only cooked vegetables, and only bottled water or other bottled drinks like beer and soda. I would only eat fruit I could peel or wash myself. I also ordered meat cooked "well done." Over many years of international travel I'd found that these restrictions were worth it – I'd never gotten any debilitating intestinal sickness.

The next morning I checked with the hotel and online about tour operators and finally found one a few blocks up the street that had good reviews. I booked a tour of the Karnak Temple and other "in town" sights for that afternoon and the Valley of Kings and associated monuments for the following

Sunset over the Nile River in Luxor

day. There was also a light show event at Karnak Temple that night, a "Son et Lumiére" (Sound and Light) show like those put on at many of the famous chateaux in France during the summer. These shows are really pageants with costumed actors playing various historically significant figures. They're often a little hard to follow even if you know the history so the real attraction is the spectacle of the light and sound playing across the ancient ruins.

It turned out I was the only one to book the tour both days so in effect it was a private tour. I was able to adjust the events to suit me, such as taking a boat along the river back to the hotel, instead of the van, after visiting the Valley of the Kings.

Like most people, I knew some of the history of these places and had seen many images and photos, so I had some idea what to expect. Even so, I was struck by the magnitude of it all and the incredible amount of work that went into the construction, all done by slaves of course. Still, to devote such enormous resources to building these things, in a culture that was still basically scraping an existence from the earth, was extraordinary. I won't go into any details about what I saw, since they are any number of guidebooks and travel resources that will explain the history and sights around Luxor much better than I could. But I will admit I succumbed to superstition and bought a small basalt scarab, an ancient Egyptian good luck amulet which I kept on the plane for the remainder of my flight around the world and on my subsequent flights to South America and Antarctica.

Through Facebook I was aware that Mark Vogler, a guy I met on my Antarctica cruise the preceding February, was traveling through the Middle East with his mother. I knew they were somewhere in Egypt by his posts but was still astonished to run into them at the Valley of the Kings. They were taking a multi-day cruise down the Nile in one of many small luxury ships that make this trip. They had now stopped in Luxor; apparently it was the terminus of the cruise. They invited me to join them for dinner onboard, an unexpected treat and congenial conclusion to my stay in Luxor.

Dubai

I was scheduled to leave Luxor at 7:00 am local time. I arrived at the airport an hour and 15 minutes early, but the handler was so efficient at managing the Egyptian exit formalities and refueling that I took off at 6:50. I filed a VFR flight plan at FL115 because the minimum enroute altitude required for IFR flights on my route to Dubai (airport code OMDB) were higher than I wanted to fly. For example, along part of the route the minimum enroute altitude is FL150 (about 15,000 feet) where I would have to use oxygen and where my plane does not run as efficiently. There was no reason for these high minimum enroute altitudes to clear terrain. Often the minimum enroute altitudes are high because the distance between ground navigation (VOR) stations is large and planes are required to fly at high altitudes to receive signals from them. With GPS navigation, however, such limitations become moot. In the US they are now resetting some minimum enroute altitudes lower where GPS navigation can be used, or defining new routes entirely that don't require reception of VOR stations. Sometimes high minimum enroute altitudes are set because of the limited range of ground VHF communication stations. I discussed this issue with Skyplan, who recommended that they file a VFR flight plan for the next leg to Dubai. They apparently had done this many times before, often for helicopters that were not capable of flying at FL150. As it turned out, after takeoff Egypt ATC assigned me a squawk code and FL110 (an IFR flight altitude) despite the minimum enroute altitude, and from then on I was treated as an IFR flight all the way to Dubai.

After leaving the fertile Nile River valley, the bleak dry desert below returned and continued until I reached the coast of the Red Sea. Amazing. To be this far from home over these legendary bodies of water. It was a little hard to appreciate the context of where I was, not just flying over another stretch of desert to the shore of a lake somewhere in the Western

Volcanic desert of western Saudi Arabia

US. As I crossed the eastern shore of the Red Sea I was now over Saudi Arabia, which turned out to be much more volcanic than I expected. In several places I was flying over prominent cinder cones, long extinct I'm sure, but a surprise when I had expected endless rolling sand dunes below me.

At about the VOR navigation station named GAS on airway number A145, they said I couldn't fly the route I had been assigned because of "military activity" so they re-routed me at the waypoint called ALMAL onto a new routing that avoided the military exercises. This new route was actually shorter but involved flying over a longer stretch of the water in the Persian Gulf.

Oil terminal in the Persian Gulf

In the western part of Saudi Arabia I observed small, widely scattered villages in the dry volcanic landscape. As I flew further east that gave way to sandy desert with much more built-up cities connected by starkly black asphalt strips of high-speed highways. The black web of highways made a blunt contrast to the shimmering desert they crossed. Arriving at the coast of the Persian Gulf, the oil fields, tank firms, and offshore tanker-loading terminals below me marked the business end of the Saudi oil boom.

Overall, the flight was reasonably smooth but hazy all the way. It was particular hazy flying into Dubai. I struggled to see some of the oddities for which they have become famous, such as a man-made offshore island designed to resemble a palm tree and another meant to look like all the continents in the world. Because of the haze I couldn't really pick them out. Along the shoreline I saw an amazing collection of high-rise structures. Among them I had hoped to see the Burj Khalifa from the air, at 2,722 feet the world's tallest building, but I could not pick it out because of the haze.

N788W on the ramp at Dubai

Coming into the airport at Dubai, I had to fly the DESDI-4T Standard Arrival Route for a time, but they started giving me vectors because I was a lot slower than the inbound jets behind me. I was vectored on to the approach for Runway 30L. At one point the controller asked if I could fly faster than my normal approach speed of 90–100 knots. I told him I could go faster, but the plane would never land! The landing sequences of faster commercial jets are finely choreographed at busy airports. A relatively slower plane like mine screws up that choreography.

As I crossed into Saudi Arabia, the ATC people I was talking to, all men, were clearly expatriates from either the United States, the UK, or Australia,

Gold souk in Dubai

judging by their accents. I had expected this from the stories of other pilots who'd crossed the Middle East. It was consistent with the Saudi's general approach to outsourcing skill jobs to foreigners rather than training their own people to do them. They certainly had the money for the generous "hardship" pay, housing allowance, and vacation months (not weeks) that are needed to induce people to live and work in Saudi Arabia for extended periods of time.

After landing at Dubai, I had to taxi a long way to arrive at stand 33 by the Executive Flight Center, where I parked my plane among corporate and private jets. Dubai is a huge airport, the biggest airport I've ever landed in. My plane N788W was by far the smallest plane I saw parked at this airport.

The Executive Jet Center general-aviation terminal itself could only be described as opulent, with leather furniture, wood paneling, and polished brass accents everywhere. There was elaborate security getting on and off the ramp into the terminal. After passing through security, I

SUV for driving the desert dunes

was escorted to a comfortable waiting room while entry paperwork was completed. A charming hostess offered me coffee and pastries. I rarely feel out of place but this was one occasion. On the long flight over the desert, where even at my altitude it was hot, I was sweating most of the way. On top of that I had drunk a couple of bottles of water and used my pee bottle a couple of times so it was now full. I walked off the ramp into this sophisticated setting of well-dressed people in my jeans, sweaty T-shirt, and with a full pee bottle in my hand. My first stop was obviously the men's room to empty the bottle and splash some water on my face.

Riding camels in Dubai

Many other pilots who have flown small general-aviation planes around the world have worn starched white "pilot shirts" with gold epaulets so they look like professional pilots. By dressing like real pilots they expect to get more respect and better treatment by handlers, fuelers, Customs and Immigration people, and others at foreign airports. Some pilots have even worn flight jumpsuits with various patches, again with the intent of looking like serious aviators. I had taken a white pilot shirt with me on this flight, complete with epaulets, but never wore it while flying. It just seemed like a ridiculous and false costume, definitely not for me. In all the foreign places where I've flown, I can honestly say I never felt like I was not respected because I wasn't wearing pilot attire. Even wearing the same casual clothes I'd wear at home I was almost always addressed as "Captain." On

Lunch Bedouin-style

the other hand, wearing the pilot shirt in the hotel bar at night can be an interesting way to meet people and find other fun adventures. It certainly worked out that way in Dubai.

Despite my degenerate appearance, everyone at the airport was very kind and helpful to me. Inside the executive terminal, I noticed there were many people standing around wearing white "thobes" (the traditional Saudi long robe-like garment) with apparently very little to do. While I didn't wear a pilot shirt, I did wear a photo ID badge around my neck which had my FAA pilot number, some wings-type logo, and some dates. I had created it myself before I left on my trip back in June, but the expiration dates I had used did not anticipate the delay in my trip so the expiration date had passed. One of these idle Saudis who had some unclear responsibility to review incoming crews noted that my badge was expired. I explained that the badge didn't really mean anything anyway so it didn't matter that it was expired. He pondered that for a long moment, then with a smile nodded "OK," accepting my explanation. The foolishness of officialdom.

Once at the hotel I realized I had left the charger for my notebook computer on the plane, so the next morning I had to go back to the airport, go through tight security, and obtain a "ramp pass" from the police just to walk 30 meters out to my plane to get the charger. It was essential though, because getting online to check weather and emails and book hotels farther down the line was essential.

At this point in the trip, having the computer was particularly crucial. Just after I arrived at the hotel the night before, I learned that there was no aviation gas at my next planned stop in Ahmedabad, India (airport code VAAH), a change that had occurred only days before on Oct. 1, 2011. The fuel my engine requires is high-octane aviation gasoline as opposed to jet fuel which is basically kerosene. Jet fuel is available everywhere. The lack of aviation gas at Ahmedabad resulted in a lot of scrambling around by me and by Skyplan to find another city in India where aviation gas was available, then

In the desert near Dubai

formulating a new flight route and obtaining landing permits for that city. The internet and my notebook computer were the only practical way to manage such a reorganizing process for this flight.

Aviation gas is pretty rare in India. What I wanted was an airport with aviation gas that is also an Airport of Entry from which I could enter and leave the country. There really was no good choice that fit these criteria except Mumbai (airport code VABB). But it is such a trial and expense to land at that huge airport, I really wanted to avoid it as everybody had advised me to do. I finally settled on flying to Nagpur, India (airport code VANP), a longer flight but an Airport of Entry which at least had aviation gas – but apparently no pump to pump it out of the barrels. When I called the aviation gas guy, he suggested using a bucket and funnel to refuel. At the time I thought that a ridiculously crude way to shift fuel from a barrel to my plane. He assigned some of his people the task of finding a pump for use at Nagpur.

Even though I knew it would be expensive, I had wanted to visit Dubai because it has become a marquee international destination. There were certainly cheaper alternatives where I could have stopped for fuel. Now that I was here I wanted to explore Dubai a bit. My hotel, the Hilton Dubai Jumeirah, was on the beach, giving me a chance to swim in the Persian Gulf. I also wandered around the marketplaces in the old city. The souks devoted to gold, spice, perfume, and more are remnants of Dubai's thousands of years of trading heritage, but I imagine they're economically irrelevant in Dubai's modern high-finance economy. I also took an organized excursion out to the desert and did desert stuff – crashing around over sand dunes in a 4x4 with tires deflated to improve traction, riding a camel, sitting on a carpet under date palms eating various nomad concoctions and drinking sweet tea as a late morning breakfast.

Construction had started on many buildings in Dubai. Incredibly vast amusement park projects had broken ground inland from Dubai city, but at the time of my visit in 2011, all the work had stopped and the workers, largely Indians and Pakistanis, had been sent home. The forest of construction cranes stood idle, reminding me of the state of condo construction in Las Vegas when the housing market crashed in 2008. The economy of Dubai seems to be all about trading and shopping – anything and everything. They've cultivated their own brand of ridiculous excess. I'm sure they'd rather have a steady growth trajectory or resolved endpoint instead of the boom and bust alternative they were then experiencing.

8

Dubai to Thailand

With no aviation gas at my originally intended stop of Ahmedabad, India, I had adjusted my route so I would fly to Nagpur, India (airport code VANP), instead. Late the night before this flight, I did get confirmation that a fuel pump would be available at Nagpur to pump the aviation gas from the barrels into the plane's fuel tanks.

If you've never heard of Nagpur, you're not alone. With all the famous tourist destinations in India, Nagpur is nowhere among them. Nagpur is in the middle of India. Because the flight from Dubai to Nagpur is some 1350 nm, longer than the flight to my original destination, Ahmedabad, I planned an early start from Dubai in order to land during daylight at Nagpur. I left the hotel for the airport at 5 am, scheduled refueling at 6 am, and planned departure at 7 am. Getting through Immigration and Customs to exit Dubai at the Executive Flight Center was quick but the fueler screwed up my early departure. He was scheduled for 6 am but arrived an hour late, and then, in classic Middle East fashion, everybody in earshot had to participate in discussing how best to park the fuel truck next to the plane, wasting another 20 minutes. My plane was also blocked in by corporate jets, which had to be moved with the tug to get the fuel truck close enough to my plane and ultimately to let me out. I had to push these people to get it all done, including filling the wing tanks and putting 170 liters in the ferry tank. I also was concerned about getting a takeoff slot, given the large numbers of commercial

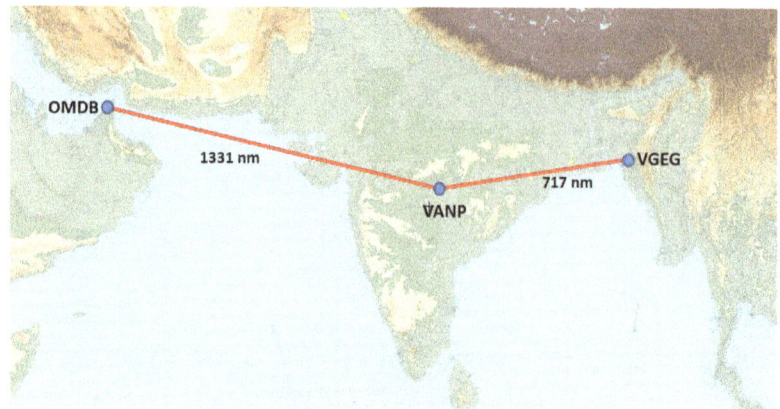

Flight legs from Dubai to Chittagong

aircraft leaving their gates at the same time. Given the fueling delay, I was lucky to get off at 7:55 am. Aviation gas in Dubai turned out to be the most expensive on the entire trip, around US$21/gallon.

Once I had my clearance delivered, ground control sent me to a run-up area for runway 30R (everybody else was on 30L). For my run-up I always test run the engine on both of the wing tanks and the ferry tank, with the ferry tank being the last one I check. I was switched to the ferry tank when I got the call from ground control that I had to depart immediately or incur a delay of several more minutes for new incoming traffic. I immediately taxied to the runway while I finished configuring the aircraft for takeoff, forgetting that it was still switched to the ferry tank.

I took off that way with no problems but several minutes into the flight I heard a loud bang. I had no idea what it was but thought maybe it was a backfire since everything still seemed to be working okay. The plane had never backfired on climb-out before. While checking through all the systems after the bang, I then discovered I was still switched to the ferry tank. I immediately switched to the left tank, my normal departure configuration, and checked the right wing tank. Sure enough, the needle was pinned to the very top of the gauge. The return fuel from the ferry tank into an already full right wing tank had no doubt overflowed the right wing tank. I started speculating that the bang I heard could have been related to the fuel overflow, maybe resulting from overflow fuel dribbling onto the hot exhaust and igniting. Nothing like that has happened since, so I really don't know what the loud bang was. The remainder of the flight was a little nerve-racking, not knowing whether

I had a serious problem, but I never considered turning back to Dubai to get it checked out. When I landed in Nagpur I checked the plane for damage or any sign of an explosion, but found nothing. This incident was a reminder of something I had failed to do at the start of the trip. With an additional tank in the plane I should have prepared a supplemental checklist, or a new checklist, that included operating that tank. Following such a checklist may have helped me avoid taking off while switched to the ferry tank.

Departing from Dubai, I had initially been assigned a Standard Instrument Departure for my clearance. The designation for my aircraft on the flight plan is COL3, a rare designation that ATC controllers don't recognize. It could have been a light jet designation they hadn't seen before. However, once I was flying and they realized I was a slower, light aircraft, departure radar decided to get me off the Standard Instrument Departure plan because I was delaying other planes behind me that were also flying this same procedure. Instead, ATC just vectored me to my first on-course waypoint, which I preferred anyway.

With full fuel and the plane overweight, the power setting had to be reduced for a climb-out rate of 400–500 fpm (feet per minute) as I did leaving Goose Bay. This power reduction was especially important here to keep the engine temperatures from getting too high in the very hot climate of the Middle East. Even for this early morning departure from Dubai, it was already very hot outside.

I was quickly out over the open water of the Gulf of Oman, so there was not much to see except occasional passing tankers and container ships. After four hours of flying over water and talking to controllers in Muscat, Oman, and Karachi, Pakistan, I finally crossed the coast into India. I had some communica-

Crossing into India

tion trouble with Muscat, but pilots in this airspace were very willing to relay my position reports to ATC – they all have had the same problem at one time or another. Once again, I asked for the next couple of frequencies down the line in case I lost contact.

When I arrived in the Karachi Flight Information Region, Karachi asked for my India overflight/landing permit number, which I read to him over the radio. I thought all was well, but when I got to the boundary with India-controlled airspace at a waypoint called TELEM, they told me to hold at that point because they were in a conversation concerning my permit with India authorities. This was not good. I did a couple of turns in the holding pattern, but when they asked about my remaining fuel supply (endurance), I told them I only had 30 minutes of reserve fuel beyond arriving at my destination in Nagpur. This wasn't true – I just wanted them to release me from the hold right away. Believing I had such limited reserves, of course they immediately cleared me back on to my flight plan route and all was well continuing into Nagpur. I really don't know what the confusion with my permit number had been all about; ultimately, the Indian authorities did get it sorted out. It could have been related to the ridiculously over-populated government bureaucracies in both India and Pakistan that stumble over themselves with too many people assigned to do a few simple tasks. Things get lost in the cracks with so much paper-shuffling.

I had meant to look for, and take a photo of, my crossing of the antipodal longitude from my starting point at Bremerton. The antipodal longitude is the longitude exactly on the opposite side of the world. The antipodal longitude for Bremerton is at about 57 degrees east longitude, or a few degrees east of Dubai. However, I was busy at the time and forgot all about it. Anyway, in terms of longitude, this flight leg marked being halfway around the globe. Even though I was on the other side of the globe, I was not yet halfway along my route in terms of total flying distance since my route would take me into the Southern Hemisphere south of Singapore.

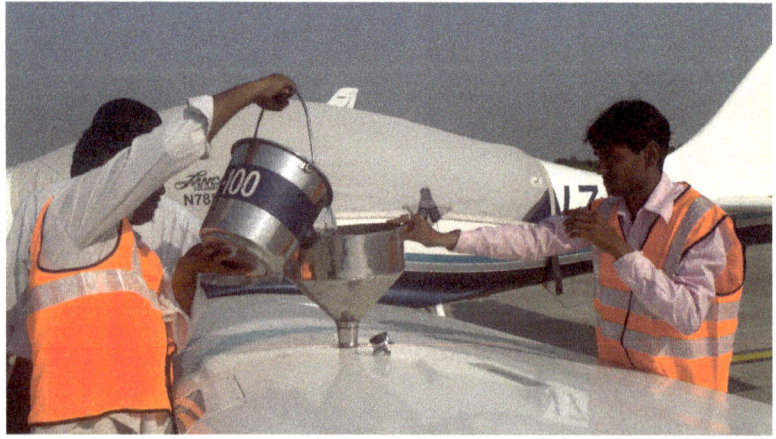

Refueling in Nagpur

Flying over India was a disappointment because it was so hazy. I could see the ground from my altitude, but not clearly. The few photos I tried to take did not show much. The haze is composed of dust and soot (black carbon), the by-product of charcoal fires being used everywhere in India for cooking. I found out later that India is one of the worst places in the world for the density of carbon-based air pollution, easily 100 times higher than typical amounts in metropolitan areas in the US.

Nagpur

Because of the delay in Dubai, I arrived just at dusk in Nagpur. They cleared me to fly the instrument approach for runway 32 with a procedure turn, something I don't do often in US because ATC can usually give me radar vectors directly to the final approach course. But it did give me a chance to do some flying, so I shut off the autopilot and manually flew (a bit sloppily at first) the full approach including the procedure turn. When the approach lights came into view as I neared the runway, I was reminded that I'm actually a pilot instead of just someone running an autopilot and talking on the radio. By the time I parked the plane it was fully dark.

I was met by the handler on the ramp. I think handlers are essential in India. The handler and I proceeded to go from one end of the airport to the other, visiting numerous offices, each of which required that some little piece of paper be signed and stamped. I had no idea what the purpose of most of these approvals were, but the handler knew them all and shook hands as we arrived at each office as I stood to the side, smiled, and said nothing.

I planned to stay for two nights, at least, in a minimalist business hotel right by the airport. I thought it would take at least a day to sort out the fuel situation and get it pumped into the plane. I also anticipated having a weather delay here. After the last few flights over the desert and ocean in clear skies with no weather concerns, I was looking at a forecast of thunderstorms and some volatile weather en-route to Bangladesh, my next stop after Nagpur, and further into Thailand. I was moving into the tropical zone and weather patterns were changing accordingly.

I arrived in Nagpur on October 20 and decided to refuel the plane the next day, which meant going back to the airport and getting ramp access, which required more visits to airport offices with the handler to get pieces of paper stamped and signed. There is actually a fuel depot at Nagpur next to the airport at the India Oil Company, so the aviation gas was nearby. It was brought from the depot in barrels in the back of a small pickup truck after I had paid for it with hundred-dollar bills. With their well-known bureaucratic excess, the manager who made out the fuel sales invoice actually wrote the serial number of each bill on the invoice. Wow.

The fuel pump that was supposed to be there that day was not there, so we resorted to the bucket and funnel approach. It seemed a little crazy when I was told that's how they would do the refueling, but I realized other pilots on flights like this had encountered the same slow, manual process and made the best of it. It was a matter of accepting unconventional (to me) yet practical ways to get things done. The refueling also went better than I expected. The bucket and funnel were stainless steel, dedicated to this purpose with the label 100LL, the grade of aviation gas being put in the plane. The funnel had a built-in filter.

After they broke the seal on a 200-liter barrel, they did a test of some sort to verify the quality of the contents. It took a while but the aviation gas got poured into the wing tanks. The total cost was US$575 for 200 liters, or a little less than $11/gallon, a little cheaper than aviation gas in Europe. Most of the aviation gas they sell from their depot here in Nagpur goes to flight schools and a handful of flight clubs in the central region of India. They only sell it in barrels. If you break the seal and take any gas from a barrel, you buy the whole barrel even if you have no place to put it all. Fortunately, with the ferry tank I could always load the fuel so I never had to leave any behind. Some pilots without my onboard fuel capacity have left fuel (and money) behind because they have no room for it. I don't know what the locals do with fuel left over in a barrel: maybe put it in their cars?

The Indian festival of Diwali was coming up and my Indian handler advised me to leave early on Sunday morning, Oct. 23, to avoid the relative crush of air traffic in the form of charter jets coming in, full of people bound for festival events. I scheduled to get away by 7:00 am, which meant another morning getting out of the hotel early like I had in Dubai. I'm an early riser by nature so this wasn't a particularly great hardship.

The handler's local guy was a very confusing young man who told me contradictory things from one day to the next about whether my landing permit had been extended for the extra day I had delayed for weather. But on departure day he managed to navigate the airport bureaucracy successfully once again, with its multiple offices, stamps, carbon paper forms, and signatures. I silently followed him around to each stop where a 5-to 10-minute seemingly argumentative conversation took place until finally all parties agreed that I was entitled to the stamp or signature or slip of paper (whatever they dispensed) and we were off to the next office. As we got to the last office I could see the ramp and my plane beckon beyond the last set of glass doors, which were,

En-route to Chittagong

of course, guarded by two soldiers with automatic weapons just as other soldiers had been positioned throughout the airport. In the end it was only 30–40 minutes to get through it all one way, either coming or going, and I was able to take off at 6:50 am, just after the first of the incoming charter jets had landed. Compared to that of other pilots I have talked to, or heard about, my experience getting in and out of India was very smooth sailing by India standards. I'm glad I had the handler, confusing as he was. I can't imagine how a pilot would

get through this labyrinth on their own. Some have tried and ended up stuck for many days or compelled to pay outrageous bribes to resolve "problems" with their permits.

India was still very hazy with no rain or clouds. I now understood this was typical for the months after the monsoon ends. Fortunately, there were no

Refueling in Chittagong

significant weather issues on my day of departure. I filed an IFR flight plan route at FL090 to Chittagong, Bangladesh (airport code VGEG), a relatively short flight of about 725 nm. The flight was pretty uneventful, but with long stretches where I had no communications with ATC. I'd gotten pretty accustomed to this by now so I wasn't bothered by it. I did get a relay at one point through a commercial airliner flying overhead. The paper versions of the Jeppesen aeronautical charts are valuable in this circumstance because they have ATC frequencies shown on the chart, something that's missing from the electronic version of the charts I now have displayed on the iPad. Maybe the frequencies are somewhere I haven't found on the e-versions. The airspace is so devoid of small planes flying at my altitude that the chances of an airspace conflict are pretty remote, greatly reducing the importance of traffic alerts from ATC about nearby planes.

Chittagong

Upon arriving at Chittagong there was some confusion because my original landing permit had not been updated in response to my re-routing to Nagpur. It still showed Ahmedabad as my point of origin, not Nagpur, and the dates had not been advanced for the weather, delay day I took in Nagpur. They had me do "left orbits south of the field" around no particular holding point while they sorted it out. After 10 minutes in my lazy hold they accepted my explanation that I had to go to Nagpur because there was no aviation gas at Ahmedabad and finally let me land. Somewhere the ball was dropped on the landing permission side of things, likely at Skyplan.

I immediately liked Bangladesh better than India. Walking alongside my handler as we passed through the international terminal, I was waved past Immigration and Customs on the strength of my phony "Air Crew" ID badge with photo and pilot number. I didn't need to buy a "Visa on Arrival" for US$180. This is the same fake badge I wore in Dubai and throughout the trip. Even though the badge is a fake, my pilot certificate number and picture are legitimate, and as a pilot I really am "Air Crew" so I guess there is some validity to how I got processed there.

The aviation gas situation at Chittagong was the same as Nagpur–fuel is purchased by the barrel. Once they break the seal, you've bought the whole barrel. It was more expensive here than Nagpur: US$655/barrel. This time they moved the fuel from the barrel to my wing tanks using a plastic jug and funnel, not as reassuring as the stainless steel bucket and funnel used in Nagpur.

Tuk-Tuks in Chittagong

I wanted to stay at the Peninsula Hotel in Chittagong, which had been highly recommended, but unfortunately it was fully booked the one night I was in the city. I settled for the Tower Inn Hotel, which was OK by Bangladesh standards but poor by international standards. It was in a noisy, obscure part of town that was a full hour's ride by tuk-tuk from the airport.

Chittagong is a lively and active port city with a huge number of ships of all descriptions anchored or moored in the river. The road traffic was a colorful, chaotic flowing river of vehicles of every description as difficult to understand and manage as any I've seen (and I've been to some crazy places).

Having planned only one night here, I had not done any research on the place from a tourism standpoint. No doubt there are interesting things to do here, and interesting food I've heard,

Streets in Chittagong

but it would have taken some time to figure out where to go and what to do. Since I had lost a day due to weather I thought it better just to move on. I was anxious to get to Chiang Mai, Thailand, where I had planned to spend three nights.

The next flight leg to Chiang Mai was pretty short, so I set my departure from Chittagong at the more reasonable hour of 10:00 am local time. Again there was confusion with the permits. I had looked at two flight routes. The longer route went south along the water, basically to Rangoon then east into Thailand. The second, shorter route went directly over the mountains of Myanmar to Mandalay and then on to Chiang Mai. I selected the longer route because I wanted to avoid the weather buildups I expected over the mountains along the shorter route. I communicated this selection to Skyplan

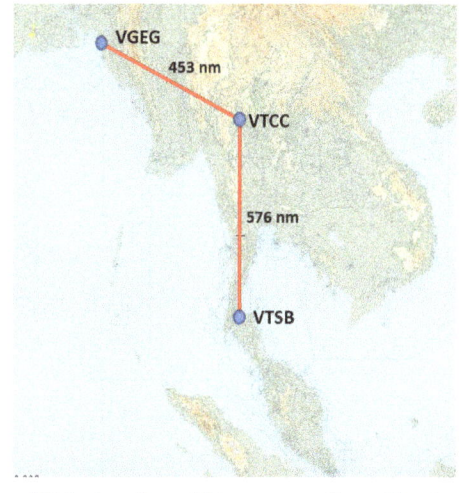

Flight legs from Chittagong to Surat Thani

Flying over verdant Myanmar

to get it filed. For some reason the short route got filed instead, but it required permission – which was never obtained –to overfly a small piece of India. The problem was resolved by filing a new flight plan at the Chittagong tower, which sent me to a waypoint just far enough south of the India section, at the waypoint called AVLED, which then would allow a left turn directly to the Mandalay VOR navigation station and then on to Thailand. The guys in the Chittagong tower were very helpful in getting this amended flight plan filed.

This route had very little to do with designated airways, and the cruise altitude of FL090 was well below what you'd expect to fly to get over these mountains. In fact, I now see that beyond the US, Canada, and Europe, where a flight plan would not be accepted if you filed for a flight altitude below the minimum enroute altitude along any section, minimum enroute altitudes didn't seem to matter much around here. Even though this was an IFR flight, I flew this route to Chiang Mai more like it was a VFR flight. I changed to FL110 and drove around buildups as needed and just told ATC about it more or less after the fact, when I had re-established communications with them.

Dinner with fellow pilots in Chiang Mai

Myanmar is a beautiful country as seen from the air: dense mountainous jungles with small clustered villages widely dispersed on ridgetops and along river valleys. Arriving over Mandalay, the widespread flooding along this extensive river system was obvious.

Myanmar was still a pretty closed country during my trip in 2011, so I felt I was enjoying a rare treat to see the country from the vantage point of a relatively low-flying aircraft. The cloud buildups I expected were everywhere – in a few cases I had no choice but to fly through the least dense part of them and accept the turbulence. They had not yet built into thunderstorms though, and no lighting was registering on the Stormscope.

Chiang Mai

Upon my arrival in Chiang Mai (airport code VTCC), I flew the instrument approach for runway 36, a great runway 11,000 feet long. However, the wind was blowing the wrong direction for a landing on this runway. The resulting 10-knot tailwind greatly extended the landing distance in a plane like mine. Apparently the Chiang Mai Airport folks like the instrument approach on runway 36 and routinely route the planes there regardless of the wind direction. I was later told they rarely switch to runway 18, partly because that approach is over the mountains to the north instead of up the flat valley.

Arriving at Chiang Mai felt like returning to modern civilization, from the professional perfection of the way the marshals on the ramp guided me to parking, to the handler waiting with an air-conditioned terminal bus, to the terminal itself, which was more modern and up-to-date than most air terminals I've seen in the US. Restaurants, shops, ATMs, everything I would expect was there. Even the taxi rank had a dispatcher that set the price, took the money, and called a driver from a waiting line to take the fare. What a contrast to the jostling rabble of limousine and town car drivers I have to weave through to get to the real taxi ranks when I get off the Bainbridge ferry on my way to the Sea-Tac Airport.

Washing elephants at Patara Elephant Farm

I had an unexpectedly great dinner the night I arrived. When I was in the UK in July I had traded emails with a pilot named Ed who lives in Phuket and flies a turboprop Malibu. He happened to be in Chiang Mai with some other pilot friends doing flood relief flights to the Thai backcountry. The five of us had a great time over dinner and drinks at the Riverside Restaurant overlooking the Ping River.

The area surrounding Chiang Mai is famous for its elephants. I spent a day at the Patara Elephant Farm, with a dozen other tourists, where we became "elephant handlers for a day." Well, sort of. This is one of the few elephant

Patara Elephant Farm

farms in Thailand that is committed to an eco-friendly approach to keeping domesticated (as opposed to wild) elephants – they are well cared for and well fed. During our day on the farm we were each basically assigned our own elephant, and, with the assistance of a regular handler, we went through a normal day of care – feeding them, checking their health (including digging through their poop to check it), and washing them in the river.

We then climbed aboard our elephant, using its bent foreleg as a foothold, for a bareback ride that wound through rice paddies then up an incredibly steep trail to a waterfall where we had lunch. We took another incredibly steep trail back to the farm. In all it was about three hours with your legs wrapped around the neck of an elephant. Remember, this was bareback, not in chairs, so by the end we were all walking weird from stretched and strained leg muscles. It was a full, tiring day but one of the more interesting side excursions I made on this trip. There are lot of elephant shows and treks in Thailand. Many use skinny, poorly cared-for elephants and really are more like

Painting above the bed in my room at Yaang Come Village hotel

circus shows with elephants kicking balls around and such, with a short ride through the jungle in a chair strapped to the elephant's back. The Patara approach offers a one-on-one interaction with an elephant which I think is a lot more interesting and rewarding.

I stayed at the Yaang Come Village hotel in Chiang Mai. For once, it was just as good as the photos on the website made it look. As a bonus, it's a short walk to city nightlife. Just around the corner from the hotel is the famous Night Bazaar – a huge collection of sidewalk stands, regular retail storefronts, and restaurants that stretches for several blocks and stays open until midnight. A few blocks further on are several great restaurants along the Ping River with live music every night. Of the new places I'd been on this trip, Chiang Mai was the most appealing – a place I would like to visit again.

The next day, October 26th, was a day to just relax around Chiang Mai and the hotel pool before starting more detailed planning for the next four flight legs that would get me to my fifth continent – Australia.

Surat Thani and Phuket

I had planned to fly into Phuket from Chiang Mai. Space for parking an aircraft is usually very limited at Phuket, although my pilot friend Ed, who lives there, said they probably could find a place for a small plane like mine. However, the normally tight parking situation was exacerbated due to flooded airports in Bangkok and surrounding areas that had caused planes to be re-positioned to Phuket. Because of this crunch I decided to go to the airport at Surat Thani instead. Surat Thani has aviation gas and is an Airport of Entry with Customs and Immigration. The drawback of Surat Thani is its distance from the ocean beaches and the hotspots of Phuket. It meant a two-hour ride from the airport to the hotel I'd booked on the beach in Khao Lak.

Compared to other flights I'd done, this was a short flight of about 600 nm. My main concern was the weather. I was now fully in the tropical weather zone where thunderstorms can pop up all over the place, usually with the heat of the afternoon. I'm used to how thunderstorms grow, develop, and move in the West and Midwest of the United States. But I have only limited experience flying in the tropics, primarily the Caribbean, and reading the weather. Weather is also easier to navigate in the United States because I can receive weather radar images on a map display in the cockpit. It's relatively easy to identify and fly around intense weather buildups when they're shown on a map. I'm a little spoiled by having that level of technology back home.

From Chiang Mai I filed an IFR flight plan to Surat Thani at a cruising altitude of FL090. As I flew south, the significant flooding around Bangkok and the areas north of the capital was very apparent. People had parked their cars on bridges and overpasses to keep them out of the water. One of the realities that aggravates the flooding here is that the water has no place to recede. Once it has flowed over a levee, it just sits there with no way to drain. Large parts of Bangkok are below sea level, like New Orleans, so once the water is in there it is only leaving through pumps and through evaporation.

South of Bangkok I was over the Gulf of Thailand and put my inflatable life vest on. The Thais seem to have better radar and radio communications coverage than countries I'd crossed since leaving Europe, probably a result of a more prosperous economy or a more aggressive and well-funded military. I was never out of communications on this flight, but I was in and out of radar coverage because at FL090 I was literally flying below their radar. My main job was driving around cloud buildups which weren't thunderstorms yet but could be pretty bumpy if I tried to fly through them. Occasionally, I'd get in the clouds and couldn't see the next buildup. I'd have to choose a route past them all while I could still see a way through, then stick to that decision.

At Surat Thani (airport code VTSB), there were broken clouds at about 1500 to 2000 feet so I flew the instrument approach for runway 04. I made an interesting video of flying this approach using a GoPro camera suction-cupped to the inside of my windshield. Once I landed, I was surprised to see several Thai military types in full dress uniforms on the ramp. There is a military air wing based here, but it's on the opposite side of the airport from the passenger terminal. Apparently, there was a VIP of some sort arriving in 45 minutes. The tower hustled me to parking – I told them I needed to refuel. No sooner had I

Sunset over the Andaman Sea

shut down the engine than the fuel cart was there and ready to go. "What great service," I thought. But their real motivation was to get my aircraft fueled, covered, and parked in an out-of-the-way corner, and to get the scruffy, sweaty American pilot who crawled out of it off their ramp before the VIP showed up, thank you very much. OK with me. I was out of the airport in record time (for this part of the world) and on my way to my beach hotel at Khao Lak. Though it was long ride in the hotel shuttle, the route wound through lush green scenery and a national park that reminded me I was in the tropics.

While in Thailand I encountered my first unexpected delay due to airspace restrictions. Making contact with Yeow Meng at Wings Over Asia, a flying club based in Singapore, I learned that there were intensive military air exercises taking place in Singapore and Malaysia through November 2. Because I had a private, low-flying, unscheduled flight, he thought it unlikely I could get a clearance to fly to Singapore, my next stop after Thailand. A call to an administrator for the military exercise confirmed this. I decided to just hang out in Thailand for a few extra days, planning my departure for November 3. There's plenty to see in the Phuket, Krabi, Khao Lak area, so it was not a hardship, but it did push back my overall schedule a bit. I'd have Skyplan adjust the dates on overflight and landing permits for Singapore and Indonesia.

With a six-day layover, I finally could completely forget about flying and enjoy this area. The beaches around the hotel were great, with

Phang Nga Bay

fantastic sunsets every night looking west over the Andaman Sea. There were several restaurants within easy walking distance, offering a wide variety of Thai and international cuisine along with more mundane choices that catered to the foreign tourists who mostly occupied the hotels here – Australians, Germans and other Europeans, primarily. I didn't encounter any other Americans.

I took several excursions from the hotel. One was a day-long voyage on a Chinese junk that toured several of the odd undercut limestone islands in the waters around Phuket known as Phang Nga Bay, including what has become known as "James Bond Island" because of the famous limestone pillar that appeared in the James Bond movie "*The Man with the Golden Gun.*" The island's real name is Khao Phing Kan and as might be expected, it was completely overrun with tourists. After taking a few obligatory photos with the rock in the background, I was happy to go relax at a café. Colorful stalls selling cheap souvenirs were everywhere. That island was one of the least appealing places I visited. The Chinese junk tour of Phang Nga Bay also included a floating village that apparently was not attached to the land in any way other than mooring buoys. They did a bit of fishing there but, again, the tourist trade was their main source of income.

A common means of transportation on Phang Nga Bay are so-called longtail boats, or Ruoa Hung Yao in Thai. These are narrow, covered wooden boats which have been equipped with large engines on the stern that are recovered from automobiles. The engine is directly attached to a propeller via a long drive shaft (the longtail). These auto engines could be six cylinder or even V8s. Instead of using a fixed propeller and a rudder to steer, the engine/propeller shaft combination is mounted on a pivot system such that the boat driver pushes the whole engine/propeller ensemble to port or starboard to steer. Pushing this large weight around seems like a lot of work but apparently the pivot is efficient enough for them to manage and the extreme maneuverability they achieve must make it worth it. These boats can make their way through very tight quarters and when it gets shallow, they can readily pivot the engine so the prop is out of the water.

Chinese junk on Phang Nga Bay

I took a second excursion on a high speed boat out to Khao Phi Phi, Bird Island, and some famous islands in the Phang Nga Bay that routinely appear on calendars as classic images of a tropical paradise, with white sand beaches, turquoise waters, the odd limestone cliffs and foliage overhanging it all. "Khao" means island in Thai. It was a relaxing day island-hopping, swimming, and snorkeling, with a final stop on the way back to Phuket at a bar situated on an almost treeless sandbar where Mai-Tais were the drink of the day, with some interesting people I met on the boat.

Of course, I couldn't leave Phuket without going to Patong Beach, or just Patong, and its collection of wild bars and clubs clustered along Bangla Road and its side streets, a place where pretty much anything is for sale. Thailand has become famous for sex tourism and Patong is a primary destination for this. I met up with friends from the boat tour for a great night wandering around this beachside town. Bar girls were in the street trying their best to seduce patrons to drink and dance or play games, or go to a room with them. They have a wide variety of bar games like Connect Four where the winners could get free shots, all ultimately designed to get patrons drunk and abandon their inhibitions. It was very competitive among the various clubs and bars to get us to stay and hang out there. Though prostitution and nudity are technically illegal here, or so I was told, it was all surprisingly out in the open. Apparently, you can hire a girl for an hour, a night, or to be your "girlfriend" for your entire stay, and either way it's a straightforward business transaction. Sometimes these transactions go badly and somebody gets robbed or hurt. The police are highly motivated to keep the tourists happy and safe, so crime is dealt with harshly and incidents are suppressed from the news. I have traveled the world for 40 years but have never seen anything quite like this. Overall, it seemed like people were having fun and getting what they wanted from their holiday in Thailand.

I probably stayed a little later than I should have that night in Patong Beach. Fortunately, I still had one more day of my Singapore-imposed layover to recover, lying around on the beach before I had to fly again.

9

Thailand to Australia

It turned out to be a long day. I had been staying at the Mukdara Beach Resort in Khao Lak, a 2½-hour drive from the airport at Surat Thani where the plane was parked. I wanted to take off at 7 am to get to Singapore before noon, since thunderstorms usually build up in the afternoon in this part of the world. That worked out to leaving the hotel at 4 am, followed by a long drive through the dark by the hotel shuttle driver and arrival at the airport already tired but still facing a 3½-hour flight to Singapore.

Exiting Thailand went pretty efficiently at Surat Thani; I managed to take off at about 7:25 am. I filed an IFR flight plan at FL110 to my destination airport called Seletar (airport code WSSL), located on Singapore Island. It's not the big international airport at Singapore, but it's well known as a small general-aviation-friendly airport where a handler isn't needed. I was told getting through Immigration and Customs with your own General Declaration forms was easy at Seletar. Buying aviation gas is also easy – they have a real fuel truck (US$2.37/liter) instead of having aviation gas pumped, or poured, from barrels. There are also maintenance facilities. In sum, Seletar is a good place to stop on a round-the-world flight like this.

The first half of the flight from Surat Thani was spent flying around new cloud buildups or remnants of storms from the day before. I asked for and got diversions to avoid the worst of it. The route I had chosen was along the east coast of the Malaysian Peninsula. Even though it was longer, I thought it

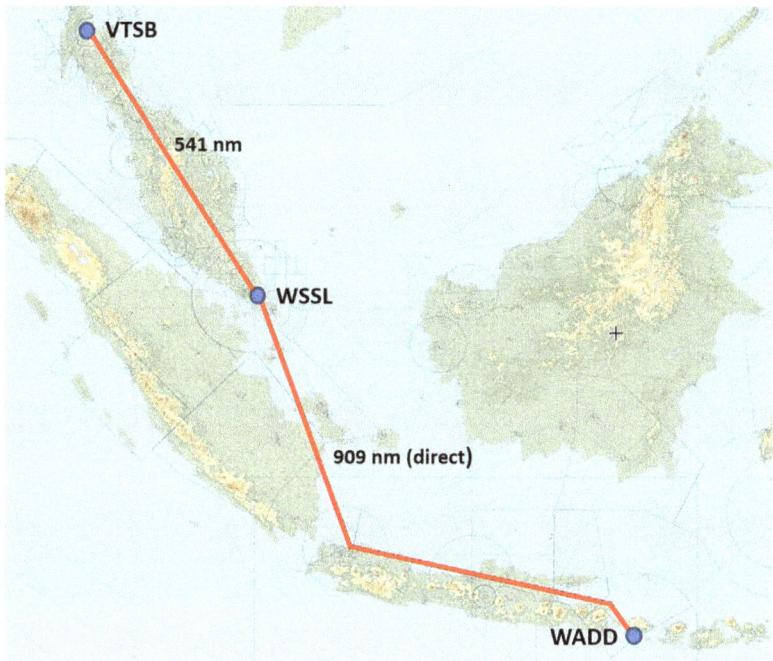

Flight legs from Surat Thani to Bali

would be better, weather-wise, than the more direct route down the west coast due to a low-pressure system building over Sumatra. As I dodged cloud formations, I looked to the west and saw it was clear – just low-hanging clouds. Oh well, you make your choice and take what you get. There was solid VHF communication all the way along on this flight route though. As I may have mentioned, I've started using the SL-30 NAV/COM radio in my cockpit for enroute communications. It works better and has more power and clarity than the VHF radio in the Garmin GNS530W GPS, which I still use when close to an airport and talking to approach/tower/ground because it's more conveniently located in my panel. The communications superiority of the SL-30 is something I've heard about from other pilots; I can now add my concurrence with their observations. I'm glad I had it on this trip.

As I got closer to Singapore the weather became socked-in so I was flying through flat rain clouds the rest of the flight, very wet but not bumpy. Singapore Control started giving me radar vectors 20 miles out, and I ended up doing what amounted to a surveillance radar approach into the Seletar. There are no published instrument approaches for Seletar, so ATC gave me a descent

Oil change in Seletar Airport, Singapore

to 1,500 feet, and vectored me on to the final approach course for a straight-in approach on runway 21. It was so rainy and misty, I didn't see any runway and approach lights until I was about 4 km away. As I flew the radar vectors as instructed, they kept asking me if I could see specific landmarks like gantry cranes for loading ships along the waterfront. This method worked fine and the landing was straightforward once I had the runway in sight, but they could use an ILS or RNAV approach at that airport. That surveillance radar approach method is something I'd learned about in instrument flight training years ago, but I'd never actually flown one until that day.

Hotel in Singapore

After landing and parking, I first got the aviation gas fuel truck to come and refuel N788W for the next flight leg to Bali. I recalled they took credit cards here for fuel payments, which was an improvement over using stacks of US cash. Paperwork for entry into Singapore was as easy as I had been told. There is a small blue sign pointing to the "Arrival Hall" that is a little difficult to see from the parking ramp after clearing Immigration. I took a taxi into town and splurged on a room at the Pan Pacific Singapore hotel downtown near the marina, a famous place I had seen in many photos of Singapore.

I was also able to arrange for an overdue oil change at Seletar. On my layover day there, I went back out to the airport to get the oil changed at the Hawker Pacific facilities on the south side of the airport. It took some bureaucratic hassling to get a pass back onto the ramp to taxi my plane across the field. Once I was at my plane, I couldn't just call ground control on the radio for permission to start the engine and taxi, I had to call apron control *on the phone* to get permission to reposition the plane. There was very tight security there.

The oil change took about two hours. When finished I had to go back through the same process to return the plane to my original parking stand A13. I had brought my own oil with me for this oil change and to add to the engine periodically when the oil level was low. The maintenance shops overseas generally do not stock the type of oil normally used in a small plane (or any oil really) so it is necessary to special order the oil before getting there if it's not carried on board. I had to have the oil ordered ahead of time when I had it changed in England.

After the oil change I had a chance to drop in at the pilot lounge of Wings Over Asia, a very active flying club based at Seletar. They have a new office with a great lounge on the sixth floor of a building overlooking the airport, just outside the security fence. I had a beer with Yeow Meng and Greg Ang and talked flying and planes. Greg is the owner of a Columbia 350 based at Seletar that he and Meng ferried in from the US the previous June. It's the only other Columbia aircraft I encountered during this entire round-the-world flight.

While planning this trip I viewed Singapore as a pivot point, essentially exiting Asia although technically that wouldn't happen until I left Indonesia. I'd be crossing the equator a short distance south of Singapore. In terms of longitude, I was about two thirds of the way around the world from my starting point at Bremerton. Considering flight miles along my route, I was now more than halfway done with this adventure. In terms of flight segments, there were only eight more flights and I'd be in Hawaii. From here the flights become more about ocean-crossings and island-hopping, except crossing Australia I suppose. Anyway, it felt good to have gotten this far, to this important milestone.

Singapore is a highly urbanized city, at least in the area where I was staying. Underground passageways tied into the metro system were the common way of getting around – people didn't really cross streets at street level. There was a wide selection of shops and restaurants to choose from, so I was happy to have a chance to eat fresh salads and vegetables that I would only eat in overcooked form in the developing countries I had been visiting. I really didn't tour the city but I did visit the famous Raffles Hotel for a Singapore Sling at the Long Bar – you can't go to Singapore without doing this! Singapore is also renowned for being a very tightly controlled and disciplined society. Stories abound of serious fines or even jail time for relatively innocuous offenses like spitting on the sidewalk or dropping a wad of gum.

On the day of my departure, I woke up at 6 am for an 8 am departure to hear thunderstorms crashing all around Singapore. I wasn't sure I was going to be able to take off on time. But the weather changes quickly around there so I proceeded as planned and hoped for clearing by my departure time. And that is more or less what happened.

Bali

The route I took from Singapore to Denpasar, Bali (airport code WADD), was not the most efficient one that went directly across the water, but instead was almost due south to Jakarta, then east along the north coast of Java. I filed an IFR flight plan for FL110 (they actually gave me 11,000 feet). This route is about 12% longer than the more direct route but I thought the VHF radio communications would be better than over the open water, and, certainly provide more interesting scenery flying along the coast and near the picturesque volcanos of Java. VHF communications were indeed pretty solid along this route I chose.

On takeoff and the climb-out from Seletar I noticed the altimeter and vertical speed indicator (VSI) weren't moving, a potentially serious problem since an accurate altimeter is critical to almost any flight. I'd seen this happen once before on this plane and quickly switched to the alternate (interior) static port. Both the altimeter and the VSI need to know the air pressure to operate correctly. They get the air pressure reading through a simple plastic tube connected to a round metal disk with a hole in it mounted on the outside of the aircraft, called a static port.

Once I had switched to the alternate static port inside the plane, the needles on the altimeter and VSI jumped and started acting normally. This time, and the time before when this had happened, the plane had been sitting around under intense rain for a few days. The static port on this plane is in a bad place – on the right side of the fuselage too far aft to be covered by the cover supplied with the airplane. Since it's a flat metal disk there's no good way to attach a cover to it the way you can with the pitot tube, which is in a more conventional location under the wing where it is better protected. I keep it covered when parked. Given its location, rain can dribble down the fuselage and into the static port to plug it up – at least that's what I think was happening to cause this static port failure. The alternate interior static port obviously is not going to get plugged up with rain water, but it will result in slightly different readings since the air pressure inside and outside the plane are slightly different during flight.

Anyway, I flew to Bali with the alternate static port selected. Eventually, on a subsequent flight, I switched back to the exterior static port to see whether it was unplugged (dried out) and working again, which it was. There are a lot of places Lancair could have put a static port to prevent this problem – they made a mistake with this location. I thought to improvise a cover out of duct tape and some plastic, since I would now be commonly encountering tropical downpours from here on, but I never got around to it.

Evil weather leaving Singapore

Singapore ATC was on top of its game and gave me radar vectors around a lingering thunderstorm to the south without my asking for a diversion. This also shortened my route a bit. Once out of the vicinity of Singapore, the clouds looked thin and flat as far as I could see.

I had thought a few times about trying to take a picture of the GPS as I crossed the equator just south of Singapore, but the thought occurred to me again almost too late. I flipped to the onscreen page on the Garmin GPS that shows the current latitude and longitude, hoping to catch a photo showing 0 degrees, 0 minutes latitude. I was 15 seconds from being there! I grabbed the camera and starting clicking off photos. The closest I got was 0 degrees, 0.12 minutes north, about 220 meters from the equa-

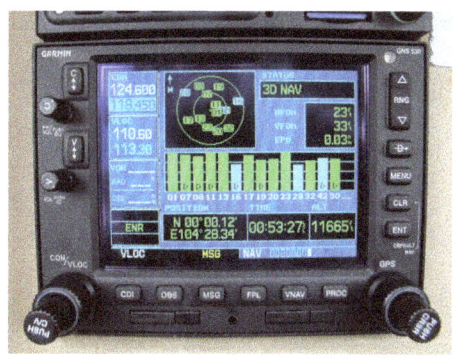

Crossing the equator southbound

tor. Pretty close, considering the plane was moving about five km/minute. If I'd thought about it, I would have switched the camera to video mode to get one frame that was exactly on the equator. Oh well, I'd have another shot at it going north near Christmas Island.

Approaching Jakarta, I could see the storm clouds building over the string of volcanos that pretty much creates the island of Java. I turned east at Jakarta, an incredibly busy seaport with literally hundreds of tankers and containers ships anchored offshore or tied up waiting to unload or load. The Stormscope on board was showing electrical activity (lightning or static discharge due to rapid updrafts and downdrafts passing each other) to the south in the mountains. My route went north of this activity for the most part. As I proceeded east I did have to fly diversions around weather buildups as most of the other pilots were doing. For the first time since Europe I heard other planes flying in my altitude range (10,000–15,000 feet) in addition to commercial jets flying much higher.

Streets of Bali

At a waypoint called ENTAS I picked up the Bali approach, who gave me a vector straight to the airport. The sky was pretty clear by now, but they had a lot of commercial traffic lined up ahead of me for the instrument approach to runway 09. They told me to overfly the airport and turn back on a right downwind parallel to the runway and they would shoehorn (not their word) me into the sequence. It worked out well, with a 10-knot crosswind I had to deal with on landing.

Rice paddy on Bali

There was good parking and handling at Denpasar, Bali (airport code WADD), although the fuelers were busy servicing the

Beach at Permuteran

Flight leg from Bali to Darwin

commercial jets, and there were about 20 on the ramp when I arrived. I didn't want to wait for them to get to me for fuel so I breezed through Immigration and Customs as Air Crew with the help of the handler and headed for the hotel. I'd have to refuel on the day of departure.

A friend had told me the northwest coast of Bali is one of its best areas, so I booked a nice hotel at Permuteran for a couple of nights. The main drawback to this area is that it's a 3½ hour drive from the airport. You can get a taste of the Bali countryside and life during the drive over, which is interesting, but after a while it is just grueling. The roads of Bali are jammed with motorbikes of every size and description: many more motorbikes than cars. And the rules of the road are best described as approximate.

The hotel was OK though, right on a beach made of dark sand; it is a volcanic island after all. The hotel put on a dance show by local performers in elaborate costumes during dinner the two nights I was there. I spent the day swimming and snorkeling along the peaceful beach. I spent my third night at a hotel back in the main town of Denpasar close to the airport. I didn't want a repeat of the Surat Thani situation with a long early morning drive before flying all day.

Darwin

Australia! This would be my fifth continent and it felt like the beginning of the homestretch to the finish line. I was anxious to get there, but the day got off to a shaky start when the handlers did a bad job getting the fuel lined up on time for my departure from Bali. I wanted to get away at 7:00 am local time, to get to Darwin before the worst of the afternoon thunderstorms typically roll in. I also knew I was going to be flying into a 15–25 knot headwind. The fuel arrived in two barrels 90 minutes after I asked for it to be there. Then they forgot the pump and had to go back to their office to get it. Once they got going, it didn't take long to fill both wing tanks and put the remainder of the second barrel in the ferry tank, but I was seething with frustration by the time they finished.

Then it was time for the cash payment for fuel, and the absurdity I'd experienced before began once again. The price was OK, about US$580/barrel, but let me tell you about money, specifically US currency. I gave these guys a stack of US$100 bills and three US$20 bills. They went through the hundreds and rejected almost all of them. I had a mix of old $100's with the small portrait of Ben Franklin (Small Head Ben) and some new ones with the big portrait of Ben Franklin (Fat Head Ben). Small Head Ben – no good! Even older printings of Fat Head Ben – no good! They wanted Fat Head Bens printed after 2003, and needless to say, no rips, tears, blemishes, discolorations, writings, or adulterations of any kind on the bills. I ran into this in Chittagong and Nagpur; thankfully the Thais didn't care and Singapore took credit cards. Drawing upon my nearly four decades of international travel experience, living and working overseas in many places, and the diplomatic tact and cultural sensitivity I've developed during that time, I explained, "Listen, you idiots! This is my national money. Small Head Ben is worth just as much as Fat Head Ben. You can go into Tiffany's and buy diamonds with a stack of Small Head Bens," an assertion that might have had more impact if they knew what Tiffany's was. They were not interested in my defense of Small Head Ben. Ever practical, if it took pristine Fat Head Bens to move aviation gas from their barrels into my airplane, then so be it. It's like the currency was artwork, not money: wrong lithograph series – no good! As artwork, US currency is pretty bland. I like the Euro better, and many other foreign currencies. The old French Franc notes were fantastic as artwork. I just hoped I had enough unblemished Fat Head Bens to buy fuel to get home.

In defense of their picky process, I will say that they have to take these US currency notes to

Storms en-route to Darwin

the bank to exchange them for local currency they can spend. The banks are actually the ones who are finicky about the money. If their banks won't exchange or deposit the notes, then these guys are screwed.

Anyway, back to flying. Thunderstorms had raged the previous night in Bali, even blowing rain under the cover of an open-air restaurant where I was having dinner. When I went to bed, setting the alarm for 5 am, the thunder was still rolling. It rained so hard that it overflowed the drainage systems at the hotel and water was flowing down the stairwells that night. In the morning, though, it was calm and not raining, but still with drifting low clouds and a high overcast layer. I filed an IFR flight plan from Bali to Darwin at FL110.

This routing was pretty much the obvious way to go: almost due east. It skirted along the southern edge of the series of islands that extends eastward from Bali. Remnants of a string of thunderstorms were just south of my course most of the way, but it was no problem to stay away from them. I did indeed get a 20-knot headwind and settled in for a long flight.

Lightning strikes on the Stormscope around Darwin

Turning southeast slightly at Kupang for a straight 500 nm run across the Timor Sea to Darwin, I eventually lost VHF radio contact with Indonesia ATC. They had assigned me an HF frequency, but I didn't have any hope it would work, so I didn't even try it. Once over the water, though, I got a call on the VHF inter-aircraft frequency 123.45 MHz from a helicopter northbound over the water in my direction. They said Brisbane Center (who handles oceanic travel in this area) asked them to give me a call for a position report, a proactive communication relay from ATC – nice. I reported my position, and also said I'd call them on the satphone which I did. The satphone worked great; I gave them a new positon report and my 8816 satphone number in case they needed to call me. While I had the phone out I called Customs at the airport in Darwin and told them I was going to be 50 minutes later than the ETA I gave them the day before, due to the fueling delay in Bali.

As I got close to Darwin, the Stormscope started to light up with lightning strikes and other electrical activity, but mainly over the land and islands

Sunset from Darwin, Australia

surrounding Darwin, which left me an open corridor over the water into the airport. Eventually I had Brisbane Center back on the VHF radio (118.15 MHz) and from there on it was conventional air traffic control to a visual landing on runway 29. There were a string of separate weather buildups ringing Darwin, but the airport was in the clear. A lot of inbound aircraft from the south were seeking diversions around these storm cells. I was concerned about what that would portend for my next flight leg due south to Uluru (Ayers Rock).

I elected to come into Darwin without using a handler at the airport, partly to see if I could do it, and partly because I had already done some of the preparation work myself at home. The specific steps to properly enter and exit Australia with a US-registered and -owned airplane are listed in Appendix E.

Once I had completed and submitted all the forms and paid the landing fee, I was done with the entry process. I got back in my plane and taxied to the north general-aviation ramp where it's first-come, first-served parking. There were many planes here, but also lots of parking spaces and the first real tie-down rings I'd seen since leaving Bangor, Maine. It's a nice setup for small planes and indicative of the importance of general aviation in Australia.

The entry process described in Appendix E has many steps, but I can say the Australians I dealt with were very helpful and good-natured in every way, quickly responding to emails and answering all my questions. The Darwin people told me a lot of planes show up in Darwin from international points having done NO paperwork ahead of time. They scramble to get it done on the spot. If they arrived just before a weekend, when government offices are closed, they could find themselves in a bureaucratic limbo for a few days: physically, but not officially, in Australia.

After I tied down and covered the aircraft, a commercial pilot at Hardy Aviation let me off the ramp through their charter business offices and even called a taxi to take me to my hotel. Nice folks at Hardy's. I would need their help again to get back on the ramp when I left Darwin. Apparently, there is a process to apply for a temporary ramp access code, but I was there such a short time I didn't bother to pursue it.

The taxi brought me to the Holiday Inn on the Darwin esplanade waterfront. From my ninth floor room I had a great view of the harbor, the boat traffic, and a glowing sunset. I went down to the bar by the pool, sipped a cold beer, and watched the sunset and lightning flashing in distant clouds. I was glad to be on the ground and not airborne dealing with such weather.

It felt great to have flown as far as Australia, yet I was just beginning to appreciate the magnitude of what I'd done. I had strung together a series of flight legs to get this far, but had always kept my head down and focused on the next flight. I had not looked too far ahead, like a football team focusing on one game at a time and not on the string of games it takes to win a championship. It was an effective way to organize my efforts, but the broad sweep of what I was doing was just now starting to emerge. I was nearing the beginning of the homestretch, something I couldn't ignore, and something that made relaxing around the pool in Darwin with a beer all that much more enjoyable.

10

Crossing Australia

Uluru (Ayers Rock)

Uluru (Ayers Rock) is one of those world-renowned places you've got to visit if you come to Australia for any length of time. Situated near the middle of the Australian continent, pretty much due south of Darwin's location on the north coast, it was on my world flight itinerary from the beginning.

Departing Darwin turned out to be easy in terms of exit formalities. It's necessary to complete an Outward Manifest (form B960) and take it to the Customs Border Protection window on the day of departure. This window is located in the main terminal building on the concourse at the west end. I had to pick up a "Certificate of Clearance," a piece of paper that I could show at other airports, if asked, that demonstrated I'd cleared Customs in Darwin. It all took about five minutes and I was ready to leave.

Logistically, it was best to take a taxi to the main terminal with my baggage and get this done, then get a second taxi for the short ride over to the general-aviation parking area, unless you're feeling energetic enough to walk carrying all your stuff, which I did. The night before my departure I called Hardy Aviation to ask if I could enter the general-aviation area through their terminal since I didn't have a ramp access code. Fortunately, Hardy had an early charter going out, so a pilot would be there who could let me through the

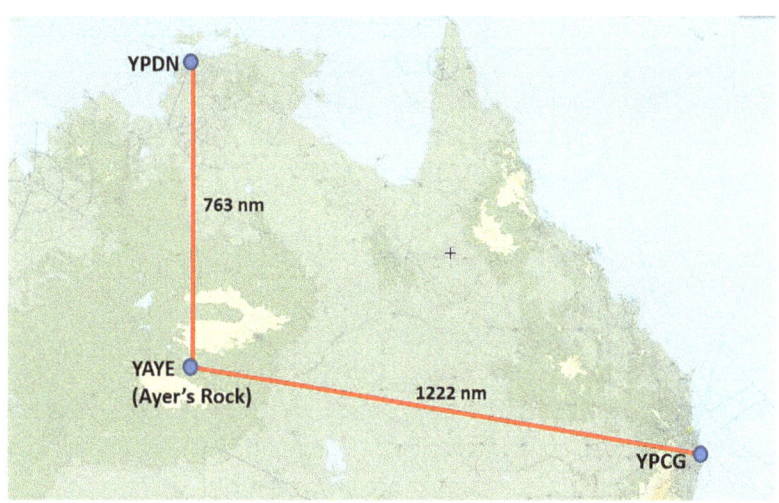

Flight legs from Darwin via Ayers Rock to Coolangatta

gate to get to my plane. The fuel guy with his truck (no barrels) was there on time and took credit cards. I taxied out and took off at close to my planned 7:00 am departure.

I filed an IFR flight plan to Ayers Rock Airport (airport code YAYE) at 9,000 feet, via a route that was pretty much direct to that airport although going by way of the Alice Springs VOR navigation station, which is a bit out of the way. There are several military operation areas along this route, but it was Saturday so they were all inactive. It was a reasonably clear day with occasional cloud buildups to drive around. The terrain reminded me of parts of the western US: dry with widely spaced signs of human activity such as long dirt roads cutting across the country connecting clusters of farm or mine buildings.

Radio communications were good. When I was handed off to Melbourne Control about 120 nm north of Alice Springs, they asked if I wanted a direct routing to Ayers Rock – of course! From there onward the terrain got more interesting, with dry lake beds and colorful rock striations running for miles. I'm not sure what I was looking at – at some point I'll pull

At Ayers Rock Airport

out a map and investigate it. The day was heating up, causing hot thermal currents to rise from the undulating land and make the air turbulent, not unlike flying over Wyoming on a warm summer afternoon.

Once at Uluru, I wanted a nice aerial view of the rock for some photographs. There is a charted scenic route at 4,000/4,500 feet in the Jeppesen chart material for the Ayers Rock Airport. The route goes both directions along the north side of Uluru and then about 20 km to the west to the Olgas, another prominent rock formation which is actually a more sacred site to the native tribes than Uluru. I flew the charted route and got a few good photos, although it remained bumpy.

A word about the names. Uluru is the native name for the rock; it has become more widely used by everybody in recent years. Ayers is the name of the sponsor for the 19th-century white-man expedition that first spotted the rock and reported it. Those explorers named it Ayers Rock in honor of the money man. The airport is named Ayers Rock Airport, and the nearby resort village is called Yulara, which is a native word meaning "place where tourists spend money." Actually, I was once told what it does mean but I've forgotten.

Ayers Rock Airport is a nice place. There's no control tower, but they do have someone on the radio speaking as Ayers Rock radio who does some coordination of air traffic in the area. It's a little like the Alaska airports in that way;

Ayers Rock from the air

they don't have control towers but do have a traffic coordinator on the radio. There are several commercial airline flights that bring in tourists every day and do a quick turnaround. There was no radar coverage but Melbourne Control also manages traffic in this area – although I never got a formal handoff to Ayers Rock radio once I had canceled my IFR flight plan to take the scenic flight around the rock. There is a reasonably large general-aviation parking area with a self-serve aviation gas pump alongside the ramp which takes credit cards. While I was refueling my plane, an airport guy came out and informed me of parking fees ($55/night as I recall). He was most helpful by giving me his business card with the ramp gate code written on the back, allowing me to let myself back into the parking area when it was time to depart.

Yulara village is all owned by the same company and offers various levels of accommodations ranging from camping to nice hotels. I stayed at the Desert Garden hotel. It was OK, but my big complaint was no internet (wired or WiFi) in the room – you had to go to reception or other public areas to get WiFi, which costs $1 for six minutes. I didn't realize how much I was using the internet for email, weather, flight planning, the blog, and other things, until I had to walk a ways to log on. I also wanted to see the outcome of the big Oregon versus Stanford college football game, which actually didn't happen until Sunday afternoon my time. In terms of time zones, I was 19½ hours ahead of the US West Coast at Uluru. There was no TV coverage, of course, but I watched the text of the play-by-play online. Oregon, my team, won comfortably 53-30.

Of the dozens of excursions offered for tourists at Yulara, I booked two. The first is called the Sounds of Silence, a sunset-viewing dinner thing out on a sand dune, which provides a somewhat elevated view of the rock from what is largely flat terrain

Ayers Rock from the ground

to the north. It was worth doing, and included a didgeridoo player and a guy explaining the night sky by pointing out stars and constellations with a powerful spotlight. We were lucky to have a very clear night. After the didgeridoo guy had played 10 minutes, an Aussie woman seated at my table remarked that he was really good. I had thought a didgeridoo was an antique, an aborigine curiosity, a dead instrument, but not so. It is widely played in Australia, and popular. In Darwin I walked past a club that advertised a duo consisting of a didgeridoo player and drummer. I should have popped my head in to see what that sounded like.

When the star guy came on he asked if we saw the Southern Cross. I've seen it many times before, but didn't see it tonight. Apparently it sets three months a year in Australia, something I hadn't known. That would not be real helpful for navigation if you were a 17th-century mariner who counted on it to reckon your position.

The Sounds of Silence excursion is the most popular excursion at Yulara – it took four buses to handle all the people. The dinner buffet was set up at a few different sites so the crowd at each one wasn't too unwieldy. The only significant downside was ants. While we stood around having a welcome drink, there were small biting ants crawling everywhere. Most people were wearing shorts and sandals so the ants easily got onto bare feet to make their tiny bites. It wasn't really painful, just annoying.

The other excursion I took was called Morning Awakenings which required us to meet at 4:30 am in the hotel lobby. Not surprisingly, it wasn't as popular. The idea was to drive out to another sand dune to watch the sunrise and the desert come awake and have some breakfast. After that we drove around the base of the rock with many stops for photos and explanations of the sacred sites (no photos allowed at these, though). We stopped at the point where the climb up the rock begins. Although the rock itself is not sacred, it has many sacred sites, so climbing the rock is very controversial. The climb has about 1,000 feet of elevation change and typically takes three hours round trip. I saw the whole trail from my plane. Although people still make the climb, our guide said it's closed 90% of the time

Cave paintings on Ayers Rock

due to high winds, high temperatures, an approaching storm, or at the whim of the park rangers. There has also been a pollution problem from people taking a toilet break at the summit. Rain runoff, which pours down the rock in many places during a storm, has apparently created a hopeless E. coli infestation in one of the rock's famous watering holes situated at the base. On the day of our tour the trail was closed due to high winds. I really had no inclination to make the climb in any event. This tour ended with the inevitable stop at the rock's information center, with many shops and demonstrations of aboriginal painting. The aboriginals have developed their own odd primitive symbols to illustrate stories in these paintings. I bought a small original aborigine painting and rolled it up to make it easier to stow on the plane.

The weather was generally clear, dry desert weather, so there were no issues that would delay my departure. I liked this place, even though it was so highly controlled by the company running the Yulara resort. In retrospect I wish I'd rented a car to explore the surrounding area, and the Olgas, on my own.

Coolangatta (Gold Coast)

Coolangatta Airport, at about 28 degrees, 10 minutes south latitude, is the southernmost point on my round-the-world flight. Over 1250 nm from Uluru, it was one of my longer flight legs extending more than halfway across the middle of Australia. I planned to take off at 6:30 am to get the flying done during the coolest part of the day, but due to some confusion on the scheduled time, my shuttle bus transport from the hotel was late. There were no taxis in Yulara. With no problems other than that, I was off at 7:00 am. Nobody was in the Ayers Rock Airport working the radio when I left, but Melbourne Control has VHF coverage on the airfield so that is the point of contact to call for engine start, taxi clearance, a squawk code, and to pick up an IFR clearance if you leave early before the local Ayers Rock radio guy shows up.

The flight plan route I filed along airways went out of the way to the north at Alice Springs. As soon as I was airborne I asked Melbourne for, and got, direct routing to the BDV (Birdsville) navigation station to shorten the flight. This flight was mostly uneventful. There was interesting terrain underneath in some places, especially one section where there were miles and miles of reddish lines running across the countryside more or less north-south. Clearly natural, maybe they were eroded or windswept ridge tops

En-route to Coolangatta

on slight terrain undulations I couldn't perceive from the air, but I really don't know what they were. As I got farther east, river beds with water, rather than dry beds, appeared along with inland lakes that held muddy brown water. Farther still, forested lands gave way to intense agricultural activity as I neared the coast.

Inevitably, there were weather buildups beginning about 300 miles from my destination. I wasted some time trying to fly around them but finally gave up, tightened my seatbelt, and flew mostly underneath them at 9,000 feet. It was bumpy but not extreme. The autopilot is going to battle the bumps, and so it's important to watch that you don't get into a downdraft and the autopilot radically pitches up in an effort to maintain altitude, which risks an aerodynamic stall. An aerodynamic stall occurs when the airflow over the wings is disrupted to the point where the wings stop generating lift, usually when they are tilted up at a high angle. I finally disengaged the autopilot and manually flew the plane – it was a bit like a rodeo ride.

Once past the cloud buildups, I was close enough to the coast to be identified on radar (always a comforting event) as I approached the Brisbane-controlled airspace. Some weeks later I heard from an Australian guy on the ground with an ADS-B receiver who was actually tracking my flight inbound to Coolangatta over this region. When I upgraded the avionics in N788W in 2010, I installed the most advanced Garmin transponder, which included so-called ADS-B Out transmissions. These transmissions allow anyone with a suitable receiver, within range, to monitor my position.

Australian Gold Coast

When I was doing the initial planning for this flight, Brisbane Airport was my first uneducated guess for a place to stop before launching across the Pacific. However, after talking to ferry pilots that routinely fly small planes to Australia from the US, I learned Coolangatta (airport code YBCG), more commonly known as Gold Coast, was the better place to go for a general-aviation-friendly airport with low fees. Following this advice, I made Coolangatta my last stop in Australia.

The weather was fairly clear coming in, though hazy, so I got a straight-in visual approach to runway 14. Ground control gave me directions to parking and even called a fuel truck to stop by my plane. I've gotten in the habit of watching the fuel guys fill the wing tanks and generally they stop filling too soon. The wing tanks on my plane are very flat. To really fill the tank, they should be filled to the bottom of the short filler neck with no space left in the top of the tank. Most fuelers leave a space which usually means the tank is 2–4 gallons short of being full. For these long-haul ocean flights, you've got to load all the fuel you can. This time I made sure the fuel guy filled all the tanks, including the ferry tank, to maximum. The next leg was only a little over 1000 nm, but when out over the ocean and prevented from landing at the intended destination for whatever reason, the alternate may be several hundred miles away on another island. I wanted to have the fuel to make it to such an alternate if necessary.

Coming in to Coolangatta I noticed multiple high-rise condos and hotels built along the white sand beach, reminiscent of southern Florida. Apparently, the Gold Coast area south of Brisbane is a very popular beach holiday destination and even has a reputation as a surfing hot spot. I booked a hotel a block from the beach for two nights so I really didn't have much time to explore the area; my one day would, in part, be taken up doing Australia exit formality paperwork at the airport. At least they had a solid WiFi connection in the hotel room, which gave me a chance to catch up on email, the blog, and other things. My layover day was a pretty day – the sun was out and the air was humid, but with a pleasant sea breeze that made it a lot more comfortable than the inland heat around Uluru. I had lunch at a beachside restaurant and watched the surfers for a while. I was actually getting sentimental about this flying adventure coming to an end.

Australian Gold Coast

Coolangatta was my exit point from Australia and the beginning of four flights totaling about 4,671 nm that would take me to Honolulu. The landing and overflight permits were in place for these flights, the barrels of aviation gas on remote islands reserved for me, and the hotels were booked. The airplane and the avionics were working well, so now it was all about the weather in what would be a six-day dash across the Pacific to Hawaii.

11

Australia to Hawaii

Vanuatu

I originally intended my flight leg departing Australia to be to Noumea (airport code NWWW), the international airport in New Caledonia. However, I found out that airport does not have aviation gas; instead, the aviation gas is at Magenta (airport code NWWM), a smaller airport 20 nm away that handles the local general-aviation aircraft, flight school, charters, etc. Going to New Caledonia would have required a stop at Noumea to clear Immigration and Customs, then another short flight to Magenta to refuel. Initially I was told I would then have to go back to Noumea to exit the country – a bad situation because it would have meant an overweight landing with full fuel. I finally learned I could get a special permission to exit the country at Magenta, but it still would have meant an additional short flight, and the runway at Magenta is only about 4,500 feet long, a little less length margin than I would have liked with an overweight takeoff.

Given all that, I started looking at other places to stop and came upon Port Vila, Vanuatu (airport code NVVV), which hadn't been mentioned to me by ferry pilots as a common place to stop. Port Vila even had aviation gas in a real truck, not barrels. The Custom and other fees are reasonable. Port Vila is also a little farther east than Noumea so the length of the two flight

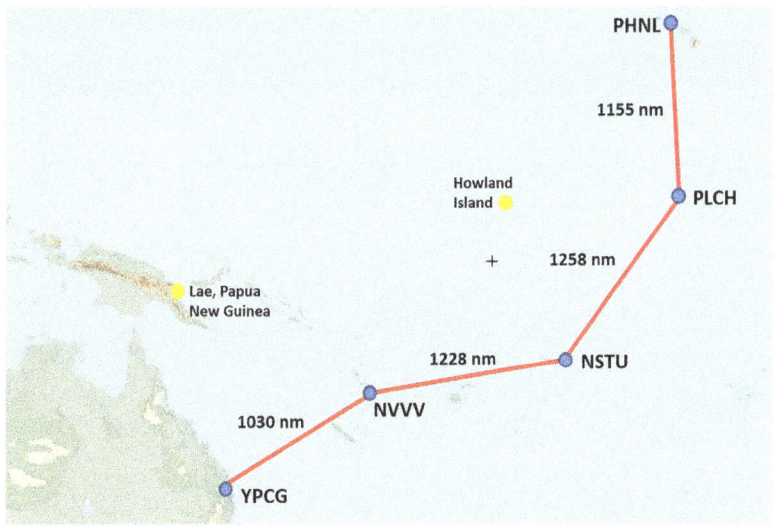

Flight legs across the Pacific from Australia to Hawaii. Lae, in PNG, was Amelia Earhart's departure point for Howland Island. She never arrived.

segments to Pago Pago (airport code NSTU) would be a little more balanced. Instead of a 750 nm flight from Coolangatta to Noumea followed by a 1400 nm flight from Noumea to Pago Pago, going through Port Vila results in a 1050 nm flight and a 1240 nm flight. The route through Port Vila is a little longer overall, but the convenience of having only one stop in Port Vila for fuel and to pass through Customs and Immigration outweighs that difference.

My departure from Coolangatta was delayed a day due to a misunderstanding about dates with the company, Skyplan, who was obtaining my permits. They had requested a landing permit at Port Vila for a day later than I wanted. I thought it could be fixed in an hour or two, so I actually went through security and Customs at the Coolangatta Airport then went out to the plane and got ready to go. I filed the exit paperwork myself which was similar to my procedure leaving Darwin, but I needed to hire a handler to escort me from security in the terminal to my plane. Of course, the control tower would not release me for departure without an approved landing permit in place at my destination. I waited a couple of hours at a friendly nearby general-aviation terminal, hoping the permit would come through that day, but had no luck. I wanted to leave early enough to avoid a night landing at Port Vila, where the weather was forecast to be poor and the instrument approaches are a little funky. There's no precision approach for low ceilings, and the other non-precision approaches don't allow you to descend below 1,000 feet above ground level.

Without a landing permit for Port Vila, I had to go back into Australia and stay another night. Technically, in terms of paperwork, I had already left. This caused a little consternation with the Immigration guy, who kept seeing me show up at his window wanting to enter or leave his country. The upside is that the Gold Coast is a nice place to be delayed if you've got to be delayed somewhere.

The permit for Port Vila came through late in the afternoon so I was good to go for the next day, November 18th. Things got off to a smooth start on the 18th with good weather at Coolangatta and a takeoff at 7:15 am local time, just 15 minutes later than the time indicated on the flight plan.

This intended route backtracked a bit to the Brisbane VOR (BN) navigation station to stay on the airways, but I expected I could get a direct routing to a waypoint on the eastbound airway R587 as soon as I got handed to Brisbane Center. That's exactly what happened – cleared directly to a waypoint called HARVS. The flight was pretty straightforward, flying high at FL110 above cloud clusters and pretty smooth air. As I left VHF radio coverage from Brisbane, they gave me HF frequencies. I tried them, but had the same result as before – I could hear them but they couldn't hear me. Before leaving the VHF coverage, I got their phone number and gave them my satphone number. I was also now including my satphone number in the Remarks section of my flight plans. I called Brisbane a couple of times with position reports; they called me once to give me the contact VHF frequency (128.2 MHz) for entry into New Caledonia-controlled airspace at a waypoint called MEPAB. New Caledonia ATC was called Tontouta Info. I was able to connect with them 75 nm from the waypoint named MEPAB and from that point on into Port Vila I had VHF communications all the way. Incidentally, as I mentioned before, the Jeppesen enroute paper charts have these frequencies (128.2 MHz, for example) printed on the chart – I don't see the same information anywhere on the Jeppesen electronic

Flying over New Caledonia

charts that come with their Flight Deck app on the iPad. I think this is one example of an important difference between the paper and electronic charts.

I had great views of the reefs around New Caledonia and the island itself as I flew over. Mining and other industrial activity was apparent. I was a little surprised to see a fairly large river winding through the mountainous sections in the north part of the island. I've traveled many parts of the world, but I admit I know very little about these South Sea island countries.

As I approached Vanuatu, the weather got murky and I was handed off to Port Vila approach/tower/ground (everything) on 120.7 MHz. The weather was a low cloud layer and rain, as expected, but reasonably good visibility at the airport. I was given the best available non-precision instrument approach for runway 11 which, oddly enough, is offset from the runway heading by 30 degrees. I descended to 2500 feet over the ocean to the initial approach fixed at waypoint DELTA. I was in solid clouds at that point and established on the localizer course of 80 degrees. Using the GPS for distance from the localizer (not runway), I followed the step-down fixes to an altitude of about 1300 feet as glimpses of the jungle-covered hills below began to appear through the clouds. They looked so close I began to doubt I had the right altimeter setting.

Finally, the airport and runway appeared through the clouds to the right, situated in a broad valley, about the only place it could have been on this island. I made the turn inbound to the runway for a nice landing. This instrument approach is very odd in that it not only relies on a radio beacon, it also includes a string of white lights on the ground in the form of a curve that is supposed to

Beaches at Port Vila

Marketplace at Port Vila

lead you to the runway threshold from the 30 degree offset approach course. I only saw a few of the lights, but by that time I had the runway in sight anyway. I wondered what it would be like to follow the curved path of lights without having the runway in sight. It is certainly one of the oddest instrument approaches I've flown, but I'm sure it's no big deal for the Air Vanuatu pilots who fly it all the time.

Ground handlers were waiting for me and everything went smoothly with refueling right away and the Customs and Immigration folks on the spot. With the plane fueled and covered up, I was off to the hotel, which was situated overlooking a lagoon, and a well-deserved drink after a seven-hour flight.

I spent a couple of nights here. I thought it was only going to be one night because of the landing permit delay. Well, guess what? On the next flight to Pago Pago I gained back the day I had lost hour-by-hour while flying east. I had scheduled to fly into Pago Pago on the afternoon of November 19th, which meant I needed to depart Vanuatu on the morning of November 20th, so that meant two nights here. I never flew on the Concorde, but I'm told that going west from Paris to New York, your arrival time would actually be earlier than your departure time! If you kept going around the world that way, you'd never get old.

I did have a chance to see Port Vila, with its community market, big and small yachts anchored in the excellent natural harbor. I had lunch on my layover day at a resort situated on an island accessible by a short ferry ride in an open boat. Vanuatu is a great island destination, one where I'd like to spend more time, with beaches, an active volcano, and an assortment of small getaway islands that can be reached by boat, helicopter, or float plane.

Pago Pago

Even though Vanuatu is attractive, I decided not to linger and took off for Pago Pago (airport code NSTU) in American Samoa pretty much as I scheduled at 6:00 am local time on November 20. As a place to stop, Port Vila turned out to be more expensive than I'd thought. The fuel price was reasonable for this part of the world and came on a truck, not in barrels, so I didn't end up paying for fuel I couldn't load. And they took US cash (Small Head Bens OK). But they charged me about $150 for "Customs" – not sure what that meant except maybe separate processing. The handler said the price can vary depending on how many Customs people are working at the time – they charge for the time for everyone working that day whether or not they actually do anything related to my arrival. A strange system, or maybe it was a bribe or a lie. Fortunately, there were only two working on the day I arrived; had it been five, I would have paid a lot more. I also paid US$50 for "Quarantine" services but never saw the guy. The handler, Air Vanuatu, was also a little expensive (US$500), but I've decided to pay for that convenience in countries where I don't feel like figuring out the airport and the Immigration and Customs formalities myself. I don't know if handling is required for transit aircraft at Port Vila as it is some places. The airport is simple enough, so I can see going through here without a handler. Anyway, this could potentially be an expensive stop but nothing like the alternative at Nadi (Fiji) where I understand they recently put in place some outrageous charges for transit aircraft on the order of several thousand dollars.

Flying over Fiji

The route to Pago Pago from Vanuatu goes right over Fiji. As with most of these inter-island routes, it's pretty obvious on the chart which route to take – there aren't many other places to go.

The climb-out from Port Vila heading pretty much due east was through dense rain clouds, resulting in instrument flying conditions up to about 6,000 feet. Above that, cruising at about 9,000 feet, I was in the blue skies with a cloud layer below. On departure I asked the tower for a transponder squawk code and they said they don't do those. When I got in touch with Nadi (Fiji) as I flew over, they said the same thing. They don't issue and use the codes. Because there is no radar service, there really is no point to having a squawk code. At some point inter-aircraft transponder awareness will have to change that. After leaving Port Vila VHF coverage I contacted Nadi Control on the satphone at +679 672 0664. At the BEACH waypoint I easily got them back on VHF at 119.1 MHz.

Flying over Fiji, and the islands off its west coast, I was reminded of a trip I made here in 1986. I spent a great week at some thatched-hut island resort full of fun-loving Australians. I spotted the same island as I flew over, distinctive for the dirt/gravel airstrip in the isthmus connecting the two prominent halves of the island. It was just a five-minute flight in a small plane not much bigger than N788W from the Nadi International Airport to this island. I wasn't a pilot in those days, but the pilot of this short shuttle flight seemed to have an easy job, though probably boring. I remember getting together with two other people and chartering him to take us across Fiji to the island of Ovalau where we spent a couple of nights, my last stop before leaving Fiji. The pilot hadn't flown into the grass strip at Ovalau before, so at least on that day of the charter his job was a little more interesting.

Runway 05 at Pago Pago

Crossing Fiji, the clouds were thickening below. I climbed up to 11,000 feet to clear them and asked the Nadi controller for weather along my route to Pago Pago. He didn't have any weather information but put me in touch with Qantas 6027 that was flying the same route, much higher and faster of course, but with weather radar and a longer range view. Those guys were helpful in reporting that they didn't see much in the way of buildups along my route. I had a chance to chat with them on 123.45 MHz, the inter-aircraft oceanic frequency. I told them I was on the last few legs of my round-the-world flight. They were on a "deadhead" (no passengers) flight to a Victorville, California, "boneyard," to park the plane in the desert along with hundreds of others waiting for a day when it might be called back into service or sold. That day may never come.

East of Fiji, actually on a north-south line passing through the Fijian island of Taveuni, I crossed the International Date Line, where in an instant November 20 became November 19. I made a short video of the GPS coordinates as the numbers spun through East 180 degrees, 00.00 minutes – geek stuff.

After leaving Nadi VHF coverage, I was briefly handed to Auckland, New Zealand Control, which I could reach on the sat-phone for a position report. I wasn't close to New Zealand so I thought it odd they have ATC responsibility here, but Western Samoa used to be a colony of New Zealand so that history may explain why this is their airspace. How airspace responsibility is divided up out here is a little strange, but I suppose somebody has to cover it all.

Shipwreck on the coast of American Samoa

The weather remained good until I approached Samoa, where a line of buildups was situated along the island chain, though fortunately not right in my path. I was finally talking to Faveolo Control at Apia, Samoa, on the VHF radio. They cleared me for a descent down to 4,000 feet, 30 miles from Pago Pago where their controlled airspace ended.

There is no control tower or radio operator at Pago Pago, so I was self-announcing my position to Pago Pago traffic as I approached, lined up, and landed on runway 05 using the instrument approach. It's a great airport with a long, well-paved runway. No other planes were in sight, and according to the handler, the airport was a shadow of its former self in terms of number of flights. There were only two international flights a week by Hawaiian Air plus local inter-island commuter flights and some military flights. Once parked, I fueled the plane with the cheapest fuel I'd found since leaving the US, at about US$9/gallon. No wonder this is a popular stop for ferry pilots.

There are two distinctive parts to Samoa: Western Samoa (or just Samoa) and American Samoa. Samoa is an independent island country and a member of the United Nations. American Samoa is a US territory where the population is hugely dependent on US aid for survival. When Western Samoa changed the name of their country to just "Samoa," there were protests from American Samoa, feeling the change somehow diminished their claim to being Samoans. I still sensed some animosity or competitiveness between the two Samoas, though I wasn't there long enough to understand any of it. Despite the similar name, geographical proximity, and centuries of shared cultural heritage, the two Samoas have followed separate paths. Novelist and travel writer Paul Theroux noted that there were marked differences between the societies in Samoa and American Samoa in his book about paddling a kayak at islands around the Pacific.

I had booked a room at the Tradewinds Hotel. The Tradewinds and Sadie's by the Sea are the best of only a few hotels on the island. There are also a few bed and breakfast places which I really didn't consider since I needed to be assured of a good internet connection. The Tradewinds Hotel is in town, not on the beach like Sadie's, but is more modern and has much better internet, I'm told.

They don't have much of a tourism industry here – there really isn't much to do – but it's something they're trying to change. The main industry is fish for export, both fresh and canned. Apparently, a new factory is being built to expand processing capacity.

During my one-day planned layover I decided to rent a car at the hotel to explore the island of Tutuila where Pago Pago is located. After only a few miles of driving, I managed to run over a sharp piece of metal on a potholed dirt road that stabbed a tire so deeply it went completely flat in one minute. I pulled into the parking lot at the Pizza Hut and retrieved a jack and tools from the trunk to change the tire. The lug nuts were incredibly rusty from the ocean climate. I was making progress but struggling to loosen the nuts when a huge Samoan guy came out of the Pizza Hut and offered to help me. The help was very welcome since the high heat and humidity were wearing me down. He made quick work of it. The spare was a small, temporary tire so I drove back to the hotel to get a different car. An hour later I was off again, this time a little more alert for debris in road. This was the first time I had driven a car since France so it felt a little odd at first – no airplane controls.

Tisa's Barefoot Bar

Tisa's Barefoot Bar is a locally famous beachside destination outside of town along the road heading north along the beach. I stopped at Tisa's for a great lunch. I shared flying stories with the owners, who handed me an engraved shot glass as I was leaving as a memento of my visit. Even the ferry pilots I talked to in the US told me to not to miss this place.

They use American money in American Samoa, so I decided to start archiving all the bills and coins of foreign currency I'd accumulated along the way, realizing it would no longer be of any use on this trip. I didn't know what money is used in Kiritimati (Christmas Island), my final stop before re-entering the US at Honolulu.

Lunch at Tisa's Barefoot Bar

Pago Pago is actually a collection of small hamlets, a few shopping districts with fast food joints, a large government complex, and not much else. Driving north along the coast road, the clusters of houses get smaller and more widely spaced, but they're still on the coast. I drove to the north end of the road. I then backtracked to a road that goes west over the crest of the mountains to the far side of the island, where there are a few more coastal villages, a national park, and some steep, towering offshore rocks where years ago young island men would show their macho by climbing the rocks to collect eggs and birds. The weather was good all day, which made the drive a pleasant break from flying.

Christmas Island (Kiritimati)

Christmas Island, my next destination and a critical fuel stop on the way to Honolulu, is the largest island in the island nation of Kiribati, and apparently the largest coral atoll in the world. My flight from Pago Pago to Christmas Island was a decision-making challenge. The crux of the weather issue was the Inter-Tropical Convergence Zone (ITCZ), basically where the weather systems from the northern and southern hemispheres converge. This zone lies more or less along the equator but can be positioned several degrees north or south depending on the season and the La Nina/El Nino cycles. In the summer months the zone can be fairly benign; in the winter months it can show its power. At the time I was there, the ITCZ was positioned about 8 degrees north of the equator, and north of Christmas Island. The forecast I had been consulting showed long lines of thunderstorms stretching along the zone with the "cherry on top" being a Category 4 hurricane, Kenneth, in the eastern Pacific, making its way west toward my flight route. How and when do I fly across the Inter-Tropical Convergence Zone?

The information I had for Christmas Island (airport code PLCH) indicated that internet communication would be difficult. If I left Pago Pago, where I had good internet service, and flew to Christmas Island, I envisioned being stuck with no way to view weather forecasts, maps, satellite photos, etc. – the things I'd come to rely on to make flight planning decisions. I needed two days of reasonable weather to get to Honolulu from Pago Pago. What I was seeing at the time were tall thunderstorms in the convergence zone. A call to the US weather briefing confirmed this. If I left Pago Pago and went to Christmas Island, would I get stuck south of the convergence zone with no good information on deciding when to cross it? Furthermore, if Hurricane Kenneth plowed westward unabated and ended up crossing Christmas Island, my plane would be out in the open because there are no hangars or tie downs at Christmas Island. N788W could be destroyed.

Satellite photo of Christmas Island

I finally decided I needed to get to Christmas Island at some point, and the weather en-route from Pago Pago on November 21 looked OK, so I decided to take "the bird in the hand," and go for Christmas Island, and not wait for an ideal weather setup for both flight legs.

Early on the morning of the 21st there were thunderstorms rumbling around Pago Pago. I got up at 5 am, looked out the window, and saw pouring rain and flashing thunder. And this was supposed to be the good (non-ITCZ) day! I went to the airport, prepped the plane, and sat in the office of the handler for 15 minutes re-checking weather information, trying to decide whether to go. The thunderstorms had abated around the island so, locally at least, it was just rain and low clouds. I decided to go.

Once in the plane I tried calling Faleolo Approach for my IFR flight clearance, but I got no response. A US Coast Guard C-130 had departed 45 minutes before, so either they had been able to make contact or they just ignored the lack of communications. I decided to self-announce my intentions on the Faleolo frequency and depart without my IFR clearance. I couldn't get them on the ground, but maybe I could get them later while in the air. At the time I didn't have a phone number to call them on the satphone.

I back-taxied out onto runway 5, turned the plane 180 degrees into the gusty wind, and looked at what I had. The rain had actually intensified, and the ceiling was low and indeterminate. The rain was so intense I couldn't see the far end of the runway. I hesitated for a few seconds wondering whether I should taxi back to the terminal and shut it down. I decided to take off into this muck, made all the more treacherous by American Samoa's high hills and a bizarre cable stretching across Pago Pago harbor, which was noted on the charts as a serious hazard to planes. With very poor visibility I wouldn't be able to see any of it. Of all the instrument takeoffs I've done, I'd have to say this one had the worst conditions. Once airborne, I was totally focused on the instrument panel – the rest of the world disappeared. And this was supposed to be the easy day!

During the climb-out I kept calling Faleolo Approach to get my flight clearance. Fifteen minutes later I finally made contact and complained about calling them several times from Pago Pago with no response. She said they were having technical problems with their radio there. Hmmm. I finally was high enough to get out of the solid clouds and the sky opened up a bit. I could hear Faleolo making test calls on their various frequencies, so maybe there really were technical problems and they weren't just sleeping late. As I flew out of range of their VHF system, I pulled out the satphone and called them on that.

The route I filed for had a bunch of waypoints defined by latitude/longitude coordinates, but the route I got actually followed airway B577. I flew via waypoints called DARMA, SAPIX, and PASSA, then directly to Christmas Island.

Arriving at Christmas Island

Once again, I was not given a transponder code. Flying around here is a little ad hoc. The weather finally cleared up, but I was still driving around cloud buildups. At one point I headed for a "cloud valley" of blue sky between two buildups, which was beginning to close; it closed just before I got there. It reminded, of the scene from the movie "Independence Day" where they just made it out of the alien mother ship before the triangular portal closed. In my case it did close, but it was just clouds I could easily fly through.

On this flight leg I came closest to Howland Island, the intended destination of Amelia Earhart's final, ill-fated flight. There is a curious illusion, flying over vast stretches of ocean. In the bright sunlight the clouds themselves can create very dark, odd-shaped shadows on the surface on the water that can be mistaken for islands, especially here in the Pacific where many islands are basically flat with no hills or mountains to distinguish them. In desperation to find a place to land, I can see a pilot chasing after "shadows" that look like islands only to find empty ocean there. A man dying of thirst in the desert would chase the shimmering mirage of an oasis in the same way.

Airport terminal building at PLCH

The farther north I flew, the better the weather got. I had time to make a video of the GPS counting down to 0 degrees latitude while crossing the equator, making up for missing it while flying south from Singapore. After the waypoint called PASSA, I was now talking to

Oakland Control in the US on the satphone, which, psychologically at least, made me feel closer to home. By the time I descended into Christmas Island – a truly immense island I could see from 70 miles away – I was really enjoying the experience of landing on a very remote Pacific island as the sun was setting. The view of the extensive turquoise lagoons was amazing. As I came in to land, the video I made with my GoPro camera suction-cupped to the inside of the windshield caught the shadow of the plane as it approached and touched down on runway 08. Nice.

White beaches of Christmas Island

The "terminal building" at Christmas Island is an open-air building; and the "control tower" a one-story, one-room shack with radio antennas on the roof. That fit what I expected, but the rest of Christmas Island did not. I've described my experience on Christmas Island in Chapter 1. Christmas Island turned out to be the most unadulterated Pacific island experience on my trip.

Even the internet communication was not as bad as I'd feared. They had WiFi at the hotel but it was somewhat inconvenient to use. However, the runway construction group staying at the hotel had set up a room with their own computers and internet connection they used to Skype with their families and for other purposes. They were gracious enough to let me use it and their computers when I explained my need to

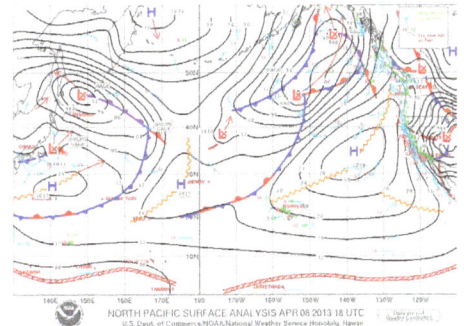
Typical weather map showing the Inter-Tropical Convergence Zone

check the weather for my flight to Honolulu. It was very helpful, confirming the information I'd received from a US weather forecaster in Hawaii the night before who advised me to delay a day before flying north.

During my layover day I had the plane refueled. Though I was very wary of the two rusty barrels of aviation gas the fuel company K-OIL brought to the airport, I really had no choice but to have them pump that gas into my plane. The only game in town was really the only game in the Pacific for me at this point.

As the only "ferry pilot" at the hotel, I was a novelty and had a good time telling people about my flight during my layover day. The time I spent with the fishermen, an interesting group of travelers of diverse nationalities and professions, made my short time on the island more enjoyable. It is on the short list of places I've encountered that I would definitely like to revisit, without the weather and scheduling demands of the flight affecting the time I could linger and relax. I might even take up fishing to sample the excitement these fishermen found traveling this far.

Honolulu

My day of delay waiting for improved weather in the Inter-Tropical Convergence Zone was worth it. I got to enjoy a day in a place that was unexpectedly pleasant, and my flight to Honolulu (airport code PHNL) would be less difficult with a gap having opened between the forecast thunderstorm clusters. I took off almost on time at 7:14 am local time, which is a bit challenging to figure out since Christmas Island is actually in the UTC+14 time zone, not the UTC-10 time zone where its geographic location would place it. UTC (Zulu time) is the Greenwich Mean Time worldwide reference. In terms of time zones, Christmas Island is in the Eastern Hemisphere even though geographically it is well into the Western Hemisphere. The hour shown on the clock is the same as the hour shown in Honolulu, except a full day ahead. I was actually leaving Christmas Island on November 24 and arriving in Honolulu on November 23. Hmmm – what dates do you put on the General Declaration form to exit Christmas Island? Even though Christmas Island is far to the east of the International Date Line, they created this time zone jog so the whole island country of Kiribati, which is spread across more than 1000 miles of the Pacific, could be in the same time zone. Kiribati also made the change so they could claim to be the first country to greet the new Millennium back in 2000.

Departing Christmas Island

My takeoff from Christmas Island was on a beautiful sunny morning. As I turned back across the island to head north, I gave the fishermen already wading across the lagoons a classic wing "waggle" salute – as the noisiest thing around on this quiet island, no doubt they saw me depart. I set the autopilot for my typical overweight climb-out at just 500 fpm to keep the engine temperatures under control, and called Oakland Center to get my clearance to Honolulu. They gave me a new set of waypoints defined by latitude/longitude (typically every 5 of latitude) until the waypoint called TARDE south of the big island of Hawaii. At that point I would enter the Honolulu Flight Information Region and be back in the US ATC system. Oakland asked me to call them on the satphone with a position report at every waypoint and every hour in between, which I did.

Inside the Inter-Tropical Convergence Zone

About 1½ hours out of Christmas Island I saw the Inter-Tropical Convergence Zone weather front I had expected. I tried to choose the most likely route through it, but eventually I was buried in solid clouds with intermittent and sometimes intense rain. It was a bit bumpy but not the worst I've experienced. I was happy to see that there was no electrical activity showing on the Stormscope, indicating there were no invisible, embedded thunderstorms I would have to avoid.

The solid clouds, rain, and turbulence lasted for about 45 minutes, but finally yielded to a miraculous sight. I popped out the north side of this front to find only blue sky as far as I could see. Looking back at it, and based on what I had experienced, flying through the zone was very much like flying though a conventional weather front. Anyway, I was very happy to be on the north side with blue skies that lasted all the way to Hawaii. There were still

Emerging from the Inter-Tropical Convergence Zone; blue skies to Hawaii

clouds below me, sometimes scattered, sometimes solid overcast, but I was in the clear. I even saw a few rainbows among the clouds below, something I don't remember seeing anywhere else on this trip.

I picked up Honolulu approach at the waypoint called TARDE and got vectored around a little by ATC before getting cleared direct to waypoint JULLE, followed by the JULLE 5 Standard Arrival into Honolulu. The weather was good with just a scattered-to-broken layer at about 4000 feet. Once underneath it, I was given a visual approach to runway 04R, one of several runways at Honolulu and the one commonly used by small private aircraft.

I taxied to Air Services Hawaii where Customs was waiting for me on the ramp. I had Skyplan, the Canadian company that had been doing my overflight and landing permits, file the Customs notifications since I didn't think I would be able to from Christmas Island, although it turned out I could have because of the runway builders' internet setup. Entry in the country went smoothly. It took maybe 10 minutes to fill out the conventional Customs arrival form, answer a few questions, get my passport stamped, and I was back in the USA!

Coming up on Mauna Loa

From there I taxied down to Anderson Aviation, where the plan was to install a second smaller auxiliary fuel tank to provide some additional fuel and extra range margin to make the long ocean crossing of 2100 nm back to California. Because I had arrived in Honolulu the day before Thanksgiving, I didn't expect much to happen with this installation or the necessary FAA paperwork until the following week. That was OK with me. The flying this past week or so from Coolangatta in Australia onward had been very demanding, with a series of long over-water flights through sometimes volatile tropical weather conditions. Having several days to relax in Hawaii worked for me.

I had booked a room at a simple hotel near the airport so that I could more easily manage the second ferry tank installation and FAA paperwork processing. To my surprise, Anderson Aviation was willing to do the installation on the Friday following Thanksgiving, though the FAA paperwork wouldn't get processed until the following week. Anderson Aviation often does ferry tank installations for planes coming from, or going to, the US, so they are accustomed to ferry pilots wanting the shortest possible delay. While parked there, I also off-loaded a lot of things that would be irrelevant for the rest of my flight – books, clothes, souvenirs, etc. – and boxed them up to be shipped to my home on Bainbridge Island. With this trip's largest fuel load and maximum weight coming on the flight leg to California, I wanted to eliminate all extraneous weight.

Landing at Honolulu

I moved from an airport hotel to a hotel on Waikiki where I enjoyed eating and drinking everything in sight, especially seafood and green salads. As I mentioned, I refrain from eating fresh vegetables and anything the least bit suspicious in developing countries, because an intestinal illness could have really knocked a hole in my plans to complete this flight. For that reason, I was probably a lot more conservative about what I ate than I would have been if I had been traveling on commercial airlines. There were also many shops on Waikiki within walking distance of my hotel where I could pick up a few extra things I was missing. Waikiki is a gaudy tourist mecca: not the kind of place I'd normally stay. But for this occasion it suited my needs.

12

Hawaii to California – The Longest Flight

Second Ferry Tank Installation

The second ferry tank installation had been efficiently done by Anderson Aviation the day after Thanksgiving, but the FAA paperwork turned out to be a different story. Fred Sorensen, who organized and signed off on the original ferry tank installation in Merced, put most of the paperwork together for this one over the weekend based on information from me and from seeing the photos I had taken of the new installation. He then FedEx'd the document package to Anderson Aviation for submission to the FAA office located just down the street. The FAA started processing it on Tuesday, finally meeting with me on Wednesday. They were OK with the installation, but they questioned me extensively about the fuel burn calculations, especially my claim that I could get

Additional 28 gallon fuel tank installed in Honolulu

165 knots airspeed with about 11 gph (gallons per hour) fuel consumption at 11,000 feet. I explained I'd just flown 22,000 nm doing exactly that. They were particularly motivated to explore this issue because of an accident a few weeks before in which a twin engine Cessna being ferried from the US to Hawaii went into the ocean 13 nm short of Hilo due to fuel exhaustion. They were hesitant to sign off on another ferry flight where there was a risk of it happening again.

Additional fuel tank in co-pilot seat

I was happy to answer their questions. Believe me, nobody in the room was more interested in being assured of getting to California than me! Review-ing the numbers and evaluating "worst-case" scenarios turned out to be important.

The FAA issued a new Special Flight Permit and associated Operating Limitations on Thursday morning. I took off on a VFR flight plan that afternoon for the short flight to Maui (airport code PHOG). Repositioning the plane to Maui had a few purposes. It gave me a chance to test the new ferry tank in flight, required by the Special Flight Permit. I had to note a successful test with an entry in the maintenance log. I had tested it on the ramp and it worked OK, but a flight test is the real measure of whether it is working as expected. Maui is also a good launching point for the flight to California. It's closer to California than Honolulu, and runway 02, which is typically in use, ends pretty much at the water's edge so if you need a shallow climb-out angle because the plane is overweight, there's nothing but open ocean in front of you. It is also a better option than Hilo (depending on where you're going in California) even though Hilo is 20 nm closer: because Maui is a bit farther north, the route heading is a little more favorably oriented in relation to the

N788W on the fuel pump in Maui ready for its crossing to California

prevailing winds aloft. With N788W repositioned to Maui, it was just a matter of waiting for a good weather day to make the flight to California, what would be the longest flight of this adventure in terms of distance and time.

The Crossing

Originally, my plan was to fly straight back to Merced, California, where TDL Aero would remove both ferry tanks, reinstall the seats, and return N788W to its original configuration. However, I continued to be bothered by the forecast of winds aloft. A "winds aloft" forecast shows the speed and direction of the wind depicted on maps at given altitudes on a given date and time. Generally, the winds over the ocean can't be forecast as accurately as winds over land because there simply are not as many reporting stations or weather balloons, as I understand it. I decided the prudent thing to do was give myself every advantage making it across to California, which meant going into the closest possible airport. In this case that airport is Monterey, California (airport code KMRY), about 60 nm closer than Merced. Monterey is actually a much larger airport than Merced with good general-aviation facilities and hotels within walking distance, unlike Merced.

I planned to depart on Saturday, December 3, but there were horrendous windstorms in California, knocking down trees, power lines, and gas station signs. There were official AIRMETs (weather warnings to airmen) for turbulence and high winds Thursday, Friday, and running into Saturday, then

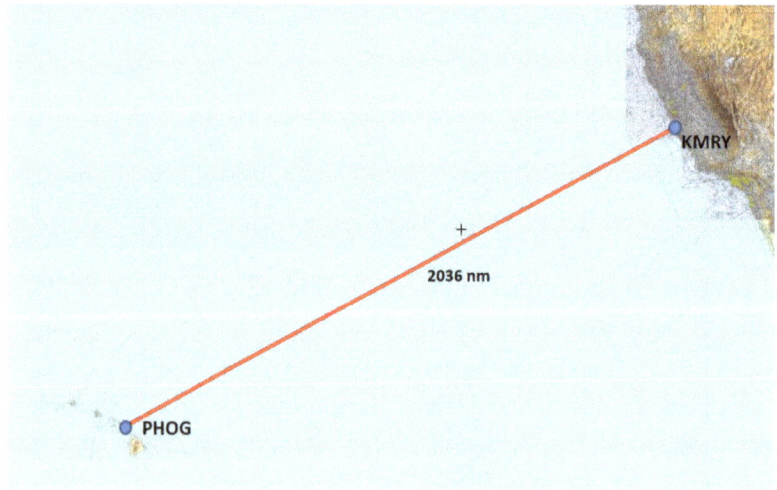

Flight leg from Maui, Hawaii, to Monterey, California

finally being lifted Saturday evening. The weather on the route was generally good – a big high-pressure system was dominating the eastern Pacific, so the few thunderstorm clusters were lingering on the edges and well off my route. On the National Weather Service's Aviation Weather Center website there is actually a Route Forecast I came across for the San Francisco to Honolulu route – exactly what I needed (in reverse, of course). It's a little hard to find, but worth the effort. For Sunday, December 4, it showed just low clouds below my flight level the whole way, and net headwinds of just 12 knots for the entire route at 10,000 feet. I ran the route through a couple of flight planning websites I used and they concurred with that headwind forecast. How wrong it turned out to be!

I planned to leave at 6:00 am Maui time (1600Z) which meant another morning of getting out of the hotel in the dark at 5:00 am, but it would be my last for this trip. To get ramp access to transient parking in front of the fire station at Maui, I needed to call airport security. I had fueled the plane when I arrived, my usual habit, so it was ready to go. I finished my pre-flight inspection in the dark with a flashlight. I also tested all the panel and position lights, something I normally don't do. I hadn't really done any night flying on this trip, and I knew I would arrive at Monterey in the dark, so it was critical that these lights be working.

Since I knew the flight would take about 13+ hours, and given the short days of winter in the Northern Hemisphere, I knew I would either have to land or take off in the dark, or take off in the evening, fly all night, and land in the morning. All else being equal, I would choose to land in daylight, but all was not equal. I chose to take off in the light at dawn and land at night mainly because the plane would be overweight on takeoff. Having done these overweight takeoffs a few times already, I knew having a real horizon was helpful in easing the aircraft off the runway and establishing a shallow climb-out angle. Upon arrival at Monterey, most of the fuel would be burned off, the plane would be light and inside its normal weight-and-balance envelope. The landing would be a conventional night landing. I didn't fancy flying all night if unexpected cloud buildups were in the way. At night over the ocean with no lights on the ground for reference, cloud buildups are much more difficult to detect and fly around.

After some confusion about the flight plan – they didn't have the one I filed for Monterey, just an earlier one filed to Merced – I was off at about 6:30 am into a nice Pacific dawn, direct to a waypoint called CLUTS. I found out later the Monterey flight plan was rejected because the estimated en-route times format I used for the waypoints was invalid. I never reviewed it to figure out why.

With the Merced flight plan adjusted to show Monterey as the new destination, the next ATC issue came up 20 minutes later as I was completing my climb to 11,000 feet. Before they would clear me beyond waypoint CLUTS, they required I establish HF radio communication with Oakland Center. I told them I would be using my satphone. Honolulu told me that was not acceptable for primary communications. For a short time they actually canceled my clearance to Monterey and told me I'd have to go back to Hawaii if I didn't use the HF radio. I explained that going back was impossible because it would mean landing overweight and risk damaging the plane, not to mention violating the operating limitations in the FAA Special Flight Permit. After talking to a Honolulu supervisor (by satphone), he got Oakland to accept me beyond waypoint CLUTS, even if the HF didn't work. Thank you! But to show good faith, I switched on the HF radio and gave Oakland a call on the primary frequency of 8843 kHz they had assigned me. To my astonishment, it worked! They heard me and called me right back. Since trying the HF on the flight from Goose Bay to Iceland and having no success (and even interference to the autopilot), I had given up on trying to use it. Now it was

Looking back on the setting sun as I get closer to California

working OK, with no autopilot interference, and for the next few position reports out beyond waypoint CLUTS I used the HF radio to call them, until finally my signal got so weak they couldn't hear me anymore. At that point I switched back to the satphone and used it (and relays) for the remainder of the flight. Any pilot contemplating an oceanic flight crossing to or from Hawaii: be prepared to deal with this HF radio issue.

From there on, the flight was a long grind. The clouds were below me, as forecast, so I was in clear skies the entire flight. I was making position reports every hour on the hour, as well as at waypoints defining my route, which were about 400 nm apart. I had anticipated worst-case headwinds of about 20 knots, the highest wind speed shown on the winds aloft forecast map anywhere in the east Pacific, in any direction. I was surprised I had that much headwind almost from the beginning of the flight. As I flew on, the headwind increased until it started to worry me. I was getting 165–170 knots airspeed from the plane as usual, but as the miles went by I watched the ground speed on the GPS progressively fall from 150 knots to 145 knots to 135 knots. By the time I reached about the halfway point at waypoint CORTT (the point of no return), my ground speed was down to 130 knots. Are you kidding me? A 40-knot headwind? Where was that on the forecast? The ground speed continued to fall and ultimately got as low at 121 knots, which meant almost 50 knots of headwind.

Now my fuel situation really became a concern. If this headwind got stronger, making it to Monterey could be in question. I did everything I could to get the most out of the airplane without increasing fuel burn – notching up RPM and power a bit, really at the edge of the engine performance. The strong headwinds persisted, so I called ATC and alerted them that I potentially had a headwind/range issue. On paper I could still make it at 125 knots ground speed all the way, but it would be close. ATC responded by giving me a block altitude assignment (5,000 to 17,000 feet) so I could look for an altitude with more favorable winds. Unfortunately, this is not always helpful unless you know a better altitude, because a lot of fuel can be wasted going up and down looking for something better. I descended to 10,000 feet, then 9,000 feet, without much improvement – I was still experiencing 120–125 knot ground speeds. I was now using relays to ATC by way of commercial aircraft and private jets flying overhead at 30,000 to 40,000 feet, which, curiously, had much weaker headwinds of 10 to 15 knots; but I couldn't fly that high. Those pilots were supportive of my situation, and a few even double-checked my fuel burn calculations and confirmed what I thought – that I could still make it OK if the headwinds didn't get stronger.

I explained to these other pilots that I was on the last, most challenging leg of a solo round-the-world flight in a single-engine piston aircraft. That led to running conversations about my flight. It was a pleasure to pass the time this way, taking my mind off my fuel situation in what was now becoming a long, grueling flight. As night descended, they could see my strobe lights far below as they passed by me overhead.

One crew of a Falcon private jet based at Sea-Tac Airport was particularly friendly and interested in my trip. I told them I was headed to Monterey; they were going to San Jose. Since they would arrive well before me, they said they would drive down and meet me in Monterey. It was a kind offer, but I really didn't expect it to happen late at night.

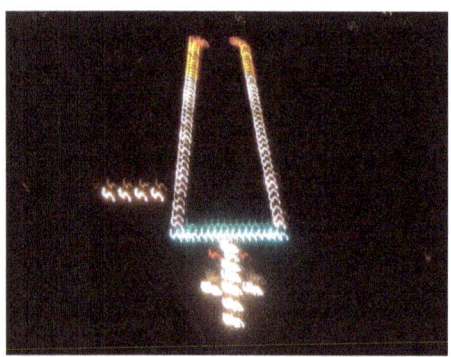

Finally! Runway lights at Monterey (KMRY)

As my flight continued, the strong headwinds continued. I decided I needed every drop of fuel from the ferry tanks. Normally, I would drain them to the point where perhaps only 5 or 10 gallons was remaining. Now, to get at all the usable fuel, I kept running the engine using the ferry tank until the engine actually started to sputter and stop from fuel starvation. I had my hand on the alternate right wing tank valve so as soon as I heard the engine start to sputter, I could immediately switch to a tank with some fuel in it, flick on the boost pump, and drive new fuel into the engine. The last thing a pilot wants to hear is the engine sputter this way. That I deliberately ran the engine out to this point reminds me how concerned I'd become about having enough fuel.

After using all the fuel in the ferry tanks and trying unsuccessfully to find a better altitude, I realized I had done everything I could do to extend my range. There was nothing left but to sit back, relax, and try to enjoy the starry night and the ongoing radio conversations with other pilots. I could see Orion, one of the few constellations I can consistently recognize on my far-flung travels, positioned in the sky above my right wing. It was reassuring to have a familiar presence alongside for this flight, a resonance that stretched across the decades and continents. When I hitchhiked around Africa in 1975, I remember getting rides on trucks hauling copper plates from the mines in Zambia to the port city of Dar es Salaam in Tanzania. Sometimes I would ride on top of the load, lying there in the cool breeze, looking up at the stars as we rumbled down the highway toward a faraway dawn. Flying across the Pacific I was still on that decades-long journey, connected by Orion and a night sky that tonight would be forgiving.

As I passed the waypoint called CUNDU, with still more than 600 nm to go, the headwinds finally began to ease. I watched the ground speed slowly creep up from 125 to 130 to 135 knots. I knew then my concerns about fuel were resolved. The moral of this story is: don't trust wind forecasts in these situations. I don't know who forecasts these winds or what models they use, but I think the NOAA wind models for this area are not much good – and potentially very dangerous. My flight circumstance is just one data point, but still as a Ph.D. engineer who has done a lot of mathematical modeling, I say there ought to be some statistical wrapper on this data, such as stating the median predicted headwind is 12 knots but there is a 10% probability it could be greater than 40 knots.

I started my flight in Maui with 204 gallons; I would finally land in Monterey with about 25 gallons of usable fuel on board. That's still 1.5 to 2 hours flying time and maybe par for the course for ferry pilots who do these flights for a living. But to me, as a conservative pilot, it was tight. I definitely needed the second 28-gallon ferry tank I installed in Honolulu. If the headwind forecasts had been reasonably accurate, or given me some indication or probability they could be much stronger

Falcon pilots who greeted me in Monterey

than the forecast, I would have waited for a better day. To other pilots contemplating long over-water flights I offer my strongest possible caution about wind forecasts – and under any circumstances, take a lot more fuel than you think you'll need.

Monterey

Coming up on the lights of Monterey from the Pacific Ocean was a wonderful sight. It was past 11 pm–the tower had closed at 9 pm–so I clicked on the runway lights with my radio and lined up for runway 10R. After nearly 15 hours in the air, what a joy and relief to feel the wheels once again touch down on my home continent.

After I landed at Monterey at 11:10 pm, I was amazed that the Falcon pilots who said they would meet me actually showed up a few minutes later. They even brought me an extra catered meal they had on board and gave me a ride to my hotel near the airport. Pilots can be incredibly supportive. We traded contact information so we could get back in touch in Seattle.

I had now flown across all the longitude meridians and crossed the equator twice. Even though I wasn't home yet, I had completed a flight around the world. After a well-deserved rest at the hotel, where I was almost too wired to sleep, I would fly the plane to Merced the next day so the ferry tanks could be removed, the seats re-installed, and the plane returned to its normal configuration. I'd leave the plane in Merced for few days, rent a car, and visit family and friends in the San Francisco Bay area.

13

Heading Home – the Final Flights

I woke up the morning of December 5 after getting maybe four hours' sleep. It was one of the easiest days I had faced in months. There was no need to check the weather or consider rescheduling flight days because of it, nor flight routes to rearrange, nor Customs and Immigration hassles, nor greedy handlers to argue with and face down. With my relief at having completed the most challenging flight leg the day before came some nostalgic sadness at seeing this adventure come to an end.

The day after arriving in Monterey late at night, I flew N788W directly to Merced, California (airport code KMCE), a short flight of only about 76 nm. The ferry tanks were installed

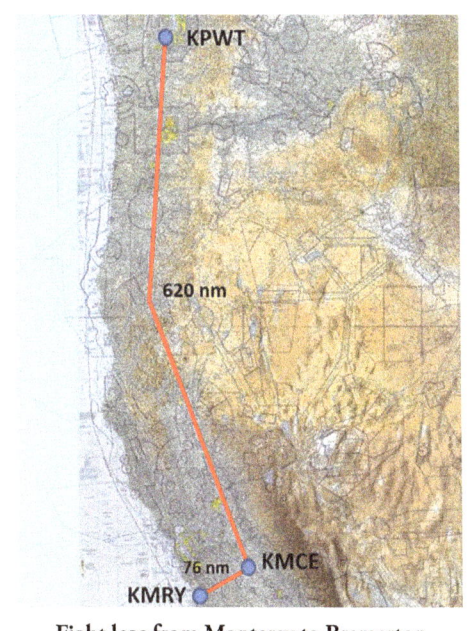

Fight legs from Monterey to Bremerton

in Merced at TDL Aero the previous June as described in Chapter 2. Now they would remove the tanks and plywood platform they installed, along with the second ferry tank installed in Honolulu, and return the fuel system plumbing to its original configuration. They also re-installed the seats and did an oil change, which was overdue. While this was going on, I was up in the San Francisco Bay Area visiting family and friends.

Flying north over Lake Shasta

On December 8 I had intended to fly from Merced back to Eugene, Oregon, where I had lived for nearly 20 years and still had a country home and ownership in a business: EDX Wireless, Inc. EDX is a software company that develops and sells PC software for designing and optimizing wireless communication networks. I founded EDX in 1985, sold it in 2000 at the peak for the tech boom, and bought it back with some partners in 2004 for pennies on the dollar. My partners now successfully run it, so relatively little involvement is required from me, freeing me to do long-haul flying adventures like this. I did want to check in with the company and attend the annual holiday party.

Mt. Shasta

However, a large high-pressure system was lingering over the Pacific Northwest, creating fog (and freezing fog) at the Eugene Airport (airport code KEUG). Even when the temperatures warmed up a few degrees in the afternoon, the ceiling would only come up a few hundred feet. These are not unusual conditions for Eugene this time of year and one of the reasons Eugene has a high performance precision instrument approach, allowing commercial jets that are suitably equipped to land in conditions with near-zero cloud ceiling and zero visibility. Well, that is not me. Rather than wait on the weather to improve in Eugene, I decided to skip Eugene and fly all the way back to Bremerton Airport where this trip really started. It has a 6000-foot runway and instrument approaches. I filed an IFR flight to Bremerton at 10,000 feet, expecting low ceilings but no fog when I landed. I would be flying along airway V23 over the Siskiyou Mountains, my usual route back home from California.

It was a sunny day in Merced with no forecast clouds on the route except low clouds and fog in the valleys of Oregon and Washington. I got direct routing to Sacramento, then north, and sat back to enjoy what would turn out to be the sunniest, most cloud-free flight on this whole trip. I was flying over countryside I had flown over many times and knew well. Flying north over Lake Shasta and along the west side of Mount Shasta was a beautiful sight in the crisp, clear winter skies. As I was handed off from controller to controller, I realized I didn't have to struggle to understand them or ask them to repeat things, something that had been commonplace during much of the past few months.

Further north I could see the familiar volcanic peaks of the Oregon Cascades – Diamond Peak, Mt. Bachelor (where I snowboard), the Three Sisters, Mt. Jefferson, and Mt. Hood. As expected, the Willamette Valley around Eugene was a flat sea of clouds. But as sometimes happens, Corvallis and Salem, somewhat farther north, were on the edges and in the clear. The headwinds were light and I was making good time. I cruised past Mount St.

Finally home! Final approach on runway 01 (now 02) at Bremerton (KPWT)

Helens, Mt. Adams, and the tallest Cascade peak, Mt. Rainier, well above me at over 14,000 feet.

Coming into the Puget Sound area, the expected overcast cloud layer was solid but thin. Winds were out of the north at Bremerton with a ceiling at 1400 feet above ground level. Easy. I flew the GPS instrument approach for runway 01 (now 02), only spending a couple of minutes inside the clouds descending through the overcast layer. What a familiar sight: runway 02 at Bremerton where I've landed a hundred times. I taxied to my hangar, shut down the engine, opened the door of the plane, and was immediately struck by how cold it was: 40° (F). It was the damp bone-chilling cold the people in the Northwest know well and a real contrast to the warm tropical temperatures I'd become used to for the last several weeks.

Pushing N788W back into its hangar seemed anti-climactic. I felt that the momentous conclusion to this flight had been my arrival in Monterey, where the hard flying was finally completed. Avian Aeronautics at Bremerton, great people who also maintain my plane, arranged a ride for me to my home on Bainbridge Island, where I'd left my car when I returned to England. My house was still standing and I knew there would be a two-month stack of mostly useless mail waiting. I would have to sort through that at some point.

It felt great to be home, but the satisfaction of completing what I'd set out to do really hadn't gripped me yet. I would still make my visit to Eugene but probably by driving. I was actually looking forward to driving around in my car listening to music – such a simple pleasure after living with an airplane, flight plans, overflight and landing permits, weather reports, Customs and Immigration agents, and hotels for the past few months.

I went down to my wine cellar and pulled out a bottle of one of my favorite Oregon Pinot Noirs from the rolling hills around Newburg. I lit a fire, something I rarely do, and sat back to savor the moment, watching the firelight flicker through the iridescent red wine swirling in my glass. It seemed too comfortable, like there was something I should be doing – researching, preparing, booking, filing, staring at my notebook screen, deciding – something. During the trip I had incrementally dialed up a high level of intensity and focus without even realizing it. It would take a while to dial it back down to suit my life at home.

Flight Summary Details

After unwinding for a few days, I managed to review my flight logs (which I keep on an Excel spreadsheet) and compile a few statistics for this round-the-world flight:

1. Total distance (via great circle paths between points): 23,937 nm
2. Total flight hours: 162.2
3. Estimated amount of fuel: 1900 gallons
4. Estimated cost: US$50,000, consisting of:
   a. Fuel
   b. Hotels
   c. Insurance
   d. Overflight and landing permits
   e. Handlers
   f. Ferry tank installation and associated paperwork
   g. Jeppesen e-charts
   h. Airport navigation and landing fees

As I mentioned at the beginning, I didn't keep an accurate tally of expenses, so these numbers truly are an estimate. But they're probably not wrong by more than 10% for my particular flight. Of course, flying with a different plane, along a different route, and spending more time along the way to enjoy the places visited would certainly affect the cost.

14

Preparations for Antarctica

My New Goal

I attended the Earthrounders Reunion (*www.earthrounders.com*) in Florida in March, 2012, a few months after completing my round-the-world flight in N788W. Earthrounders is an informal group of pilots from all over the world who have either flown around the world in small planes or have ambitions to fly around the world in small planes. Having successfully completed my flight, I was honored to be counted among pilots with a similar accomplishment. I was given the coveted "Earthrounders" decal by Claude Meunier, one of the founders of Earthrounders, and keeper of the Earthrounder web page. I now display that decal on the side of N788W.

After completing my round-the-world flight, I said I would never do it again, even though some pilots have done it two or three times. I may never do a round-the-world flight again, but that doesn't mean I wasn't interested in new challenges involving long-distance international flying. This reunion inspired me to consider what those challenges might be. While the Earthrounders group had discussions about flying to many countries and continents, the ultimate rare, elusive destination emerged as Antarctica.

Only one reunion participant, Bob Gannon from the US, had flown there solo in his Cessna. Only two others were known to have flown there solo in small planes – Polly Vacher from the UK and Matevz Lenarcic from Slovenia.

Many other pilots had flown to the southern tip of South America, either to Ushuaia in Argentina or Punta Arenas in Chile, but had not attempted a flight to Antarctica. Others had attempted, but not completed, flights from New Zealand. Although the flight was not particularly long to reach the nearest landing strip in Antarctica, the difficulties were daunting: highly volatile weather, no nearby alternate airports (you basically have to fly back to South America if you can't land at one of two available landing strips), and most significant of all, getting permission to land. There are no airports open to the public in Antarctica. The few landing strips that are available are controlled by individual countries for military and research purposes only.

Given the challenges involved, flying to Antarctica was exactly the kind of project that could really engage me, to break the humdrum pattern of life at home that had already begun to set in after the round-the-world flight. It would also require me to fly the length of South America and back, something that would involve stopping at many places along the way that could be interesting and fun.

My goal for this flight was therefore to fly the length of South America, across the Drake Passage, and land in Antarctica. In doing so, I would complete solo flights in my single engine Lancair Columbia 300 aircraft N788W to all seven continents. This became my new "Mt. Everest."

The Route

Timing was important for this flight. The weather in Antarctica is only viable for this kind of trip for a few months a year, roughly from late November to March, our winter and their austral summer. Even cruise ships only visit during these months. Rather than leaving in the summer as I had done for my round-the-world flight, I would be leaving in the winter and plan to attempt my flight to Antarctica around the end of January.

My planned route to Antarctica began at the Creswell, Oregon airport (airport code 77S) near Eugene, rather than from Bremerton, Washington, the nearest airport to my primary residence on Bainbridge Island. To avoid the winter weather in the northern United States, I planned to fly straight south through California, then east across the southern US to Florida. From Florida I planned to fly along the Caribbean Islands to Grenada, which would be my last stop before entering South America. My route would then take me to French Guiana, then Belem, Brazil. From Belem I planned to follow along the east coast of Brazil, partly to avoid the rainy season and thunderstorms across the Amazon Basin (January is their rainiest month), but also to enjoy several beautiful stops along the Brazilian coast. My exit point from Brazil would be at Iguazu Falls where I would make the very short flight across the river and enter Argentina. The planned route would continue south through Argentina, including stops at Buenos Aires and El Calafate, the heart of Patagonia. From El Calafate the next stop would be Punta Arenas in Chile (airport code SCCI), the jumping-off point for the flight to Antarctica.

Fuel tank installation and O2 tank

In Antarctica the two gravel airstrips within range for a small plane are the Chilean base on King George Island (airport code SCRM) and the Argentine base on Marambio (airport code SAWB). Of the two, the first is closer to South America, about 500 nm of open water across the Drake Passage between Cape Horn and King George Island. This air strip also has webcams showing the runway, routine weather forecasts (called TAFs) and weather observations (called METARs), and a small village that accommodates researchers who stay over during the summer months. The 4200-foot gravel airstrip is used by some commercial operators who fly tourists to King George Island to stay for a day or two, as well as other tourists who board small cruise ships sailing farther south along the Antarctica Peninsula. Those visitors want to avoid the delay and what is often very rough water during the two-day crossing of the Drake Passage. Because of the better weather information and greater activity overall, I set King George Island as my destination.

There is another jumping-off point for Antarctica at Ushuaia, Argentina (airport code SAWH), that others have used. It's only 530 nm from King George Island, compared to 670 nm for Punta Arenas, so it's more desirable for that reason. Flying from Punta Arenas means flying over or around the southern end of the Andes Mountains at altitudes of 11,000 feet or higher, which often means icing conditions may be present. Ushuaia is located right on the coast of the Beagle Passage, which provides a simple low-altitude route out to the Drake Passage. From there it is a straight shot south over the water to King George Island.

The problem with Ushuaia is getting permission for the flight. Ushuaia is in Argentina, so there is some unclear issue about getting a clearance to depart Argentina for a flight to a Chilean airbase where there is no Customs and Immigration. This issue is pretty murky because no country has a legitimate, recognized claim to any territory in Antarctica, but Chile certainly controls who lands at their airbase. Departing from Punta Arenas for a flight to King George Island meant I would at least be staying inside Chilean jurisdiction and my chances of getting permission to make the flight would be better. Also, the route from Punta Arenas to King George Island is far and away the most heavily traveled air corridor to Antarctica, with detailed weather forecasting along the route. In spite of the longer distance and having to negotiate a path over or around the southern end of the Andes Mountains, I chose Punta Arenas as the jumping-off point for my flight to King George Island.

Fuel

On my round-the-world flight I had a 78-gallon ferry tank that gave my plane a range in excess of 2000 nm miles. While it was great to have this range to minimize the number of stops I'd need and give me flexibility in the event of bad weather, it had several limitations. Foremost, installing a ferry tank connected to the fuel system requires a Special Flight Permit from the FAA. The Special Flight Permit or "ferry permit" is intended for the sole purpose of getting a plane from point A to point B as expeditiously as possible, so it's not for cruising around the world with extended range. For my round-the-world flight, I basically needed two ferry permits – one that allowed me to fly from Merced, California, to Honolulu the long way around, and the second which allowed me to fly from Honolulu back to Merced the short way around, thus completing the around-the-world flight. Such a flight objective is not really the intended purpose of a Special Flight Permit, but it's technically acceptable to the FAA. Given these restrictions, the five pages of operating limitations that go along with it, and the requirement to get prior permission from foreign countries that are crossed, I decided to make life easier on this flight and do it without the ferry tank and associated paperwork and permits. The spacing of airports with aviation gas along the planned route made this possible.

However, the flight leg from Punta Arenas to King George Island in Antarctica is 670 nm. There is no aviation gas at the airstrip on King George Island, so the round trip is right at the maximum range of my Columbia 300 using just the fuel available in the wing tanks. But after landing at King

George Island, I would have the opportunity to refill the wing tanks on the ground. Therefore, I decided to take the extra fuel as *cargo* in a tank in the back seat where the ferry tank would normally have been installed. It would not be plumbed into the aircraft fuel system as the ferry tank had been, so a Special Flight Permit would not be needed.

I researched the regulations on carrying aviation gas as cargo to determine the capacity limitations. The regulations are difficult to interpret and depend on the type of container, but from that research, I concluded I could carry about 58 gallons in a tank made of metal (i.e. aluminum). With this information, I had a custom aluminum tank constructed that would be strapped down in place of the back seats. I would bring a manual rotary pump to transfer fuel from this cargo tank to the wing tanks once I was on the ground at King George Island. That would provide me with full wing tanks for the return flight to Punta Arenas.

New HF radio installation

I did a trial run with this cargo tank and pump setup while still at home, flying to a nearby airport on San Juan Island and filling my wing tanks from the cargo tank. I wanted to make sure I had all the tools, hoses, and other pieces I would need. It all worked as I had expected.

Other Equipment

In addition to the custom fuel tank and pump, the additional equipment I'd carry was pretty much the same things I took on my round-the-world flight – a covered life raft (by Winslow), a new Mustang immersion suit (OC8000 model), the Iridium satphone, and the HF radio. I spent some time during the summer improving the HF radio installation from the awkward location and operation I had for the round-the-world flight. I disconnected the control head from the radio and mounted it in the radio stack in front of me, with the main body of the radio and antenna tuner mounted in the baggage area. I also installed an interface box made by PS Engineering so I could connected the HF into my audio panel as a third radio, allowing me to use my headset to talk on the HF radio instead of using the hand mic and speaker. I could also more easily monitor the VHF communications with this configuration when I was using the HF radio.

During my round-the-world flight, I transitioned from using paper charts to using electronic charts on the iPad. I'm now fully committed to the e-charts, and even bought a second iPad I could carry back and forth to the hotel for flight planning while the primary iPad stays in the plane. The second one also provides a backup in flight. I bought the Jeppesen e-charts subscriptions for the Caribbean and South America that work with their Mobile FlightDeck application. I replaced the GoPro Hero camera I used to record flight videos with a newer model (the Hero 2) which has an external audio input jack, a big improvement. By plugging the camera input into the aircraft audio system, the videos I make would have a soundtrack with my narration and the radio transmissions between me and air traffic control.

Permits

The landing and overflight permit process for foreign countries I crossed en-route to Antarctica was largely the same as for my round-the-world flight. I enlisted the help of the same agency I used before, Skyplan, in Calgary, to obtain these permits. They were relatively inexpensive and saved me a lot of hassle compared to doing it myself. On my round-the-world flight I was never delayed because permits weren't ready on time, except once when there was confusion about my departure date resulting from time zone shifts.

The very difficult permit challenge was for the last leg from Punta Arenas to King George Island. I would have to do this myself. I will explain it in some detail because this is a primary stumbling block for general-aviation pilots who want to fly to Antarctica. The process I went through was specific to flights from the US for a United States citizen ("expedition" in the parlance of Antarctica). For flights originating in other countries with different aircraft registrations and citizenship, part of the process I describe will not apply.

Antarctica is not a country; it is an international Treaty Area. The Treaty Area is everything south of 60 degrees south latitude. As such, the process to get a flight permit requires going through diplomatic channels rather than dealing with the civil aviation authority of any particular country. It is actually a two-track process, one for the US and the other for Chile. I will explain both.

As a US citizen starting an "expedition" from the US, my first stop was the US State Department where I communicated with the Senior Advisor for Antarctica, who at the time was Susannah Cooper. She asked me to complete form DS-4131, which is an advance notification for a US expedition to Antarctica. Based on the information on the form, they classified my expedition as a US expedition, which initiates the next two steps. Susannah put me in touch with Julie Roemele at the Environmental Protection Agency and Nadene Kennedy at the National Science Foundation. Note that these people were in these positions in 2012 when I was attempting to arrange my flight for January 2013. The people in these positions change from time to time, as job assignments in the government are changed, so the names given here may no longer be the correct.

Julie sent me directions on how to complete an Initial Environmental Evaluation (IEE) document, which was required for them to approve my expedition to Antarctica. There is no form for the IEE, but several elements have to be addressed as required by Treaty obligations. Previous IEEs submitted by other expeditions ranging from small yachts to cruise ships are publicly available from the EPA to use as a guide. You can also hire people who make their living writing such documents. I decided to do it on my own, using a previously submitted IEE for a yacht as a format guide. The IEE I produced, which was ultimately approved (after a few iterations), was 15 pages long. Like the others, it is now publically available from the EPA to use as a guide on how to write one. I have also included it verbatim in Appendix G.

The US Antarctica Program is part of the National Science Foundation. The National Science Foundation requires a Waste Permit Application. In this application I had to basically explain what I would do with all the waste generated on my expedition in the Antarctica Territory. Again, there is no form, but Nadene Kennedy gave me guidance on what needed to be included. In fact, much of it was the same information I'd already written for the IEE. A copy of the Waste Permit Application is also included in Appendix G.

Approval of the IEE by the EPA and the Waste Permit Application by the National Science Foundation were both contingent on getting approval from Chile to land at King George Island. Getting permission from Chile is the second process that needs to be pursued in parallel with the US government process. To get permission from Chile, I approached their DGAC to request permission to fly to King George Island. DGAC stands for Direccion General de Aeronautica Civil, Chile's equivalent to the FAA.

The process of applying for permission from Chile to make this flight is spelled out in a section of Volume I of Chile's Aeronautical Information Publication (AIP) referenced in Appendix G. It is written in both Spanish and

English, listing several pieces of basic information that must be submitted to apply for permission. This constitutes the application to the DGAC, which was sent to them as indicated in the referenced document. The second Chilean document referenced in Appendix G provides further information. As part of their application approval process, the DGAC will seek approval from both Chile's Antarctica research group and, more importantly, from the Chilean Air Force who actually control the airstrip at King George Island. Appendix G includes a verbatim copy of my application to the Chilean DGAC for permission to land at King George Island.

However, a problem arose because the DGAC in Chile would not give permission until I had approval from the US, and the US would not give approval until I had permission from Chile. It was a classic "catch-22" situation where I couldn't get permission until I had permission. I resolved it by asking the EPA to give me conditional approval of the IEE, the one condition being approval from Chile. I even modified the IEE to state explicitly that if I did not receive permission from Chile, I would cancel the expedition. Since I needed to refuel at King George Island, landing was certainly essential for the expedition to happen. The EPA granted this conditional approval, and Chile quickly followed by issuing a clearance number for the flight to King George Island at the end of January 2013. So after several months pursuing these two parallel tracks, I finally had the permits I needed.

All the people I dealt with on this process were helpful and friendly. They had their rules to follow and necessary Treaty obligations to fulfill, but they were supportive in getting my "expedition of one" approved. Susannah Cooper at the State Department was especially helpful, since she was the contact with her counterparts in Chile's Foreign Ministry who ultimately signed off on my flight. Susannah made sure all the pieces were put together so my expedition could take place.

Ready To Go

As a last step, I brought the plane in for an annual inspection at Avian Aeronautics at the Bremerton Airport who normally do the maintenance work on N788W. I fixed and replaced some things I probably would have left alone if it weren't for the planned flight to Antarctica, like installing a new battery, replacing an old vacuum pump, and replacing worn parts in the brakes. With the special equipment and the critical Antarctica flight permit in place, I was ready to begin my trip.

15

Oregon to Florida

Creswell is a small town about eight miles south of Eugene, Oregon. I had lived in Eugene for about 20 years before moving to Bainbridge Island; I still had a country home on 20 acres near Eugene. When I visit Eugene, I fly into Creswell's Hobby Field (airport code 77S) where I have had a hangar since I began flying in 1998. My first plane was a 1979 Piper Archer II (N3048T) which I bought right after getting my private pilot certificate and kept at the Creswell Airport. I sold the Archer when I bought N788W in 2010. Even though I am based at Bremerton Airport where I have a more spacious hangar, my earliest flying adventures in the Archer began while based in Creswell, so I decided to begin this flying adventure to Antarctica there as well.

Creswell is typical of many small community airports I have flown into across the US, at this point more than 300 of them. With a 3100-foot runway, fuel, a good mechanic, and a couple of flight schools, it has everything needed for basic flying. Creswell doesn't have any instrument approaches for landing in bad weather, but with GPS-based approaches now viable without the large expense of ground-based radio beacons, an instrument approach may soon come to Creswell.

Of course, Creswell is in the Pacific Northwest. Having flown in this region's winter weather from the beginning of my interest in flying, I am well aware that it's possible to get trapped by low, wet clouds that make even instrument flying over the surrounding high mountains treacherous because of

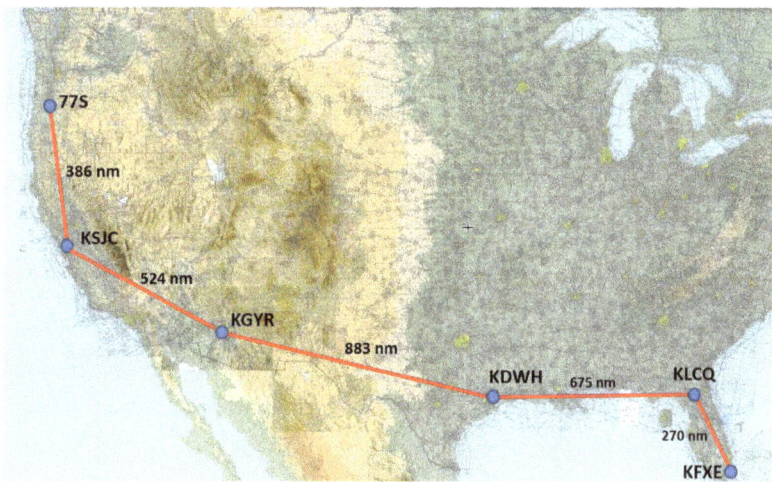

Flight legs from Oregon to Florida

the potential for ice formation on the plane. Small planes like mine are rarely equipped to prevent the accumulation of ice. The weight of the ice, and its buildup changing the shape of the wing and tail airfoils, can lead to seriously bad consequences. The ice problem is especially true going south over the Siskiyou Mountains. If getting over the mountains is a problem because of ice, going out to the coast and flying at a low altitude south over the ocean is the alternative. I don't like to fly that way if I don't have to, since it carries its own risks.

A series of monster storms coming off the Pacific Ocean was forecast for my original departure date of December 23, so I took advantage of a relatively clear afternoon several days before that to reposition my plane to Redding, California (airport code

Creswell Airport (77S) general-aviation terminal

KRDD), which is south of the Siskiyou Mountains. From Redding, I'd have flat terrain and warmer temperatures flying to my first stop in San Francisco.

The weather cleared in San Francisco on December 24, so I made the instrument flight from Redding to San Carlos Airport (airport code KSJC), a small airport on the peninsula south of San Francisco but probably the

On the ramp at San Carlos (KSJC)

most accessible general-aviation airport for visiting San Francisco. San Francisco International is closer to the city but the landing and parking fees are exorbitant. Besides, ATC really doesn't want small, slow planes flying in there.

The flight plan I filed sought a fairly direct route from Redding to San Carlos, but naturally I got re-routed south and east via Manteca so I actually arrived at San Carlos Airport from the southeast. The weather was clear, though, giving me a wonderful view coming into the San Francisco Bay area. Unfortunately, I forgot to take any photos, partly because

Departing the San Francisco area on a nice day

there were a lot of planes sightseeing with this sunny break in the weather so I was busy avoiding them. I realized I hadn't yet gotten into my long-distance flying mode where I always have the camera ready.

Expecting a lot of people flying in for the holidays, I was worried about finding a parking spot at San Carlos Airport, but no worries. They have 60 transient spots so there was plenty of room when I arrived. Only $10/night to park the plane at San Carlos – parking a car in San Francisco costs way more. The fuel truck arrived within a few minutes of my arrival, so I was immediately fueled up and ready to leave after Christmas. As I've mentioned before, I always like to fuel the plane when I arrive rather than on departure. Too many times on my world flight I was left standing around, anxious to depart, while waiting for a fuel truck shows up.

I had a great Christmas holiday in San Francisco with my brother Jim, his partner Lois, and his family. We took an afternoon drive down the Pacific coast past Half Moon Bay, where I lived in a little house for about four years from 1977 to 1980. All in all, it was an enjoyable few days and a nice way to embark on the long flight to Antarctica.

Phoenix

I departed San Carlos on December 27 into nice weather and a good forecast along my route to Phoenix's Goodyear Airport (airport code KGYR). In the past I've departed airports in complicated, busy metropolitan airspace like San Francisco with an instrument flight plan, thinking it gave me an advantage by not having to figure out and comply with the sometimes-complex altitude and airspace restrictions. However, the departure procedures for small airports under busy international airport airspace have gotten more complex, so I'm beginning to question this strategy. The

Snowy mountains north of Los Angeles

instrument departure from San Carlos southbound begins with a visual flight portion. I don't know if there is a real instrument departure plan from San Carlos – for example, if you had 300-foot ceilings, only departure minimums are shown in the charts. Anyway, the departure procedure went like this: departing runway 30, remain on the runway heading until past the diamond-shaped waterway, then a right turn to 120 degrees, remain at or below 1,100 feet until past the Oakland VOR station (OAK) 165° radial, then climb to 2,100 feet and fly directly to the Woodside VOR station (OSI). I've seen departure procedures more complex than this.

Salton Sea

The weather was fine heading south over Salinas and the San Joaquin valley. I stayed with the instrument flight plan, with a routing that periodically changed as I proceeded south. North of Los Angeles it was a bit bumpy, and my originally filed altitude of 9,000 feet got pushed up to 11,000 feet to get over high terrain, but I didn't have to contend with any icy clouds. After being vectored around a bit to avoid LA-bound traffic, I finally got vectored onto airway V64/V16 for a straight route east to Phoenix, leading to a visual approach and landing at Goodyear.

Goodyear Airport is southwest of Phoenix and a good place to go if you're just looking for a quick stop to refuel or to stay overnight. It avoids most of the busy Phoenix airspace. It also has a great general-aviation terminal – Lux Jet Center – who arranged a free shuttle for me to a nearby Holiday Inn with discount air crew rates. When the Jet Center manager came out to greet me, he noticed the cargo fuel tank on board. I told him I'd flown around the world in N788W a year before. He said that over the past five years they've had three round-the-world flights pass through this airport. I wondered who they were and if I knew them. The airport is clearly a good stop if you're zipping across the southern part of the US.

Clear morning departing Phoenix

There are a number of defunct or retired DC-10s, 747s, and other large commercial aircraft parked at Goodyear. It's a small "boneyard" similar to a few others in the dry desert climate where hundreds of old airliners are parked. On my round-the-world trip, flying from Vanuatu to Pago Pago, I remember talking to a Qantas crew flying overhead who were ferrying a plane to a boneyard in California. It's a little sad to see all that technology and capability sitting idle.

Houston

The next flight leg on December 28 took me directly east across the American Southwest and Texas. My flight route was some 906 nm long, close to the longest flight I'd ever done in N788W using only the fuel in the wing tanks. With economy cruise engine power settings at around 10,000 feet, I typically get 165–170 knots airspeed with a fuel burn of about 11.5 gallons per hour. With 98 gallons of usable fuel in the wing tanks, that theoretically yields a range of about 1400 nm with no reserve. Of course, I never want to push it to that limit. When the fuel gauges fall below even 20 gallons in each wing tank, I start to get grouchy.

All fuel gauges in airplanes like this have limited accuracy because they are simple float gauges that bounce around as the aircraft does. Like many modern planes, though, I have a device called a fuel totalizer (mine is made by

Shadin) that provides pretty accurate assessments of how much fuel has been burned and how much is left in the tanks. Fuel totalizers are basically little paddlewheels in the fuel line. Counting and totaling each revolution of the paddlewheel provides a very accurate indication of how much fuel has gone into the engine, and by subtraction, how much remains in the wing tanks. I rely on the fuel totalizer on these long flights.

As mentioned before, an issue I've encountered with the Columbia wing fuel tanks is that they are very flat. The fuel guys typically leave a half inch of space between the bottom of the filler neck and the fuel level when I ask them to top off the tank. When I checked the levels before departure on the morning of December 28, the fuelers had again failed to fill the tanks all the way to the top. I should have watched them. However, I wasn't very concerned about fuel because I knew I had a good tailwind and I didn't want to take the time getting the fuelers back to really top off the tanks. I did resolve to watch the fuelers do their job from now on to get the tanks really full.

Low mountains in New Mexico

Because the forecast weather en-route to my next stop in Houston was so good, I decided to depart without a flight plan, flying under visual flight rules (VFR). It had been cold that night in Phoenix, but I was still surprised to find the wings and tail covered with frost in the morning. Leaving Redding a few days before, I'd found a coating of ice had formed on the wings overnight. That morning I spent some time with a piece of cardboard and a plastic card cleaning it off. While visiting my brother's place in San Francisco, I tried to find a plastic ice scraper used on car windshields without success. As I was leaving there, however, my brother's partner Lois loaned me the one from her car. I put it to good use that morning in Phoenix. I guess that ice scraper has now earned a ride all the way to Antarctica.

I headed directly to the Stanfield VOR navigation station after flying under sections of the Phoenix-controlled airspace. Goodyear apparently has a very large, active flight school; before takeoff I had to hold short of the runway for nearly 10 minutes while a string of Bonanzas from the flight school came in to land, or do touch-and-go's, a common method to efficiently train pilots to land and takeoff.

Once out of Phoenix airspace, I picked up Flight Following from Albuquerque Center. "Flight Following" is a service offered by ATC in which an aircraft is assigned a transponder squawk code to identify it and ATC provides alerts about nearby aircraft so midair collisions can be avoided. Flying east at 9,500 feet was a pleasure. The sky was clear with a few clouds below. Occasionally, I spotted interesting terrain or other features that are only apparent from the air, like a large open pit mine.

Open pit copper mine

Passing El Paso, the vast flat plains of West Texas stretched out in front of me. Occasionally, there was light turbulence, but not bad compared to crossings I've made of similar terrain in Wyoming. As I proceeded east, the tailwind got stronger; by the time I got to Houston it was 35 to 50 knots, so I got the quick trip the flight plan said I'd get. Flying VFR this way, I generally follow airways to stay clear of restricted airspace, unless the routing by airways is too inefficient and out of my way. In that case I fly directly between waypoints.

As I crossed the VOR navigation station at Navasota to start my descent into Houston's David Wayne Hooks Airport (airport code KDWH), the broken layer of clouds below me had congealed into a solid overcast. As I was handed off to Houston Approach, I asked for and got an IFR clearance from where I was into the airport via radar vectors to get me below the cloud layer. Hooks Airport was still reporting a 2,000-foot ceiling so I thought I could make a visual approach once I was vectored below the overcast layer, which I did. The winds, though, were a bit of a challenge – 15 knots gusting to 25 knots with varying direction that included a quartering tailwind. It was one of the more demanding landings I've made in N788W, but I needed to get used to such landings. From what I've read of other pilots' experiences in Patagonia and the southern parts of South America, winds like this, and worse, are typical.

Gill Aviation, the general-aviation FBO at Hooks, arranged a rental car since the hotel I booked was some distance away and had no shuttle. My stop in Houston was a good intermediate layover between the West Coast and Florida. It also gave me a chance to have dinner with an old friend from my days living in Quincy, Illinois, whom I hadn't seen since 1983. Reminiscing is engaging, but sometimes it's sad, reflecting on all the years that have gone by.

Lake City

Houston was cold overnight, but it's still Texas, and on the Gulf of Mexico (nearly). Yet for the third time I came out to my plane in the morning to find the wings and tail covered with frost and ice. Once again I pulled out the ice scraper and put it to good use. Hmmm…I wondered how far south I'd have to fly until I didn't have to scrape off my plane in the morning. If I was still doing this when I reach the blazing sun of the tropics, I'd know I was in the grip of some climate anomaly that was following me around.

Departing Houston under a flat sky

It was mostly clear but cold departing Houston. Given the good weather, I decided on another VFR flight instead of filing an IFR flight plan, again using Flight Following from ATC to provide alerts of nearby aircraft. My route followed along airways due east to Florida. After takeoff on runway 17, I turned northeast and leveled off at 1,500 feet to

Rivers meandering into the distance

stay below the Houston airspace until the Hooks tower handed me to Houston Approach control who cleared me to climb up to 9,500 feet. I turned east and saw vast open sky in front of me. I didn't have the strong tailwinds that I had coming into Houston, but I still had tailwinds that added 10 knots or so to my ground speed.

I've flown to and landed in every state in the USA, most of them in my former plane, but I'd never flown east or west along the Gulf Coast like this. It is dead flat, with water and land making tentative, uncertain transitions from one to the other. It's curious to see the hand of nature with meandering waterways and fragmented shorelines juxtaposed to the hand of man with dead straight canals, causeways, and roads carved across the landscape.

Tank farm on the Gulf Coast

There are many airports in this region and the good weather on a sunny Sunday brought many weekend pilots into the sky, producing a lot of radio chatter. Occasionally, ATC scolded these pilots for their clumsy excursions, nearly flying into restricted military airspace. There's a lot of such restricted airspace along the Gulf Coast, especially around Pensacola Naval Air Station.

I could see Lake City (Gateway) Airport (airport code KLCQ) from 30 miles away, so I dropped the Flight Following from ATC and headed down to an easy landing straight in on runway 10. It's a big airport for a relatively small town – there must be military or some other flight heritage to the place. Taxiing up to the general-aviation terminal, I was further surprised by the building: brand new and first class in every way, better in some ways than many general-aviation terminals I'd seen that cater to a jet-set crowd. I don't imagine they get too much of that kind of traffic in Lake City, but maybe they aspire to.

N788W on the ramp at Lake City (KLCQ)

In contrast, Gill Aviation, the general-aviation terminal at Hooks Airport in Houston, that handles a lot of private and corporate jet aircraft, had been a very humble facility. The service at Lake City was also much better than at Gill, with the terminal manager coming out to marshal me in, help tie down the plane, drive my rental car out on the ramp to load my luggage, and then refuel the plane. Nobody greeted me from Gill until I carried my bags through the door of the building after parking and tying down the plane myself. I guess only the jet jockeys were entitled to a ride in the golf carts they had sitting around.

I was not impressed with Hooks Airport nor with Gill but I was impressed with Lake City and its operation.

I was in for another treat that evening – dinner with Thom Kane and Veronica Baird, who have also flown around the world in Thom's Cessna 180. It amounted to an Earthrounders mini-reunion. They invited me to their home in the countryside southwest of Lake City along a private airstrip, Little River residential airpark (airport code FL10). Thom and Veronica would like to make a trip to South America and Antarctica someday, so we talked about the planning and permit issues. It was a fantastic dinner and great fun to swap stories about our adventures flying little planes to faraway places.

With Veronica Baird and Thom Kane

Fort Lauderdale

The flight from Lake City to Fort Lauderdale is a short one, about 290 nm, so I got to the Lake City Airport later in the morning and was happy to see no frost on the wings of my plane. There was a forecast for a low broken cloud layer at Fort Lauderdale Executive Airport (airport code KFXE), my destination, so I filed an IFR flight plan even though the weather was forecast clear along the whole route up to arrival at the coast. After initially being given a clearance route different from the one I filed, then having it changed again once airborne, I ultimately ended up flying the route listed in Appendix D at 7,000 feet. It was an easy flight, with a 15-knot headwind at Fort Lauderdale blowing right down runway 08.

I'd been to this airport several times before in my Archer II, en-route to the Bahamas in 2004 and the Cayman Islands via Key West in 2005. There is a great general-aviation terminal here – Banyan Air Services – which has everything from normal general-aviation services to aircraft maintenance and a large pilot shop. I had the oil in the Archer changed here once. Since my last visit, their facility had undergone a complete upgrade; it's not even in the same old place at the airport. Everything was still first rate, with prompt service

Short final, runway 08 at Fort Lauderdale

from the line guys and the desk staff. Fort Lauderdale is a popular jumping-off point for private flights into the Caribbean, so they have a lot of current, first-hand, practical advice for making these flights. They also rent life rafts and other emergency equipment if needed or desired for over-water flights. Although I'm pretty much prepared for where I'm going, I knew if any last minute questions or equipment needs came up, I probably could deal with them at Banyan.

I treated myself to a hotel overlooking Fort Lauderdale's famous beach for New Year's Eve. It was finally warm, the sun was shining, and a parade of cargo and cruise ships coming and going from the busy port added motion to the ocean scenery. Like always, the Fort Lauderdale beach promenade was full of people, some on the sand, some just strolling along the sidewalks on either side of the A1A beach highway. There was great reggae and rock music in the restaurants and clubs along the beach highway that night. I hung out late, enjoying the music along with tropical food and curious pastel-colored alcoholic concoctions garnished with fruit, knowing I wouldn't have to fly the next day. I almost drunk-dialed a former girlfriend who now lives in Fort Lauderdale. Surprisingly, restraint overcame vivid memories.

Fort Lauderdale beachfront

The next day I looked at my flight log for this trip. I had already covered about 30% of the way to Antarctica. But I was still on familiar ground so it really didn't seem like I'd gone anywhere at all. There would be no flying New Year's Day, a day off, but then on January 2 I would move on to Providenciales (Provo for short) in the Turks and Caicos Islands. This would definitely be new territory for me.

16

Crossing the Caribbean

Providenciales

Flights outside the US require a few more steps than domestic flights. The first step is the electronic Advanced Passenger Information System (eAPIS) set up by US Customs and Border Protection to gather information on who is leaving and who is entering the country in small planes (and vessels). I've used it before, but I don't use it often enough to be fluent in how it works; I have to re-learn it every time. The password to gain access also expires after 90 days (I'm told), so if you use it infrequently like I do, it will probably be necessary to reset the password as I did. Flying beyond the US's air defense zone (ADIZ) also requires a pilot be in communication with ATC, so it's necessary to have either an IFR flight plan or fly VFR using "Flight Following" as described earlier.

I talked to a charter pilot at Banyan about preferred routing to Providenciales (airport code MBPV), my next stop. He told me not to bother with an IFR flight plan when the weather is good. He advised me just to ask for VFR and Flight Following and fly direct. I planned to do that, but I filed an IFR flight plan as a backup. When I called Miami clearance delivery at Fort Lauderdale Executive after engine startup, she started rattling off my clearance so rapidly I didn't have a chance to interrupt and tell her I didn't want it, that I

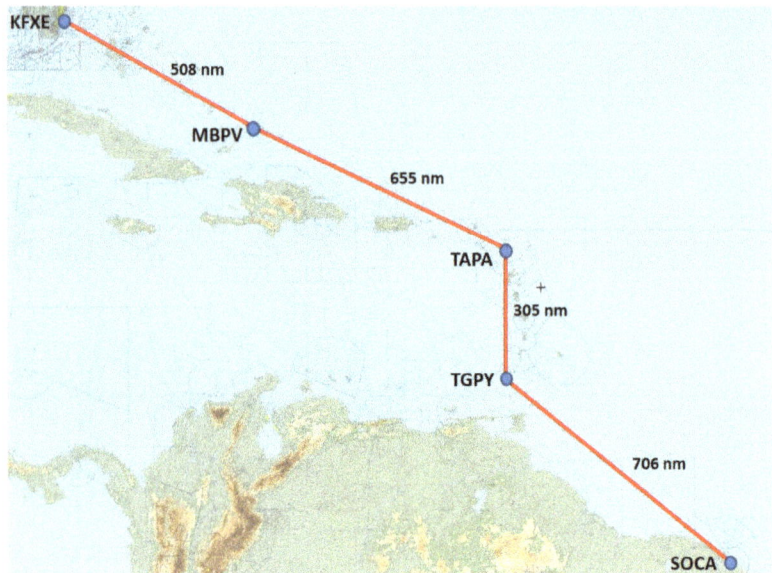

Flight legs crossing the Caribbean

was going VFR. So I took the IFR clearance she gave me, which wasn't much longer than the direct route anyway.

The weather was brilliant: just low clouds hugging some of the islands strung out along my route. The larger ones have names I found on the charts, but there are many, many others. I'll never tire of flying over islands rimmed with white sand beaches and surrounded by turquoise water.

Along the way I flew into a new air traffic control zone above the transition altitude so I reset the altimeter to 29.92 inches and started using flight levels (FL090) instead of altitudes in feet. This was all familiar from my round-the-world flight. Miami Center kept communication, control, and radar coverage all the way to the waypoint called BTLER where I was handed over to Providenciales ATC (Provo Approach) for my descent into Providenciales Airport (Provo). There were a few gaps in communications, but I got picked up again at Mayaguana Island. I really don't know the extent of Miami's radar coverage.

Caribbean islands

There were 20-knot surface winds at Provo – fortunately blowing right down the runway so landing wasn't a drama. I started to turn off the runway at the first turning but was instructed to taxi all the way to the end (to Charlie taxiway) where the Provo Air Center and general-aviation parking is located. They apparently don't have a parallel taxiway connecting the commercial ramp with the general-aviation ramp.

The tower told me to expedite my taxi, so I barreled down the runway at 50 knots because I knew there was a plane landing right behind me. Fast taxi, but not fast enough: the guy coming in behind me elected to abort his landing and go around because I was still on the runway. If I'd known the spacing was that tight, I could have landed long and gotten off sooner. One thing I learned on my round-the-world flight is that nobody outside the US knows my plane type so they don't know what it can and can't do. Maybe they thought it was a jet and needed the whole runway. I remember aggravating the tower guy in Dubai (an American) because he put me in the landing sequence with the commercial jets, but I was too slow and screwed things up a little ("Can't you go any faster?").

I was listening to XM satellite radio all the way down to Provo. The XM satellite coverage footprint ends somewhere outside the borders of the US

Nassau

Final approach runway 10 at Providenciales

Grace Bay beach

Grace Bay

Grace Bay, departing Turks and Caicos

but I didn't know exactly where. I guessed I'd find out when I ventured farther south to the point where it finally does disappear.

TCI (Turks and Caicos Islands) Immigration and Customs is available right at the general-aviation terminal, so it was a breeze to get through and jump on the shuttle they provided, which took me to the hotel. I'd booked a nice place on Grace Bay beach. After staying in some really low-level places on the round-the-world flight, I was determined to enjoy myself during the stops on this trip wherever I could.

Sixty minutes after landing I was at the beach bar, starting my way through the list of drinks with little umbrellas. In Seattle this time of year, drinks come with little Gore-Tex parkas. I spent three nights on Turks and Caicos Islands making the most of the beach, the fine weather, and the fine dining. While there are a number of mostly aquatic-based excursions available on the island, I didn't stray very far, instead content to ride the hotel bicycles around the local roads. I've done plenty of parasailing, snorkeling, sailing, and other similar activities at other tropical places over the years.

Flying over Puerto Rico

Antigua

My next stop was planned for the island country of Grenada for three days. Normally, this would be a single hop from Turks & Caicos in N788W, but given the strong easterly headwinds I'd been experiencing, I decided to make a fuel stop in Antigua.

One thing I wanted to experiment with on this trip was online flight planning software for filing flight plans outside the US. I have used CSC DUATS for years and have a number of flights stored there, so I tried it first even though the user interface workflow is clunky. It worked fine for filing the flight plan for Fort Lauderdale to Provo, but when I tried filing a flight plan from Provo to St. John's in Antigua (airport code TAPA), it didn't know or recognize the airport code TAPA. OK, so I moved on to FltPlan.com, a very popular and well-regarded flight plan filing website that I also have on my iPad and iPhone. It planned flight routes for both Provo to St. Johns, and from St. Johns to Grenada (airport code TGPY). I filed the one for Provo to St. Johns, but it said it couldn't file the one for St. John's to Grenada. OK, so then I moved on to the AOPA flight planning tool, which accepted both routings but when it came time to file the flight plan, it presented the old FAA domestic flight plan form – useless outside the US. Maybe there's a switch somewhere to get to the right form but I didn't see it.

Finally, I went back to EuroFPL, which I had used to file flight plans crossing the Atlantic and in Europe on my round-the-world flight. It really was designed to obtain validated flight plans from EuroControl, but has expanded use outside of Europe. It accepted and filed both flight plans and even provided an address list for the relevant airspace control authorities where the flight plan was being sent, a list that can be can added to manually. It also provides nice email notices of when the plan is filed and acknowledged. So EuroFPL won the flight plan filing contest. Incidentally, another tool called RocketRoute, which is a great tool for Europe, didn't recognize the Caribbean airport codes I entered. These observations about flight planning software were current as of January 2013, but I would expect the capabilities of many of these flight planning alternatives to have improved since then.

On the ramp at St. Johns, Antigua

I guess the most commonly used book by US and other pilots flying the Caribbean is called *Bahamas & Caribbean Pilot's Guide*. This probably is a good place to offer my critique of this book. In my opinion it is only a somewhat successful collection of information. First, a good portion of the pages are advertisements, some of which may be useful, but the thickness of the book makes it look deceptively comprehensive when the hard-core flying information is only a fraction of the bulk you think you are buying. It

Rainbow climbing out of Antigua

also attempts to be a travel guide, but in this respect falls far short of other common travel guides from the usual sources – Fodor's, Frommer's, Lonely Planet, etc., which are much cheaper. The *Pilot's Guide* would be better if it just stuck to piloting matters. As a piloting guide, its strengths are several color photos of airports so you have an idea what you're going to see when you get somewhere, along with information on Immigration and Customs hours, fees, and general-aviation terminals/handlers (if any), entering and exiting the US, and basic airport details.

These days, however, you can get similar basic airport details for free for any airport in the world at the WorldAeroData website listed in Appendix B. Entering any airport code (even SCRM for the gravel airstrip in Antarctica) in the WorldAeroData website will bring up basic information and a satellite photo you can click on and zoom in to the point where you can see small aircraft parked on the ramp. You can also get the same bird's-eye view via Google Earth and rotate and tilt the image so you get a simulated view of what it looks like to fly the final approach and land on a given runway. Of course, none of this replaces having real enroute or VFR charts and instrument approach plates.

A further weakness of the *Bahamas & Caribbean Pilot's Guide* is that it has some bad and obsolete information. Flight plan filing is a case in point. For example, in the Eastern Caribbean section on page 295 (2012 edition) it says you can file flight plans using the online tools I tried, as discussed above. Well, no you can't, not everywhere. It also says you can print the flight plan form, fill it out, and fax it. Really? Fax it where? To the tower, to the general-aviation terminal? Not clear. Probably all of the above, and the *Pilot's Guide* does have a lot of fax numbers. Fortunately, the Caribbean is generally a laid-back place so you can often do things ad hoc at the general-aviation terminal if there is one, or in the tower at the last minute, and get by.

For the flight from Provo in Turks and Caicos to St. Johns, Antigua, I filed an IFR flight plan at FL090. After the waypoint called HARDE, I was cleared direct to VOR navigation station COY. Fltplan.com said the net headwinds would be 15 knots, but they turned out to 30–35 knots, so a planned 4½-hour flight turned into 5 hours. I was really glad I had planned a fuel stop. Surface winds were gusting up to 20–25 knots at St. Johns; the tower even cautioned me about wind shear on the final approach as I came in to land. It's a busy airport, but they have a good general-aviation terminal in FBO2000, which is on the south side of the field toward the end of runway 07, on the opposite side of the airport from the commercial passenger terminal.

Sun going down, flying south from Antigua

Even though FBO2000 is a good terminal, stopping here just for fuel (a so-called technical stop for large planes) turned out to be inefficient and somewhat expensive. Just stopping for fuel, I had to go through the country entry procedure with associated fees. It was fairly quick, but I really didn't enter the country since I didn't leave the airport. I should have been able to skip this. Maybe there is a way and I failed to ask.

The fuelers were from a different company, not FBO2000. They told me they could sell me only 20 gallons of aviation gas because they were running low and needed to ration it. That was a surprise, but I took what they

Final approach runway 10 at Grenada

would sell me; it was enough. After the fueling was finished, they had to drive back to their office with my credit card to run the charge. I complained to the FBO2000 guys about the fuel limit – they were angry and called the fuelers and argued with them. I really didn't care – I just wanted them to come back with my credit card so I could leave. So the stop was a little confused and slow at a time when I was in a hurry to get to Grenada before dark.

With more fuel on board, I was ready to taxi and already late. Several commercial jets were in the sequence for departure, a process aggravated by the absence of a parallel taxiway. So I was surprised when the tower instructed an Air Canada jet to back-taxi on runway 07, and then told me to back-taxi right behind him. Hmmm, how's this gonna work? Air Canada taxied to the beginning of runway 07, but the tower told me to stop and turn around at the 1000-foot markers. OK, I get it – he then cleared me for takeoff ahead of Air Canada because I didn't need the whole runway. I've never done that before, but it's probably common practice when you have no taxiway and a busy airport. Sometimes there are advantages to having a little airplane.

XM radio coverage became intermittent just south of Grand Turk VOR navigation station and then dropped completely. I didn't check to see whether XM weather information was still there. Anyway, when returning northbound to the US, it should be possible to start picking up US XM weather info around Grand Turk or at a place at a corresponding latitude further west.

Grenada

The flight out of Antigua for St. Georges, Grenada (airport code TGPY), was pretty uneventful. I saw some nice rainbows over Antigua, created by quickly passing rain showers as I climbed out and headed south. I had filed for FL090 but eventually asked for and got FL110 to get over some thickened clouds on a route direct from Antigua to Grenada. This route is pretty much over open water. A more conservative approach would be to follow airways A312 and A324 along the chain of the Leeward Islands, and then the Windward Islands, so if a problem arises, land is closer and maybe an airport as well. The route along the islands is not a lot longer than the direct route over water which I took.

Beaches on Grenada

Since I was now headed almost due south (magnetic course of about 195 degrees), the headwinds were gone, replaced with about neutral winds. It was cloudier here, compared to the first flight leg to Antigua. The approach controller at Antigua handed me off at the boundary of his airspace to Montserrat Approach. For the next three controllers (including Martinique) I had a mix of French and English on the radio. I didn't notice any gaps in VHF radio coverage for this entire flight. In the Windward Islands I was again talking to controllers from old English colonies. Joshua approach in St. Vincent: "N788W, you gettin' cleared to flight level 110, mon," and a similar thing arriving at Maurice Bishop International Airport, just south of St. Georges in Grenada. Accents on the radio and no radar coverage (instead I was reporting estimate en-route times to various waypoints) reminded me that I was now in new territory and getting back into the long-distance flying groove I had on my round-the-world flight.

It was a long day of flying, but I now had the long over-water flight legs for my expedition to Antarctica behind me. From here on, there would be a short over-water crossing south to Trinidad, then onto the South America mainland across the countries of Guyana and Suriname to my next overnight stop in Cayenne, French Guiana.

The time I spent on Grenada was relaxing, but the grander flying mission was never far from my thoughts. I used the local public bus to ride into the main town of Saint George where I toured the local historical sights and had a great lunch on the harbor. I also had a couple of great dinners at the best restaurants along the beachfront where I was staying south of Saint George. In retrospect, I should have rented a car since there are many beautiful spots in the more remote areas around the coast of Grenada that I missed. Getting to them on public transportation was too cumbersome and slow, but it does provide a chance to ride with the local people and have some conversation.

Hotel in Grenada

Cayenne

Getting through Immigration and Customs for departure at Grenada was straightforward with the help of SVG Air walking me through the process. They had helped me park the plane and called for the fuel truck when I first arrived. I paid the fuel guy in cash, drawing from my packet of fresh, up-to-date Benjamins for the first time. Credit cards had worked up to this point for all airport and fuel purchases. SVG Air is listed as being a general-aviation terminal (FBO), but it really is a local airline and handler. The airport fees were small. SVG didn't have me on the handling list so hadn't figured out what to charge me. I gave them $200 cash for services and three nights' parking and they were happy with that.

For my next flight leg to Cayenne (airport code SOCA), I filed an IFR flight plan at FL090. Climbing out in rainy, windy, cloudy weather that morning, definitely instrument flying conditions, I had the first important failure I've had on N788W during these long international flights. The pitch control on the STEC 55X autopilot went berserk. Pitch is the angle of the nose of the aircraft relative to the horizon. In simple terms, when the nose is pitched up the plane is climbing, pitched down and it is descending, on the horizon and the plane is cruising at a constant altitude. With the failure, I couldn't set a particular climb rate or hold an altitude with the autopilot: it kept trying to climb at a high rate. Fortunately, the roll control in the autopilot (the more critical of the two functions) was still working. Actual pitch mechanics (elevator control) and electric trim were still working OK – I could manually use the electric trim for pitch control. Later, reading some information on the STEC autopilot, I was reminded that it has its own internal barometer and accelerometer to make decisions about climbing, descending, and holding an altitude. It doesn't take any information from the aircraft's altimeter or vertical speed indicator. So apparently I had a problem in the STEC control box. I have no idea what may have brought on this problem, and I really didn't know if there would be any place down the line I might get it fixed. If it was a failure in the control box, it would mean a replacement box, which would take time to get. There is an avionics shop at the San Fernando Airport (in Buenos Aires), one of my planned stops. Could they fix it?

On final approach to runway 08 at Cayenne

The problem with the autopilot wasn't a real crisis that seriously concerned me. The plane was still perfectly flyable, I'd just have to do more work in terms of manually climbing and descending, and using the electric trim to hold altitude. In other words, the old fashioned way. N788W is fairly stable.

By using electric trim to hold an altitude, I could let several minutes go by without adjusting it if the air was reasonably smooth.

Unfortunately, during this flight leg I had thick cloud layers below me which meant I didn't get much of a view of Trinidad or anything else I was flying over, just occasional glimpses of jungle and water. I got some direct routings from ATC to shorten the flight, finally arriving at Cayenne at about the expected time. I flew the instrument approach to runway 08 under a broken layer of clouds at about 2500 feet.

Cayenne is a little piece of France, and once inside the Cayenne Flight Information Region, ATC was speaking French to pilots so-equipped, or French-accented English to people like me. My French is better than my Spanish, but still not good, though I could get the gist of what ATC was saying to other pilots. Aviation-specific vocabulary is pretty limited.

There is a daily flight from Paris to Cayenne and a lot of local shuttle flights to small airports throughout the country. I hired a handler to facilitate entry and exit from French Guiana. The handler called the fuel truck, who was there a few minutes later, took US cash, but didn't have change. He actually drove back to his office and returned with change – in US dollars no less. I would have been OK with Euros, the currency used in French Guiana. I appreciated the fuel guy going to that trouble.

Regarding using a handler, one issue with trying to do it yourself is figuring out which doors to go through to get to Immigration and Customs and the police. At Cayenne, before entering the terminal, there was a small, inconspicuous, unmarked wooden building with Customs people. They did a cursory search of my luggage and both the han-

N788W On the ramp at Cayenne

dler and I were "wanded" for weapons. From there we went into the terminal to the police for a passport stamp, and I handed over one of my preprinted General Declaration forms. Since I preprinted them with all the basic information, I only have to fill in the date, the ICAO codes for the departure and arrival airports, and then sign it. Once out of the terminal, the handler drove me to the Novotel hotel, one of the few nice places to stay in Cayenne.

I'll have more to say about using or not using handlers later, but generally, using them, at least when entering a country, seems to be the easiest way to avoid offending somebody because you don't know the process. It can also save of lot of wasted time wandering around a strange terminal with your bags trying to figure out what to do. I never would have figured out to go to the little wooden building for the luggage search. If the cost for the handler is reasonable, it is worth the money when entering a country.

Cayenne was only a one-night stop, really designed to break up the flight to Belem, Brazil, into two pieces so I didn't arrive in Belem in the afternoon when the thunderstorms are most likely to fire up. It worked in that respect, though the hotel was too expensive for what it was. The handler picked me up the next morning at 8 am for a planned departure to Belem at 9 am. In total, the handler charged me about US$320 for what he did, including transportation to/from the hotel. I'm OK with that – flying these international flights is an expensive proposition. Airport fees were only US$24 – they took US cash.

Looking back on the Caribbean crossing from Florida to Cayenne, no overflight or landing permits are needed for Guyana, Suriname, or French Guiana. The same is true for all the island countries throughout the Caribbean. You can basically file a flight plan and go – from Florida all the way to entering Brazil where the comprehensive paperwork obligations for entry and landing begin.

Landing in Cayenne was significant in another way. I had now landed my aircraft on a sixth continent, one step closer in achieving my goal of solo flight to all seven continents. I was exactly on the schedule I'd laid out months before – so far, so good.

17

On to Brazil

While neither visas nor overflight and landing permits are required for the Caribbean countries and French Guiana, entering Brazil is a different story. I needed a visa to enter Brazil which I had to obtain ahead of time from the Brazilian consulate in San Francisco using a visa service. It's the only country I went to in South America where I couldn't get a visa automatically upon arrival. Brazil also has a well thought-out but elaborate paperwork procedure for entering and exiting the county in a private aircraft.

Belem

Blowing rain clouds were on hand for my departure from Cayenne. It seemed a busy place when I arrived, and the approach controller even mentioned I might have to fly in a holding pattern because of the number of planes that were inbound at that time. That didn't happen on arrival, and when I left about 9 am local time the next day I was the only plane moving. I filed a simple IFR flight plan to Belem (airport code SBBE) at an altitude of FL090.

This was a short flight of about three hours. Checking the weather in the days leading up to this flight, I saw that Belem had been experiencing regular rain and thunderstorms in the afternoons. I wanted to land before any of that could fire up. At FL090 I was clear of the clouds most of the way but, as usual, had to drive around a few buildups to avoid the worst of the turbulence. I don't

Cloudy weather en-route to Belem

Flying over the Amazon

think they had any radar coverage once I was beyond Cayenne-controlled airspace. They kept asking for estimated times to enroute waypoints – a sure sign they really couldn't see where I was. At the OIA waypoint, the point on the boundary of the Cayenne Flight Information Region, I was given the Brazilian controller frequencies and warned that it might be some distance before I could talk to them. They also gave me a backup frequency, which turned out to be the first one that worked. It was another 220 nm to the waypoint named MADRE before I could make solid VHF radio contact with the Belem ATC Center.

During those times I wondered: if something were to happen with the plane, an engine failure or something serious, "Who ya gonna call?" I could hear some other aircraft talking to Center, but in Portuguese, so a distress call even to them might not be effective. Below me were broken clouds, and below that jungle and brown water, no doubt full of endless varieties of creeping, crawling, squawking things Darwin would have been giddy to study.

Final approach to runway 06 at Belem

There were only a few breaks in the clouds, but I did manage to get a photo as I started flying across the Amazon River at its mouth, which was about where VHF radio communications resumed.

Descent and approach into Belem via an instrument arrival

procedure and approach was through many bumpy clouds. The controller left it late to give me a vector to intercept the course for the instrument approach on runway 06. Because of this, I overshot the course to the runway, but it didn't matter. Below 3000 feet I had the runway in sight all the way.

Brazil Entry Procedure

For foreign aircraft entering Brazil, they have a relatively new online procedure for obtaining your landing and overflight permit. That procedure is described in Appendix E. A few days before arrival I went through the preparation steps listed there.

After arriving in Belem, I completed the final step of the entry process, which was to validate the permit. I did this by going to Customs when I arrived at Belem and having them issue a document whose name I forgot, but whose acronym is TEAT (which you don't forget). When the TEAT is issued, the permit is validated. When I arrived at Belem, I was directed to park on the ramp outside the Customs office. I had, however, hired a handler, so they took over guiding me through the entry process. I have more to say later about the experience with this handler, and the whole subject of self-handling in Brazil specifically, in Appendix F. Suffice it to say here that it took about 30 minutes with the Customs guy pecking away at his keyboard to validate the permit. They wanted to see hard copies of all the documents I submitted

Flight legs from Cayenne to Natal

online earlier, except the medical, as I recall. They asked when I would exit Brazil. I told them the actual date, which was stupid because it didn't give me any flex time. On their own they added five days to what I told them, giving me a total of 15 days in Brazil.

I now understood this is not just about flight permission, this is also about controlling and tracking the import and export of aircraft; that's probably why Customs drives this process. The entry/exit procedures in Australia are driven by Customs considerations in the same way. From that perspective, it's a little baffling that every country doesn't track the entry and exit of private aircraft to make sure that any plane brought in actually leaves. What's to stop someone from bringing the plane in and selling it, if Customs never knows whether it left the country?

Shoreline sand dunes en-route to Natal

Anyway, TEAT in hand, I went back out to the ramp, moved the plane to the south side of the airport and parked it outside the handler's hangar. I had them call a taxi, which took me into downtown Belem to my hotel in the Nazare neighborhood. I was officially, legally, physically and otherwise, in Brazil.

Shoreline sand dunes

I had scheduled two nights in Belem to get oriented since I'd be here for the next several days. I did take my day off from flying to visit a local zoological museum focused on Amazon flora and fauna, wander around the old and new docks and the old part of the city with classic houses built under the influence of various colonizing countries. It was a chance to walk around some, a treat when most days I'm cooped up in the cockpit. However, the rain showers were repetitive and intense. I copied the locals' technique of dashing under cover (like a storefront awning or an entry alcove) during 15 minutes of downpour and then moving on a bit further when it subsided. The locals seemed surprisingly averse to getting wet. For me, it was not so bad because the rain was warm and I was just walking around in a T-shirt. I left the parka on the plane for the colder southern climate to come. Imagine that. In the Pacific Northwest, my home, walking around in the rain in a T-shirt is an invitation to hypothermia.

Natal

My flight to Natal (airport code SBNT) would take me almost due east (a little southeast), but more importantly, out of the Amazon basin to the Brazilian coast where generally it is much drier. Most of these airports where I've stopped have standardized arrival procedures and standardized departure procedures. These published procedures are designed mainly to control and organize the flow of commercial aircraft into and out of an airport. But even for my little plane, if they have them, they're going to use them. It is more efficient than reading the details of an

Final approach runway 16L at Natal

arrival or departure route to a pilot over the radio. So even for a simple flight plan to Natal, they gave me the JANES 1 departure, which, as I got the plane warmed up and the GPS programmed, sent me scrambling to the Jeppesen procedure documents on my iPad to see what they were talking about. Well, they could have just told me: direct to the waypoint called JANES because that's what that procedure was (pretty much). Oh well. Lesson here: have all the standardized arrival procedures, standardized departure procedures, and approach plates available for these flights if you're going fly IFR flight plans – you never know what they'll ask you to do. I guess I could have told them I didn't have the procedure so just give me vectors, or read me the procedure, but that really defeats the purpose and probably would annoy them.

Heading east on the G677 airway, the cloudiness continued to diminish: out of Amazonia and into the clear. I now saw the G677 airway I was following as the "Route 66" for flying the Brazilian coast. Hey, maybe there's a song in

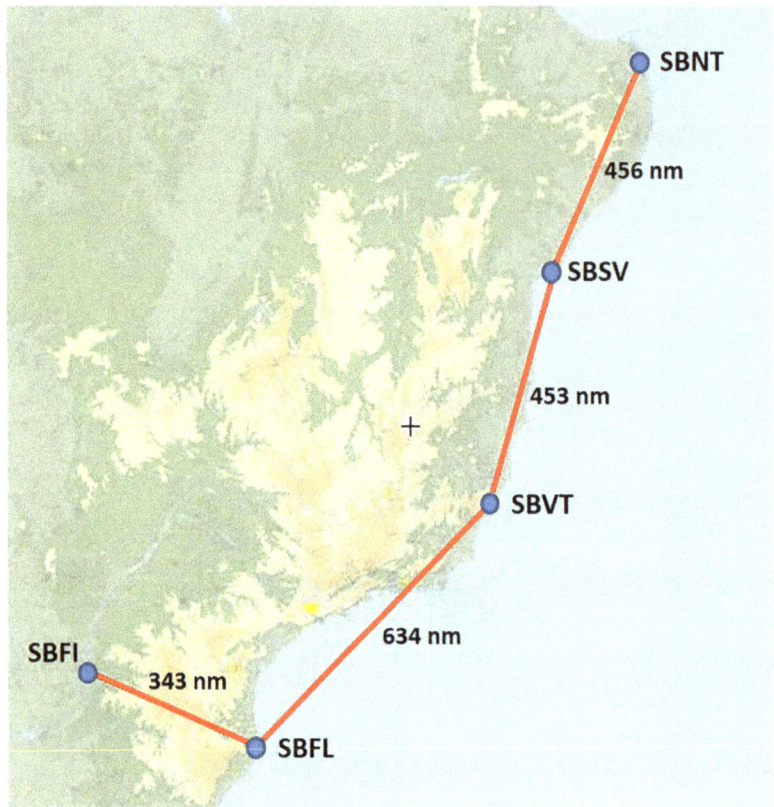

Flight legs from Natal to Iguazu Falls

that – lots of stuff rhymes with seven. G677 begins in Belem and wraps all the way around Natal, Recife, and down to Salvador Bahia, then continues on to Vitoria where it finally ends.

The flight to Natal was long: 868 nm and almost 6 hours with a pretty familiar 15-knot headwind. Descending into Natal was surprisingly bumpy, and landing was into a 20-knot headwind while an airliner patiently held short of the runway for my plane to slowly descend and land into that wind.

On departing Belem, I told the handler I used there that I would like to use their company again in Natal. While flying there, though, I changed my mind and decided to try to get by without a handler. After parking and engine shut-down, the handler's van pulled up next to the plane. I explained that I decided not to use the handler because it was too expensive. The guy was nice about it and told me if I had any questions I could ask him. He then drove back to his office. Navigating the airport at Natal turned out to be pretty easy. The step-by-step process, and even photos of the doors to walk through, can be found in Appendix F.

Before shut-down I told the guy in the tower I needed aviation gas, so he said he would send a truck. Filling the plane was easy enough, but when it came time to pay, I offered him US dollars. That meant he had to convert the price in the Brazilian money called Reais to US dollars, which required a calculator and several calls back and forth to his office.

Surfers and coconuts at Natal's city beach

I tried to tell him he could give me change in Reais, but I'm not sure he understood. Anyway, it took 20 minutes just to get the payment figured out, with many interruptions from others who were calling on the radio about getting fuel.

My hotel in Natal was a couple blocks up the hill from the beach. It was just OK but with a great view overlooking the coast. I spent a little while on the city beach below the hotel, which was pretty trashy. I've seen photos of really fine beaches just outside of town. This was a one-night stop; I was still on a demanding schedule to get to Punta Arenas in Chile. Someday I would like to visit Brazil in a more leisurely fashion.

During WWII, my dad, as a naval aviator (a radioman, not a pilot), was stationed for a time in Natal as part of a crew that flew PBY Catalina amphibious patrol planes out over the Atlantic Ocean hunting for German sub-

Endless beach south of Natal

marines. Given the main theaters of war in Europe and the Pacific, few know how widespread the fighting actually was. I'm sure at the time Natal was a pretty sleepy little town, surprised to be drawn into the conflict on any level. I don't know how many, if any, submarines they found and sunk on the missions they flew from Natal. Actually, I'd be interested to know. Things certainly heated up when my dad's squadron was redeployed to Dunkeswell, England, and they traded the PBY Catalina's for B-24s and a much more dangerous set of missions.

Salvador

Things went smoothly exiting Natal. In fact, doing my own handling now, I had my most on-time departure yet on this trip. I filed a flight plan following along airway G677 at an altitude of FL100. As they did at Belem, the control tower gave me a departure procedure, the SAFUC departure, but I was ready for it this time. Climbing out was bumpy, because even at 9 am there was a 16-knot surface wind blowing down the runway.

Fueling at Salvador

Once handed over to the Recife controller, I was given direct routing to the navigation station called MCE to shorten my route. I have to say, the ATC controllers I'd dealt with on the whole trip so far, especially in Brazil, had been great. They said to me, "Good morning," when I first contacted them, and "Have a nice flight," when they handed me off to the next controller. They were patient and friendly when I didn't understand an instruction and asked them to repeat it. This experience was the complete opposite of the experience a couple of other general-aviation pilots had when they flew across Brazil the previous spring. ATC didn't even want to talk to them in English. I suspect the difference may be because I was flying a heavily traveled international flight corridor and ATC was used to dealing with English-speaking pilots. These other small-plane pilots were flying straight north from Iguazu Falls across the center of the country, routes that don't see so many international flights. Anyway, I had no complaints about ATC: it was working very well for me.

The weather along the coast was reasonably clear, so I got better views than on the previous few flight legs. FL100 worked pretty well, keeping me above the clouds. Arriving in airspace controlled by Salvador Bahia (airport code SBSV), I was cleared directly to the waypoint called BONF, which is on the standard arrival. From there I was cleared direct to the DUNA waypoint, which is the geographic fix (reference point) to fly the instrument approach for runway 10. The clouds were scattered to broken at 3,000 feet, so once ATC cleared me through this bumpy layer to 2,000 feet, I had the whole of Salvador Bahia spread out below me. Turning onto final approach for landing, I again was flying into a 15–20 knot headwind. With the runway in sight, but with ground speed reduced to 70–80 knots due to the headwind, it was almost like being suspended in space as the runway threshold seemed to barely creep closer compared to what I was used to when landing with less headwind.

Pelourinho, the old historical district in Salvador

Once on the ground, I told Ground Control I needed general-aviation parking for a couple of nights. He gave me taxi instructions to "Apron 4." Salvador is a much larger airport than Natal, and somewhat complicated, with two runways and a lot of construction in preparation for the then-upcoming World Cup matches. I was taxiing for 10 minutes or more to get to Apron 4. Along the way, I taxied past other ramp areas where private jets were parked outside hangars where, no doubt, the handling companies reside. I continued to taxi to the end, to Apron 4, parking for the

Street musicians in Pelourinho

"unwashed" (those not blessed with a handler). Surprisingly though, as I turned into the parking area there was a guy there from Infraero marshaling me into a parking spot with his yellow truck parked nearby. Infraero is the Brazilian entity that runs the airports. Once I'd shut down the engine and opened the door, I asked him about getting fuel. He said in perfect English, "I don't speak English." So I said, "Gasolina" and he smiled and nodded and said "Shell? Petrobras?" I said "Shell." He get on his handheld radio and made the call. OK, now we were on the same page.

About languages: Portuguese is spoken in Brazil. I don't speak any Portuguese and only some Spanish. So, when in a pinch, I'll try the Spanish words which are sometimes close enough to the Portuguese that I can be understood.

Beaches along the coast to Vitoria

Ten minutes after my conversation with the Infraero guy, the Petrobras fuel truck showed up. All right, he's got aviation gas, away we go. After he started pumping, the Shell guy showed up. I spread my hands in the international sign of apology, pointed to the Petrobras guy and said "El primero." The Shell guy smiled, nodded and drove away. I paid the fuel guy in cash with the last of the Reais I had. I didn't want the challenge of a conversion to US dollars which had turned out to be a little comical at Natal.

Getting from Apron 4 to the airport terminal to grab a taxi, I relied on a helpful mechanic at a nearby charter business. I describe that experience in Appendix F. If I'd thought about it, I would have asked the Infraero guy to stick around until the fueling was done so he could drive me to the terminal. Anyway, once in the terminal I replenished my supply of Reais from a cash machine and grabbed a taxi for a long ride in to town.

For something different I booked a hotel in the old historic section of Salvador called Pelourinho, an interesting, colorful, musical place. On the ride in from the airport the old taxi driver warned me in a mishmash of Portuguese and Spanish that this was a bad neighborhood with many drug dealers and prostitutes. Despite the caution, I didn't see any problems while staying there, no doubt due to a heavy police presence. It's a popular tourist destination, so they are certainly motivated to suppress any crime.

I took a day off from flying in Salvador. Ahead of me were maybe two days of weather-challenged flights south. So far, though, I was right on schedule and hadn't had to cancel or amend any hotel bookings I made weeks before.

I had a good time in Pelourinho in a somewhat funky boutique hotel where I was staying along with a wide variety of young travelers from many countries. The colorful nightlife in the streets and the variety of bars and restaurants that stayed open late made this one of the more interesting stops on this trip so far. Salvador is another place I would like to visit again when I have more time.

Vitoria

My plan for the next day of flying was to stop in Vitoria (airport code SBVT), refuel, and then continue on to Florianopolis (airport code

Cloudy descent into Vitoria

SBFL). It would be a long day, and I would be crossing the river of bad weather around Rio de Janiero and Sao Paulo in the afternoon when the thunderstorms are usually at their worst. It's the South American version of the Inter-Tropical Convergence Zone I crossed on the round-the-world flight between Christmas Island and Hawaii, though now it was south instead of north of the equator.

There was a second problem. The airways from Vitoria south as far as the RDE ground navigation station have minimum enroute altitudes of FL150 and FL160 (about 15,000 and 16,000 feet, respectively). My plane has a service ceiling of 18,000 feet. It's not turbocharged, which means the power and performance is degraded at these higher altitudes. The sweet spot altitude for N788W's performance is 10,000 to 12,000 feet where I get the most performance (speed) for a given amount of fuel burn. There are no good reasons for these high enroute altitudes that I could see: no terrain clearance issues, nor communication or navigation gaps. I didn't know

Final approach runway 05 at Vitoria

how flexible ATC would be with assigning lower altitudes for an IFR flight, so I filed a VFR flight plan from Vitoria to Florinapolis at FL105. Given the weather, I didn't really know if such a flight avoiding clouds would even be possible.

When I start to make these compromises and rationalizations, my piloting instincts tell me I'm making a mistake. So before departing for Vitoria, I decided to forget the VFR flight plan for the second leg to Florianopolis and stay for the night in Vitoria to re-evaluate what I would do for the next leg. Accordingly, I filed an IFR flight plan from Salvador to Vitoria at FL100.

I had to climb through a 6,000-foot-thick layer of clouds on departure from Salvador, but above that it was a pretty smooth flight under blue skies and a high layer of cirrus clouds. By the time I got to the Vitoria-controlled airspace and started my descent, the cumulus cloud buildups had already started. I had no choice but to fly through the very bumpy clouds via the vector instructions ATC was giving me. Ultimately, I ended up flying the GPS (RNAV) approach for runway 05, which has some tight turns that I needed to anticipate when arriving from the north. This GPS approach also comes close to some high rocky hills right under the descent path. When I see things like this I sometimes wonder if the designers of the approach were maybe cutting corners on the terrain clearance standards normally applied when creating an instrument approach for an airport.

After landing, I was surprised to get a call from Ground Control asking me to report to the Traffic Control Office because there was a problem with a document. I couldn't imagine what that might be. I was marshaled to parking again by an Infraero guy who tried in Portuguese to explain something, without success. Instead, I went through my usual process of getting fuel first, then dealing with the airport. After fueling, the Infraero guy drove me to the airport office where they were nice enough to track down a woman who worked for Infraero and spoke pretty good English. She explained that Vitoria is a Prior Permission Required (PPR) airport. Oops. I had landed without prior permission. They were all very nice about it and explained that the airport is very small and there is very little room to park. Indeed, the ramp space is very limited, unlike Belem, Natal, and Salvador, where there is no requirement for prior permission. I told them I'd be leaving first thing in the morning. I wondered how I could have missed this important piece of information. Back at the hotel I booked, just off the airport, I researched Vitoria and couldn't find it flagged as a PPR airport. It may be buried in the Notices to Airmen somewhere for this airport and I missed it.

Cabo Frio en-route to Florianopolis

I felt good about my decision to delay continuing on to Florianopolis as I watched the satellite weather pictures on my computer that afternoon showing numerous thunderstorms and heavy lightning activity across what would have been my flight route south. I expected flying this stretch in the morning hours the next day would work out much better.

For convenience, the Vitoria hotel I booked was the closest one to the airport. Unfortunately, I really didn't take the time to see any of the city, so I can't offer any comments about it.

Florianopolis

Re-evaluating my plan to get to Florianopolis, I decided to file an IFR flight plan at FL160 departing at 9:00 am local time and get this 4½-hour flight done mostly in the morning hours. My hope was that I could "finesse" my way to staying at a preferable lower altitude like FL120. Fortunately, no finesse was required. I accepted the filed flight clearance to FL160, and as I climbed out, passing through FL100, I simply called ATC and asked them to amend the clearance altitude to FL120. No problem! They made that change and I flew the rest of the way to Florianopolis at FL120. The flight altitude/performance issue I thought would impact this flight turned out to be a non-problem.

Thick weather south of Rio de Janeiro

The first half of the flight was in pretty nice skies; I had some great views of the Brazilian coast and the hilly country inland. Unfortunately, the W6 airway I was assigned to fly does not pass close enough to Rio de Janiero to get any good photos of the place, plus mist and low clouds obscured what might have been stunning, crystal-clear views. Although I could make out some main features like Sugarloaf Mountain, my attempts to take zoomed-in photos really didn't produce anything worth sharing.

Flying farther south, the weather got murkier at FL120 and I was finally inside solid clouds, but it was a flat cloud layer with a little rain and light turbulence. As I got closer to the RDE VOR navigation station, I broke into the clear again just long enough to see a huge wall of clouds right across my flight path. No way around it or over it, I'd have to fly through it. As I flew into this weather turmoil, turbulence increased and the rain really intensified, completely obscuring anything through the windshield. When flying at 170 knots, almost 200 mph, even rain falling straight down hits a plane as if it were driven by a Category 5 hurricane. Flying so far on this trip had been reasonably pleasant – this was the first real weather challenge I'd faced.

Praia Mole, one of Florianopolis's famous beaches

Then an intense cluster of lightning strikes popped up on the Stormscope about 25 miles to the east. I immediately made a 20 degree turn to the west. Seeing my turn on radar, ATC called me and said "N788W, confirm heading to FLN" (the VOR navigation station at Florianopolis). That's a polite way for them to say, "Where do you think you're going?" I responded "N788W diverting 20° west for bad weather," which is the polite way to say "I'm flying where the lightning ain't." She approved the diversion. After that I had to wrestle the weather for another 15 minutes or so, but fortunately no cluster of lightning strikes popped up in front of me. I quickly left behind the ones I had detected to the east.

Promenade in Florianopolis

Eventually, I broke out of this weather and had a fairly clear and pleasant flight the rest of the way into Florianopolis. When I crossed the controlled airspace boundary, the controller asked if I could speed up, no doubt to get me in ahead of other inbound traffic. I told him I could only speed up if I started my descent. He approved that so I roared down into Florianopolis at 190–200 knots, got under the scattered layer of clouds and made a visual approach for a landing on runway 14, glad to be on the ground after dealing with the bad weather en-route.

I taxied back on the runway while a TAM commercial jet was taxiing to the threshold to turn around for takeoff. I'm getting used to operations with no parallel taxiway. Again, I had an Infraero guy marshal me to a parking spot, the fuel truck was there in 10 minutes, and an air-conditioned shuttle waited to take me the short distance to the terminal. If I had a handler, I really don't know how it could have been any more efficient or comfortable, except maybe through having a translator. When things are going well, generally I'm happy to try a language I don't know and learn some words in the process, even if it means stumbling around and using hand gestures to be understood. It's part of the fun of international traveling. Like in Vitoria, there was limited parking in the general-aviation ramp at Florianopolis, but there is no Prior Permission Required restriction. However, they did want to confirm I would leave first thing the morning of January 17th. With that, I walked out in the reverse direction through the crew/ramp security portal, into the terminal, had a bite to eat and a beer, grabbed a taxi, and was off to the hotel.

Surfers at Praia Mole in Florianopolis

Florianopolis is a pretty famous beach resort and surfer hangout. I stayed at a hotel along the waterfront with several great restaurants within walking distance. Since I was going to be here three nights, I took the opportunity to have the hotel do my laundry. I made excursions during the day out to the white sand beaches, some of which were very crowded. There were a few clubs around the hotel for the evening hours where many English-speaking tourists were hanging out. I made a few new traveler friends for the first time on this trip.

As my trip into Brazil progressed, I was getting more experienced at making my way through Brazilian airports on my own, using a few relevant words of Portuguese I had picked up. The morning at Florianopolis went pretty well as a result. When I bought aviation gas on arrival three days ago, I only had US$100 bills, so the fuel guy owed me about US$43 change. He said he'd bring it when I left and true to his word, he came by as I was doing the pre-flight inspection and gave me the change.

Iquazu Falls

Iguazu Falls

Iguazu Falls is a famous, spectacular, multi-part, multi-level waterfall that is often referred to as one of the natural wonders of the world. Any trip to Brazil should include a visit here.

Iquazu Falls

The flight to Iguazu Falls airport was a relatively short flight of less than three hours, and for the first time, I didn't have to fly through any clouds. I filed an IFR flight plan at FL090 to Iguazu. The routing goes almost due north, out of my way, but I was hoping to get a direct routing to Iguazu once airborne, and so I did. The controller at Navegantes asked me if I could fly direct to FOZ, the navigation station at Iguazu Falls, some 300 nm away. I told him no problem. He assigned me an altitude of FL100, I dialed "FOZ" as the destination into the GPS and let the autopilot take over. I had a pretty nice flight over scattered and broken cloud layers far below.

The land I passed over was green farmland and forest, a change from the seemingly much drier Brazilian coast that was almost desert-like in places. The farther west I flew the clearer it became, until eventually I was under open blue skies as I lined up for the GPS approach to runway 32 at the Iguazu Falls airport. Naturally, I hoped I would be able to fly directly by the Falls themselves. The approach course was close – I could see the upstream side of the Falls and the mist billowing up farther downstream – but not close enough to see the face of the Falls which are quite spread out.

Iguazu Falls

Unlike the last few airports, there is a reasonable amount of parking space for private aircraft at Iguazu, part of the scene that included a number of commercial passenger jets coming and going. As a world-renowned place, Iguazu Falls attracts a lot of visitors, requiring several commercial flights coming in every day to carry them.

The fuel guy here spoke more English than the last several I'd recently dealt with. When I wrote down my name for the fuel order, he said "Mr. Anderson, like in *The Matrix*." He had a good time calling me "Mr. Anderson, Mr. Anderson" while fueling the plane and getting paid. Curiously enough, the fuel guy at Florianopolis could only take US$ cash, while this fuel guy could only take Brazilian money in cash. I guess the lesson is to come supplied with both. Actually, I had stocked up on Reais in Florianopolis, so I was happy to start getting rid of them since I would only be in Brazil a few more days.

Iguazu Falls

I treated myself to the nicest hotel around on the Brazilian side of the Falls, the Belmond Hotel das Cataratas. I could actually see the Falls from my hotel room window, just across the roadway. Of course, I spent the afternoon taking photos and then the next morning, took the obligatory tourist boat ride up the river and under the Falls where they promise you'll get soaked, and I did. That night at the hotel, sitting on the veranda outside the bar with a Chivas on the rocks in my hand (a simple drink for a simple man), I was seeing the first pretty sunset I'd seen since entering the Caribbean. My route had been on the west edge of the Atlantic Ocean – not the best place for prolonged, colorful sunsets. It was sublime moment; I was glad I had decided to stay at this hotel.

18

Southbound Through Argentina

Buenos Aires

Because of a few logistics mistakes I made dealing with exit formalities leaving Brazil at Iguazu Falls, I was late departing into a clear blue morning sky. My destination was only 8 nm away, the Argentine airport at Iguazu Falls (airport code SARI) just across the river from the Brazilian airport at Iguazu Falls. I filed a simple VFR flight plan to make the short flight across the river into Argentina at an altitude of 2,500 feet. Departing runway 14, I was given a left turn to loop back around to intercept the runway approach course for runway 13 at Iguazu Falls in Argentina. On the radio, I changed from the Brazil airport tower to Brazil approach control to Argentine approach control to the Argentine airport tower in about four minutes, a lot of frequency changes in a hurry. As I was landing in Argentina, I was directed to parking position 5. Again, I wanted to fly over the Falls to take photos but judging by the radio traffic there were already a few planes doing that. Wanting to keep things simple, I didn't bother to ask ATC for permission to do that.

After landing and engine shutdown in Argentina, I was greeted by a guy with no uniform who wanted to see the aircraft's Registration and Airworthiness documents. He took them off somewhere to make copies

– already unusual. Next two police officers showed up who needed a General Declaration document, which provides the details about the flight, the flight crew, and any passengers.

At this point the process got a little convoluted. One of the police officers, a young guy, escorted me to various places in the terminal building, eventually to the Customs person at the incoming Immigration desk who needed six(!) copies of the General Declaration for my flight arrival. One of these was their own version in Spanish which I filled out, the rest were my preprinted forms in English. She stamped and signed all of these and kept two. Then

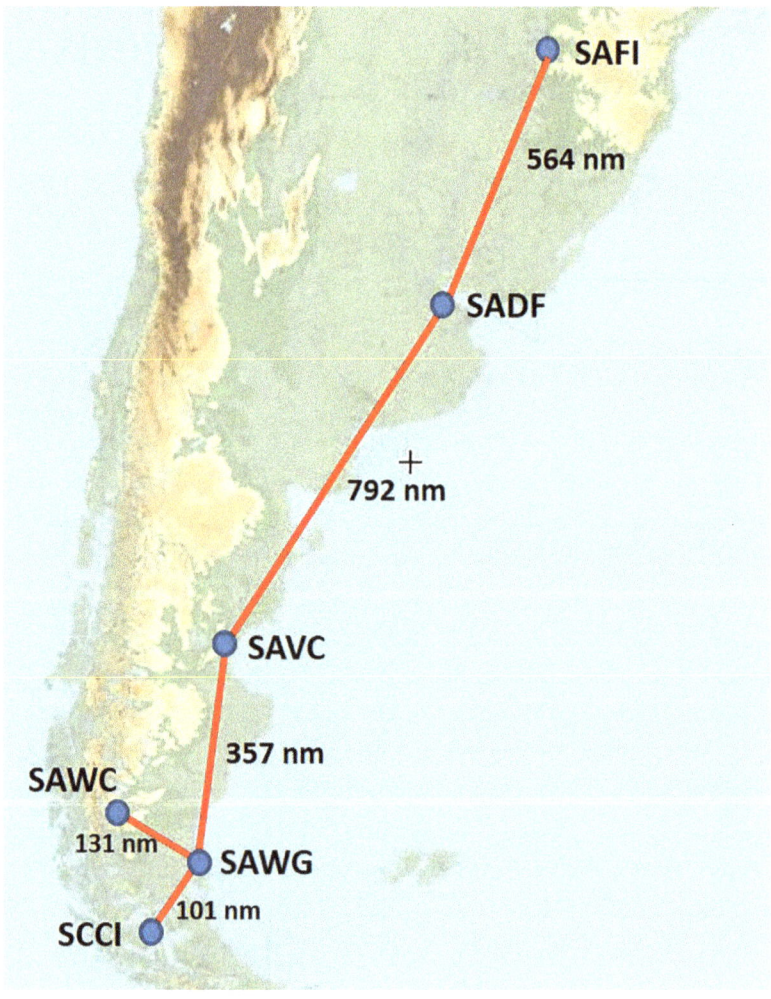

Flight legs from Iguazu Falls in Argentina to Punta Arenas in Chile

the young officer and I waited around for nearly half an hour for someone, I wasn't sure whom at the time. The young guy spoke almost no English and I struggled with my limited Spanish to understand why we were waiting. It turned out we were waiting for a Customs guy who needed to initial the General Declarations. There was a discussion about whether I needed to pay any fees (I think). Their conclusion was "no" so we headed back out to my plane where they wanted to see the inside. They brought along a sniffer dog. A policewoman in uniform was also videotaping the whole event as they pulled a couple of bags off the plane (but not all my bags) and put them on the ground for the dog to sniff. It seemed like a training exercise to me. They concluded that all was OK, we shook hands, and I asked "OK to go?" (Todas esta bien?) They gave me a thumbs-up. At least Spanish was the right language I didn't speak and not Portuguese. Having already entered many countries with my plane, this entry process was the most elaborate.

I called the tower for permission to start my engine. They said they couldn't find my clearance and asked me to come to a room at the base of the tower. It turned out the clearance had been canceled, either because it had expired due to my late arrival and the Argentine entry process taking a long time, or because I hadn't paid the airport fees. The tower guys helped me file an updated flight plan and calculated the airport fees which turned out to be just US$9 – I don't know why I wasn't asked to pay the fees in the first place, although I still would have had to re-file the flight plan.

Reservoir in northern Argentina

Anyway, I was not too impressed with how all this went as my first exposure to Argentine airport operations. I would have several stops in Argentina – I needed to understand their process better.

Now almost two hours behind schedule, I was finally off the ground en route to San Fernando Airport (airport code SADF) on the outskirts of Buenos Aires, the heavily used general-aviation airport on the northern edge of the city. I filed an IFR flight plan at an altitude of FL100.

This altitude worked pretty well that day, keeping me above the cumulus clouds that were building in the afternoon heat. I flew over vast farmlands, cities, and meandering rivers whose names I didn't know. Approaching Buenos Aires, the clouds thickened into a solid layer and I was flying on instruments for most of the descent to San Fernando, breaking out into the clear around 2,500 feet.

There is no weather radio broadcast for this airport, so once I was handed off to the control tower, I asked them about the wind direction and the runway in use. The wind was from 120 degrees at 10–15 knots and they were using runway 23. What? How about going the other way? There must be some noise abatement or other restriction that caused them to prefer using runway 23 because runway 05 made more sense for this wind. Anyway, I was going to have to deal with a quartering tailwind.

Refueling in Buenos Aires

Anyone who has flown a Lancair or Cirrus aircraft with their laminar wing designs, or looked at the performance curves, knows that they are not good with tailwinds – the landing rollout distance increases sharply with increasing tailwind speed. Normally, I like to take a photo of the runway as I'm about to land, but this time I put the camera aside and focused my full attention on this landing. With a tailwind, the plane lands with a lot more ground speed than normal (the airspeed is the same). The trick is to manage the dissipation of that speed and energy as the plane touches down and rolls along the runway.

The arrival procedure at San Fernando is to park on the apron in front of the tower so the police can collect another General Declaration from you (their Spanish version) and inspect the plane. I also understand they will sometimes bring out a sniffer dog, but they didn't with me. Once cleared through this process, I could taxi to parking. San Fernando is a very busy, very crowded general-aviation airport with planes parked all over the place on the grass and aprons at odd angles, fitted together in "puzzle-piece" fashion to make the most of the space. Fortunately, I had emailed an Argentine pilot friend to arrange a parking space for me at Hangar Uno, one of the larger operators on the field and a dealer for Piper aircraft and Robinson helicopters. The Hangar Uno line guys called the fuel truck and the plane was quickly fueled. I paid them in US cash but got change in Argentine pesos. They put the plane in the hangar ($115/night including tax). The girl at the desk arranged a taxi for me into central Buenos Aires where my hotel was located and where there was a beer at a sidewalk café with my name on it.

I'd been to Buenos Aires many times, beginning in 1980, so I wasn't interested in any tourist activities, having done them before. I just wanted to relax and enjoy the great food, great restaurants, and sunny seaside climate. With its older architecture, many parks, and broad avenues, I'd always thought of Buenos Aires as a European city in a California climate. A newly developed area along the now little-used ships basin had become home to many waterfront restaurants within easy walking distance of my hotel.

I was also now south of the tropical zone so I would be facing different weather patterns as I flew on toward Punta Arenas. The few days I had in Buenos Aires gave me a chance to review the overall plan for Antarctica and recalibrate if necessary. I was still exactly on my original spreadsheet schedule. I may have actually been getting good at international trip planning and flying. The plane was doing fine except for the failed altitude hold on the autopilot. I'd gotten used to maintaining altitude manually by adjusting the electric trim, so living with this failure was not a major hardship.

I considered having the oil changed at San Fernando since there are definitely competent mechanics here who work on small planes. I'm sure a Cirrus mechanic could be found, which would have been ideal since the engine in the Cirrus SR22 is the same as mine. However, I needed to have arranged it ahead of time since I had arrived on Saturday and was leaving on Monday. It would have been a challenge to find someone to do it over the weekend. Besides, I felt like I was on a roll and didn't want to risk messing up anything by having a strange mechanic do any work on the engine, even something as straightforward as an oil change.

Comodoro Rivadavia

Departing from San Fernando, even for a domestic flight, requires taxiing to the ramp in front of the tower to park for another police inspection. Once parked, I needed to go into the terminal through a door on the right-hand end of the building as I faced it from the ramp. The police are located here. I needed to fill out two General Declarations, their Spanish version. They stamped and signed both, kept one, and gave the other to me to take with me and turn in at my next destination. The police also came out and inspected the plane, which only took five minutes. Then I was released to go.

To get to Comodoro Rivadavia (airport code SAVC), I filed an IFR flight plan at an altitude of FL100. After departing runway 05 at San Fernando, they had me stay on the runway heading for about ten minutes before instructing me to turn south, direct to the La Plata VOR navigation station, followed by a direct course to the GBE navigation station. From there I followed airway W18 south. This routing was not quite as direct as what I had asked for, but no doubt was intended to keep air traffic like me away from the busy international airport south of Buenos Aires. The weather was good, with a broken cloud layer at about 6,000 feet. I was in clear skies for the whole flight of about 850 nm to Comodoro Rivadavia.

Flying south past Buenos Aires

The landscape below was very flat with ranches and farms spread out as far as I could see. Flying further south, it got drier and the landscape more closely resembled a prairie, then drier still, almost like northern Nevada with few towns spread far apart. There were long, straight paved highways below with large trucks rolling north and south.

Comodoro Rivadavia is on the southern bank of a large river. The tower assigned me a visual approach to runway 07 in the left traffic pattern, which actually has an interesting little hill to watch out for at the final turn to line up with the runway. There was a military twin engine turboprop plane doing touch-and-go's in the right traffic pattern, which doesn't have the hill. Touch-and-go's are a flight training procedure where the pilot lands, coasts for a few seconds on the runway, then applies full power to take off again without taxiing off the runway. The pilot then flies in a tight oval around the airport to do it again. The purpose is to maximize the number of practice landing and takeoff repetitions in a given training session.

Dry coastline en route to Comodoro Rivadavia

After landing, I taxied to the fuel stand at the west end of a very large ramp, the first fuel pump (instead of a fuel truck) I'd seen since the US. At my request, the tower called the guy who runs the pump from his office in a small building about 50 yards from the pump. He filled N788W with aviation gas, then we went back to his office where I was able to pay with a credit card. There were no designated general-aviation parking areas at this airport. After calling the tower, they told me to just push the plane into a position along the edge of the ramp between the fuel stand and the taxiway. From there, it was about a hundred yards' walk to the terminal building, where I handed in the General Declaration I'd retained from San Fernando and grabbed a taxi into town, a 20-minute ride.

Comodoro Rivadavia was meant as an overnight fuel stop before proceeding to El Calafate (airport code SAWC), where I wanted to spend a few days. I had checked the weather for the next day, which showed rain at El Calafate, but it was still fairly clear that afternoon. I considered the idea of continuing on from Comodoro to El Calafate since the weather was still favorable. In retrospect, I probably would have had an easier time getting to El Calafate if I had gone that afternoon.

Coastline en route to Rio Gallegos

There wasn't much going on in Comodoro Rivadavia. It's a seaside town with a convenient but uninteresting downtown where my hotel was located. I wandered around a bit as afternoon turned to evening, eventually finding a great little restaurant with an outdoor terrace. I skipped the hotel bar that night and made it an early evening.

El Calafate

The curious thing about the El Calafate Airport is that there is (as of January 2013) no aviation weather data available online – no terminal forecasts, no hourly observations, nothing. El Calafate doesn't even show up on the worldwide list of weather reporting stations. This is in spite of the fact that it is one of the most popular and well-known tourist destinations in Argentina, with numerous scheduled commercial flights each day. The lack of aviation weather data meant I had to revert to other online sources like the Weather Underground maps and Accuweather (listed in Appendix B) to figure out what was happening. Those forecasts showed 60% chance of rain for the next day. The winds aloft maps for an altitude of FL100 showed 40-knot winds from the west and temperatures hovering around zero, introducing the potential for ice.

Final approach runway 25 at Rio Gallegos

Because of my uncertainty about the weather, I decided to do this relatively short flight (about 330 nm) in two stages. I would first fly from Comodoro Rivadavia to Rio Gallegos (airport code SAWG), a flight almost due south along the coast. During this flight I could make my own visual evaluation of the weather to the west, since El Calafate is located only about 100 nm inland. I could also note the temperature at altitude to decide if ice might be an issue. Using this information, I could decide whether to fly the second leg from Rio Gallegos to El Calafate that day. It's a short flight, only about 130 nm, less than an hour in my plane.

Breaking out of the clouds above Lago Argentino

I filed an IFR flight plan to Rio Gallegos along airway W18 at FL080. During the flight I was in the clear with a high layer above and the usual scattered to broken cloud layer below. The weather stayed like that all the way, so I was able to make a visual approach and landed on runway 25 at Rio Gallegos.

I was now seeing the high winds of Patagonia I was warned about. The wind was a steady 25 knots, gusting to 35 knots, but blowing right down the runway. Even after the wheels were on the ground I had to carefully control the rollout since the strong winds still created some lift and made the plane light on its wheels, resulting in reduced traction and braking ability.

From the weather I saw to the west, I decided I could fly the second leg to El Calafate. I went into the terminal, a really nice new building, and turned in the General Declaration form as usual. I then called Skyplan and had them file a flight plan to El Calafate. Even though it costs a few bucks, sometimes it's easier to call them and have them file what I want than wander around an unfamiliar airport trying to find the office where I could fill out and file a paper flight plan myself.

Off the ground again in about an hour with a route along airway W52, I climbed up through a cloud layer and was in the clear for a while. Clear skies turned into solid clouds at FL090 with the temperature hovering at +2 to +3° Celsius. As predicted, I was flying straight into a 40–50 knot headwind bringing my ground speed down to about 130 knots. It was a short flight but seemed to take forever; fortunately the clouds weren't too bumpy. I called ATC and asked for weather at El Calafate, which she gave me in detail. They actually do have at least METAR (observation) data. I couldn't understand why it wasn't available online.

Iceberg in Lago Argentino

Nearing the airport, the tower told me to remain at FL090 until directly over the airport. Normally I would have started my descent long before that, but the tower knew something I didn't – there was a huge hole in the cloud layer above Lago Argentino and the airport, which is on the lakeshore. As I got within 10 nm of the airport, I suddenly and dramatically broke out of the clouds to see an amazing vista of Lago Argentino, the airport below, the town of El Calafate to

Upsala Glacier dropping into Lago Argentino

Spegazzini Glacier

the left, and the Andes, wrapped in clouds, in the distance. It was amazing! I reported the airport in sight and did a rapid descent for a visual approach and landing on runway 07.

General-aviation parking is at the aeroclub ramp, which is just off the east end of the main ramp. I had previously sent an email to Pablo Argiz, of the aeroclub, informing him of my arrival date. He was on the ramp working on his helicopter. He knows a little English, so I explained I wanted to buy some aviation gas. There is none available commercially at El Calafate, but the aeroclub has a supply. He sold me 75 liters, proving himself a very helpful guy to know at El Calafate.

I went through the usual General Declaration process with the police, then passed through to the modern terminal building and had some lunch before proceeding to the hotel. Two short flight legs that day, a little more work than usual, but I was now only about 230 nm from Punta Arenas, Chile (airport code SCCI), my departure point for the flight to Antarctica.

El Calafate is located in Los Glaciares National Park. It has become famous worldwide for its glaciers, mountains, and lakes where a wide variety of outdoor activities are available. As the taxi rolled into town, it seemed like every other shop along the main street was advertising tours and excursions of one kind or another. I stayed at Posada Los Alamos, maybe the nicest hotel in town and a short walking distance to many restaurants, shops, and places to book tours. Probably the most popular tour is the boat excursion on the lake that passes close by the faces of the several glaciers that descend into the lake. The most famous of those is Perito Moreno Glacier, which actually comes down a mountainside and crosses the lake to stop at the opposite shoreline.

Perito Moreno Glacier near El Calafate

The glacier lake tour was interesting and a major attraction for South Americans who have fewer opportunities to get up close to such snow and ice compared to people from other parts of the world. Overall, the number and size of the glaciers found here is not that impressive when compared to other places in the world like Glacier Bay or Prince William Sound in Alaska.

There were many travelers in El Calafate from a wide variety of nations, ranging from wealthy tourists to young backpackers bumming around South America. I fell into the former category now, though I remember decades before being the impoverished backpacker hitching around Africa, Europe, and the Middle East. Over the years I've speculated on which way of traveling is better. With money, traveling is certainly easier and more comfortable, but the money also insulates me from experiences I would have had, and people I would have known, if I had been staying in hostels, or camping, and traveling on the cheap. I'm too old to go back to that now, I think, but it's impossible not to wonder about what I might be missing, especially in a place like El Calafate.

I spent three nights here, which gave me some time to relax and interact with people I met. The flight to this point had seemed like an insistent rush, for no particular reason except that's how I had planned it, but I could tell my urge to accomplish the Antarctica flight was the underlying driver for the schedule and everything else I was doing. I was not on a tour; the intermediate stops were necessary for rest and fuel, but the thought that I needed to push on with the primary mission never left my mind.

At El Calafate I started checking the weather in earnest at King George Island in Antarctica, where my destination airport (airport code SCRM) is located. I was also looking at weather patterns in the Drake Passage, the stretch of often-violent water I would have to fly over to get from the tip of South America to Antarctica. I was already bothered by the fact that the forecasts and what the weather turned out to be often greatly disagreed. Weather forecasts would become my obsession for the next several weeks.

19

Waiting in Punta Arenas

Punta Arenas

In miles, the flight to Punta Arenas from El Calafate was the shortest flight on the trip, but completing it led to one of the more frustrating days. El Calafate is designated as an Airport of Entry on the airport information websites I consulted. Well, it really isn't, or rather it can only be temporarily turned into one with 48 hours' prior notice. This led to several problems for my departure to Punta Arenas (airport code SCCI).

The many scheduled commercial flights that come to El Calafate are all Argentine airlines arriving from, and departing to, other cities in Argentina; they are domestic flights so there is no need for Customs and Immigration services. Because those services are not normally provided at El Calafate, I suppose the 48-hour required notice gives them time to get an Immigration and Customs agent to the airport from somewhere else. When I arrived three days before, I tried to explain to the man in the airport office I would be departing to Punta Arenas, Chile. Although I didn't know about the 48 hours' prior notice at that time, I was hoping I might have accomplished that notice three days ago. Apparently not.

Two Argentine pilots from Buenos Aires, flying a Cessna 182 around Patagonia and also headed to Punta Arenas, were encountering the same problem as I and fortunately spoke reasonably good English. They explained the problem to me, which they said could be solved by writing a letter to the airport chief asking for temporary Airport of Entry status, which he might grant sometime that day. This did not seem particularly likely. Alternately, we could fly back to Rio Gallegos which is a full-time (sort of) Airport of Entry and depart to Punta Arenas from there. That seemed like the better course, so I wrote out a new flight plan for Rio Gallegos and away I flew. The Cessna 182 guys were put off by the high surface winds at the airports in Patagonia. When I last talked to them before I left, they were thinking of leaving Patagonia and flying north where the wind and weather were calmer.

Requesting engine startup, I was surprised again when the guy in the control tower would not speak to me in English even though I came to realize he knew more aviation English then I knew aviation Spanish. It was the first time I'd run into this anywhere in the world. There was definitely a nationalistic, cultural attitude with this guy – maybe he was offended by my presumption that I could impose English speaking on him. I certainly hadn't encountered a language problem with the guy in the tower when flying in three days before. The guy in the tower for my departure bluntly explained in Spanish that El Calafate is a Spanish-speaking airport. I did my best to mix in what Spanish I knew, listened to his taxi instructions and repeated them back, got the squawk code, until finally I was off the ground and headed to Rio Gallegos. I was happy when he handed me off to Comodoro Control, who were perfectly willing to speak to me in English.

Punta Arenas airport (SCCI)

The weather was clear but very bumpy on descent into Rio Gallegos. When I got handed to the tower, he told me surface winds were 32 knots, mostly blowing along runway 25 but varying +/- 20° from that direction. The wind was actually gusty, which he didn't tell me, but I managed an adequate – though not very elegant – landing. I walked back into the terminal I had visited just a few days before. With a new flight plan for Punta Arenas, I was asked to come to the tower where an English-speaking guy told me that they needed to call the Immigration and Customs people to the airport. It would take at least one hour, since they are normally only at the airport when scheduled international flights are arriving or departing. I also needed to pay fees, which turned out to be about US$10.

Once the Immigration and Customs people arrived, I handed over the two stamped and signed General Declarations I'd been given when I entered Argentina at Iguazu Falls. There was more swapping, stamping, and signing of General Declarations – I lost count on how many but I was glad I had an ample supply with me. Finally there was a cursory inspection of N788W and I was released to go.

N788W's long-term parking spot at Punta Arenas

I'll note here that that the procedure with handing in and receiving General Declarations with the Police Federal works for domestic flights only. When leaving the country, hand in the last General Declaration that got you to the departure airport. Then it's a transition into the hands of Immigration and Customs people to fill in many General Declarations required for leaving the country. Finally, there is a visit to the airport office to pay fees.

As I taxied out to the holding point for runway 25 at Rio Gallegos for takeoff, the plane shaking and being pushed around by the wind, the tower told me the wind was 30 knots, then he corrected himself and said 38 knots. I know a few planes that would be flying on their own in wind like that.

N788W at Punta Arenas with IL-76 in the background

The flight to Punta Arenas is only about 100 nm but took some time because of the headwinds. Fortunately, the sky was clear, though I had the same situation with strong surface winds when landing at Punta Arenas. The approach and landing was a slow creep down the approach course to runway 25 and bumpy enough that I didn't get a runway photo. In my plane

I normally cross the runway threshold (the beginning of the runway) at an airspeed of about 80 knots. This time I glanced at my ground speed on the GPS – 48 knots – by subtraction, a 32-knot headwind!

I arrived in Punta Arenas on January 25, 2013, exactly the day I had planned on my spreadsheet months before, which was a little amazing. No weather delays I couldn't compensate for. That was going to change dramatically.

I hired a handler (Aerocardal) at Punta Arenas, partly to help me through Immigration and Customs but mainly to connect me to the right people in the DGAC (Chile's FAA) and the Chilean Air Force. I needed to coordinate my flight to/from King George Island in Antarctica with them.

I went through Immigration and Customs, loaded US$1000 worth of aviation gas on N788W, including filling the cargo fuel tank full for the first time, and then removed the wheel pants which took over an hour. I had asked the handler to find some hangar space for me so this task could be completed inside but none was available. So, at my parking spot out in the gusting wind with my tool bag open, I laid on the tarmac and undid the screws and bolts to get the wheel pants off. Then I wedged foam sponge material in between the main gear strut and its fairing, since those fairings are no longer secured to the plane with the wheel pants removed. I finally wrapped the whole thing in duct tape to hold it in place. I took the wheel pants off because the gravel runway at King George Island is reported to be rough from handling large military planes. Removing the wheel pants greatly increases the small ground clearance on the main landing gears (wheels) and eliminates the possibility of breaking them on the rutted runway. I'd devised and tested flew this ad hoc configuration back home. With the wheel pants off, the plane is a few knots slower at high speeds but otherwise flies the same as with the wheel pants on. With that task done and the fuel loaded, the plane was ready for the flight to Antarctica.

N788W with main gear wheel pants removed

The weather forecast for the following day, Saturday, January 26, looked favorable for the flight, though it was sooner than I expected to go. Nonetheless,

I told the handler I wanted to prepare to go on Saturday, so we went to the airport office to file a flight plan and also meet with the chief of the DGAC at Punta Arenas, along with two other DGAC guys, to discuss the flight. The chief, who spoke excellent English, was completely familiar with what I intended to do, had copies of all the emails I'd exchanged with the DGAC office in Santiago months ago, and offered his team of people there to support me in whatever way they could, starting with calling

Torres del Paine in the clouds

the Air Force and making sure there was no conflict with my flight if I flew on Saturday. These guys are very familiar and knowledgeable with flights of all kinds to Antarctica, and looking around the hangars and other facilities at

the airport, it was clear that this was the hub for air traffic from South America to Antarctica. As an example, while I was at the airport that day, a large Russian-built Iluyshin IL-76 cargo jet left for Union Glacier in Antarctica, about 80 degrees south latitude, where a private company has established a base to support many types of private expeditions in Antarctica ranging from mountaineering to ski trekking. The early Antarctica explorers, like Shackleton, also used Punta Arenas as a staging point to provision their wooden sailing ships for voyages south to Antarctica.

It was for me to decide when I would make the flight, based on weather, so with the handler I

Torres del Paine

Torres del Paine

also made a stop at the weather office (Meteo) for the latest updates. Saturday still looked favorable but I wanted to wait and make a final decision later that night based on the latest forecast that came in from King George Island airstrip (SCRM). If I didn't actually use the flight plan I had filed, it was no big deal. After the trying day I'd had getting out of Argentina, I also was asking myself if I was ready for the "summit pitch" to Antarctica on this long flight south. In the end, the weather forecast worsened a bit, I didn't feel up to this flight after the day I'd had, and so I decided to delay.

It was a mistake. Getting up Saturday morning, I checked the webcams at King George Island, which showed lots of open sky. I should have made the flight. At the time I didn't know how long it would be before another favorable day like that one would come along. There are interesting things to see and do around Punta Arenas and Puerto Natales. While I waited on a new window of good weather, I had time to explore the area.

Torres del Paine

One of the more interesting places in this part of Patagonia is Torres del Paine, located north of Punta Arenas and Puerto Natales. One-day excursions from Punta Arenas are available, but it's a long drive. The van leaves early and returns late, although at this time of the year at these latitudes there are many hours of daylight.

Lago Grey in Torres del Paine

I took this excursion on a day when the flying weather to Antarctica was certain to be bad. Ironically, Torres del Paine is actually much closer to El Calafate than to Punta Arenas but a border crossing is required to go there from El Calafate. Nonetheless, tours from El Calafate do go to Torres del Paine.

On the drive north from Punta Arenas in the small van, we experienced the same strong surface winds I encountered at the airport. The van was being blown back and forth across the road. We passed through Puerto Natales, where we stopped for gas, and then farther north at a road junction we stopped again for coffee and snacks. We passed the airport at Puerto Natales which had a small, modern terminal building but not much else – no planes on the ground, large or small, that I could see. It's fairly wide open with a runway that is not oriented in the best way for the prevailing winds that normally blow from west to east.

Our excursion took us in through the east entrance of the park and out the south entrance. Along the way we had fantastic views of the distinctive dark and light banded peaks with the many lakes and rivers that make this park spectacular. We stopped at several places with awesome perspectives just made for photos. At a few stops we could take short hikes to waterfalls or across a glacial moraine to get close views of small icebergs.

There were many other people on the road, ranging from backpackers hitchhiking around Patagonia, to climbers loaded with their gear, to tourists like us just there for sightseeing. There were several campgrounds and a few very high-end hotels near the south end of the park. These hotels would be great for a relaxing luxury stay. Everywhere we went, though, the wind was unrelenting, especially in the open area crossing the moraine on Lago Grey. It was a long day but definitely worth it. I enjoyed doing something interesting and fun for a change instead of just hanging around Punta Arenas waiting for the weather in Antarctica to change.

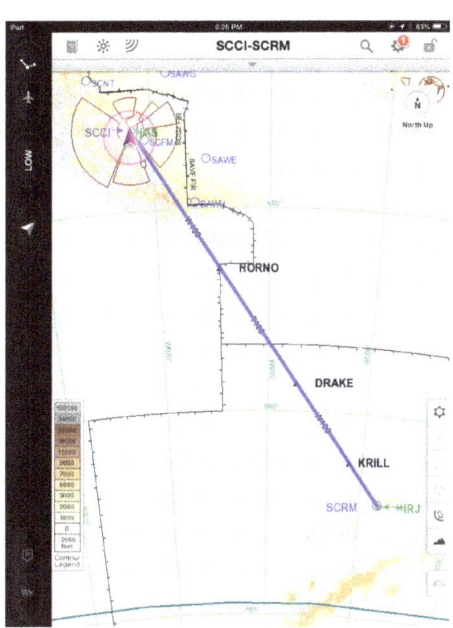

Flight route from SCCI (Punta Arenas) to SCRM (Antarctica)

A Reconnaissance Flight South

It was not the flight I planned to make, nor the flight I wanted to make, but it was the flight I was able to make.

For two weeks I had been held up in Punta Arenas waiting for suitable weather at the airstrip on King George Island and along the route across the Drake Passage. I was checking current and forecast weather a few times a day and utilizing whatever other forecast resources I could find. But the weather was not just marginal, it was continuously bad, with fog much of the time. It even grounded or delayed flights by DAP, a small, specialized air carrier that flies scheduled and charter flights to King George Island a few times a week using a BE30 (King Air) or a regional jet (BE46). The BE46 is used to ferry Antarctica cruise ship passengers to King George Island to board their ship, an expensive alternative that bypasses the two-day, stomach-churning crossing of the Drake Passage. Even the BE46 was delayed by fog to the point where some passengers to whom I spoke, destined for a Quark Expeditions cruise, were concerned about literally missing their boat. Even when there was no fog, the forecast and actual ceilings were continuously below 1000 feet, with visibility that varied from a few hundred to a few thousand meters.

Andes Mountains south of Punta Arenas

Having flown there many times, the DAP pilots are of course accustomed to this and no doubt have devised their own techniques for landing under such poor conditions. There are two published instrument approaches for landing at King George Island. The runway is nearly at sea level with a flat, low-altitude approach over the water to the threshold possible. I expect that's what the DAP pilots are doing.

Even if there isn't fog at a given time, the temperature-dew point spread is typically only 1° C which means that a small change in either the temperature or the dew point can quickly and unexpectedly turn low ceilings and low visibility into fog. Fog typically occurs when the temperature and dew point are the same or very close. For this reason it was essential to be able to fly to an alternate airport in the event the one at King George Island suddenly became fogged in.

Looking south from the Drake Passage turnaround point

Though I probably would attempt a landing under these conditions at an airport back home, for me this was too risky given where the airport at King George Island is located. It made me realize I was actually under-equipped for this flight given my strategy to refuel from a cargo tank once on the ground at King George Island. If I flew to King George Island and was unable to land, I would have to return to the nearest alternate airport where a landing was certain. The two possible airports are 530 nm miles to the north at Puerto Williams (airport code SCGZ) or Ushuaia (airport code SAWH) which has a precision instrument approach for landing in bad weather conditions. Unfortunately, flying all the way to King George Island, being unable to land, then flying all the way back north to Puerto Williams or Ushuaia would be right at the limits of my range with wing tanks only. Variable and poorly forecast headwind conditions could well make it

Islands north of Cape Horn

impossible to get back, so trying this simply was not a viable option. Instead of taking the fuel as cargo, if I had gone through the FAA process and installed a ferry tank into the aircraft fuel system instead, I would have had adequate fuel to abort the landing at King George Island due to fog and comfortably return to one of these alternate airports.

Being under-equipped for the flight and weather conditions translates into requiring a much narrower and more ideal set of weather conditions so that landing at King George Island would be a certainty. Hence, a long wait for those assured conditions to appear which, after two weeks, had never appeared (except that first Saturday).

I was frustrated by waiting and by having my plane beat up by vicious surface winds on the ramp at Punta Arenas Airport. The winds were sometimes gusting to 65 knots and twice bounced my plane out of its nose wheel chocks. I finally asked the question: if I couldn't make the flight to King George Island, what flight could I make? I devised a flight plan in which I would fly out over the Drake Passage as far south as 60 degrees south latitude, the official boundary of the Antarctic Treaty Area, some 500 nm south of Punta Arenas and 170 miles short of King George Island, and then turn around and fly back. I told myself it would be a "reconnaissance" flight. I'd gotten fed up watching weather reports and weather maps, so I'd fly down there and see for myself what the Drake Passage was all about.

I picked a day with good weather in Punta Arenas, with a front moving across the mountains south of Punta Arenas, but with the potential for clear skies at the waypoint called DRAKE near my turn-around point. I filed a VFR flight plan at an altitude of FL120 and took off at around 1200Z, about 7:00 am local time. I climbed up to FL120 to get over the front and the Andes Mountains south of Punta Arenas. I continued south with a nice tailwind and the temperature continuously dropping, ultimately getting to -9° C at the turn-around point. If I'd been in the clouds instead of clear skies, the plane would have been iced up and I would have been forced to descend to warmer temperatures nearer the ocean's surface.

The clouds below me did open up halfway between the HORNO and DRAKE waypoints. I was over the blue water of the Drake Passage with whitecaps everywhere showing strong surface winds. When whitecaps look big from 12,000 feet, it's a strong wind. I made it to my turn-around point, but realized I faced a strong headwind going back north so I dropped down to FL030 with the idea of flying under the clouds, hopefully with a temperature above zero. The temperature did rise to +5° C but the headwinds really didn't weaken much, and I really couldn't fly under the clouds in spite of going down to about 1200 feet over the water. At that point I was in clouds for the most of the next two hours with ground speed falling to 110 knots. I also realized that the missing wheel pants where having more of an effect on airspeed than I'd realized. I should have made some longer test flights at home with this oddball configuration so my flight planning would have been more accurate. I obviously was cheating on my VFR flight plan during this phase but it didn't really matter. There were no planes around here over the ocean doing what I was doing, so no possibility of a collision in the clouds.

I became concerned about having enough fuel to get back to Punta Arenas, knowing I would need to climb higher to get over the mountains. On returning to the HORNO waypoint going north, I told ATC via the satphone I was going to my alternate airport at Puerto Williams. Incidentally, outbound I successfully contacted ATC on my HF radio at HORNO, which was satisfying given the work I'd done to improve the installation the preceding summer and interface it to the audio panel as the third radio. However, I couldn't contact them on HF at the DRAKE waypoint, so I was now on

Isla Navarino where Puerto Williams is located

my satphone.

From HORNO to Puerto Williams I climbed up to FL060 in anticipation of flying the instrument approach at Puerto Williams. I was still in the clouds crossing Cape Horn, unfortunately denying me a view of this landmark. But just north of there, the clouds finally opened up and I had some astonishing, though intermittent, views of this wild and rugged landscape. Flying further north, the sky opened up so I could easily see all of Isla Navarino (where Puerto Williams is located), the Beagle Channel, and Ushuaia farther to the west. Flying east over the Beagle Channel, I made a right turn back to the west for a visual approach into Puerto Williams.

At some point on this trip I was hoping to re-connect to places I had visited two years before on a cruise to Antarctica. The cruise left from and returned to Ushuaia via the Beagle Channel; the Beagle Channel became that connection. I have clear memories of standing outside on the upper deck as we departed Ushuaia in the evening, cruising east along the channel heading for the Drake Passage. While standing on deck that night I noticed the little airport I hadn't expected to see at Puerto Williams, the airport where my plane was now parked.

Puerto Williams

Puerto Williams is in Chile, on the south side of the Beagle Channel which runs east-west forming part of the border between Chile and Argentina in Tierra del Fuego. Puerto Williams has the distinction of being the southernmost airport in South America, a few miles farther south than Ushuaia which is on the north side of the Beagle Channel. Puerto Williams is not visited often by light aircraft because no aviation gas is available. There is aviation gas at Ushuaia about 25 nm west. As a consequence, Ushuaia is the southernmost airport where small plane pilots usually stop before turning around and heading north again.

With a cargo tank full of fuel, the lack of aviation gas at Puerto Williams was not a problem for me. Since I was still in Chile, I didn't have to pass through any entry formalities which would have been required if I'd gone to Ushuaia. In the event someone had to make an emergency landing at Puerto Williams for lack of fuel, a guy with the DGAC at Punta Arenas told me they have arrangements to bring aviation gas from Ushuaia by boat.

In some respects I was glad to get a chance to use the cargo tank to refuel my plane. I figured out all the details of how I would do this, researched compact plastic rotary pumps, and gathered together the plastic hose, clamps,

N788W refueling by hand at Puerto Williams

and other pieces I'd need to make it work. I even brought along a spare pump and fittings. Once parked at the ramp at Puerto Williams, I got the pieces out, screwed the pump into the cargo tank, ran the plastic hose to the wing tank inlet, and pumped away. It took about 10 minutes to replace the 30 gallons in the left wing tank. I moved the pump to the bung on the other side of the cargo tank and put the remaining fuel in the right wing tank. Altogether, it took about 20 minutes to complete this operation. Everything worked the way I planned it. I would have been disappointed to have carried all this stuff 10,000 nm to the tip of South America and never put it to use.

The ATC/tower guy at Puerto Williams was great. He came out to greet me on the ramp, spoke English well, and asked whether I was going to stay the night. I told him all my stuff was in the hotel back in Punta Arenas so

I would be going back right away. He directed me to the office in the little terminal building where I could file a flight plan.

In the meantime, a commuter flight from Punta Arenas arrived to unload and pick up passengers, then head straight back to Punta Arenas. One of its pilots came over to chat while I was refueling, so I asked him about the weather along the route to Punta Arenas. He said it was clear above FL110. It doesn't get any better than that for weather info – a pilot report just 20 minutes old along my exact flight route. After the weather I had flying north over the Drake Passage, I was due for an easier flight. While we were standing there, a guy came by with a drum of jet fuel to put in their turboprop commuter plane. He pulled up to the plane with the fuel drum on a trailer, pulled out a rotary pump and hose, and started pumping away. Hey, it works on planes big and small. My unusual approach to refueling my plane was normal in Puerto Williams.

Ushuaia on the north side of the Beagle Channel

I filed a VFR flight plan at FL100 to avoid the high minimum altitudes required for IFR along the route. Climbing out westbound from Puerto Williams I had beautiful views of this incredible countryside along the Beagle Channel. It's a raw and

Mountains northwest of Ushuaia

remote place that few venture to see, to me much more compelling in that way than some high-profile attractions, like Torres del Paine, which are usually overflowing with tourists. I really don't know if the areas around Puerto Williams are accessible with hiking trails, campsites, etc. I do know that Chile is trying to promote Puerto Williams as a tourist destination. A few nice lodges have been built near town and the scheduled flights from Punta Arenas make it easy to get there.

I was able to climb fast enough to get above the clouds as I went west, but flying straight into the prevailing winds, which are typically from the west, made progress slow. Turning northwest direct to Punta Arenas at a waypoint called DARIN improved the wind situation somewhat. Over the mountains, updrafts and downdrafts kept me busy maintaining the correct altitude manually. I'd been doing that since that altitude hold on the autopilot failed departing Grenada. This was the first time it was actually a lot of work to maintain altitude.

Re-Evaluating

I first arrived in Punta Arenas on January 25. My reconnaissance flight into Antarctica Territory occurred on February 9. I had some decisions to make on what I would do next. I didn't think there was a realistic chance weather conditions at the airport on King George Island would improve sufficiently to make the flight, given the technical limitations of the plane and fuel loading that I explained previously. The morning of February 10th I checked the current and forecast weather again at King George Island. It was the same old story – fog, drizzle, low visibility, low ceilings, and a small temperature/dew point spread. The few tools I use for longer range forecasting beyond 24 hours, mainly Accuweather and Weather Underground, showed nothing hopeful in the coming week. These websites hadn't been all that accurate in this part of the world anyway, sometimes showing sunshine for the next day only to see the forecast collapse overnight to the same old thing of cold low clouds and low visibility.

Descending over the Straits of Magellan toward Punta Arenas

The wheel pants were still off the plane. Once I put them back on, I would be done with trying to make it to Antarctica. I was frustrated and berating myself for my poor fuel planning. To some extent it was born of arrogance from my round-the-world flight. That flight had been so trouble-free, and except for the flight from Hawaii to California, had never really challenged me. I looked at the flight leg from Punta Arenas to King George Island: only 670 nm! Hey, a walk in the park compared to the long ocean legs I had flown. What an idiot I was not to connect the ferry tank to the fuel system!

I decided to stick around a few more days and see if the weather might surprise me. I had prepaid for the hotel room for a few more days in any event, so I thought I might as well make use of it.

I've rarely discussed specific hotels in this book, but with my extended stay in Punta Areas I got to know three of them pretty well. I'd had to change hotels a few times because I didn't want to book more than a week ahead since I didn't know when I'd be leaving. The hotel would get fully booked during the week and I couldn't extend my stay. The two best hotels that have a reasonable number of rooms are Hotel Dreams del Estrecho and Hotel Cabo de Hornos. The third is a notch down – the Best Western Finis Terrae. Hotel Dreams is a modern glass monstrosity on the waterfront with an attached casino. It's comfortable and has large rooms with great views, but the all-glass exterior can make the rooms beastly hot on sunny days – there is no air conditioning. I prefer the Hotel Cabo de Hornos. It's an older building right on the main plaza, recently remodeled though, and has a more artistic personality in the public areas like the lounge and restaurant, compared to the large anonymous public areas in Hotel Dreams. It's also got a better wine cellar. The LAN air crews stay at Cabo. Large tour groups, research teams headed for Antarctica, and those waiting for cruise ships or flights to Antarctica, stay at both Cabo and Dreams. The Quark Expedition passengers I talked to waiting for their fog-delayed flight to Antarctica were staying at Dreams. All three of these hotels are within a few blocks of each other in downtown Punta Arenas, so they offer easy access to all the restaurants, the waterfront, the museums, and the other attractions in the city center. Both Dreams and Cabo have good restaurants, but there are many others.

Here are a few specific operational details for pilots flying out of Punta Arenas toward Antarctica. The enroute charts show the Argentine Comodoro Rivadavia Flight Information Region has control along part of the airway to King George Island. Actually, this is not the case. Punta Arenas will have control of the flight the entire way. The HF contact frequencies given to me were 6649 kHz primary, 10024 kHz secondary.

The Meteo office is right next to the Operations office at Punta Arenas. An easy way onto the ramp is through the Operations office, where they will just wave you through once they recognize you. I'd at least achieved that much, waiting here for nearly three weeks and periodically going to the airport to check on the plane. An even easier "secret" way to the ramp is through the Petrobras fuel office, which I've seen other Antarctica air crews use. Additional details can be found in Appendix B.

20

Giving Up and Going North

The Decision to Leave Punta Arenas

After 2½ weeks in Punta Arenas I decided to give up on making the flight to King George Island. Without the reserve range that would be provided by a ferry tank, the risk profile for the flight was too high, unless a very good day of weather occurred and was accurately forecast. I had not seen such a day since I arrived. There had been a few days when the weather was acceptable at King George Island but those weather windows lasted a matter of hours, not days. And on more than one occasion they occurred contrary to the forecast. Such windows of reasonable weather at King George Island seemed to occur every seven to ten days.

As I mentioned earlier, in 2011, I took a two-week cruise to Antarctica that sailed south of the Antarctic Circle. During that cruise I enjoyed the highlights of Antarctica that most people go there to see – the wildlife, the ice and rocks, the primeval vibe that comes from being in such a remote, relatively untouched place. My flight to King George Island was not about doing any of those things. Although I didn't reach my goal of landing at King George Island, landing there would have been simply a trophy event, not another dose of the Antarctica experience. If I had landed there, I would have immediately refueled the plane and returned to Punta Arenas before the weather could change. I wouldn't have spent any time looking around.

GIVING UP AND GOING NORTH | 223

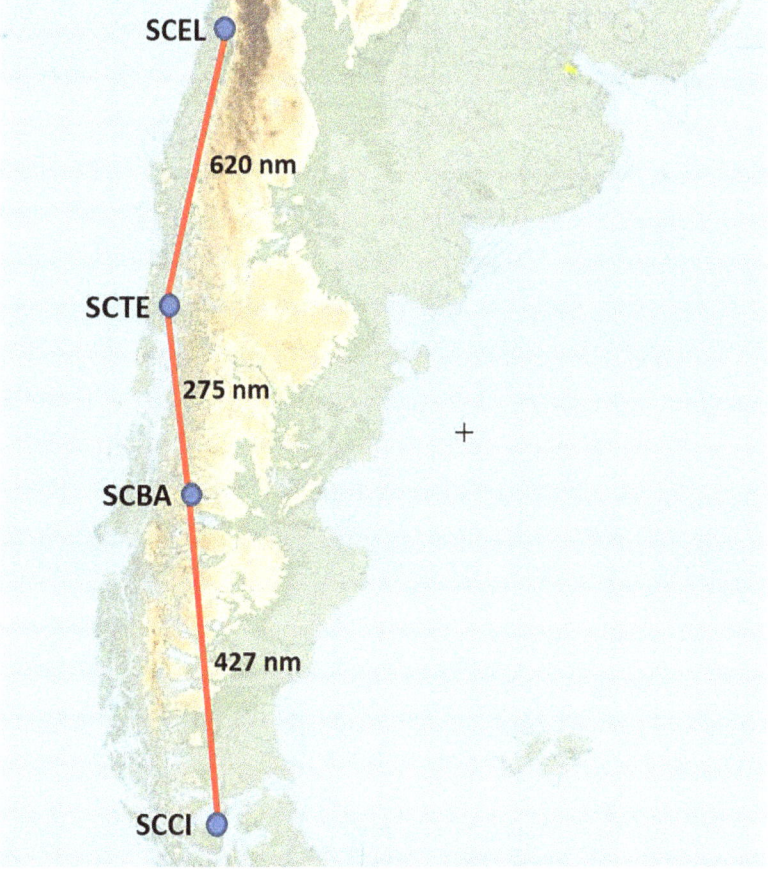

Flight legs from Punta Arenas to Santiago

At the time of my decision to abandon the flight to King George Island I wrote the following in my flight blog: "With the flight I did make to 60 degrees south latitude, I think I got the genuine experience of a flight to Antarctica even without landing there. I'm satisfied with that. My regret is not getting some aerial photos of interesting places we passed on the cruise like Deception Island." Well, that turned out to be a lie. I was not satisfied with that flight to 60 degrees south. By the time I had flown back home to Bainbridge Island I had resolved to address the issues that caused me to abandon this flight and decide whether it was feasible to try again.

There was another factor that limited my time down there, which I'll explain with a short digression. During my round-the-world flight in 2011, I was retired from a professional job and could devote an unlimited amount of

Climbing out of Punta Arenas headed north

time to the flight. That changed in the fall of 2012, after I had gotten all the permits to land at Antarctica, when I decided to take over as CEO of a small software company where I am majority owner. EDX is a company I founded in 1985, sold in 2000, and bought back again with some partners in 2004. Since 2004, my partners have been running the business and successfully rebuilding it. By returning as CEO I hoped to accelerate that success. However, it also meant I had responsibilities and demands on my time now that I hadn't had during my world flight. When I embarked on this flight to Antarctica, I didn't want to be out of the loop for more than six or seven weeks. My time was up. I needed to fly north to Santiago where I'd park the plane and take a commercial flight back to the US to resume my role as CEO at EDX for several weeks to keep things there on track. I would return later to Santiago to pick up the plane and fly it back home.

Balmaceda

The first flight leg north to Balmaceda directed my attention to weather patterns over the Andes Mountains in a region I hadn't been watching. The Andes Mountains, especially the volcanoes, are one thing I wanted to see from the air. Weather Underground showed a high pressure system moving eastward from the Pacific, so I timed my departure and route north so I would be

View from Coihuique

flying by the volcanoes when the sky was clear. The first leg was to Balmaceda, Chile (airport code SCBA). There is a direct route from Punta Arenas to Balmaceda along the G550 airway, but this follows close to the eastern slope of the Andes. The weather was still cloudy along this route on the day I left, and flying in the leeward side of a mountain range

Flying over the Andes Mountain range

like this, especially with the high winds from the west, will almost guarantee a very turbulent ride. I opted for a route further east via Rio Gallegos that is 70 nm longer but bound to be smoother.

This worked out well – I had clear skies the entire flight. When looking to the west along the direct route, I could see some nasty weather building in the mountains, which I was now happy to be avoiding. Turning directly west at the waypoint called MIKIM, I was flying straight into the wind. I was amazed, but not surprised, to see the ground speed fall to 100 knots in spite of an airspeed of 170 knots. Approaching Balmaceda Airport, which is located in a broad valley, the surface winds were intense. On final descent, a quarter of a mile from the runway threshold, the tower gave me a final wind check: 300 degrees at 41 knots – that works out to about 20 knots of crosswind. My landing was reasonably solid – I think I'm getting better at handling these high winds after all this time in Patagonia. I might forget how to land a plane when the wind is a paltry 10 or 20 knots.

There is aviation gas at Balmaceda, so I had the plane refueled first. In the high surface winds, the weight of the fuel in the wings helps to keep the plane on the ground. Like most places outside the US, there were no tie-down rings so I relied on chocks on all three wheels to keep the plane from blowing away.

There really is no town at Balmaceda, just the airport which has a few LAN flights daily from Santiago and Puerto Montt. The nearest large town is Coihuique (also Coyhuique) some 55 km away. There is a fleet of shuttle vans from the airport to Coihuique which cost 4000 pesos but I think they only show up at the airport to meet commercial flights. If you fly to Balmaceda and want to stay overnight in Coihuique, check the LAN flight schedule so you arrive about the time they do, and the shuttles will be available. I stayed overnight in Coihuique mainly as a way to time my next two flight legs for the clear weather along the volcanoes.

Flying over the Andes Mountain range

Coihuique is a thriving little town and the capital of the Aysen region of Chilean Patagonia. It is situated on the Austral Highway route 7 which winds its way along the Andes and provides access to the many national parks, fantastic scenery, and mountain activities that abound here. There is definitely a lot to see and do in this part of Chile, but unfortunately my time was limited. I think it's worth a future visit.

Puerto Montt

I wanted to depart Balmaceda by 9:00 am, which meant leaving Coihuique no later than 0800 local, well before the fleet of shuttle vans departs to meet the first commercial flights. Because of this, I had to take a taxi for the 55 km ride to the airport which cost 25,000 pesos (about USD$50).

I filed my flight plan in the Operations office, located at the base of the tower at Balmaceda. Even though it was Sunday morning, someone was there. The man there that morning didn't really speak much English, but in the fashion I'd become accustomed to (between his bit

Refueling at Puerto Montt

of English and my bit of Spanish) we got the flight plan for Puerto Montt filed. He also wanted me to fill out a manifest, as I had when departing Punta Arenas, showing me as the pilot and only crew, no passengers. With the paperwork done in about 10–15 minutes, I did my pre-flight check on the plane (only 20-knot surface winds!), started the engine, and taxied to the runway for takeoff.

There is a direct airway route (T102) from Balmaceda to Puerto Montt (airport code SCTE) with a minimum enroute altitude of FL110. It runs right along the slope of the Andes, but as with the previous flight leg, I opted for a route further west over the water, where I expected the air to be smoother. The Andes were still under a blanket of clouds at this point, so flying closer to them would not have yielded better views. I filed an IFR flight plan at an altitude of FL120.

Climbing out of Balmaceda was very bumpy (not a surprise), but as I climbed above FL100 it smoothed out and I had a very nice ride all the way to Puerto Montt. In the section of the flight that cuts almost directly west across the mountains, there were occasional breaks in the clouds, giving me the opportunity to capture a few good photos of the exposed Andes summits.

Northbound, over the water, I passed many islands to the east and west of my route. From time to time I would spot homesteads on these islands or the pens of commercial hatchery operations. Further north I was flying along the eastern shore of Chiloe Island, which, along with nearby islands, had established agricultural activities with farm field boundaries clearly delineated. There were also more ships of various kinds plying the waters, including large cruise ships.

I landed at Puerto Montt via a straight-in approach on runway 35 under a broken cloud layer at about 3,000 feet. Fuel is available at Puerto Montt at a small park-

Volcano Osorno across Lago Llanhuique

ing area beyond the north end of the main ramp. Actually, there is a small taxiway off the main taxiway that leads to the aviation gas fuel pumps. After fueling, I was directed to park at location 9 at the south end of the ramp alongside a King Air. There were also some Cessnas parked there, in what is

Volcano Osorno

apparently the general-aviation section of the ramp, the first small planes I had encountered in a while.

I had wanted to stay in Puerto Varas, an attractive little community on the shores of Lago Llanquihue about 20 km north of Puerto Montt. But unfortunately, all the good places were booked so I stayed in Puerto Montt instead. I had arrived in Puntas Arenas as scheduled so I was able to stay at all the places I pre-booked along the way. However, flying north from Punta Arenas, the trip and schedule were now ad hoc – I hadn't pre-booked anything because I had no idea how long I would be staying in Punta Arenas. It was also the summer high season here, so it wasn't surprising the best places were fully booked.

Although Puerto Montt was not my first choice, it was OK. I arrived on a Sunday afternoon when everyone was out strolling the streets and along the waterfront promenade, enjoying better weather after several days of heavy rain. I turned a corner and came across a small church choir on the sidewalk entertaining passersby with religious songs. I sat and listened for a while – a pleasant way to spend the afternoon. On the walk back to the hotel I came across a McDonald's – the first I'd seen since Buenos Aires. I couldn't resist popping in for cheeseburger. It still amazes me how they can get their food and its taste so consistent across their vast worldwide network.

I did plan one day off here. With great weather predicted, I booked a day-long tour out to Petrohue and Lago Todos Los Santos and then on to Volcano Osorno where I rode the rickety chairlift up to its highest point on its slopes. Osorno is renowned for its classic snow-covered volcano cone shape, rivaling Mt. Fuji in that way. A beautiful blue-sky day meant some great photo opportunities as the tour wound around the valleys and lakes.

Volcano Osorno and its glaciers

There were a few other excursions I would have taken if I had more time. One goes east from Petrohue across three lakes, with roads connecting the lakes, crosses the border into Argentina, and arrives in Bariloche. It takes 12 hours each way, so an overnight stay in Bariloche is required. The second excursion I considered was taking the ferry across to Chiloe Island. This also is a day-long excursion but according to a couple of people I met who had done it, not worth the time. There is some interesting architecture on the island, and some nature reserves, but apparently it's a long day on the road for a relatively minor payoff. My tour to Petrohue and Volcano Osorno, an iconic symbol of this part of Chile, was certainly worthwhile.

Santiago

I planned for a 9:00 am departure from Puerto Montt, pushing me out of the hotel at 8:00 am for a 20-minute taxi ride to the airport. The Operations office at Puerto Montt is in the building under the tower, but has a larger office with a small lounge, a step up compared to Balmaceda. I

Climbing out of Puerto Montt above the clouds

imagine they are more used to general-aviation aircraft of various kinds going through here. Again, they wanted a paper flight plan (the one already filed online was not enough), and a manifest of who was on board the flight – the usual stuff. I was through the Ops office and on the ramp in 10 minutes or so. It occurred to me then that since arriving in Chile, my luggage and I had never been through a scanner at any of the three airports I'd visited, nor my aircraft inspected. I had always gotten back on the ramp through the Operations office where there are no scanners. It certainly makes things easier and is a perfectly practical way to handle general-aviation flights.

I called for engine start-up and my clearance, and they only cleared me partway to Santiago. I was headed for the main international airport at Santiago (airport code SCEL). Because they couldn't know when I'd actually get there to slot me in with other arriving traffic, they told me I'd get further clearances along the way as the flight progressed. I'd elected to go to the main airport at Santiago because N788W was way overdue for an oil change. There is a Cirrus Service Center at the Aerocardal, a general-aviation handler, at Santiago. Of course, N788W is not a Cirrus but a Lancair Columbia; still it has the same IO-550N engine as the Cirrus. Since my plane is rare outside the US, nobody works on it specifically. However, it is possible to find Cirrus service centers, so I elected to take my plane to Aerocardal where presumably they would know the engine.

Volcano flying north to Santiago

I had filed my flight plan for an altitude of FL100. I mostly flew the assigned route except that at one point they gave me routing to the Talagante NDB navigation station. An NDB station is an old-style radio beacon using mediumwave frequencies below the AM radio band. I don't have an NDB receiver on board, but all NDB stations are in the navdata database in the GPS so I could easily dial it up and fly there. From Talagante, ATC gave me radar vectors to the instrument approach for runway 17L at the main airport at Santiago.

Leaving Puerto Montt, I climbed through an overcast cloud layer from 1,500 to 3,500 feet. Above that I was in the clear all the way to Santiago with pretty much neutral winds until the last 150 nm when I picked up a 15-knot headwind. To the east of my flight route, Chile's famous string of volcanoes were laid out in a fashion that very much reminded me of the volcanoes of the

Pacific Northwest from Mount Shasta northward. The airway I was flying was a bit too far away from these mountains to get great photos, but nonetheless it was a very impressive sight. I was glad I waited for a sunny day for this flight leg. Halfway along the flight, the marine layer of clouds below me cleared away and I got good views of the fertile inland valleys that run north and south between the Andes and the coastal hills. Extensive agricultural operations and vast commercial forests were apparent.

Mountains descending into Santiago

It became increasingly warm as I descended into Santiago and landed on 17L at around 1530Z. It was time to leave the parkas and fleeces on the plane. The main airport at Santiago is a large one that I didn't know at all, other than the rudimentary Jeppesen layout diagram, so after I'd taxied off the runway they sent a "Follow Me" truck to lead me to the Aerocardal complex. Aerocardal said they would be able to do the oil change that afternoon or the next day.

As I explained, my original plan was to park the plane in Santiago for about a month, take a commercial flight back to the US, return to pick up the plane, and then fly it back home. I was seeking a secure place to park the plane for that month. I asked Aerocardal about the cost of leaving the plane in their hangar; the cost was very high but not surprising given the value of hangar space at an international airport like this. My alternative plan was to fly the plane to a nearby small airport called Tobalaba (airport code SCTB), which is partly owned by a local aeroclub and has outdoor parking space available for a reasonable price. Once the oil change was done, I planned to move the plane over to Tobalaba.

Short final runway 17L at Santiago

To make the most of returning to a sophisticated city like Santiago, I booked a 16th-floor room at the Marriott Hotel with a great view of the mountains – a nice hotel along Avenida Kennedy with all the modern amenities and a huge shopping complex next door with a wide variety of restaurants. I booked a commercial flight back to Seattle that would give me a few days in Santiago to relax and enjoy the city.

Tobalaba

I was fortunate to have fellow Earthrounder pilot Flemming Pederson put me in touch with Madeleine Dupont de Bock, a well-known pilot and flight instructor in Chile who had done a long solo circumnavigation of the Northern and Southern Hemispheres. She was one of two pilots who flew a single engine piston aircraft into King George Island in Antarctica in 2006, a V-tail Bonanza with ferry tanks and TKS de-icing. I met Madeleine the day I arrived in Santiago and told her I was looking for hangar space for about a month at Tobalaba. She got on the phone and in a short time had found a space for me at a fair price. After the oil change at Santiago I moved the plane over to Tobalaba, put it in the hangar, and gave the owner his deposit.

N788W parked in a hangar at Tobalaba

Having the plane in a locked hangar was a much better option than parking it outside, not so much because of the weather, which generally is pretty great in Santiago, but because of security. With a 3/32-inch hex wrench in hand, an evil pilot could break into my plane and remove a bunch of very expensive avionics without much effort.

I left for Seattle on Saturday, February 23, a hiatus to the USA motivated both by business and personal reasons and by the fact that my FAA medical certificate was about to expire and needed to be renewed. While there were many practical reasons for the hiatus, I was actually forced out of Chile. As a result of my being there, the entire country had run out of pisco sours! I had to leave for a while and give them a chance to replenish their supply. While at home, I had friends over for dinner and, of course, served pisco sours – a pretty good batch. If you don't include the egg white and dash of bitters you're really not serious about a pisco sour. I think I made a few converts.

21

Chile and Easter Island

Sunriver, Oregon

During my five-week absence from Chile, I got a lot done at home I had planned to do, but was also faced with the unexpected task of dealing with the consequences of frozen and burst pipes in my vacation home in Sunriver, Oregon. It was a big mess that occurred in mid-January. I only found out about it when I returned to my home on Bainbridge Island and listened to a message on an answering machine I never access remotely. Fortunately, a contractor working near my Sunriver house noticed monster icicles hanging off the deck, looked through the window, saw the damage, and took the initiative to have the water shut off. Insurance would pay to dry out the house, fix the damage, and restore it to its pre-damage state, less the deductible I had to pay. I got new floors and carpet out of the restoration. Still, one more thing to deal with that I hadn't planned on. This event was the final straw that convinced me to sell the house later in 2013.

Since buying that house in 1996, I'd had great fun staying there – snowboarding on nearby Mt. Bachelor, mountain biking on the dirt roads crisscrossing the National Forest just on the other side of the Deschutes River, hiking South Sister and backpacking to campsites around the pristine mountain lakes in the area. At that time I was living in Eugene. Sunriver was an easy two-hour drive for a spontaneous getaway weekend any time I wanted one. After moving to Bainbridge Island in Washington State, however, I found myself using the Sunriver house less and less, even with the convenience of being able to fly there; Sunriver has a great little airport (airport code S21). I still like Sunriver, but I don't spend enough time there to justify owning a house. It was time to sell it.

Return to Santiago and Easter Island

I flew back to Santiago on March 29 via a pretty efficient flight sequence on American Airlines from Seattle connecting through Dallas. I had booked a short trip to Easter Island, ironically, on Easter Sunday, March 31. As long as I was in this part of the world it made sense to see this curious place. Easter Island is about 2300 nm west of Santiago, a flight that some small planes have made with suitable ferry tanks following the southern round-the-world route. N788W was not outfitted for a journey like this, and there is some question about aviation gas being available at Easter Island anyway, so I jumped on a LAN commercial flight to spend two nights and one full day on Easter Island. I was pleasantly surprised to get upgraded to first class on this flight.

Easter Island Moai at the quarry

Moai with eyes

I booked a day tour that was supposed to be a group tour. However, I was the only one who booked it so it turned into a private tour with the guide throwing in several stops not normally on the itinerary. Of course, the huge stone carved heads (the moai) are the real draw of Easter Island, but their creation is wrapped in a

Moai re-erected along the coastline

strange story of growth, abundance, in-fighting, and ultimately destruction that reduced the Rapa Nui population from a peak of around 15,000 to only a few hundred.

When the first Europeans arrived at Easter Island (on Easter Sunday, 1722) the population of the island had been reduced to 2,000–3,000 and some moai had already been yanked down from their perches during fights between competing clans. The civil wars continued to the point where basically all the moai had been toppled. The moai seen standing today are restorations of the broken and toppled originals – much of the restoration done by the Japanese, oddly enough. Most of the moai photos from Easter Island show blank stone faces, but in fact they all had eyes made of while coral with obsidian for the pupil of the eye. The eyes make them really creepy. I can't imagine walking around centuries ago with these things staring at you as they all faced inland. Currently, only a few of the re-erected moai have had the eyes restored.

As many have done, it's easy to draw parallels between the fate of the Rapa Nui and life in our "global village" on planet Earth. As the population grew on Easter Island, the handful of clans that had divided up the land began to compete for diminishing resources and fight over the limited space. Knocking down another clan's moai was the ultimate humiliation – if you

Crashing surf on Easter Island

managed to break the head off in the process, all the better. By the time the Europeans arrived, the circumstances of the Rapa Nui were much diminished, a plight accelerated when slave ships rounded up the Rapa Nui and sent them to South America and elsewhere. Our global village knows a lot more about what is happening to it than the Rapa Nui did, and what might be done about it, but whether anything *is* done is another matter. It's easier to knock down someone else's "moai."

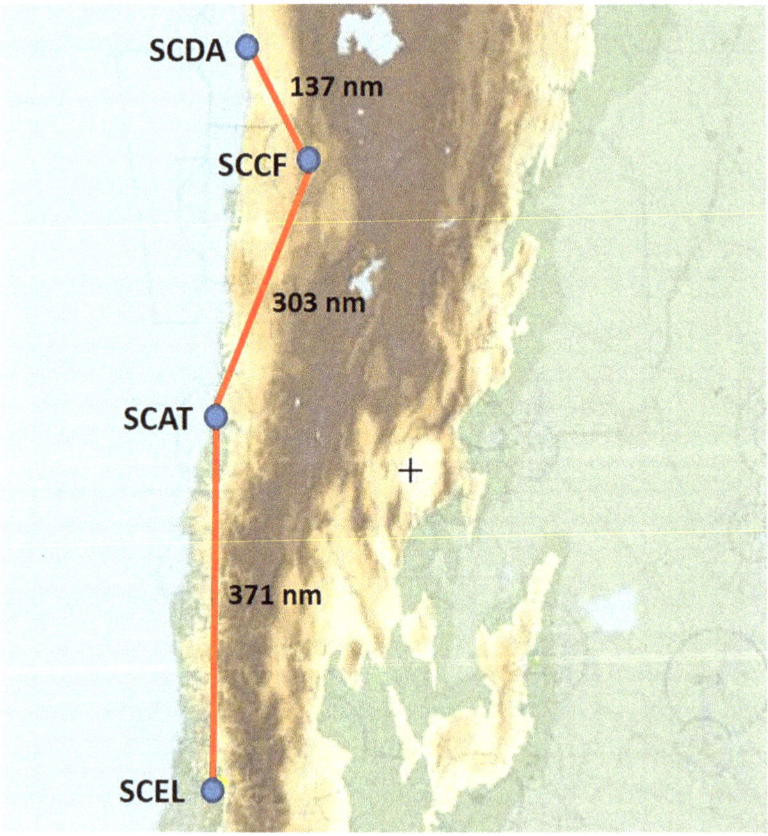

Flight legs from Santiago to Iquique

Currently, Easter Island has a population of about 6,000. Most are from Chile rather than descendants of the Rapa Nui. Almost all make a living from tourism – maybe as fragile an existence as that of the Rapa Nui. Given the apparent affluence of the residents (lots of cars and trucks driving around), I suspect there are significant subsidies from mainland Chile supporting the place.

Beyond looking at the moai, there are adventure tours of all kinds on Easter Island and the usual "how the people lived" cultural venues. Having seen many primitive cultures in my overseas travels, I really don't have much remaining interest in ceremonial villages and learning how they ground up their food or how they buried their dead. The moai are the unique, extraordinary feature at Easter Island and definitely worth seeing.

Calama and San Pedro de Atacama

After Easter Island, I was finally back in the cockpit. Rudder pedals, side stick, instruments and gauges – it all looked familiar, all these things must do something. I picked up the plane at Tobalaba on April 3 and flew north to Calama, Chile (airport code SCCF), gateway to the Atacama Desert, the driest place on earth. The guys at Tobalaba had pulled N788W out of the hangar that morning so it was ready to fly. The engine started with no problem. When I re-fueled at the pump along the main taxiway, I found this was one of the few airports on this trip that accepted payment for fuel via credit card.

I had a quandary for this 725 nm flight. I could not confirm that aviation gas was available at Calama. The next flight leg after Calama to Iquique, Chile (airport code SCDA), was only 150

Coast en-route to Atacama

nm, so technically well within the range of N788W with full tanks. But if Iquique was closed from some reason, the alternate was another 150 nm away. Tobalaba is at an elevation of 2129 feet, and the runway is only about 3700 feet long, and the temperature was hot. Being conservative, I did not want to put fuel in my cargo tank and take off overweight on a hot day from this relatively short runway. In general, the length of the runway an airplane needs to take off safely increases with increasing elevation, increasing temperature, and increasing weight. A headwind blowing down the runway helps a plane take off, so this can mitigate the other factors to some extent. I decided to be prudent. I left the cargo tank empty, filled the wing tanks, and planned to make an intermediate stop to refuel at Atacama (airport code SCAT). I therefore filed two flight plans at FL120, one from Tobalaba to Atacama and the second from Atacama to Calama.

Valle de la Luna, San Pedro de Atacama

Tobalaba has no instrument approaches, but it does have three Standard Instrument Departures that go to a navigation station named AMB. They cleared me for one of those, then cleared me further up the coast to the Atacama Airport. There was a low cloud deck over the coast extending inland, so I really didn't see much during this flight leg.

I wanted a quick fuel stop at Atacama but I got delayed. The fueling itself was quick, but when I went to the Operations office to file the flight plan for the second leg to Calama, I got in an argument with the DGAC people about flight payments, aggravated to some extent by the language barrier. It turns out when I arrived in Punta Arenas on January 25th, I paid for just 30 days of use of the Chilean airports and ATC system. I thought I had paid for 90 days because the piece of paper they gave me from Customs (Aduanas) allowed me to stay 90 days. I learned they are two different things.

Anyway, it costs about 22,000 pesos (about US$50 at the time) for each 30-day period. When I finally understood this, I paid another 44,000 pesos for the additional two 30-day periods during which I had parked my plane in Chile, and was now flying again since my return. I apologized in my broken Spanish for arguing about it; it was totally my misunderstanding.

The northern part of Chile is an incredible desert, especially interesting because it starts at such a high elevation that eventually descends right down to sea level. There were desert peaks

Llama in the high desert

above me as I flew along the coast at FL130. There were rich colors, deep canyons, and vast plains crossed by stream beds that may not have seen water for a hundred years.

I was also now using my oxygen bottle, required for aircrew on flights of more than 30 minutes above 12,500 feet. I hadn't used it so far on this entire trip. I have an oximeter that clips on my finger and gives my specific oxygen absorption rate as well as pulse. Any absorption rate below 90% is cause for concern and may indicate a looming oxygen deficiency and impaired judgment. I'd never seen my rate fall below 92% with or without supplemental oxygen.

The elevation of the airport at Calama is 7,613 feet, the highest airport I have flown to in N788W. The highest airport where I had previously landed, years before in my Piper Archer II, was Taos, New Mexico, at 7,095 feet. Given the temperature, pressure, and humidity levels when I landed at Calama, the density altitude was more than 10,000 feet. Density altitude is the actual elevation corrected for temperature and barometric pressure to give a value that is relevant to how the airplane performs; i.e. the actual elevation may be 7,613 feet but the airplane performs as if it were at 10,000 feet.

The airport was under construction, with the DGAC office temporarily located in blue trailers east of the main terminal. Chatting with the DGAC guy on arrival, I found out there was aviation gas at Calama but not immediately available at the airport. A phone call could be made to have a truck come to the airport for refueling.

4x4 truck rented at Calama

Calama has the look of a boomtown from the western US. That's not surprising since the multi-year worldwide boom in copper demand has brought riches to Calama. It was definitely suffering growing pains with huge new shopping malls served by an inadequate road system. The nearby Chuquicamata open pit copper mine is the largest in the world. I didn't go for a tour, though you can, but from miles away as I flew in I could see the rising smoke and dust from operations there.

For the first time on this trip I rented a car, actually a 4-wheel drive Hilux pickup. Most of the rental car inventory at Calama airport was 4x4 pickups of one type or another, a very practical choice for this desert country with many gravel roads.

After a comfortable night at a Calama hotel, I headed south in the truck to San Pedro de Atacama, a small town with mostly adobe buildings housing a wide variety of hostels, tour operators, and tourist shops. Beyond that veneer

Volcano Lincancabur near San Pedro de Atacama

there are authentic things to see here – the beautiful decaying chapel is one of them. There are also natural wonders outside of town that I visited, like the Valle de la Luna, the flamingo sanctuary, and the high volcanic desert.

In the center of San Pedro de Atacama is a very interesting museum of artifacts from the many groups of people that have populated this area over the centuries. Some had direct contact with the Incas to the north in Peru. Some had learned to smelt copper, the first people to exploit the easily available metal resource lying at the surface in these mountains.

There is also a human-built wonder nearby at the recently

Chapel at San Pedro de Atacama

inaugurated ALMA project, a deep-space millimeter wave radio observatory located 15 miles southeast of San Pedro de Atacama. No tours were available here though. There is also a small paved airstrip at San Pedro de Atacama with absolutely nothing around it and no services.

It was fun ripping around the desert in the diesel Hilux. I managed not to get stuck, a good thing since cellphone coverage was almost non-existent. San Pedro de Atacama is also a lively little hamlet with many travelers from all over the world hanging out. I regretted not staying here instead of in Calama.

Iquique

I flew to Iquique because I thought it was the farthest north Airport of Entry in Chile so an appropriate place to exit Chile and fly to Peru. As it turns out, you can also enter and exit Chile at Arica, right on the border with Peru. Iquique is a very popular beach town with many hotels and condominium buildings overlooking the water. The flight was only about 150 nm from Calama. I flew this leg VFR to avoid climbing to the high minimum IFR altitudes on such a short flight. The guy at the DGAC office in Calama the morning I left was a character. He pointed at the chart on the wall to an active "Restricted" military area and said "No va aqui – pow, pow, pow!" I managed to avoid the "Restricted" zone and not get shot down en-route to Iquique.

The fuel stand at Iquique is at the far south end of the airport. Parking for me was at the far north end of the airport, the north ramp. Iquique Airport is very spread out – walking to the terminal from the parking area is a long distance, and given the busy cargo operations along the way, they probably wouldn't let me walk it anyway. However, the DGAC did provide a "Follow Me" car that led me to the fuel stand and after fueling, to the parking area. When I unloaded my bags, he then drove me to the terminal.

Refueling at Iquique

With the short flight done in the morning, I had the afternoon to preview the formalities I needed to complete the following morning to exit Chile for my flight to Peru. Unfortunately, the preview only raised concerns. There are a large number of international cargo flights out of Iquique but almost no passenger flights. Of those, most go via Santiago to get some place else, so are not international flights. This created a concern about whether the Immigration Police would be available to stamp my passport when I wanted to leave early the next morning. I checked airport information, which seemed to indicate that two hours' prior notice

Ocean terminal en-route to Iquique

was required. Customs was supposedly available 24 hours a day, but the Aduanas office I found on the Arrival floor of the airport in the early afternoon was closed and dark. The number I called for them just had an answering machine.

I spent the afternoon making phone calls, trying to sort out what would happen the next day on departure and get prior notice to the Policia (if that's what was needed), but my limited Spanish was a hindrance. I really needed to get to Lima on

April 6th since I'd booked a flight/hotel/train for April 7th to Cusco and then Machu Picchu. If I didn't get there on the 6th, that whole side trip would be screwed up. I was even willing to pay a handler to help in the morning but I couldn't find one that was available and spoke English.

I was filing for a departure time of 9:00 am so I decided to get to the airport early at 7:30 am to get things sorted out then. Given all my experience to date with exiting countries with the plane, I was confident it wouldn't be a big problem, especially in Chile since it had been very reasonable and accommodating thus far. The airport at Iquique is far from town, about 30 minutes, a 15,000-peso taxi ride. I was out of the hotel at 7:00 am. The weather was forecast to be good all day, so even if my departure was delayed by getting exit formalities done, I could still easily get to Lima on the 6th.

22

Peru and Machu Picchu

Lima

I arrived at the Iquique airport at 7:30 am as planned. The taxi dropped me at the base of the tower, which looked new. Alongside the tower is a one-story building, also new, where I presumed the DGAC Operations office was located. The sun was barely up and I had to try a few doors to find one that was unlocked. I wandered around for a few minutes until I came upon the right office. Inside was a bright young woman who, in two minutes, resolved my concerns from yesterday afternoon. She'd already printed out the online filed version of my flight plan and was on the phone to the terminal to notify Customs and Immigration that I would be coming over soon. She asked me to fill out the paper flight plan form, no surprise, but this time she stamped and signed it and told me I needed to get it signed and stamped by Customs and bring it back. She called one of the DGAC ramp guys who came by with a truck to take me to the terminal. The Customs office is not where I had gone the day before. It's located on the second level at the far right end of the ticket counters as you face the counters. They stamped and signed the flight plan form, and also in the box marked "Salida" (exit), signed and stamped the Customs form I had received at Punta Arenas. They then kept that form as a record of when the plane had arrived in, and departed, Chile.

The last thing I needed was Immigration (the Policia International) to stamp my passport and collect my entry form, a small piece of paper I received when I arrived in the country. This took a little more doing, but the police at the security checkpoint latched on to a guy who seemed to have the run of the airport and a big stack of keys. He disappeared for five minutes then came back and directed me to a typical Immigration kiosk where a young woman had magically appeared. She went through the normal exit passport stamping routine and I was finished, and very glad I was getting out on time. I walked down a convenient jet way to the ramp via the side stairs where the DGAC guy took me back to Operations. I turned in my stamped flight plan form, and then was taken to my plane. I actually took off at 9:10 am so arriving at the Operations office at 7:30 am was just about right.

Flight legs from Iquique to Guayaquil

I had filed an IFR flight plan at an altitude of FL100. On departure, though, they gave me a clearance directly to a navigation station in Peru that shortened the flight a bit. I expected more desert as I climbed out and that's what I saw. Entering Peru airspace was seamless: there was no confusion about the landing or overflight permit as some pilots have experienced. I now always include the number of the landing/overflight permit in the Remarks section of the flight plan form.

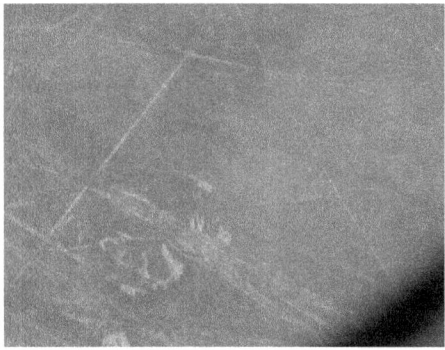

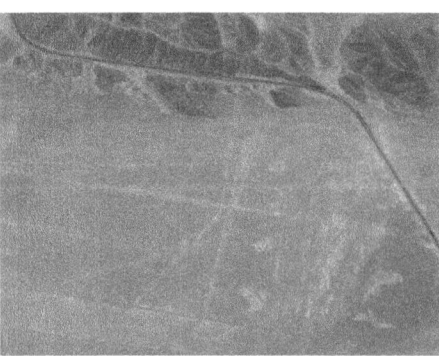

Nazca Lines in Peru

The main point of interest I was looking for on this flight leg was a glimpse of the Nazca Lines just northwest of the waypoint called ERISA, which was on my flight plan route. I climbed up to FL120 to get over some terrain just south of ERISA then asked for and was cleared to FL080. I didn't know the protocol here, but there was no radar coverage, so lingering a bit in the area to get a view of the Nazca Lines seemed reasonable. It was clear enough to get some photos, including one with a tour airplane circling at a much lower altitude. There are organized flying tours of the Lines which apparently depart from the small airport located at the town of Nazca. They fly at a much lower altitude, affording them a closer look at these curious drawings of enormous scale that stretch across the land.

These lines have been an enduring source of speculation about whether they were constructed by extraterrestrials centuries ago for navigation and landing purposes, because it's hard to make sense of them unless you're flying overhead. It turns out, though, that you actually can make out the designs from the tops of surrounding hills. So local tribes would have had their own artistic or other motivation to make them. Moreover, extraterrestrials with technology sophisticated enough to come to the Earth from a faraway planet would not need crude scratchings on the Earth's surface for landing or navigation. A similar argument can be made to dismiss the idea that the pyramids in Egypt were constructed by aliens as navigation markers.

After the Nazca Lines, I had about 200 nm to fly to get to Lima, via Pisco on the coast. The sky was clear blue during the whole flight so I opted for a visual approach instead of an instrument approach on runway 15 at Lima (airport code SPIM). It was hot, but I was glad to have arrived on schedule. My side trip to Cusco and Machu Picchu, which began the following day, would not be derailed.

I decided to use a handler at Lima at the last minute because I'd read varying accounts of the difficulty of dealing with this airport. If it weren't for the planned side trip to Cusco via a commercial flight leaving from Lima, I probably would have considered stopping in either Pisco or Trujillo as a fuel stop, the only

River valley en-route to Lima

other two places in Peru that have aviation gas, I'm told. Both are smaller, but are Airports of Entry, and no doubt are easier to get around. By email I did negotiate a lower fee for handling but it was still around US$400. There is no real general-aviation terminal or ramp at Lima: a little surprising. I was directed by the tower to park in an area where an odd assortment of old military planes was parked along with some corporate jets. There is a small group of transient parking stands numbered 71, 72, 73…

With the handler, I quickly got through Immigration and Customs. The handlers generally have pass cards to get in the back doors around large terminals, which streamlines access. I questioned him about where everything was, so I could do this myself if I ever returned, but without a pass card I'm not sure how I would manage. The handler was not particularly helpful explaining the layout and sequence of stops we made.

I stayed at the hotel at the airport since my flight to Cusco was early the next morning and I heard Lima traffic can be a nightmare. I didn't want to risk missing my flight, stuck in traffic in a taxi. The hotel at the airport is very convenient but far too expensive for what it is.

Cusco and Machu Picchu

Flying to Cusco on a commercial flight is much quicker and cheaper than it would be in my plane. The weather is often cloudy over the mountains between Lima and Cusco. The required minimum altitudes are typically at FL230, higher than my plane can fly.

Arriving in Cusco early in the day, I had a chance to wander around a bit. Cusco turned out to be more interesting and attractive than I had expected, with the center consisting of several old but well-maintained colonial-style buildings. I booked two nights in a hotel near the main plaza with the full day in between dedicated to going to Machu Picchu.

Machu Picchu is actually northwest of Cusco and at a much lower altitude. From Cusco there is a four-hour train ride to Aguas Calientes, the station stop for Machu Picchu. From Aguas Calientes, a 30-minute bus ride takes you up a switchback road to Machu Picchu itself. However, the first part of the rail line

Machu Picchu – the classic view

near Cusco had recently suffered damage due to heavy storms so the first third of the journey was traveled on a bus provided by Peru Rail to an intermediate station where we then boarded the train. The train is small and the journey slow along a river canyon with occasional interesting views. The train was fairly full even in this relatively off-season time. I had booked my round-trip ticket ahead of time online at the PeruRail website.

At Aguas Calientes the exit from the train station leads directly into a rabbit warren of a marketplace with no clear path to the place where the buses leave to ascend the hill to Machu Picchu. I wandered around town for a few minutes until I found a bridge across the river that led to the ticket office and bus stop for the ride to Machu Picchu itself.

The Peruvians restrict the number of visitors daily to Machu

Machu Picchu terraces

Machu Picchu

Picchu. It's a good idea to check the website to see if it will be overrun on the day you plan to visit. At the time of my visit Machu Picchu was limited to 2500 visitors a day, so many bought their tickets online where you will also find out the number of tickets still available for the day you want to go. I didn't do this, but it was no problem – there were still around 1200 tickets available for the day I traveled there. I bought a ticket at the office in Aguas Calientes that was poorly marked and a little difficult to find. I also picked up a nice walking map of Machu Picchu at this office, which few people seemed to have; they wouldn't have had the map if they had booked online and had not gone to this ticket office. The cost of the ticket was S/.128 (Peruvian Sols) which was about US$40 at the time. From there I went to buy a bus ticket for another S/.48 round trip. There are many buses making this 30-minute trip, one leaving every 5 to 10 minutes.

Nazca Lines in Peru

I won't go into any of the history of Machu Picchu. There's plenty of information online and numerous guidebooks that explain it all in detail. Given its world-famous significance, I was concerned that I hadn't left enough time to see the place by just allocating one afternoon. I was wrong. By the time the bus got up the hill to Machu Picchu, it was 1:00 pm. My return train to Cusco left at 5:27 pm, so I had the whole afternoon, which turned out to be plenty of time. In two hours wandering around the ruins you can see all the high points. Many people up there were just sitting around eating lunch on the grass. Others groups were being lead around by tour guides. I found the places where the iconic photos of Machu Picchu have been taken so I felt like I'd experienced the best of it though no doubt I missed many interesting details that a guided tour might have provided.

Machu Picchu – tightly fitted stonework

I took the bus back down the hill to Aguas Calientes. Many people I'd seen walking around Machu Picchu were now wandering the little streets and tourist shops, or sitting in restaurants, essentially killing time until the train left for Cusco. Aguas Calientes is one of the most tourist-oriented hamlets I'd ever seen, perched as it is in a narrow canyon straddling the river, with trinket shops and restaurants and small hotels crammed into almost every viable space. It's not particularly attractive, but not surprising given the draw of Machu Picchu. Clearly, Machu Picchu is their "rice bowl" and they have to make the most of it.

Returning from Machu Picchu on the train, I met a beguiling young American woman who had an unquenchable enthusiasm for traveling, for the sights and sounds and people of the places she'd visited around the world. Curiously, though, she claimed to be from New York originally, but because she lacked any trace of an accent I suspected that was a lie. She also appeared to have some hideous skin disease on her legs; as she sat down next to me I wondered whether she was contagious. She turned out to be contagious in many ways.

Dusk faded to darkness as the train rolled southeast back to Cusco so it wasn't possible to see anything interesting outside. A surprise fashion show set to rhythmic local music made the journey a little livelier. The train personnel were showing off a variety of alpaca apparel and tourist trinkets, not of any interest to me. Occasionally, a guy dressed like some sort of hairy goblin with an evil mask danced up and down the aisle between wardrobe changes, shaking his wooden staff festooned with colored cloth at the passengers. The regulars riding the train picked up the spirit of it all, clapping along with the music and feigning distress at the goblin's antics.

As the train continued along the narrow, winding rail line carved between the Rio Vilcanota and the mountainside, from time to time rocks would cascade onto

Waiting to take off at Lima

the roof of our car from the cliff overhead. Nobody seemed bothered by this, but taken together with the goblin, the insistent music, the fashion show, the darkness, and my train companion's bewildering saga, the whole scene was a little strange.

As we had on the outbound trip, because of flooded tracks we transferred from the train to a bus along the way. We finally arrived in Cusco around 11 at night under a dazzling canopy of stars pivoting around the Southern Cross and the celestial South Pole.

My flight back to Lima left the next morning. I wished I had planned another day in Cusco. There are several interesting places to see in the city and nearby. The population is easy-going and judging by the large number of young backpacking travelers of all nationalities I saw and talked to, it's a popular place to hang out in Peru.

Guayaquil

The excursion to Cusco and Machu Picchu was the last side trip I had planned for this South America adventure. I had already visited Ecuador several times in the past, notably during a trip to the Galapagos Islands in 2007. These famous islands are definitely worth visiting when in Ecuador. From here on I was going to make my way back north and home as expeditiously as possible.

I got the handler at the Lima airport going early for a 9:00 am departure. When I'd arrived a few days before, there would have been a long wait (one hour) to get the fuel truck out to my plane, so rather than stand around on the ramp in the heat, I broke my rule and agreed to re-fuel the morning of my departure. The handler was on the job that morning, though, and the minute I arrived at the plane for the pre-flight inspection the fuel truck showed up too, so it all worked out. I paid for the fuel, the handler, and the airport fees in US dollars on the spot. The airport fees (parking, landing, navigation for the entire length of Peru) added up to several hundred dollars – much more expensive than Chile, Argentina, or Brazil.

Refueling at Guayaquil

I filed an IFR flight plan to Guayaquil (airport code SEGU) at FL100. My route essentially went north along the coast of Peru before cutting across the western edge "bulge" of South America to arrive at Guayaquil in southern Ecuador. Taxiing out to the runway at Lima, I had to join the queue behind several commercial jets taking off ahead of me. With that delay, and waiting on inbound traffic to land, it was 20 minutes after engine start before I actually took off. They gave me the standard departure procedure they give everyone departing runway 15, but because I was slower than the commercial jets, they soon got me off of that routing and gave me a vector heading of 270 degrees, essentially straight out to sea. After the faster traffic behind me cleared out, they gave me a heading back on course northbound.

This flight was pretty uneventful. I was well above low clouds and most of what I saw was a continuation of the dry desert landscape I'd seen south of Lima. As I got to the border with Ecuador, more greenery appeared and along with it some cloud buildups I had to work around. After contacting Guayaquil approach, I descended through the bumpy clouds, following vectors to intercept the approach course on runway 21. The vectors had sent me far to the north to put me in sequence behind other landing traffic.

At Guayaquil there actually is a real general-aviation ramp and terminal close to the south end of the airport. I pulled in there and parked. I had negotiated a price for handling services by email before arriving here (it was getting cheaper and cheaper!). I told them I wanted fuel immediately when I arrived, so as I shut down the engine the fuel truck pulled up. Yes! This is the way it should work, and maybe an advantage to having the handler call the truck. I paid for the fuel in US money on the spot. US dollars happen to be the official currency in Ecuador anyway.

The handler said they used to have Immigration and Customs available at the little general-aviation terminal 30 meters from where I parked the plane, but that service had recently been discontinued. We had to get in a vehicle and drive to the main terminal for processing. There is an entry door off the ramp for air crew (by Puente 18, I think) that leads straight to Immigration, then past that into Customs, where my luggage was run through a scanner. Scanning arriving luggage is something that had become common in South America airports. From there it was out the door and into a taxi to the hotel. There are many comfortable business hotels a five-minute drive from the terminal. I was only staying one night so I didn't choose to stay at any place special.

I had been in Ecuador and Guayaquil a few times before, going back as far as 1982, so I had no inclination for sightseeing. They have accomplished some impressive improvements here in recent years, however, in particular upgrading and restoring the old city center and building the Malecon, a long, very modern promenade along the banks of the Guyas River within easy walking distance of the old city center.

As the afternoon rain deluge and thunderstorms began, I spent my time reviewing the weather forecasts and patterns for tomorrow's flight, which would take me 850 nm to Cartagena, Colombia (airport code SKCG). Once again I would be crossing the Inter-Tropical Convergence Zone and the thunderstorms and bad weather usually found there.

23
North to the USA

Cartegena

To get an earlier start ahead of potentially bad weather, I moved my departure time up to 8:00 am. I got up at 6:00 am, opened my notebook computer, and started checking the weather along my route across the Inter-Tropical Convergence Zone to Cartagena. The clear, dry days I had experienced so far flying north along the west coast of South America would be coming to an end.

When I evaluate the weather, I usually start by looking at the METARs (current weather observations at airports) and TAFs (weather forecasts for 24 hours in the area around an airport) on the Aviation Weather Center website listed in Appendix B. I looked at weather reports and predictions at both the departure and destination airports and at any other airports along the route. Unfortunately, along my route there were essentially no airports with area forecasts and only a few with current weather observations – not enough information to construct a picture of the weather along my route.

I next looked at the AC weather network website, also listed in Appendix B, at the page specific to South and Central America. This site is a compendium of different forecast sources including Jeppesen, US, and other government sources. The US government high level (above FL250) maps showed a gap in forecast thunderstorm activity along my route up to 1800Z (Greenwich Mean Time). The Jeppesen forecast map showed potential isolated thunderstorm activity everywhere. Other maps here showed recent lightning activity along my route.

Finally I look at the Weather Underground website, also listed in Appendix B. The maps shown on this website provide a very useful satellite view of cloud formations, current and past. The cloud formations are colored according to how high they are. Red, purple, and white clusters indicate very tall cloud buildups, a pretty reliable indication of thunderstorm activity. Unfortunately, as I evaluated the map the morning of my flight I saw a couple of orange and red cells situated along my route. The weather patterns I'd seen, though, usually had the buildups coming in the afternoon, maturing into thunderstorms with rain in the evening and at night, then dissipating in the morning from cooler night air. The whole pattern repeats day after day.

From this perspective, I expected the tall cells along my route as shown on Weather Underground to dissipate rather than build up as the morning progressed. I checked the map again every 30 minutes as I got ready to leave for the airport, and again after I arrived at the airport, using my iPad connected to the WiFi hotspot in the handler's office. The buildups did seem to be breaking up, so I delayed departing until 9:00 am. This approach worked out well. By the time I got to the last locations shown for the weather cells, there was nothing remaining except lingering high cloud layers.

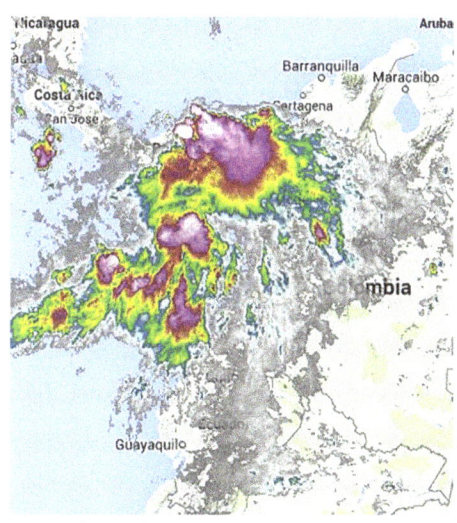

Typical Weather Underground satellite image of cloud formations over Colombia

For the flight to Cartagena (airport code SKCG) I filed an IFR flight plan at FL100. The flight plan route of 842 nm followed the coast and stayed out of the mountains. Instead of dry desert, I was now flying over flat green jungle as I continued north. Brown rivers twisted their way through the greenery with occasional hamlets and fishing villages situated along the bends. Clouds were building up to the east over the mountains where Cali and Bogota are

Flight legs from Guayaquil to Key West

located. I was in the clear until about 200 nm south of Cartegena when I had to start flying some wide diversions and climb to FL120 to avoid new cloud buildups. VHF communications coverage was pretty good generally on this route, as it was throughout South America. However, there were some gaps at the point where I needed diversions.

Finally in VHF radio range of Cartagena, I made contact with ATC who cleared me for the instrument approach to runway 01. Even though technically

I was flying in VFR conditions (I was not in the clouds), it was very hazy so I actually had to fly the instrument approach just to find the airport. Runway 01 appeared through the haze about four miles out.

They have a nice general-aviation ramp at Cartagena where several other small planes and jets were parked when I arrived. I

Cloudy weather en-route to Cartegena

think Cartagena is a standard stop for light aircraft coming across the Caribbean flying north or south. I engaged a handler at Cartagena, the cost now down to US$225. That's pretty much what I'm willing to pay anywhere at an Airport of Entry to smooth the way through Immigration and Customs and deal with any other local requirements.

The night before my flight I was notified via Skyplan –who obtains my landing permits – that their Colombia agent advised me to make sure I did the notifications required for entering, landing in, and departing Colombia. I had the landing permit but apparently these notifications were in addition to that. I had no idea what this was about, since no other pilot account I had read of flying in Colombia mentioned these notifications. However, it did sound similar to the multiple notifications required for flying into Australia.

Thinking this was just a ploy by the handler to get me to hire them, I checked via email with a competing handler at Cartagena to see whether these notification requirements were really necessary. They said yes. I hired the handler who then made the notifications, which turned out to include (1) notification of entry into Colombia airspace, (2) notification of intention to land, (3) notification of arrival, (4) notification to the anti-drug police to inspect the airplane, and (5) notification of departure.

Before engaging the handler, I asked if there was a website

Village along a river in Colombia

Cartagena old town

where I could do the notifications myself. He pointed me to a website for the Customs service explaining how to do these notifications, but the website was entirely in Spanish and incomprehensible to me. So as I write this I can't offer any useful advice about the notifications. They may be important and it may be risky not to do them. Or it may be like Australia where pilots show up in-country without any notifications and it's all worked out after arrival; other than getting scolded by the local officials, it's not a serious offense.

Cartagena is a famous old colonial trading/military outpost, a classic walled city with restored battlements. There are slick new resorts along the beach outside of the old walls, but for me the only interesting place to stay is in the old city inside the walls. I booked a small boutique hotel there: nothing special, but comfortable and in a perfect location. I had the afternoon to wander around taking photos while scouting out a place

Cartagena old town

for dinner. I watched a spectacular sunset from the top of a battlement and then headed off to dinner at a great restaurant facing one of the several small plazas scattered around the old city. It was one of the best meals I'd had on the trip, and given the charm and character of the buildings around me, I regretted not staying in Cartegena longer than one night. Cartagena is actually an easy 900 nm flight from Key West with a fuel stop (if needed) in Jamaica, so it is more accessible than you'd think given the fact that it's in South America.

I was very happy to be north of the thunderstorms and other difficult weather associated with the Inter-Tropical Convergence Zone in Colombia. Checking the forecast for the next day along my route north across the

Caribbean, I saw nothing but blue skies for my 530 nm flight north to Montego Bay in Jamaica.

Montego Bay

The flight to Montego Bay (airport code MKJS) in Jamaica was relatively short but almost all of it was across the Caribbean Sea. The forecast was sublime – no clouds or weather in the picture. The flight route was the easiest on the trip, just one airway.

I filed an IFR flight plan at FL100. They gave me the departure procedure, which essentially sent me straight north after takeoff to the first waypoint called VARON on the G430 airway. Once again, it was very hazy climbing out of Cartagena up to about 7,000 feet. I had no useful horizon and for me that meant flying by instruments even though I could see the ocean below me.

Cartagena city wall

I filed for FL100, they assigned me 10,000 feet, and they gave me a barometer setting of 1013 (29.92 inches) so I reported level at 10,000 feet at waypoints along the route. I really don't know what the transition altitude is around here unless they have adopted the US standard of 18,000 feet. They cleared me direct to a waypoint called KILER, a little over halfway to Jamaica. I had an easy cruise above the water, with large whitecaps visible below. I expected to lose VHF radio contact at some point, so I was surprised when I was able to maintain communication with Colombia (Barranquilla Control) all the way to KILER,

Short final runway 07 at Montego Bay

where Kingston Control in Jamaica could pick me up. Most likely, they're using high elevation VHF antenna sites on both sides to extend their coverage areas.

Arriving over Jamaica at around noon I had some clouds to descend through en-route direct to a waypoint called OMAXI, the final fix for the instrument approach on runway 07 at Montego Bay.

Arrival at Montego Bay

I had contacted the local FBO, IAM Jet Center, ahead of time by email. They were waiting for me when I arrived and had the fuel truck on the way. Immigration and Customs is available right in the Jet Center so it was very easy getting to the street. IAM promotes itself as a FBO with a modest fee (US$75) for handling but they charged additional fees for all kinds of other things. It is sort of a "transition" general-aviation service, a transition between expensive full-service handlers in South America and the free general-aviation services typically found in the US.

Beach and ocean from hotel room terrace

As a treat, I splurged on a high-end resort along the beach east of the airport. There seemed to be many gaggles of well-dressed people around this place, the kind of beach resort where people get married on the beach or in the tropical courtyard. Maybe I could have found a wedding to crash, but sadly I left my jacket and tie at home – not needed in Antarctica – so I doubted I could fit in as a long-lost uncle. It was relaxing but expensive there, full-blown upscale civilization lubricated by and for people with a lot of money.

Key West

I spent one day more than planned at Montego Bay, partly because it was a nice place but also because the Customs office hours at Key West Airport (airport code KEYW) had changed and they were now closed on Sundays. Their advertised hours at the time were 8 am to 8 pm, Monday to Saturday, so I delayed departure from Montego Bay until Monday. I had been through Customs at Key West many years ago when returning from the Cayman Islands and it went pretty smoothly then. I was hoping for a similar experience this time.

I got my Cuban overflight permit via Skyplan, who had done all my permits, but this time there was confusion about the route. I filed an IFR flight plan at 10,000 feet. At the last minute (my engine was already started), the Cubans rejected the routing. Instead, Montego tower gave me a clearance along the G430 airway, which doesn't go to Key West but goes north toward Miami and terminates at a waypoint called TANIA just inside the Miami-controlled airspace. I really didn't know how this was supposed to work, but I figured I'd sort it out with Miami Center when I was talking to them.

Island off the north coast of Cuba

I had clear weather going north, but low clouds over Cuba so I couldn't really get any good photos. When I flew to the Cayman Islands in 2005, the Cuban VHF radios were very bad – we had to do communication relays between planes approaching and departing Cuban airspace. Their radar was somewhat better than their radios. I'm happy to report this has all dramatically improved. As soon as Jamaica handed me over to Havana Center, I had solid radar contact and VHF communications with them until they turned me over to Miami Center.

Landing at Key West – almost back in the USA

Apparently, there were several US Military Warning Areas active the day of my flight to Key West. Many of the flights were out of the naval air station east of Key West which complicated my flight route somewhat. But after passing north of the Cuban coast, the Havana controller in consultation with Miami gave me a direct routing to a waypoint called TADPO, then directly to Marathon to avoid the Warning Areas, followed by direct to Key West. Key West approach control gave me vectors for a visual approach to runway 27. On the radio I was hearing repeated traffic alerts for F-15s and other military aircraft taking off – not the usual thing you hear.

In the Customs box at Key West

After landing at Key West, I taxied to the box outlined on the ramp in front of the Customs building at the very east end of the runway. When I'd called that morning to notify them I was coming, they'd asked me to stay in the plane until they came out, but I opened the door because it was beastly hot in the cockpit once I stopped moving. The Customs guy was nice, and he asked all the right questions. He looked at my passport and gave me permission to step out of the plane. We spent five minutes at the plane but he didn't really search it, just looked inside. I didn't need to fill out any forms – not even the standard Customs arrival form. We then went into the building where they scanned and stamped my passport and I was done. Ten minutes start to finish: amazing!

Fort Lauderdale

After passing through Customs at Key West, I took off again right away, since I didn't need fuel. This time I was flying VFR back to Fort Lauderdale Executive Airport (airport code KFXE) and Banyan FBO which had been the departure point for this trip on January 2. My weather radar display was now working again, since I was once again inside the XM satellite coverage footprint. It showed several rain showers and buildups along my short route to Fort Lauderdale, which confirmed what I could see ahead of me. It was so great to have my cockpit weather resources back. I worked my way over and around the buildups, then dropped down and called Miami approach to get vectored into Fort Lauderdale.

I've only been in and out of this airport a few times, but it was much busier that day than I had ever seen it. They were trying to land and take off on crossing runways 08 and 13 by interleaving traffic. This is tricky enough when the traffic is all commercial jets with similar approach profiles, but with an odd mix of traffic from C172 trainers to planes like mine to King Airs to small jets, all with different approach speeds, it is a nightmare. The woman in the tower was a little rattled. I had a King Air on my tail so I was going 15 knots faster than my normal approach speed. The tower told me "minimum time on runway." I touched down going fast and abused the brakes getting off the runway as quickly as I could.

The US is a wide-open place for flying compared to other countries, but the downside is a lot of traffic, to the point that some busy airports like Fort Lauderdale ought to limit or prohibit students doing laps in the pattern or practicing instrument approaches. I don't know how that would work, but quieter airports are better suited for training than a busy one like Fort Lauderdale Executive.

While in Montego Bay I had decided I simply had too much to do at home to spend the two or three days it would take to fly the plane home right away. Consequently, I decided to park the plane at Banyan for a couple of weeks and fly back on a commercial flight from Fort Lauderdale-Hollywood Airport (airport code KFLL) to Seattle. With that schedule, I could take my time later on the return flight across the country and see a few new places rather than rush it right then. Flights to Seattle from Fort Lauderdale are surprisingly cheap, and I could park my plane outside on the ramp at Banyan for an entire month for only $185.

24

Westward and Home

Flying West

I returned to Fort Lauderdale on April 28, 2013. The next day I picked up my plane at Fort Lauderdale Executive Airport and headed west on an IFR flight plan. I'd flown this Gulf Coast route a few times, so really had no interest in stopping anywhere to look around. I did need fuel stops, however, so the first stop I just picked off the map at Hammond, Louisiana (airport code KHDC). It was about the right distance and the general-aviation terminal there, Hammond Air Center, had great reviews on the AirNav website that has general information about airports across the country. As the guy at Hammond was fueling my plane, he saw the "Earthrounders" decal on the side next to the door. He told me he had always wanted to do a flight around the world, so I did my best to encourage that ambition. We took several photos standing in front of the plane. As a side business he makes craft beer and root beer. As a parting gift, he gave me a six-pack of each – nice guy. By the way, if you put root beer in a square glass it becomes just beer.

After refueling in Hammond I flew VFR on to Georgetown, Texas (airport code KGTU), another place I'd never been. But it was located at about the right distance, north of Austin, with good reviews for the FBO. I planned to spend the night here. I prefer these small, outlying airports to bigger airports like Austin because they are less busy and usually less expensive. The downside is there may be a lack of services and facilities. That was the case with Georgetown. The airport and FBO were great. They even put my plane in the hangar overnight for a modest charge – they had the room. However, the handful of hotels out near the airport where I was staying had no restaurants; the only places to eat within walking distance were fast food joints and gas station food marts. There was one taxi in town, which took me from the airport to the hotel. After a long day of flying, some of it dodging thunderstorms and cloud buildups, I didn't feel like getting a taxi just to go to dinner, so I settled for the fast food joint. I didn't mind.

Marfa, Texas

Marfa, Texas, has frequently been used as a movie location for high profile Western and other films including *Giant*, *There Will Be Blood*, *Andromeda Strain*, and *No Country for Old Men*. Since I was in this part of the country and had the time, I decided to check it out, after first doing some tourist flying along the Rio Grande.

After spending the night at Georgetown, I took off VFR for Big Bend National Park, the park and mountains situated along the border between Texas and Mexico where the Rio Grande makes a big loop to the south. The park itself is a mountain outcropping among the volcanic peaks that punctuate the whole region south of the West Texas oil country flatlands. At Fort Stockton, I turned south and followed along the river, flying just a few miles inside the United States, north of the river. I knew this was potentially drug runner's country and considered the fact that my flight could be interpreted as

Confluence of rivers with the Rio Grande

Big Bend National Park, Texas

suspicious. The weather was clear so I circled interesting features a few times anyway to get photos.

There is an airport at Marfa – that is, a runway with a few buildings – but not much else. There's no real general-aviation terminal or place to rent a car, which was what I needed. So instead of Marfa I landed at Alpine, Texas (airport code E38). A phone call the day before had arranged a rental car from a small local company. The car turned out to be a huge old Chevy. It was parked outside the humble little general-aviation terminal building with the keys left in it.

Before the car, though, I created a little issue for myself taxiing in to the fuel pump. Customs and Border Protection run their border flights in helicopters from Alpine Airport. As I taxied to the fuel pump I stopped, rather obviously, to take a picture of one of their black helicopters as it was spinning up. That, I think, earned me a visit from one of their officers as I was pumping gas. He asked, politely, to see my pilot certificate and medical certificate. I knew they had the right to inspect these documents, but they didn't have the right to do anything else, such as search the plane. The guy claimed he was really just interested in seeing my plane, which is a little unusual, so I diverted the conversation to international flying. The Earthrounders decal is always a good conversation-starter.

Big Bend National Park in Texas

He was a copter pilot so I asked him if drones were going to put him out of business. He said the only advantage of the drones was greatly extended time aloft; otherwise the copters are better. Much of what they do is rescue lost or injured hikers, which the drones obviously can't do. Given that I really dislike talking to law enforcement of any kind, overall, this interaction was OK. The guy was nice enough instead of being the usual overbearing macho jerk you sometimes encounter. I don't know if my stopping to take a photo of their air operations prompted this encounter or if they stop and question any strange plane that arrives at the Alpine.

Cruising around West Texas with the windows down in a full-size Chevy seemed like a perfect afternoon. I stopped for lunch at a local café in Alpine,

Hotel Paisano lobby in Marfa, Texas

then headed west along US 90 to Marfa. It was interesting country, with historical markers showing where the first Spanish explorers had made their way north from Mexico into this, for them, unexplored country.

There is a mystical phenomenon that many have reported seeing, called the "Marfa Lights." The Marfa Lights appear far out across the flat prairie from a location a few miles east of Marfa. The story has become so popular, and such a tourist draw, that they actually built a modern viewing pavilion and parking lot along the highway. As I passed it headed west to Marfa I decided to return that night to see for myself.

The only good place to stay in Marfa is the Hotel Paisano in the center of town. It has been a temporary home to many actors while on location filming their movies. Over the years they've kept track of who stayed in which room, so naturally I couldn't resist booking the James Dean room. The hotel lobby and staircase are impressive but the James Dean room, not so

James Dean room at the Paisano Hotel

Suspicious pilot

much. At least it had a balcony and French doors so I could look out across the little town to the open country beyond.

The best place for dinner in Marfa is also the restaurant at the Hotel Paisano. I took a chance and ordered a pisco sour from the bar – it completely missed the mark. That evening's meal was pretty pleasant, sitting in the shade on the outdoor plaza filled with people having dinner or drinks at tables situated around a great old tile fountain. I picked up snatches of local news and gossip from conversations overheard at nearby tables. Some merchants were bemoaning the slow commerce they were currently experiencing. Business was slow in Marfa before the annual film festival and the tourist season began.

After dinner I felt a little stupid, like a rube tourist, asking the woman at the front desk the best time to try to see the Marfa Lights. She answered politely with barely a note of derision in her voice. I headed out after dark at around 10 pm to the viewing pavilion I had passed. I stayed there an hour as several other people came and went. I saw nothing: big surprise.

Los Angeles

I drove back to Alpine the next day to return the rental car and pick up the plane. I headed west VFR to Goodyear Airport (airport code KGYR) in Phoenix, where I had stopped overnight flying eastbound some months earlier. It was a good FBO so I decided on a fuel stop and free snacks for lunch. My plan was to visit long-time friends living near Calabasas west of Los Angeles. From Goodyear I filed an IFR flight plan for Van Nuys Airport (airport code KVNY). Getting into a busy urban airport like Van Nuys can sometimes be easier if you are on an IFR flight plan and can get slotted into the landing traffic pattern ahead of time along with the other arriving aircraft.

As I approached the LA area I saw a large column of dark smoke right in front of me. It hadn't been there 15 minutes before. A brush fire: the fire season was under way early in LA. This fire clearly had just ignited. As I flew by I could look down and see the first fire trucks arriving on the scene and uncoiling their hoses. No doubt a Temporary Flight Restriction zone would soon be put in place to reserve airspace for aerial tankers fighting this fire.

Past the fire, flying further west, I got vectored around a bit before being given an inbound course and clearance to land at Van Nuys. It's a busy place, as I expected, the traffic aggravated by a runway that was shortened for construction at the time. The FBOs here normally cater to larger planes and corporate/private jets, so are pretty posh when compared to many others. They had a rental car waiting for me, so I headed off to Calabasas for a great dinner and overnight stay with my long-time friend Lynn Smith and her husband Andy. As the sun was setting we sat on their terrace and watched new fires popping up to the west. We could smell the smoke and speculated on whether it might move fast enough to initiate an evacuation order for their neighborhood. That would have made it the ultimate classic LA experience.

Back in Eugene

I left Van Nuys on May 3, 2013, for the 600 nm flight back to Creswell, Oregon, where this long adventure to South America had begun just before Christmas. I flew VFR north at 10,500 feet into perfect weather. Flying through clear skies over farmland and lakes and mountains I had flown over many times before, I had a chance really to reflect on what I had accomplished and what I had failed to do.

With the around-the-world flight I had visited five continents, and with this flight added South America as the sixth. The objective of flying to all seven continents was now really beginning to haunt me. At various stops along the way home, I had done some online research and realized that there were most likely only three other pilots who had flown solo in a single engine plane to all seven continents. Fewer than the number of people who had walked on the moon! There's no official tally, of course, but pilots who had accomplished such a thing would have probably informed the community of small plane pilots who make long international flights about it through the Earthrounders website or some other means.

Through this pattern of thinking I was trying to magnify the seven continents objective to the point where it really was worth flying all the way

N788W back in my hangar at Creswell

back down to the tip of South America to try it again. It seemed like a crazy, expensive, time-consuming task just to add that "pelt" to my wall. It would involve a tedious retracing of my route south followed by the repetition of the flight back home north from Punta Arenas and across the US, the flight I was just now completing. As I said at the beginning, I don't "love" flying – the uneventful routine of it can be stupefying, especially when you're flying along routes you've already flown. Most of the time on these long flights I'm just sitting there while the autopilot flies the plane, and I'm hoping something important doesn't break.

Besides the flying, I'd have to repeat the permit process with the US and Chile to make another attempt to fly to King George Island. I expected I could get the US permits again; they had no reason to deny me. Chile was another matter. They have no obligation to give me permission to land at their airstrip – there is nothing positive in it for them, but there is the distinct risk that something could go wrong with my flight and they'd be stuck with a rescue effort. Would the fact that I'd abandoned the flight once because of bad weather work in my favor, showing them I was a prudent pilot who didn't take risks when the conditions weren't favorable? Or maybe they would think I was just a flake who didn't know what he was doing? I had no way to know. It was already May. If I were going to try again in January 2014, I needed to make that decision soon and start on a new set of applications for permission to land in Antarctica.

As I descended into Creswell I heard Paul, a Creswell flight instructor and familiar voice, respond to my inbound radio call. "Harry, you sound bored." I laughed and said, "Yup!" Well, that pretty much clarified the situation; I knew what I was going to do.

25

Re-Thinking Antartica

I had committed myself to making another attempt to fly my plane to Antarctica. A second attempt would be wasteful, and perhaps just as unsuccessful, if I didn't carefully consider and thoroughly understand the factors that ultimately caused me to abandon my attempt to make this flight in 2013. In reviewing what happened, and determined to return for another attempt with a much better chance of success, I broke the problems down into three parts:

Fuel

To avoid the FAA paperwork hassles with an auxiliary fuel tank (ferry tank) plumbed into my fuel system, in 2013 I took extra fuel as cargo in a 58-gallon tank that I installed in place of the back seat on N788W. I brought a hand rotary pump that would allow me to transfer the fuel quickly from that tank to the wing tanks once I was on the ground. The problem with this arrangement is that the extra fuel was not available to me in flight.

The distance from Punta Arenas to King George Island in Antarctica is 670 nm. If I were unable to land at King George Island for any reason (sudden fog, for example, which is not uncommon), I would have to fly back to my alternate airport at Puerto Williams, 500 nm miles to the north. The total of 1170 nm is at the limit of the range of my plane with just the fuel in the wing tanks in calm air. If potential headwinds are taken into account, this distance could be beyond the range of the plane, and I might end up crashing into the water when the fuel ran out.

My 2013 strategy violated a pretty basic tenet of instrument flying: have enough fuel on board to fly to the destination airport, and from there fly to the alternate airport, and then fly for 45 minutes more beyond that. I didn't even have that much fuel on board in 2013, and in this case I was dealing with some of the most volatile weather on the planet. The remedy to this mistake was obvious: put the ferry tank back in and connect it to the fuel system so that I had abundant fuel available to return to my alternate airport if necessary. I would just accept the FAA paperwork hassle associated with doing this. With the ferry tank installed, I had a range of over 2,000 nm. The rational way to address any uncertainty created by volatile weather is with the certainty of more flight options – in this case, more fuel and much greater range. Having the ferry tank would substantially lower the risk profile of the flight.

Ice

It is possible to fly at low altitude across the Drake Passage, at maybe 1,000 feet above the water, which will usually be below the cloud base and in temperatures above freezing until you get far enough south to about King George Island where the surface temperature tends to hover around freezing during the austral summer. Launching from Ushuaia, it is possible to fly east along the Beagle Channel, then turn right and fly south at low latitude across open water to King George Island. A least one pilot I know went to Antarctica (actually Marambio Base) this way. To me, though, this is a risky way to fly. If the engine fails, there is essentially no time to prepare for hitting the water or to diagnose the engine problem and try to restart it. Flying at 10,000 or 12,000 feet is safer, since that altitude provides several minutes of glide time before hitting the water as well as some time to try to restart the engine. Engine fuel economy is also much better at the higher altitudes. The downside of flying at those altitudes is that there is a risk of ice accumulation. Flying in the clouds at temperatures between 0 and say -15° to -20° Celsius, there is a good chance of ice accumulation on the aircraft, which can be a quick killer.

To give myself more options in dealing with such cold, cloudy conditions at that altitude, I decided to install a TKS de-icing system on N788W. A TKS de-icing system pumps glycol de-icing fluid from panels in the leading edges of the wings and tail, and from nozzles on the propeller, to inhibit the formation of ice. There is an existing FAA authorization for this installation on my Columbia, but it's a very expensive aftermarket addition. I probably now have the only Lancair Columbia 300 with TKS! I justified the expense knowing that it would definitely be useful for wintertime flying in the Pacific Northwest where I live, and the Minimum Enroute Altitudes over mountains are often at altitudes with temperatures that are in the ice zone. The downside with these TKS systems is the limited de-icing fluid in the reservoir tank: it only lasts about 1½ hours. The system is not really intended for an extended flight in icing conditions. Using the TKS was Strategy A to deal with icing conditions.

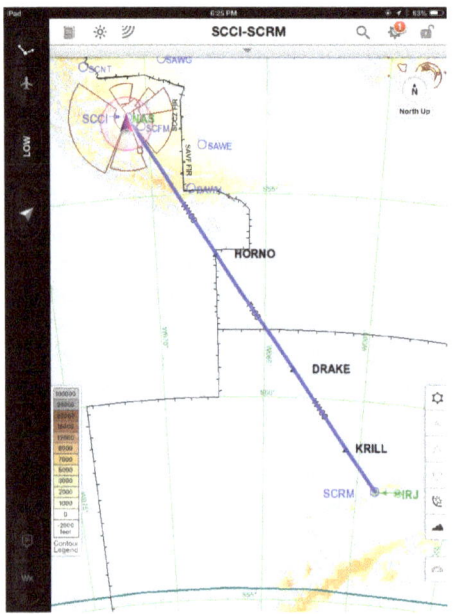

Flight route from SCCI (Punta Arenas) to SCRM (King George Island in Antarctica)

Beyond equipping the plane with TKS, I also did a few trial flights at 15,000 and 16,000 feet, where I normally don't fly. My engine is less efficient and I need to use oxygen at those altitudes. I always carry supplemental oxygen on board, so that is really not a problem. Over the Drake Passage, the temperatures at these altitudes will often be below -15° C, so the water vapor in the clouds already is crystallized into ice particles rather than in liquid form, and therefore usually won't stick to a plane as ice. Flying at these higher altitudes was Strategy B to address icing if needed.

Strategy C was the one I already mentioned: drop down to 1,000 feet to warmer temperatures and fly just above the water to King George Island. Flying from Punta Arenas, however, you must fly over the southern end of the Andes Mountains, where the Minimum Enroute Altitude is about 11,000 feet, potentially in the ice zone. Once past these mountains, though, dropping down to just above water level is viable.

Finally, anticipating a worst-case scenario where I might need all the TKS fluid in the tank for the flight south to King George Island, I brought three gallons of de-icing fluid in plastic jugs in my cabin to refill the TKS reservoir tank once I was on the ground in Antarctica, to be used for the return flight.

Time

During my attempt in 2013, I waited quite a while in Punta Arenas for good weather. I finally realized the wait could be indeterminate, and I had other business and personal commitments back home I needed to tend to. I couldn't wait forever. To economize on my time with this second attempt, I decided to hire The Flight Academy in Seattle to ferry my plane to Santiago, Chile, and also arrange installation of the new ferry tank and associated FAA paperwork. This saved me about three weeks so I could focus all my time away on completing the flight to King George Island. It was another expense, but an hour of my time as CEO of my software business is worth a lot more than an hour of a ferry pilot's time. Fuel, hotels, handlers, the airport, and navigation fees would all be the same whether I was flying or the ferry pilot was flying. Besides, I had already flown the route along the west coast of South America northbound in 2013, visiting the destinations that interested me, like Machu Picchu and Easter Island. I wasn't missing anything I wanted to see by having the plane flown to Santiago by a ferry pilot.

With solutions in place for the three issues that had caused me to abandon my attempt to fly to Antarctica in 2013, I turned the plane over to the ferry pilot, Chris Anderson, in early January, 2014, to fly first to Tracy, California, for installation of the ferry tank, and from there to Santiago, Chile.

While I was constructing my flight strategy for the second attempt at flying to Antarctica, I was concurrently submitting the documents to the US and Chilean governments to obtain permission to land at King George Island. Some of the people I had dealt with in the US in 2013 had been replaced, but the new people were just as helpful. I was basically able to update my previous submissions, and follow the same procedures, to get a new clearance to land at King George Island in 2014. As far as I know, there were no negative consequences resulting from my abandoned attempt at this flight in 2013.

Back to Santiago

I took a commercial flight from Seattle to Santiago, arriving there on January 25, 2014. I took a taxi directly from the commercial terminal to the general-aviation terminal, Aerocardal, to inspect the plane, which Chris had delivered there two days before. Everything was in good shape. I also got Chris's data on oil and fuel consumption during his flight to Santiago. All the numbers were typical for the performance of N788W, so no problems had arisen. I had the plane fueled, including fuel in the ferry tank, and got ready to fly farther south the next day, January 26th.

26

Santiago Southward

New Ferry Tank

Fueling the plane on Saturday in Santiago for a Sunday departure southbound, I filled both wing tanks and put about 40 gallons in the ferry tank. I didn't need the range – it's only 497 nm from Santiago to my destination at Puerto Montt – but I wanted to test the newly installed ferry tank system. This ferry tank system worked differently than the one I used on my round-the-world flight in 2011 and I wanted to experiment with it.

The ferry tank system on the round-the-world flight had two valves: one to control flow from the right wing tank to the engine and the second to control flow from the ferry tank to the engine. Using the fuel in the ferry tank meant closing the valve from the right wing tank and opening the valve from the ferry tank. There was no fuel return to the ferry tank so as the ferry tank fuel was used, some would go to the engine and some would go back into the right wing tank, essentially refilling it. Once refilled, I would reverse the valve operation – open the valve to the right wing tank and close the value to the ferry tank so the engine would draw fuel from the right tank again. This back-and-forth process was repeated until there was no usable fuel left in the ferry tank (or I landed).

The ferry tank system installed for this second attempt at Antarctica used a simple Tee fitting in the fuel line for the left wing tank. The left wing tank was used instead of the right wing tank because the installation of the TKS de-icing system pump blocked convenient access to the right wing tank fuel line that we had used with the 2011 installation. Using the Tee, there is only one valve that opens flow from the ferry tank into the Tee. A ramjet was installed on the belly of the plane to provide replacement air and pressure via a hose into the top of the ferry tank. With this system, the fuel from the ferry tank is being combined with the left wing tank fuel and that combination sent to the engine. Any fuel not used by the engine is returned to the left wing tank. With the fuel from the ferry tank mixing with the fuel from the left wing tank, the left wing refilled much more rapidly than with the system I had used in 2011.

Puerto Montt/Puerto Varas

I was flying southbound from Santiago to Puerto Montt along a route I had flown northbound in 2013. My takeoff from Santiago was a little weird. I'd forgotten how to manage the extra weight and aft center of gravity with the extra weight of the ferry tank in the back seat. When the plane is light with only me on board, the usual case, I'll get into the bad habit on takeoff of getting up to takeoff speed of 70 knots and yanking the plane off the runway by pulling back on the sidestick. This usually works OK when the plane is light, but not with the extra weight from the fuel in the ferry tank. I tried taking off from Santiago this way, at a density altitude of 2,000 feet. The plane complained and briefly settled back on the runway until I picked up more speed to positively lift off. The best way to take off with the extra weight in this plane is keep the plane on the runway until the airspeed is up to 80 knots then nudge the stick back to lift the nose wheel, and let the plane fly off the runway on its own at a low rate of climb.

Looking across Lago Llonquihue from Puerto Varas

Once airborne, I got vectored around a bit until being released on my flight plan route to Puerto Montt at FL110. After draining 10 gallons from the left wing tank, I opened the ferry tank valve. The engine kept running (that's a good thing) and the left wing tank pretty rapidly refilled, in maybe 10 to 12 minutes. Closing the valve, I once again drained 10 gallons from the left wing tank, then repeated the procedure.

Well, this was actually easier than the ferry tank system I had on the round-the-world flight. I realized, though, that it more heavily relied on the back pressure from the ramjet connected to the ferry tank pushing fuel into

Puerto Varas waterfront on a Sunday

the Tee junction, since it was competing with the fuel pressure from the left wing tank. I don't know much about fluid dynamics but it seems to me the source with the higher pressure will win in terms of which fuel gets to the engine. I then understood why some ferry tanks have manual air pumps in the cabin so the pilot can put additional pressure into the ferry tank and force all the fuel out. I didn't have such a pump. When the left wing tank was no longer being refilled with the ferry tank valve open, I concluded that no more fuel could be extracted from the ferry tank so I was left with the fuel in the wing tanks only. When I landed in Puerto Montt, I opened the cap on the ferry tank and looked inside with my flashlight. There were maybe 1 to 1.5 inches of fuel remaining, about 3 to 4 gallons out of a total tank capacity of 70 gallons. With the results of this test run, I then knew how much usable fuel I had to work with for the flight to Antarctica.

Coming back to Puerto Montt (airport code SCTE), I was reminded of my stop here last year going northbound. I knew where everything was, the fuel pumps and the Operaciones office where one guy remembered me, "el Norteamericano loco" who is flying to Antarctica.

This time I planned ahead to stay in Puerto Varas, about 10

On the ramp at Puerto Montt

km from Puerto Montt. Puerto Varas is a small hamlet, mainly for tourists but right on the shore of Lake Llanquihue so there are beautiful views across the lake to the snow-covered volcanoes in the distance. I stayed a couple of nights there and had a couple of great steak dinners. My stay at Puerto Varas was my one concession to tourism en route south to Punta Arenas. The Lake country in Chile that extends south from Puerto Montt and Puerto Varas in the foothills of the Andes is one of the most attractive parts of Chile. There are many small airports in this area, usually near remote lodges. It would be a wonderful place to linger in the summer and take short flights to these lodges. But from now on, it would be all business for me until my mission to Antarctica was completed.

Punta Arenas

South from Puerto Montt I was once again dealing with Patagonia weather, the "roaring forties" as mariners call it. I had become a "weather forecast obsessive" in need of an intervention! I had at least a half dozen weather forecast sources bookmarked on my notebook computer, like the Weather Underground and Accuweather sites I've mentioned before, in addition to a variety of aviation-specific forecast sites like AWC (see Appendix B). The Weather Underground and Accuweather sites provide longer-range forecasts than the aviation weather sites, but those weather forecasts are often misleading (and often disagree with each other). That bright yellow sunshine icon they might display for tomorrow's weather can, overnight, turn into clouds and rain when I check it at 5 am the next day. The Weather Underground interactive map (Wundermap™) is an honest picture of existing conditions from satellite imagery, both visual and infrared. It's my go-to source for what I really will be facing on a given day, in addition to the airport-area forecasts and observations I access via AWC.

Flying over the Andes southward

On January 28, my day of departure from Puerto Montt for Punta Arenas, I saw evil things in the satellite image along the most logical route to Punta

Arenas, near the mountains on the east side of the Andes in Argentina. To avoid this weather, I opted to take the long way around by flying all the way to the Argentine coast at Comodoro Rivadavia, then south to Rio Gallegos, then to Punta Arenas. It was 70 nm farther than the route near the mountains, but I expected it would be a much smoother flight. What do I care, I've got plenty of fuel and all day to fly there.

I filed an IFR flight plan at FL110 that crossed the Andes straight west to east. The initial altitude of FL110 was bumped up to FL130 between a waypoint called GUTIN and the ESQ navigation station in order to meet the minimum enroute altitude for crossing the Andes. This worked out pretty well. Crossing the Andes at this spot was easy with light winds and not much turbulence. I was motivated for the first time on this trip to pull out the camera and take some photos from the cockpit.

There is a VHF communications gap on this route at this altitude between ESQ and the CRV navigation station, but it doesn't last long. Flying south along the Argentine coast, then turning west at Rio Gallegos to descend into Punta Arenas–controlled airspace all seemed familiar. I flew through some dense rain showers and clouds approaching Punta Arenas, but I was in the clear by the time I got to the Punta Arenas Airport. I made a visual approach to runway 30 with a surface wind of 25–35 knots varying from 280–310 degrees. It wouldn't be Tierra del Fuego without these unrelenting winds. For all the time I've spent in Punta Arenas,

Flying over the Andes

I don't think I'd ever seen surface winds at the airport less than 12–15 knots, with 20–30 knots being normal. This time I planned ahead for these winds and brought wheel chocks for all three wheels.

It was like old times being back at Puerto Arenas, but in reality just 11 months had elapsed since I left here. I knew where to go for fuel. When fueling was done I went into the Operaciones office and told them I had parked on a small ramp area outside the aeroclub the year before. They said fine, do that again.

An ironic comment on US currency. On my round-the-world flight in 2011, I ran into the problem of fuel people and others not wanting to accept old US$100 bills, the ones with the little head of Ben Franklin or even Big Head Bens with old issuance dates. This time I had current Big Head Bens but also the latest, greatest multi-color space-age US$100 bills. Guess what? The fuel guys didn't recognize the new $100 bills, they looked at them like they were a joke! Nope, they didn't want those, just recent Big Head Bens. OK, well, I hoped I had enough of those now. Note to US Treasury: just decide on a money design, then leave it alone for like 30 years so the rest of the world knows what it's supposed to look like.

A year ago I went to a lot of trouble to remove the wheel pants from the main wheels on my plane, expecting the runway at King George Island to be so rough that ground clearance might be a problem. Removing the wheel pants seemed to take 8–10 knots off the speed of the plane and aggravated the range problem. The process took over an hour lying out in the open on the windy ramp by the aeroclub. This time I decided: forget it, I'd leave them on. If I break one landing at King George Island, I'll take them off then.

Once parked by the aeroclub with all three wheels chocked, I headed back to the DGAC building and straight to the Meteo (weather) office, which is right next to the Operaciones office. Meteo is a great weather office with 3-D computer graphic tools for analyzing the weather along the route from Punta Arenas to King George Island. I told them, "I'll go tomorrow!" They said, "Nope." They said the best day would be Friday. There was a six-hour window when the weather at King George Island would be OK and the weather along the Drake Passage route would be OK. After 6 hours, Punta Arenas weather would turn bad, a big weather front would be coming through. I said, "OK, so I'll fly to Marsh on Friday and come back on Saturday." Yes, thumbs up, smiles. "Marsh" is the shorthand name they use to refer to the airstrip at King George Island. The actual name of the airport is Teniente Rodolfo Marsh Martin. I like these Meteo people; they speak "weather English" and I get their computer graphics – very thorough. They admit their models break down looking a few days into the future; it's refreshing to hear weather people be realistic about what they are telling me. They told me to come back Thursday afternoon to double-check that the weather pattern they were seeing was still in place.

With a plan and schedule in mind, I went to the main terminal and grabbed a taxi into town. The hotel I finally preferred in Punta Arenas is Cabo de Hornos. I made multiple consecutive reservations here for a few days each with the intention of canceling the ones I didn't need once my flight to King George Island was completed. I could cancel two days ahead of the arrival date with no penalty.

Cabo de Hornos has the best lobby bar in Punta Arenas, where an interesting collection of Antarctica research groups often congregate before embarking to, or after returning from, Antarctica. It's got a vibe I like. The bar makes a perfect pisco sour, and when combined with their selection of tasty empanadas filled with beef and chicken and crab, provided the ideal "welcome back" to Punta Arenas. The rooms here are OK; the best have a view over the water. The restaurant, though, seemed to have gone downhill since I was there the year before. I'd come to prefer the restaurant at the Dreams Hotel, one of the other places I stayed in Punta Arenas. There are many other restaurants around town I like – too many to mention – but a lot of choices everywhere.

So I waited for Thursday afternoon.

27

King George Island, Antarctica

On Thursday afternoon, January 30, I was back at the Meteo weather office at the airport. The forecast they'd given me when I arrived on Tuesday was still holding, so I committed myself to fly to SCRM at King George Island on Friday morning and return the next day, with the expectation that I would miss the big front passing through Punta Arenas Friday night. The plane was already fueled and ready to go.

    The one part of this plan where there was no plan: where do I stay overnight on the island? I had originally planned to fly down and back in the same day. There are no hotels or restaurants on the island, although I found a few travel websites that falsely claimed there is a hostel. There is a small block of rooms the Chilean Air Force maintains for military visitors, but this is by invitation only and, as I found out later, requires a request 30 days in advance. It was far too late for that. Well, I was going and if I had to sleep on the plane I guess I could. The temperatures on the island that time of year are around freezing and really don't vary much daytime to nighttime. Just like camping out in the mountains, right? But if they have space available, I'd have been surprised if they didn't give me a room. To some extent I was counting on the hospitality of the Chilean Air Force or somebody else in this little village to take pity on me and give me a warm place to sleep at least for one night.

Friday I was keyed up and got to the airport early. With the flight plan filed, I headed out to the plane. I took off around 7:30 am local time (1030Z). There were clouds around but a nice big hole of blue sky to the south which I climbed through up to my cruising altitude of FL110.

The waypoints along the route have interesting names: HORNO, DRAKE, and KRILL. Krill are the tiny crustaceans that whales and other sea creatures eat. I was soon above the clouds and pretty happy: blue skies ahead of me as far as I could see, with an overcast layer below me which occasionally opened up to reveal the Andes Mountains and, later, the waters of the Drake Passage. The HF radio worked, sort of, at the HORNO waypoint, but I switched to the satphone so I could provide a reliable position report. I used it again at DRAKE and KRILL, where they handed me off to the VHF tower frequency at King George Island. The guy in the tower there spoke good English. I didn't need the limited aviation Spanish I had prepared for the occasion: "Quiero aterrizar a pista 11!" ("I want to land on runway 11.")

A curious thing occurred while over the Drake Passage – Antarctica disappeared! At least it disappeared on the Garmin moving map display on the panel in my aircraft. South of about 60 degrees south latitude, what should have been water and the land masses of Antarctica were replaced by cross-hatching. The location and route line to King George Island, and the VOR navigation station at King George Island (IRJ) were correctly marked, but the land display of the continent itself was gone. I really didn't need it, but the fact that Garmin omitted it reminded me of how rare it was to fly down here. The Jeppesen charting software on the iPad still showed the Antarctica land mass correctly and my position relative to it.

The forecast for King George Island was scattered at 2500 feet – brilliant! Once I got down there I wanted to make a short detour

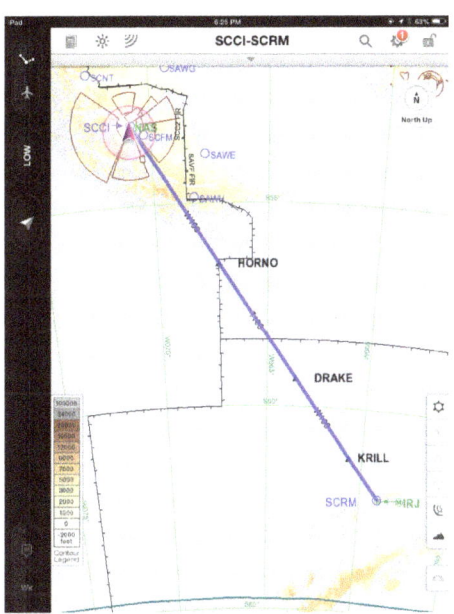

Flight route from SCCI (Punta Arenas) to SCRM (Antarctica)

En-route to Antarctica

Climbing out of Punta Arenas into clear skies

70 nm farther south to take aerial photos of Deception Island and Half Moon Island, places I had visited on the Antarctica cruise three years before. Unfortunately, and not surprisingly, the forecast was wrong and that was not to be.

I was in contact now with King George Island tower on VHF, and he reported scattered at 1500 feet and overcast at 2500 feet. Well, this was still an easy landing using the instrument approach, but I wasn't going to fly around under a 2500-foot layer in unknown territory trying to get a few photos of Deception Island, especially when the Garmin was not providing me with any terrain mapping. These islands have mountain peaks higher than 2500 feet.

I was cleared for the instrument approach for runway 11, with surface winds of 10–15 knots at 150 degrees. I turned on the TKS de-icing for the descent through the overcast layer; the temperature was definitely below freezing as I descended. I turned inbound at the initial approach-fix waypoint called TEMPA and shortly thereafter broke out of the clouds at around 3000 feet, where I could see King George Island in the distance. I shut off the TKS de-icing and the autopilot, but the island looked like all snow and rock. I really couldn't pick out a runway. The approach course was there on the GPS, however, and I followed it toward King George Island knowing it would lead me to the runway.

Through hundreds of instrument approaches and landings, a pilot develops a dispassionate routine that results in getting on the ground safely. The emotional high from finally arriving at a long-dreamed-of destination is suppressed almost instinctively. After all the effort I'd put into getting here, this was not just another landing. But I had to treat it like one, as did the guy in the tower, who stuck to business and refrained from any extraneous communications even though he knew my arrival was a rare event. There is also a certain realization that takes over at this point, almost a fatalism, that the situation is what it is, that I've made the best effort toward achieving success. If it turns out badly for an unexpected reason, that's just fate, bad luck. Pilots don't fear death as much as they fear screwing up.

Once I had King George Island in view, the approach across the water took several minutes. As I got closer I mostly noticed the cold black water crashing against rocks laying offshore. Eventually, I was close enough that only one patch of gravel in front of me could possibly be the runway. Closer still, the runway lights came into view, so I lowered the flaps to slow the plane and create more low-speed lift while reducing power to set up my final descent to the threshold of runway 11. Using de-icing on the descent had left remnants of fluid on the windshield that now obscured my view forward as I got within a few feet of the runway surface, slightly impairing my ability to see exactly where I was which resulted in a touchdown that was a little more abrupt than what I would consider a great landing. But I was here! The plane was rolling and slowing, ground features and equipment I'd seen a million times in the weather webcams from my home – stared at to the point where they became almost mythical – were now right in front of me.

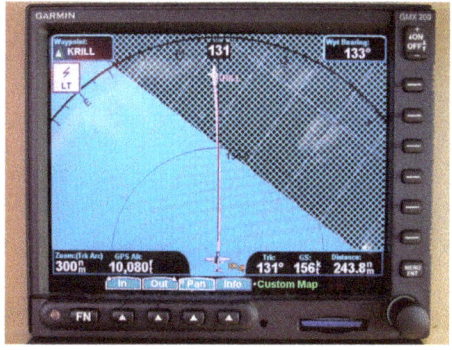

Garmin display missing Antarctica!

I landed at King George Island at 1455Z, January 31, 2014, exactly one week after getting on a commercial flight in Seattle to fly to Santiago. The landing turned out to be easy, with a wide gravel runway smoother than I had expected. I found out later the other end of the runway is where the heavy planes usually touch down, so that section is more chewed up. As I had at several places on my round-the-world flight, I made a video of the final few minutes of the approach and landing at King George Island using my GoPro camera. A link to that video on YouTube can be found in Appendix B.

But a landing is not complete until the plane is stopped and parked. The tower guy came on the radio and told me to exit the runway to the right where ground personnel would direct me to a parking place. Applying some brakes, I steered off the runway through some small patches of snow and mud

At King George Island, Antarctica

puddles to the point where I could see the guy lining me up to park. I made a sharp pivot to the right, and stopped as he crossed his arms over his head in the universal sign to stop. I shut off the avionics and radios, shut down the engine, and opened the door, still running my shutdown checklist in my head.

Several Chilean Air Force guys were standing there watching my arrival. Once the engine was shut down they approached the plane. As I climbed out of N788W and stepped off the wing onto the ground, they welcomed me with handshakes all around; several spoke pretty good English. A few were the resident pilots that flew the helicopters and turboprop aircraft for local flights. There were many photos taken of everyone in front of N788W.

I was so busy meeting and greeting people that the significance of the moment really didn't hit me. I'd spent so many days thinking about this event, spent so many days looking at the webcams showing King George Island, that I thought I already knew the place. No delirious relief grabbed me now that I had achieved the goal that eluded me the previous year. I didn't drop to my knees and kiss the ground. I got the plane ready to spend the night, like it was just another stop on what had become a worldwide, seven-continent odyssey. To be sure, I still had to fly back to Punta Arenas, but now that I had actually landed in Antarctica, I could pick my moment to return.

While inbound, before landing, I'd told the King George Island tower guy I was going to need to stay overnight because of the weather front going through Punta Arenas. He had passed the request to the Air Force, so the guy in charge greeted me and said he would ask his boss in Punta Arenas if I could stay in one of their rooms. He told me I should have made the request 30 days ago; I said the weather changed my plans at the last minute. I also told him I had cash and could pay. Word came down a couple hours later that it was OK for me to stay. They actually have a standard room rate of US$100, plus $17 for dinner. It's not a hotel, but since it functions like one on occasion, they've accepted that reality and have set up standard rates. I was delighted with this news – a warm bed for the night.

That left me the afternoon to explore the island but, of course, the first stop was the weather office in the tower, perched on a rock outcropping, to check the forecast for the next day. Yup, the forecast was still holding, and they had great graphics of the front moving across Punta Arenas and disappearing to the east during the night. They said I should expect one small front to fly across, about 200 km south of Punta Arenas, which was maybe 100 km wide with cloud tops around 12,000 feet. OK, I could live with that.

Control tower at King George Island

After an interesting lunch with an Air Force guy named Manuel who ran the visitor rooms and commissary, and Angel, the tower guy I had talked to inbound, I got the camera and wandered about one kilometer down the hill to the village called Villa Las Estrellas. There are several portable building trailers, and even inflatable shelters, that house Air Force, Navy, DGAC, and other personnel from Chile, and a research group from Russia. There was also a rock beach where they bring in the zodiac inflatable

King George Island

boats that transport people to cruise ships. Several other countries have research stations at outlying points on King George Island and nearby islands. I was happy to be here. Everything had worked out pretty well, except not getting aerial photos of Deception Island and Half Moon Island. But overall I had accomplished what I set out to do.

Zodiac inflatables at King George Island

I had dinner with the Air Force guys while a group of researchers and a film crew from Uruguay assembled to be flown back to Punta Arenas. These folks were standing around for quite a while at the commissary waiting for their C-130 to fly in and pick them up. I got in an interesting conversation with two of them who were also small-plane pilots. I showed them my plane and talked about my international flying adventures around the world. They told me more about Uruguay, a country I had flown by the year before without stopping. Everything I'd heard about that country is favorable; I regret not having stopped to visit. I'd have to add it to my travel list, which seems to grow longer rather than shorter the more I travel.

Their C-130 finally arrived, the propellers kicking up a large cloud of dust as it landed and taxied to a nearby gravel ramp intended for larger planes. Shuttle vans took the Uruguayans out to the plane which, after another hour, finally taxied out for takeoff. I took a photo of its takeoff and departure climb-out into the open sky and lingering Antarctica twilight. That photo became one of my favorites among those of my visit to King George Island.

Villa de Las Estrellas buildings

My accommodations that night were simple: a room with a window at the end of the hall, furnished with twin beds and a dresser connected to a private bathroom, and most importantly, heat. I've never had to sleep on the plane before, so I was happy not to face that challenge here. Some of the other rooms in this one-story annex were occupied on a long-term basis by various military and research personnel I passed in the hallway but never met. "Long-term" in Antarctica usually means the four or five months of the austral summer. During the much more brutal winter months, this base and outlying research stations run by various countries are either abandoned entirely or run by skeleton crews since re-supply is so difficult. The transitory nature of people and activities at King George Island was one of my lasting impressions.

N788W at King George Island

Returning to Punta Arenas

This time of year and this far south, the nights are short. I was up and outside at 5:45 am looking at the sky and seeing large patches of blue to the north. I wanted to get going. The day before, I had told the Operaciones guy at the tower that I wanted to go at 8 am. At 6 am, not a single other person was up and moving around anywhere. I had thought a military base would get going early. The wind was calm, the air cold and clear. Standing there alone on this island, on the little rocky control tower hill overlooking the runway and nearby glaciers coming down to the water, I again had a taste of the solitude and grandeur of Antarctica.

Before trying to get anybody else going, I busied myself getting the plane ready. Moisture had settled on it overnight and frozen into a thick layer of frost. I got out my ice scraper and started cleaning off the wings and tail – 20 minutes later it was okay.

C-130 taking off

They had offered to let me put my plane in the hangar overnight but foolishly I'd declined. I thought it would be a hassle to get it out for an early morning departure, which it would have been. But had I done that, I wouldn't have had to scrape frost off the wings. Always take free hangar space when offered.

C-130 departing into the Antarctica twilight

I also got out a plastic bottle of TKS de-icing fluid and topped off the wing tank, replacing what I'd used descending into King George Island. I was careful but spilled a bit. So I made use of the absorbent pads from the spill kit I brought to clean up the ground as I promised to do when I filed the environmental impact assessment with the EPA for this flight. At least I didn't bring the spill kit all the way to Antarctica for nothing.

I was a little concerned about getting the engine started with these cold temperatures. I pulled the propeller through several revolutions by hand to get some oil up in the cylinders. Then I went back to the room, packed my stuff, and put it on the plane. I finished the preflight and had nothing left to do but go up to the tower and file a flight plan. I filed for the reverse route back to Punta Arenas at an altitude of FL120.

The hole in the sky to the north was closing as the overcast layer filled in. At the Operaciones office I woke up the guy on duty, who was asleep on the sofa, and filed the flight plan. I told him I wanted a 7:00 am departure, in 15 minutes. He smiled and told me nobody was in the tower. He got on the phone and started calling people. In the meantime, I went back to the plane, where an Air Force line guy had finally showed up. The Operaciones guy came down from the tower with a bunch of weather printouts for me. They have a good way of dividing the forecast into latitude bands from Punta Arenas south, with winds and temperatures at several altitudes, and also forecast cloud cover with the altitudes of those clouds. I asked if I could start the plane to warm up the engine, something you normally don't do outside the US until the flight clearance has been issued, followed by permission from the tower. The engine took a few tries to catch but I got it running.

While N788W was warming up, the tower guy came racing by in his pickup truck and drove up the hill to the tower. A few minutes later, he was on the radio and delivering my IFR clearance. By now the hole in the sky was closed; so unavoidably I would be climbing through an overcast layer, but I expected it would not be very thick.

I taxied for departure on runway 29, the opposite direction from which I had landed, and encountered the rough patches of runway where the heavy aircraft touch down. I applied full power and accelerated down the gravel strip that I had obsessed over from 10,000 miles away on Bainbridge Island. As I climbed out, the tower asked for the base and tops of the clouds which turned out to be 4,000 and 5,000 feet, respectively. Climbing at 1,000 feet per minute, I was in the clouds only about a minute and didn't bother to turn on the TKS de-icer. Above that layer I had open sky. As I leveled off at FL120, I saw layered clouds ahead that looked okay.

Farther north, about where I was told to expect a weather front, the clouds rose above my altitude. I couldn't see ahead, but I could see cloud definition around me, so I really wasn't in solid clouds. I left the TKS off but watched for ice buildup. Another 15 minutes and I was on the other side, in more blue sky but with another wall of clouds to fly through beyond that. I was gauging where I was relative to the point where I would be past the mountains so that, if needed, I could drop down to a lower altitude and warmer temperatures over the Straits of Magellan. Once I was less than an hour away from that point, I knew I could use the TKS to deal with any clouds and ice and have enough juice to make it through. I did turn it on for 10 minutes in the clouds over the mountains that were a little bumpy, but overall it was an easy flight through and out to the open sky over the Straits.

Punta Arenas radar picks up coverage about 100 nm south of the airport. I gave them a call on the VHF radio and got an immediate reply. If there was ever a point where I felt like I was home free on completing this mission, that radio call was it. From there on, coming into Punta Arenas and landing on runway 25 was routine – 25-knot surface wind again, of course.

So much had gone into getting this done, it almost felt anti-climactic to land, like the flight itself was just the epilogue to the real story of logistics, preparing the aircraft, planning, and the arduous task of applying for Antarctica permission with two countries, two years in a row! I celebrated that night with too many pisco sours and too much wine, knowing I had the luxury of sleeping in the next morning, and for once, not having to check weather forecasts at 5 am.

Epilogue

I made it back to Punta Arenas from Antarctica on Saturday, February 1, 2014. The next day my hometown team, the Seattle Seahawks, won the Super Bowl. How's that for an awesome weekend?

Since I had gotten to King George Island with only a few days' delay for weather, I decided to use the week following my return to insert another adventure. I had filed the appropriate applications and gotten permission to land in the Falkland Islands, a relatively short flight east over the Atlantic Ocean. I planned to make this flight on Tuesday, delayed a day for weather, and finally went to the airport and filed a flight plan to depart Wednesday. I was literally minutes away from going out to the plane and starting the engine when the tower called the Operaciones office and told them my clearance across Argentine airspace had not been granted. They hadn't denied it, they simply didn't respond to the request when the flight plan was filed. I called Skyplan to see if they could help. They started making phone calls, which eventually led to the conclusion that overflight permission would not be forthcoming. Because of the political tensions that still exist between Argentina and the United Kingdom over the unresolved conflict in the Falkland Islands and over who owns them, Argentina is obstructive and unhelpful for people who want to visit there. Apparently overflight permission can be obtained, but it takes several months of effort. Ironically, they told me it is actually easier if you depart from an airport in Argentina. I cancelled my plan to visit the Falklands – it had not really been a goal of mine anyway, but just a way to add a new place as long as I had already flown this far south. With that idea scratched, I left Punta Arenas and headed back north to Puerto Montt on February 9.

I had now completed my mission, my solo flight to seven continents in N788W. Rather than exuberant joy, I felt mostly relief, like a huge burden had been lifted from my shoulders, albeit a burden I deliberately put there. I still had to fly my plane back home, but I would be following along a route I had already flown. I expected to make it a quick trip with only a few layover days along the way.

I always considered myself a very goal-oriented person, driven to check off accomplishments, to hang a trophy on the wall and move on to the next challenge, whether in business or my personal life. It seemed to me this was the only way to marshal the energy and ambition to take on these difficult tasks. I've had some travelers tell me it's the journey, the process, which matters. That's the thing to be enjoyed, to be savored. Arriving at any particular destination, achieving any defined objective, is just an artificial way of giving the journey some structure and direction. I can see the value to this perspective. I wish I could be more aligned to that attitude, because soon after achieving a goal like flying to all seven continents the glow of satisfaction fades and I'm left with the question, "What next?" It's a junkie's addiction: after one fix fades, I'm thinking about where the next fix will come from.

After returning home I wasn't surprised when friends asked me what my next flying adventure would be. I'd mumble some speculation about flying over the North Pole from Canada to Svalbard Island in Norway– certainly a feasible flight that many others have done. It was a superficial response; I had no real desire to fly over the North Pole just to have another trophy. The truth is: I have no meaningful answer to that question.

There is always the appeal of a faraway place, the rarely-visited, remote, little-known mystery circumstance. I was recently in Barrow, Alaska, where a small community college had been built catering to "outlying" villages. Outlying? I thought Barrow was outlying. The lines of civilization, of human activity, get increasingly stretched, ultimately broken, moving beyond the last signpost, the end of the road, the hesitant smile, the final conversation. Further. Passed the last trail, the disappearing footprints, the lonely, windy mountaintop where recognition is a memory. Further still. Beyond process and reason, merging here and there, blurring yesterday and tomorrow, until finally arriving at a last thin space between the shadow and the silence.

Appendix A – Aviation Terminology

Throughout this book a number of acronyms and other aviation terminology have been used. In most cases, when an acronym is used the words associated with it are spelled out in the text. However, the words do not necessarily explain the meaning of that term or its significance to actually flying an airplane. The purpose of this Appendix is to provide a single location where several common aviation terms are spelled out and explained.

AIRMET – A term used for a formal warning to airmen (pilots) about weather conditions that are potentially hazardous to flying such as high winds, poor visibility and icing.

Airport code – There are different standards for setting airport codes. International airport codes are assigned by the ICAO (International Civil Aviation Organization). International codes are always four letters (i.e. KSEA). The assigned letters usually indicate something about the location of the airport. In addition, airports have domestically-assigned codes that are three letters (i.e. SEA). Three letter codes are used when booking commercial air flights. In this book the ICAO four letter airport codes are used throughout.

Airway – To provide organized control of aircraft in flight, the airspace has been crisscrossed with "airways", essentially highways in the sky that are identified by letters and numbers just as highways on the ground are identified. Airways are shown on aeronautical charts. The flight plans routes listed in Appendix D reference many airways by letter and number. Generally, planes on IFR flights are flying along airways but sometimes, to shorten the flight or for other reasons, ATC will tell (clear) an aircraft to skip some turns on the airways and fly directly to a more distance point (waypoint) along the route. In this book when I refer to being cleared by ATC to fly "direct" to some waypoint, that is what ATC is telling me to do.

AOE – Airport of Entry. In any given country only some airports are designated as AOE's where planes arriving from outside the country, or departing to locations outside the country, must first stop to pass through Immigrations and Customs.

Approach – A general term used to describe the flight path of an aircraft when it is near an airport and lining up to land on a particular runway.

Approach course – The magnetic heading a pilot flies that leads to the runway threshold to land. It may also refer to various headings the pilot flies before finally be lined up to land on a runway.

ATC – Air Traffic Control. This term is generally used to describe the entire network of people and equipment used to manage air traffic, including controllers managing traffic along a route of flight, approach and departure controllers around busy airports, people in an airport control tower, and people who manage the movement of planes around the airport on the ground. In the US we typically use the terms "Center", "Approach", "Departure", "Tower", and "Ground" to designate different elements of the ATC system. In other countries they may use other names like "Radar" or "Radio" when addressing an air traffic control operation.

Avgas – Aviation gasoline. Small aircraft with piston engines, like those in a car, use higher octane gasoline than normally used in a car. It may have different octane levels and contain lead, or low levels of lead, but it is all gasoline and referred to as "avgas". It is totally different from jet fuel which is used in jets and in turboprop propeller planes. Jet fuel is basically kerosene and cannot be used in piston engines.

CHT – Cylinder Head Temperature. The temperature of the cylinder heads in a piston engine. These temperatures, along with oil temperature, are primary indicators of whether the engine is running too hot. An instrument in the cockpit displays the cylinder temperatures.

DME – Distance Measuring Equipment. This is equipment in the aircraft that can show the distance from the plane to a VOR station (if so equipped) or a few other types of ground navigation stations.

Density Altitude – The altitude above mean sea level but adjusted for barometric air pressure, temperature and humidity. Pilots often refer to density altitude because it's an indication of how their aircraft will actually perform. Aircraft performance generally decreases with increased density altitude. At airports at high elevations with high temperature and low humidity, the takeoff distance an aircraft needs is much greater than at an airport at lower elevation with lower temperatures and higher humidity.

eAPIS – Electronic Advanced Passenger Information System. This is an online system that planes entering and leaving the country must use to notify the US Customs and Border Protection Agency about the details of the flight and the crew and passengers on board.

FBO – FBO stands for Fixed Base Operator but those words don't really explain what FBO's are. An FBO can be one of a wide variety of businesses that provide aircraft services, maintenance, supplies, etc. that are located at an airport. Most commonly it refers to the business at the airport where small general aviation planes can park and the pilot can do such things as buy fuel, rent a car, check weather on computer terminals, use the rest room, or just hang out and wait for bad weather to pass. Passengers can also be picked up and dropped off. FBO's can be very sophisticated facilities that mainly serve corporate jets and provide a wide range of support services, even on-site conference rooms and catering. Because of all these services, an FBO can be thought of as a general-aviation terminal compared to the regular commercial-aviation terminal that most passengers use.

FIR – Flight Information Region. FIR's are large geographical areas delineated on aviation charts showing which ATC agency has responsibility for controlling and communicating with aircraft in that area. As an aircraft flies its route, it may transit from one FIR to another requiring the air traffic controller in one FIR to hand off responsibility for that aircraft to the air traffic controller in the next FIR.

FL – Flight Level. Aircraft are assigned altitudes, and refer to altitudes, in two ways. An aircraft may be assigned an altitude in feet (i.e. 10,000 feet). To establish this altitude, the pilot must adjust the altimeter in the plane so it is referenced to a local barometer (air pressure) reading on the ground. Alternately, a plane may be flying at a flight level like FL100, essentially equivalent to 10,000 feet. Aircraft altitudes are rounded to the nearest 100 feet. Flight level altitudes are always referenced to an altimeter barometer setting of 29.92 inches (1013 milliBars or mB). Flight levels provide consistent altitudes regardless of the barometer reading on the ground. In the US, flight level altitudes are used for aircraft flying above 17,999 feet (the transition altitude). Elsewhere in the world, the transition altitude can very considerable from a few thousand feet up, and be localized around a given airport.

Ferry Flight – A ferry flight is a one-way flight that relocates a plane from one place to another, usually because the plane has been sold and the new owner wants the plane flown to his local airport. Ferry flights, or ferrying an airplane, is the common means of moving a plane from the US to Australia, for example. It is usually more economical than taking the wings off the plane and shipping it in a crate. Several companies and individual pilots make their living ferrying planes around the country and around the globe.

fpm – feet per minute. The climb and descent rate of aircraft are given in feet per minute.

GA – General Aviation. General aviation is a somewhat vague, catch-all term that can include pretty much any aircraft operation that isn't a scheduled commercial airline operation. General aviation includes aircraft ranging from small piston-engine powered aircraft like mine to private, corporate and charter jets to helicopters, gyro-copters, etc. GA aircraft are generally parked in a different part of the airport away from the commercial terminal. The services they require are also different.

GENDEC – General Declaration. A standard one page ICAO form that contains information about an arriving or departing flight including details about the crew and passengers. One or more copies of GENDEC forms are almost always required when flying into or out of a foreign airport.

gph – gallons per hour. The unit typically used for fuel consumption in a small plane.

GPS – Global Positioning System. A constellation of satellites circling earth transmit special signals that can be received by GPS receivers in planes, boats, cars, watches, phones, and many other devices. The GPS receiver interprets the signals to accurately and precisely determine the location of the GPS receiver. Navigating using GPS positions has become the dominate form of navigation in modern aircraft.

Handlers – Handlers are people or companies working at airports that basically provide a variety of support services to general aviation aircraft. In the US and some other countries with active general aviation communities, FBO's provide handling services so the term "handler" is not often used. In other countries handlers are useful for efficiently getting through Customs and Immigration, refueling the aircraft, parking the aircraft, and arranging other services for the flight crew and passengers like ground transportation, hotels, etc. The cost of a handler can range from a few hundred dollars to more than a thousand dollars depending on where it is and the services provided. A pilot can save money by arranging for the needed services at an airport without using handler. Some airports require the use of a handler.

Heading – The magnetic compass direction where the nose of the plane is pointing. Depending on the wind, the heading may be different than the actual magnetic course the plane is flying.

HF – High Frequency. This refers to long distance shortwave communications in the frequency band from 3 MHz to 30 MHz. Normally aircraft use the VHF radio band from 118.00 to 136.0 MHz to talk to Air Traffic Control. Over the ocean, however, or large expanses of unpopulated land, VHF signals may lack the range for successful communication with ATC. In such cases HF frequencies are used instead. Commercial airliners and long-range private jets are typically equipped with HF radio equipment. However, small planes very rarely have HF equipment because they don't fly over the ocean. For those times when a small plane does fly over the ocean, an HF radio is temporarily installed for communications.

IFR – Instrument Flight Rules. A set of rules for flying an aircraft that are used throughout the world. Under IFR, a pilot may fly in the clouds where he may not be able see other aircraft. The plane's location is monitored and controlled by ATC which has the responsibility to ensure one aircraft doesn't collide with another since the planes may not be able to see other in the clouds. An aircraft flying on an IFR flight plan must always fly the assigned route at an assigned altitude and be in radio communication with ATC.

ILS – Instrument Landing System. A radio beacon system built on a runway that communicates with a navigation radio receiver in the cockpit. It allows the pilot to fly the plane precisely to the beginning (threshold) of a runway even if there are very low overcast clouds or fog at the airport. ILS's are installed at airports around the world. In some cases they are being supplanted by GPS-based landing systems that don't require the radio beacon system the runway.

IMC – Instrument Meteorological Conditions. Generally, IMC means the pilot is flying in the clouds and must reference instruments in the cockpit to maintain controlled flight since no visual reference (i.e. the horizon) is available to keep the wings level and make controlled turns.

Intersection – The place where two or more airways intersect. An intersection is almost always assigned a unique five level designation to identify it; i.e. SHEDD or WUMOX. Intersections are also referred to as waypoints.

Lean-of-peak – A term used to denote how the fuel flow to an engine is adjusted. Lean-of-peak is an adjustment that economizes on fuel consumption during cruise flight at lower power settings.

MEA – Minimum Enroute Altitude. The MEA is the minimum altitude an aircraft may fly along an airway. MEA's are primarily established to ensure the aircraft maintains adequate clearance above terrain. The MEA may also be set so the aircraft is flying high enough to receive navigation signals from VOR stations on the ground and communicate via VHF radio with ATC.

METAR – Meteorological Aerodrome Report. This is a standardized report of the current weather conditions at an airport at the time of the report. It usually includes the date and time of the observation, the wind direction and speed, the cloud conditions and altitude, the temperature and dew point, and the barometric pressure. It may also include notations for other weather conditions such as rain, snow, hail, fog, etc. and the presence of thunderstorms at or near the airport. METAR reports are usually issued every hour but sometimes more often if warranted by changing conditions.

Missed Approach – When a pilot is flying an instrument approach to an airport and decides not to actually land because he cannot see the runway or because he is just practicing instrument flying, the pilot executes a "missed approach" in which he does not land but instead climbs back up to a known altitude and follows a route that is documented for that runway and airport. A missed approach route often leads to a holding pattern from which the pilot can attempt the instrument landing again.

nm – Nautical Miles. Distances in aviation are always given in nautical miles. One nautical mile = 1.15 statute miles = 1.852 km. A nautical mile was derived as 1 arc minute of the circumference of the earth; i.e., the circumference of the earth divided by 21,600.

Pre-flight inspection – Before flying, a prudent pilot will makes checks of critical systems on the airplane to ensure they are working correctly. The pre-flight inspection includes a walk-around inspection of the plane to make sure nothing is broken or otherwise amiss.

Ramp – A general term used for the area of an airport where planes park or are taxied while moving from a parking place to a taxiway before actually getting to a runway. Sometimes the ramp is referred to as the apron.

RNAV – Area Navigation. Today RNAV almost always refers to GPS navigation but in the past it referred to navigation via LORAN and other systems that could provide general aircraft position in latitude and longitude.

Runway numbers – Runways are usually aligned so the local prevailing wind blows along the runway direction. Runway orientations are given in magnetic compass directions and rounded to the nearest 10 degrees. For example, a runway oriented in a compass direction of 20 degrees with be referred to as "runway 02". Since you can land and takeoff on essentially every runway in both directions, the same runway (strip of asphalt or concrete) is also a runway shifted by 180 degrees. Therefore, the same strip of asphalt or concrete is BOTH "runway 02" and "runway 20", for example. A pilot will refer to either runway 02 or runway 20 depending on which direction is being used for takeoff and landing.

Satphone – Satellite Phone. An alternative to using HF for communication over the ocean is to use a satellite phone instead to communicate with ATC. I used a standard Iridium 9555 satphone on my international flights. Of course, to use this method you must have the international telephone numbers of the ATC operations serving a particular area of flight (FIR).

SID – Standard Instrument Departure. To organize the flow of aircraft departing an airport, and simplify issuing instructions to those aircraft, the airport publishes SID's which are specific instructions for headings and altitude that an aircraft must fly after taking off. Large, busy airports may have dozens of SID's which can be assigned depending on the runways in use and the destination of a departing aircraft.

Squawk code – a four digit code such as 4320 uniquely assigned to an aircraft on a given flight. The plane's transponder transmits the squawk code when scanned by ATC radar. It shows up on the ATC radar screen to uniquely identify each plane.

STAR – Standardized Arrival Route. STAR's are the same as SID's except they provide standardized heading and altitude instructions for planes arriving at an airport. Large, busy airports may have dozens of STAR's.

TAF – Terminal Area Forecast. A forecast of weather conditions in the area of an airport, usually within a 5 mile radius. TAF's are usually issued 4 times a day and forecast about 24 hours into the future. They contain pretty much the same weather information found in a METAR.

Touch and Go's – When a pilot is learning to fly, considerable practice is required to learn how to approach and land. For efficiency, in a "touch and go" operation the pilot does not stop after landing and taxi off the runway but instead, after landing, applies full power and immediately takes off again. Using this method, many more practice landings can be made in a given hour of training time.

Transition altitude – See the discussion for **FL** (flight levels).

Transponder – A device on the aircraft that transmit a squawk code and other information when scanned by ATC radar.

Vector – A vector in aviation generally refers to a magnetic heading an aircraft is instructed to fly by ATC, usually to avoid other aircraft or to position the plane to land. A pilot may refer to being "vectored around" by ATC.

VFR – Visual Flight Rules. A set of rules for flying an airplane that are used throughout the world. Basically, flying using VFR requires a pilot stay a certain distance away from, and out of, clouds so they can see other aircraft and avoid collisions. It differs from IFR in which a pilot can fly in the clouds. With VFR, a pilot does not need to fly an assigned route or at an assigned altitude, nor does he need to be in radio communication with ATC. In some countries like the United States, a pilot can fly using VFR without filing a flight plan.

VOR – VHF Omnidirectional Radio Range. VOR's are radio stations on the ground transmitting on assigned frequencies in the VHF frequency range of 108.1 MHz to 117.9 MHz, just above the FM radio frequency band. The signals from VOR stations are transmitted in such a way that a receiver in the cockpit of the plane shows the pilot the direction to the VOR station and, in many cases, the distance. For many years navigating a plane by flying from one VOR station to another was the conventional way to follow a flight route. VOR's are still widely used in this way but are being replaced by GPS navigation which does not rely on VHF ground stations and their coverage limitations.

Waypoint – One of thousands of ground locations defined around the world and shown on aeronautical charts that can be used for directing the flight of, or reference the location of, an aircraft.

Zulu time – Zulu time is Greenwich Mean Time (GMT). Most aviation times are given in Zulu time and denoted in the form such as 1800Z which is 1800 hours GMT. GMT is a constant time standard that does not vary with daytime savings time of other local time adjustments. Converting from Zulu time to local time can sometimes be confusing because countries decide themselves what local time they want. The time they choose may not be very consistent with its location in the world. There are even places that use ½ hour local time offsets instead of one hour. In this book I use both Zulu time and local time which I denote as 1800L, for example.

Appendix B – Resources and Websites

This Appendix presents a lot of miscellaneous information I gathered while completing these flights which I think will be useful to pilots contemplating similar long-distance international flights. Let me also preface this by saying this information was current and useful for my flights in 2011, 2013, and 2014 but over time it will become obsolete. In gathering information from other pilots about flights in years past, some of it had become obsolete or wrong so it's important to double check any information, including mine, before relying on it.

Weather Websites

Of course, weather is a critical element in completing long distances flights in light aircraft. In the US, I was accustomed to having excellent weather information in my cockpit including METARS, TAF's, radar images, etc. via XM Weather so if a weather issue developed after takeoff it was feasible to recognize it and adjust for it as the flight progressed. These in-cockpit weather resources are not available outside the US, at least not for my avionics setup, so more thorough pre-flight weather considerations are necessary.

I used a variety of weather websites during my flight. The first stop was always the AWC website run by NOAA at:

http://www.aviationweather.gov/

You can enter the ICAO airport code for any airport in the world (not just the US) and get current METAR's and TAF's if available. In addition to the wide variety of weather information, wind aloft forecasts, satellite images, etc. available via the front page menu, there are "hidden" files of weather forecast maps that you can't get at directly from the menu, at least I didn't find a way. These maps are found at:

http://www.aviationweather.gov/data/products/swh/

The files have odd coded names indicating the region of the world and time for which they are valid. By clicking on a few of the file names and displaying the associated map it's possible to figure out which codes correspond to which regions of the world.

A very useful site I came across after starting my route-the-world flight is the AC Weather Network blog at:

http://acweather.blogspot.com/

This site doesn't present any new weather information but instead pulls together, in a convenient from, a lot of weather maps from a variety of sources including the NOAA maps in the hidden files, Jeppesen current surface and forecast maps, lightning strikes in the last hour, etc. The information is divided by regions of the world which can be selected on the top line of the opening page. After the AWC site, this was usually my next stop.

For Europe and the North Atlantic I found a few region-specific websites that provide additional information about temperatures and winds aloft and the potential for icing. These sites are:

http://131.54.120.150/index.cfm

http://www.flyingineurope.be/aviation_weather_maps.htm

http://www.weathercharts.org/index.htm#aviationweather

http://www.weatherroanoke.com/natlantic.html

Finally, for a general "consumer-type" presentation of a long range (several day) weather forecast I used the Weather Underground site at:

http://www.wunderground.com/

By entering any ICAO airport code, Weather Underground will provide a multi-day weather forecast for that location along with a useful satellite-derived map depicting cloud heights which can be used to assess chances for thunderstorms. Since most aviation weather forecasts don't go much beyond 24 to 36 hours into the future, the Weather Underground site can be helpful for getting approximate forecasts several days in the future. If you know a better day is coming, sometimes it pays to delay your flight.

Communications

I had two VHF radios in the panel – the one in the Garmin GNS530W and the SL-30 NAV/COM. The SL-30 proved to be a much better radio than the one in the Garmin so I often used it when I knew I would be at the ragged edge of VHF radio coverage. In the US the VHF radio coverage is available essentially everywhere while on a IFR flight plan. On international flights you can forget about having solid coverage at the lower flight levels like FL110 where I typically was. You will occasionally fly out of VHF radio contact before you can be handed off to the next controller. For that reason, while still in contact I made a habit of asking the controller for the next frequency I would be handed to. That way, if I lost contact - which sometimes happened - at least I could switch to the new frequency and start calling them. Eventually I'd be in range and make contact. Occasionally I would find a commercial aircraft flying at a higher altitude with better VHF range that would relay for me. If that failed, then I knew I'd eventually fly near an airport for which there are published approach or tower frequencies. I could call one of them and find out who I should be talking to. I only had to resort to this once - in India. Overall, it was not a big concern to lose radio contact – I just kept flying my clearance and eventually I'd be able to contact somebody.

The HF radio I had on board was a ham radio rig modified to transmit on aviation frequencies – an ICOM 760MKIIG with the AH-4 automatic antenna tuner. The ICOM has a maximum peak transmit power of about 100 watts. After ramp checking OK, on my first experience using it in flight I could hear ATC but they couldn't hear me. As a wireless engineer by profession and ham radio operator since the age of 9, this was a little frustrating (embarrassing?). I didn't expect much from this ad hoc HF radio installation done by others because the antenna installation strung under the fuselage was put there to be convenient, not designed in any way to be effective. Generally I relied on my satphone for oceanic communications. In retrospect, I wish I'd put more effort into making the HF more useful, including wiring the HF's audio into the plane's audio panel instead of using the hand mike and speaker. Mounting the removable HF radio control head on the plane's instrument panel (instead of over my shoulder) would make it much easier to tune. The biggest improvement would come from a better wire antenna installation. It would take some calculated experimentation with different options to find the best configuration.

For my flight to South America and Antarctica in 2013 I made these improvements to the HF installation. The improvements did yield better communications results but I'm still seeking more effective solutions for the HF radio problem.

The satellite phone is essential, not only for oceanic communications but also for getting weather and other information at remote locations. I had a couple of important conversations on the satphone from Christmas Island regarding weather in the ITCZ and issues related to my landing permit at Honolulu. The satphone coverage was generally good, though occasionally it would take a few minutes to lock on to a satellite.

Telephone Numbers

This is a list of telephone numbers I used for oceanic ATC communications on my satphone in the eastbound order I used them:

Gander radio: +1 709 651 5328

Iceland radio: +354 553 3022

Brisbane Center: +61 7 3866 3314

Melbourne Center: +61 3 9235 7492

Nadi (Fiji) Radio: +679 672 0664

Auckland Radio: +649 275 9817

Faleolo (Samoa) Center: +685 12530

Oakland Center (from PCHL to PHNL): +1 510 745 3403

Oakland Center: (Hawaii): +1 510 745 3415

San Francisco ARINC: +1 925 371 3920

For ramp access at Maui (PHOG) call +1 808-872-3875.

The following are phone numbers to use when crossing the Drake Passage:

Punta Arenas ATC: +56 61 745474.

Punta Arenas Operations office: +56 61 745417

Punta Arenas Meteo (weather) office: +56 61 745467

In addition, I started putting my satphone number (the Iridium 8816 number) in the "Remarks" or "Other Information" section of the flight plan so ATC would have it on file if they needed to call me. ATC may also ask for it.

Charts

Before starting the round-the-world flight I had been using the Honeywell AV8OR ACE Electronic Flight Bag (EFB). This device basically shows you digital versions of aeronautical charts that can be viewed and manipulated with a seven inch touch screen. It has VFR and IFR charts, approach plates, etc. covering the US. Although I had been using this, I wasn't particularly happy with it. I have now transitioned to using a 32GB iPad 2 and the ForeFlight HD Pro application for the iPad which is a great software application for displaying charts and planning flights. The iPad screen is much large, and the touchscreen response much better, than the AV8OR ACE. The iPad is also a lot cheaper and more versatile than the ACE.

While ForeFlight works great in the US, at the time it did not have charts for any areas outside of the US. The chart problem gets more difficult because electronic charts are generally only available from Jeppesen and are expensive. For the small part of Canada I crossed, I bought paper charts and the book of instrument approach diagrams from Canada which are excellent. Canada's enroute chart coverage on the Atlantic also extends to Iceland and the Azores.

For Europe, low altitude enroute and approach plates are available for the ACE so I didn't bother getting paper charts. However, it turned out to be difficult to use these charts for flight planning. Also, no VFR charts are included. European VFR flying is complicated so paper charts are definitely needed for those areas where VFR flights are intended. I ended up buying a VFR chart in England covering southern England for some short VFR flights I was making in that area. I finally ended up buying a set of Jeppesen paper enroute charts which made flight planning easier.

For the countries I was visiting in Europe, all of the detailed terminal charts (STAR's, SID's, approach plates, text) are available from public sources on the internet. At the time a convenient way to get them was to subscribe to EuroFPL. EuroFPL provides route planning with EuroControl route validation. It will also prepare trip kits which include all the terminal charts from these public sources for the departure and destination airports. Using these trip kits, and the Jeppesen enroute paper charts, I had essentially all the chart information I needed for flying IFR across Europe with stops in the UK, France and Greece.

Beyond the US, Canada, and Europe, the only consistent source for charts (paper and electronic) is Jeppesen, although many countries offer complete airport terminal charts as pdf files on the web site of their FAA-equivalent government organization (Australia is a good example). I initially bought Jeppesen paper trip charts for the Middle East, SE Asia, and the Pacific which amounts to a lot of paper. To minimize the amount of paper I would have to carry, I extracted all the enroute charts and only the terminal charts for the dozen or so airports on my route. However, once the trip started, and I got better information on which airports to visit, I changed my original route resulting in the paper charts I had on board being useless - I didn't have the ones I would need. The solution to this, which is what I should have done in the first place, is just accept the additional expense of buying JeppView electronic chart coverage for the Middle East, SE Asia, and the Pacific. These charts along with software to access them resides on my laptop and on the iPad running the Jeppesen's Mobile FD application. I use the iPad for all charts in the cockpit in place of the AV8OR ACE. The AV8OR ACE became a GPS backup.

After flying around the world and setting the new objective of flying to all 7 continents, I followed the same approach for charts. I bought the e-chart coverage from Jeppesen for the Caribbean and South America which worked seamlessly on the iPad in the cockpit.

E-charts are also much more accessible than paper charts. If a diversion due to weather or a mechanical issue is needed, the charts for the diversion or alternate airport are immediately available in the cockpit on the iPad and much easier to search than multiple Jeppesen binders full of paper. The iPad is also nice because travel guides can be downloaded from Amazon in Kindle format for display on the iPad (I used Frommer's eBooks for some areas). For a flight like this which was also about touring, not just flying, using eBooks for travel guides also eliminated the need for carry these paper guidebooks.

Early in my trip I went to the trouble of printing backup chart copies from the e-charts. This can be done at the business center (or front desk) at the hotel or using a portable printer. I bought a Canon ip100 portable printer with battery pack for this purpose and for printing the multiple copies of General Declarations (GENDEC's) that are sometimes needed when arriving in a new country.

Ultimately I bought a second iPad to carry with me for flight planning while leaving the primary iPad on the plane. The Jeppesen chart Mobile FD license and the ForeFlight license allow more than one installation. With redundant iPads, both containing the ForeFlight and Jeppesen e-charts, I grew confident enough in the e-chart solution that I stopped printing any backup paper copies or keeping any other paper charts on the plane. I also stopped carrying the portable printer. Getting away from paper charts of any kind reduced weight and streamlined the whole flight planning operation.

Flight Plans, Overflight and Landing Permits

There are a number of companies that are in the business of obtaining overflight and landing permits when flying over, or to, foreign countries. Most of these companies cater to private and corporate jet flights but some are willing to take on clients with small pitonpengine planes like mine.

I used a company called SkyPlan in Calgary, Canada, to obtain my overflight and landing permits for my round-the-world flight and my flights through South America. Skyplan is a full service company that can also file flight plans, arrange handlers, hotels, ground transportation and pretty much anything else a plane arriving at an airport might need. They also have a substantial staff that is available 24 hours a day if you have a problem to resolve. They are not the least expensive, but the least expensive are often one-person operations that are not always available and may not always be successful at obtaining permits in a timely fashion. On my flights I was never delayed because a permit was not in place when I needed. I've heard stories of pilots who have been delayed several days because the company they used to get permits was not very good at doing it for some countries.

For filing flight plans in the US I initially used DUATS which I had used for years. For the last few years I've been using FltPlan.com instead which is much more versatile. For flight plans in Europe I used EuroFPL which can provide a validation check for the flight plan with EuroControl. Rocketroute.com is an alternative to EuroFPL which includes its own route finding engine and also provides a EuroControl validation check but is not free. For flight plans beyond Europe as far as Honolulu, I devised my own routes and communicated those to Skyplan who filed the flight plans. Skyplan would then validate the route and altitude I selected and file the flight plans with the appropriate agencies. This was a relatively inexpensive process and worth it to get the flight plans sent to the right people along this part of my route.

Handlers

I didn't use any handlers in the US or Canada, I just parked and bought fuel at FBO's. The only place I used a handler in Europe was in Greece where GoldAir would do handling for 30 Euros at the time. Airports in Greece often require prior permission (PPR) so the handler is a convenient way to notify and obtain such permission, as well as pay airport fees. Otherwise I was just using local FBO's in Europe where I bought fuel and paid airport fees.

Starting with Egypt I used handlers selected by Skyplan. A "handler" in the context of a light aircraft really doesn't handle (push around) the plane as they might with a private jet, but rather facilitates processing through the airport (Immigrations, Customs, paying airport fees, scheduling fuel service, etc.) Some airports require you use them, others don't. For their services alone, excluding fees they may pay on your behalf, handlers can cost from as little as US$50 (like Greece) to US$500 or more depending on what they do for you and where they are. For me they were a convenience that minimized the bureaucratic time-wasting I would have endured without them. The handlers Skyplan normally uses were not necessarily the least expensive so if you are trying to save money, shop around for handlers and get written quotes via email for their services. You can also figure out airports where handlers are not required at all and try to manage yourself. Some ferry pilots I talked to were experienced enough at particular airports to navigate their own way through without a handler and save some money. Because I was confident I could manage on my own, like in Europe I didn't use a handler at Singapore (WSSL), at the Australian airports, or after arriving in Honolulu.

Spares and Tools

I'm capable with hand tools but I'm not a mechanic, especially not an aircraft mechanic, so I had no illusions about being able fix my plane myself if something serious were to go wrong. Fortunately nothing serious did go wrong - the plane ran perfectly, owing in part to the low time engine and airframe. When I bought N788W in June, 2010, it had only 288 hours total time on the engine and airframe - enough to get past the break-in period but still a very low-time plane. It had just 350 hours when I started the round-the-world trip. I planned on changing the oil twice so I took 2 oil filters and 16 quarts of 20W-50. I bought more oil along the way when I could find 20W-50 so as to preserve the stock I had on board, but ultimately I used it all for oil changes and in the course of flying. I had a set of spare spark plugs already gapped for my plane and the odd length spark plug socket and ratchet to change them, though I never inspected the spark plugs nor did I have a fouled plug. I'll note here that the cowling on the Columbia is a pain to remove with 25 screws and two piano hinges along the sides. The tools I had were just basic hand tools - wrenches, screwdrivers, duct tape, VOM meter, etc. for simple repairs. The weight of tools also impacted my thinking about what to take.

I'll point out that FAA N-registered planes like mine (not used in commercial service or instruction) are only required to have annual inspections, not 50 or 100 hour inspections, so I wasn't violating inspection requirements on this trip. This round-the-world flight took 162.2 hours to complete - not excessive hours considering what might be expected in a year of normal flying between annual inspections.

Fuel

Jet fuel is widely available because commercial aircraft use it. Avgas (100LL/100/130) is a different story. The availability of avgas will affect routing. Availability also changes with time. For example, I had planned to stop in Ahmadabad, India, but they ran out of avgas 10 days before my arrival so I had to change my destination to Nagpur, India. At Christmas Island they had been out of avgas for several weeks, but got a new shipment in a few weeks before I arrived. It's important to stay informed of avgas availability at any airport along your route where it may be in doubt.

Antarctica Approach and Landing YouTube Video

As mentioned in Chapter 27, I made a video of my approach and landing at King George Island using my GoPro Hero 2 camera suction-cupped mounted to the inside of the windshield. The audio input for the camera was plugged into the airplane audio system so the video also recorded the radio calls between me and the tower guy at King George Island, as well as comments I made along the way. The link for the YouTube is:

http://www.youtube.com/watch?v=9ks8QlUHJpk

Appendix C – N788W Weight and Balance

The ability to successful control and fly an airplane, especially a small airplane like mine, is very dependent on the overall weight of the aircraft and how the weight is distributed long the nose-to-tail axis. The later involves a calculation of the center-of-gravity (CG) using the weight and location of everything in the plane, and the plane itself. Pilots call these calculations "Weight and Balance" calculations. Technically, they should be done before every flight but most pilots are flying their planes with loading configurations they have used many times before so they already know that the weight and balance are within acceptable limits. That said, though, there have been some high-profile charter and commercial aircraft accidents as a result of the planes being overloaded or loaded so the center of gravity was beyond the acceptable range.

For my flight, N788W was equipped with auxiliary fuel tanks located in places where fuel tanks normally don't go. With a full fuel load the plane was almost 500 pounds over the certificated maximum takeoff weight (MTOW) of 3,400 pounds, one reason a FAA Special Flight Permit was needed. Because of these excesses, very detailed weight and balance calculations were done for N788W to make sure the CG was within the acceptable range with the overweight configuration.

Table C1 shows those detailed calculations. Cabin items that were removed, like seats, where subtracted. The precise locations and weights of even small items inside the cabin were measured and included in the calculations. This is a much more comprehensive approach than most pilots use when calculating weight and balance for their planes.

Table C1

Lancair Columbia LC40-550FG, N788W, s/n 40022 – Weight and Balance with Two Ferry Tanks				
Item	Weight (lbs)	Arm (inches)	Moment (lbs-inches)	% of MTOW
Aircraft empty weight per POH (6/14/2011)	2358.69	103.33	243723.44	
remove rear seats	-20.00	141.40	-2828.00	
remove right front seat	-15.00	110.00	-1650.00	
added plywood floor for fuel tanks	12.00	133.00	1596.00	
added HF radio system	6.00	133.00	798.00	
added 78 gallon fuel tank #1 (empty)	27.00	133.00	3591.00	
added 28 gallon fuel tank #2 (empty)	18.00	110.00	1980.00	
Revised Empty Weight	**2386.69**	**103.58**	**247210.44**	

Pilot	190.00	110.00	20900.00	
Survival equipment (at co-pilot station)	35.00	110.00	3850.00	
Pilot luggage (at co-pilot station)	25.00	110.00	2750.00	
Tool kit (co-pilot foot well)	15.00	95.00	1425.00	
O2 tank (behind ferry tank #1)	12.00	148.00	1776.00	
Main baggage	0.00	166.60	0.00	
Baggage shelf	0.00	199.80	0.00	
Fuel in wing tanks (98 gallons)	588.00	118.00	69384.00	
Sub-Total with no fuel in ferry tanks	**3251.69**	**106.80**	**347295.44**	**95.64**

Fuel in ferry tank #1 (78 gals max.)	468.00	133.00	62244.00	
Fuel in ferry tank #2 (28 gals max.)	168.00	110.00	18480.00	
Total ramp weight with fuel	**3887.69**	**110.10**	**428019.44**	**114.34**

Fuel for taxi, run up, take off roll (1.5 gallons)	-9.00	118.00	-1062.00	

Takeoff Weight	**3878.69**	**110.08**	**426957.44**	**114.08**

Appendix D – Flight Plan Routes

Flight around the World

There were a total of 27 flights to complete the around-the-world portion of the seven continents flight in 2011. This total does not include the initial flight from Merced, CA to my home base of Bremerton, WA after the ferry tank was installed and two local VFR flights made in England. The routing and altitude I requested are listed in Table D1 for those 27 flights. It should be noted that the flight plan routes I filed for and the clearance I was actually given were sometimes different. It was not unusual to be given a modified routing somewhere during these long flights, a practice which is also common and routine for flights inside the United States.

Flight to South America and the First Attempt to Fly to Antarctica

The flight plan routes and altitudes for the flight segments to South America and around the continent in 2013, and for my first attempt to fly to Antarctica, are shown in Table D2.

Second Successful Attempt to Fly to Antarctica

The flight plan routes and altitudes for my second trip to South America and my final successful attempt to fly to Antarctica in 2014 are shown in Table D3.

Table D1. Flight Plan Routes and Altitudes, Flight Around the World

City	Country	ICAO Airport Code	GC Dist. from last airport	Cummulative Distance	Arrival date	Departure date	# of nights	Flight Plan Route To Next City	Altitude
Merced, CA	USA	KMCE	0	0		6/13/11	8	VFR, no flight plan	10,000 ft
Bremerton, WA	USA	KPWT	620	620	6/13/11	6/21/11	6	VFR, no flight plan	various
Quincy, IL	USA	KUIN	1,435	2,055	6/21/11	6/27/11	2	not recorded	9,000 ft
Bangor, ME	USA	KBGR	1,033	3,088	6/27/11	6/29/11	6	KBGR MLT PQI GRINS YYY YZV CYYR	7,000 ft
Goose Bay NFL	Canada	CYYR	608	3,696	6/29/11	7/5/11	2	CYYR LOACH 58N50W 62N40W 63N30W EMBLA BIRK	10,000 ft
Reykjavik	Iceland	BIRK	1,339	5,035	7/5/11	7/7/11	2	BIRK DCT OSKUM DCT RATSU DCT DEVBI STN330085 STN AID GOW EGPF	FL070
Glasgow	UK	EGPF	720	5,755	7/7/11	7/9/11	1	EGPF TOC PCS WAL MONTY RETSI TOD PERUP ERNOK EGGD	FL070
Bristol	UK	EGGD	277	6,032	7/9/11	7/10/11	9	VFR, direct	2,000 ft
Gloucester	UK	EGBJ	37	6,069	7/10/11	7/19/11	81	EGJP N0165F090 MALBY L9 CPT N859 SITET A34 KOVAK H20 DOMOD A3NEV R31 MTL R161 ABDIL LFMD	FL090
Cannes	France	LFMD	622	6,691	7/19/11	10/8/11	3	LFMD N0165F090 SODRI A3 MIRSA L127 ELB M729 PNZ M603 SOR/N0165F110 M742 LUXIL L995 TIGRA LGKR	FL090
Kerkyra, Corfu	Greece	LGKR	629	7,320	10/8/11	10/11/11	1	LGKR N0165F110 MALED A14 MIL LGSR	FL110
Santorini	Greece	LGSR	326	7,646	10/11/11	10/12/11	2	VFR, direct	4,500 ft
Heraklion, Crete	Greece	LGIR	65	7,711	10/12/11	10/14/11	0	LGIR VFR SIT IFR A10 PAXIS A727 GESAD L551 DBA B12 KHG A145 LXR DCT HELX	FL090
Luxor	Egypt	HELX	697	8,408	10/14/11	10/14/11	3	HELX DECT ASRAB A145 LABIS V169 KIA A415 DOH B415 ADV A419 LUDER DCT OMDB	FL110
Dubai	UAE	OMDB	1,229	9,637	10/17/11	10/20/11	3	OMDB DCT RIKET B525 LALDO B505 NADSO B524 ALPOR M504 TELEM G472 UPTAR DCT VANP	FL110
Nagpur	India	VANP	1,331	10,968	10/20/11	10/23/11	3	VANP N0164F090 DCT NNP G450 CEA B465 DAKID DCT VGEG	FL090

Table D1 (continued). Flight Plan Routes and Altitudes, Flight Around the World

City	Country	ICAO Airport Code	GC Dist. from last airport	Cummulative Distance	Arrival date	Departure date	# of nights	Flight Plan Route To Next City	Altitude
Chittagong	Bangladesh	VGEG	717	11,685	10/23/11	10/24/11	1	VGEG DTC AVLED HDG080(M) DCT MDY R207 DCT VTCC	FL090
Chiang Mai	Thailand	VTCC	453	12,138	10/24/11	10/28/11	4	VTCC DCT CMA A464 BKK G458 STN DCT VTSB	FL090
Surat Thani	Thailand	VTSB	576	12,714	10/28/11	11/3/11	6	VTSB DCT STN W17 HTY A334 PASVA DCT VKB VPK V469 VMR A224 VIR DCT JB DCT WSSL	FL110
Seletar	Singapore	WSSL	541	13,255	11/3/11	11/6/11	3	WSSL DCT SJ A464 TPG W24 PLB W12E BIKAL G461 SBR W34 ENTAS W45 BLI DCT WADD	FL110
Bali	Indonesia	WADD	909	14,164	11/6/11	11/9/11	3	WADD DCT BLI W33 KPG A458 ALEGO DN DCT YPDN	FL110
Darwin	Australia	YPDN	954	15,118	11/9/11	11/12/11	3	YPDN DCT DN A461 AS J64 AYE DCT YAYE	9,000 FT
Ayers Rock	Australia	YAYE	763	15,881	11/12/11	11/15/11	3	YAYE AYE J64 AS W344 BDV W369 CV W356 OK W270 AMB W196 CG DCT YBCG	9,000 ft
Coolangatta (Gold Coast)	Australia	YBCG	1,222	17,103	11/15/11	11/17/11	2	YBCG DCT CG H185 BN R587 VLI DCT NVVV	FL110
Port Vila	Vanuatu	NVVV	1,030	18,133	11/17/11	11/19/11	2	NVVV DCT VLI B598 NN G224 SETTS DCT NSTU	9,000 ft
Pago Pago	American Samoa	NSTU	1,228	19,361	11/19/11	11/21/11	2	NTSU DCT DARMA SAPIX PASSA DCT PLCH	9,000 ft
Kiritimati	Kiribati	PLCH	1,258	20,619	11/21/11	11/23/11	2	PLCH DCT 05N157W 10N15630W 15N15600W TARDE KONA PHNL	9,000 ft
Honolulu, HI	USA	PHNL	1,155	21,774	11/23/11	12/1/11	8	VFR, direct	2,000 ft
Maui, HI	USA	PHOG	87	21,861	12/1/11	12/4/11	3	PHOG DCT CLUTS CEBEN CIVIT CORTT CUNDU CREAN	11,000 ft
Monterey, CA	USA	KMRY	2,036	23,897	12/4/11	12/5/11	1	VFR, direct	5,500 ft
Merced, CA	USA	KMCE	76	23,973	12/5/11	12/8/11	3	KMCE NEBBY V23 EUG V481 CVO V495 UBG V165 OLM KPWT	10,000 ft
Bremerton, WA	USA	KPWT	620	24,593	12/8/11				
Total route (nm)			24,593				164		

Table D2. 2013 Flight to South America and Antarctica Attempt

City	Country	ICAO Airport Code (or waypoint)	GC Dist. from last airport	Cummulative Distance	Arrival date	Departure date	# of nights	Flight Plan Route to the Next City	Altitude
Creswell, OR	USA	77S	0	0		12/23/12	0	VFR to Redding (KRDD). IFR from KRDM to KSJC via V23 SAC EGA CEDES	11,500 ft
San Francisco, CA	USA	KSJC	386	386	12/23/12	12/26/12	3	KSJC OSI V25 SNS V137 PMD APLES V442 PDZ NIKKL V64 BXK KGYR	11,000 ft
Phoenix, AZ	USA	KGYR	524	910	12/26/12	12/28/12	2	VFR, no flight plan filed.	9,500 ft
Houston, TX	USA	KDWH	883	1,793	12/28/12	12/29/12	1	VFR, no flight plan filed.	9,500 ft
Lake City, FL	USA	KLCQ	675	2,468	12/29/12	12/31/12	2	KLCQ OCF V157 LAL V511 NEWER KFXE	7,000 ft
Ft. Lauderdale, FL	USA	KFXE	270	2,738	12/31/12	1/2/13	2	KFXE BAHMA ZQA A555 BTLER MBPV	FL090
Providenciales	Turks & Caicos	MBPV	508	3,246	1/2/13	1/5/13	3	MBPV GTK A555 COY ANU TAPA	FL090
Antigua	Antigua	TAPA	655	3,901	1/5/13	1/5/13	0	TAPA ANU DCT TGPY	FL090
St. George	Grenada	TGPY	305	4,206	1/5/13	1/8/13	3	TGPY GND A324 TIM G443 CYR SOCA	FL090
Cayenne	French Guiana	SOCA	706	4,912	1/8/13	1/9/13	1	SOCA CYR G443 BEL SBBR	FL090
Belem	Brazil	SBBE	438	5,350	1/9/13	1/11/13	2	SBBE BEL G677 NTL SBNT	FL090
Natal	Brazil	SBNT	838	6,188	1/11/13	1/12/13	1	SBNT NTL G677 SVD SBSV	FL100
Salvador Bahia	Brazil	SBSV	456	6,644	1/12/13	1/14/13	2	SBSV SVD G677 VTR SBVT	FL100
Vitoria	Brazil	SBVT	453	7,097	1/14/13	1/15/13	1	SBVT VTR W6 RDE W45 FLN SBFL	FL120
Florianopolis	Brazil	SBFL	634	7,731	1/15/13	1/17/13	2	SBFL FLN W48 CTB A431 FOZ SBFI	FL090
Foz do Iguacu	Brazil	SBFI	343	8,074	1/17/13	1/19/13	2	VFR, no flight plan filed.	2,000 ft
Cataratas del Iguazu	Argentina	SARI	8	8,082	1/19/13	1/19/13	0	SARI IGU B687 POS B688 GUA W11 ENO SADF	FL100
Buenos Aires	Argentina	SADF	564	8,646	1/19/13	1/21/13	2	SADF FDO EXE W29 GBE W18 CRV SAVC	FL100
Comodoro Rividavia	Argentina	SAVC	792	9,438	1/21/13	1/22/13	1	SAVC CRV W189 GAL SAWG	FL080
Rio Gallegos	Argentina	SAWG	357	9,795	1/22/13	1/22/13	0	SAWG W52 SAWC	FL090
El Calafete	Argentina	SAWC	131	9,926	1/22/13	1/25/13	3	SAWC W52 SAWG	FL090
Rio Gallegos	Argentina	SAWG	131	10,057	1/25/13	1/25/13	0	SAWG GAL A570 PALIX VA570 NAS SCCI	FL080

FLIGHT PLAN ROUTES | 319

Table D2 (Continued). 2013 Flight to South America and Antarctica Attempt

City	Country	ICAO Airport Code (or waypoint)	GC Dist. from last airport	Cummulative Distance	Arrival date	Departure date	# of nights	Flight Plan Route to the Next City	Altitude
Puntas Arenas	Chile	SCCI	101	10,158	1/25/2013	2/9/2013	15	SCCI NAS W100 HORNO DRAKE PWL SCGZ	FL110
Waypoint	Antarctica	60 S. degs lat	500	10,658	2/9/2013	2/9/2013	0	SCCI NAS W100 HORNO DRAKE PWL SCGZ	FL100
Puerto Williams	Chile	SCGZ	400	11,058	2/9/2013	2/9/2013	0	SCGZ PWL VW115 DARIN VW115 NAS SCCI	FL120
Punta Arenas	Chile	SCCI	163	11,221	2/9/2013	2/15/2013	6	SCCI NAS VA570 GAL T658 MIKIM BAL SCBA	FL100
Balmaceda	Chile	SCBA	427	11,648	2/15/2013	2/17/2013	2	SCBA BAL VW101 PAR VW101 MON SCTE	FL120
Puerto Montt	Chile	SCTE	275	11,923	2/17/2013	2/19/2013	2	SCTE MON VG551 AMV SCEL	FL100
Santiago	Chile	SCEL	495	12,418	2/19/2013	2/21/2013	2	VFR, no flight plan filed.	5,500 ft
Santiago (Tobalaba)	Chile	SCTB	13	12,431	2/21/2013	4/3/2013	41	SCTB AMB T112 TOY DCT DAT SCAT	FL120
Atacama Desert	Chile	SCAT	371	12,802	4/3/2013	4/3/2013	0	SCAT DCT FAG DCT LOA SCCF	FL130
Calama	Chile	SCCF	303	13,105	4/3/2013	4/5/2013	2	VFR direct	FL120
Iquique	Chile	SCDA	137	13,242	4/5/2013	4/6/2013	1	SCDA DCT IQQ VW202 ARI L525 LIM DCT SPIM	FL100
Lima	Peru	SPIM	647	13,889	4/6/2013	4/10/2013	4	SPIM LIM V1 URA G675 SRV G437 GVV SEGU	FL100
Guayaquil	Ecuador	SEGU	612	14,501	4/10/2013	4/11/2013	1	SEGU GYV G437 ESV R564 TCO W5 MTR W8 CTG SKCG	FL100
Cartagena	Columbia	SKCG	797	15,298	4/11/2013	4/13/2013	2	SJCG CTG G430 SIA MKJS	FL100
Montego Bay	Jamaica	MKJS	501	15,799	4/13/2013	4/15/2013	2	MKJS SIA G442 UCL G448 UVR TADPO DCT KEYW	10,000 ft
Key West, FL	USA	KEYW	421	16,220	4/15/2013	4/16/2013	1	VFR, no flight plan filed.	various
Ft. Lauderdale, FL	USA	KFXE	131	16,351	4/16/2013	4/29/2013	13	KFXE LBV V157 LAL V7 SZW V198 CEW SJI PCU	10,000 ft
Hammond, LA	USA	KHDC	601	16,952	4/29/2013	4/29/2013	0	VFR, no flight plan filed.	various
Georgetown, TX	USA	KGTU	376	17,328	4/29/2013	4/30/2013	1	VFR, no flight plan filed.	various
Alpine, TX	USA	E38	312	17,640	4/30/2013	5/1/2013	1	VFR, no flight plan filed.	10,500 ft
Goodyear, AZ	USA	KGYR	480	18,120	5/1/2013	5/1/2013	0	KGYR BLH V16 PSP V388 PDZ V186 VNY KVNY	10,000 ft
Van Nuys, CA	USA	KVNY	309	18,429	5/1/2013	5/3/2013	2	VFR, generally along V23	10,500 ft
Creswell, OR	USA	77S	619	19,048	5/3/2013	5/3/2013			
Total route (nm)			19,048				131		

Table D3. 2014 Second Antarctica Attempt

City	Country	ICAO Airport Code (or waypoint)	GC Dist. from last airport	Cummlative Distance	Arrival date	Departure date	# of nights	Flight Plan Route to the Next City	Altitude
Santiago	Chile	SCEL	0	0		1/26/14	1	SCEL AMB VGS51 MON SCTE	FL110
Puerto Montt	Chile	SCTE	386	386	1/26/14	1/28/14	2	SCTE MON L775 GUTIN L775 ESQ W50 CRV W18 GAL A570 PALIX VA570 NAS SCCI	FL110/ FL130
Punta Arenas	Chile	SCCI	524	910	1/28/14	1/31/14	3	SCCI NAS W100 IRJ SCRM	FL110
King George Island	Antarctica	SCRM	883	1,793	1/31/14	2/1/14	1	SCRM IRJ W100 NAS SCCI	FL120
Punta Arenas	Chile	SCCI	675	2,468	2/1/14	2/9/14	8	SCCI NAS VA570 PALIX A570 GAL W18 CRV W50 ESQ L775 MON SCTE	FL100/ FL120
Puerto Montt	Chile	KFXE	270	2,738	2/9/14	2/10/14	1	SCTE MON VGS51 AMB SCEL	FL100
Santiago	Chile	SCEL	508	3,246	2/10/14	2/12/14	2	SCEL AMB VGS51 TOY T100 IQQ ARI SCAT	FL100/ FL120
Arica	Chile	SCAR			2/12/14	2/13/14	1	SCAR FL100 ARI L525 ILO/FL140 ESIRA/FL100 L525 LIM SPIM	FL100/ FL140
Lima	Peru	SPIM			2/13/14	2/14/14	1		
Total route (nm)				3,246			20		

Appendix E – Entry Procedures for Australia and Brazil

Australia Entry Procedures

There are several steps involved in bringing a foreign –registered and owned aircraft temporarily into Australia, in their terms, temporarily import it and then re-export it. I've listed the various steps here which were current in 2011 when I arrived in Darwin on my round-the-world flight:

1. Early on before leaving home, get a visa if you need one – U.S. citizens do need a visa but it is easy to get, all done online and costs $25. It's tied to your passport number in their system so you don't need to carry a piece of paper.

2. While at home, get a "Security" for your aircraft. A Security allows you to import and re-export your aircraft without paying any duty. It is basically a pledge that you will re-export the aircraft before a given date, which you can choose, otherwise you owe them duty on the import which is about 10% of the value of the aircraft. To get the Security you fill out a couple of forms, send them in by email, and they will email you a letter and a number. The best contact for getting a Security at the time was: Bill MacKay, email: bill.mckay@customs.gov.au

   He'll send you an email with the forms and instructions on how to fill them out. No money is needed. Choose a re-export deadline that is more time than you think you'll need; i.e. well beyond your expected departure date from Australia with the plane. Even then, you can get it extended if needed. Without the Security you run the risk of getting your plane impounded for a few days while the paperwork is completed. If you arrive just before a weekend, it may be several days.

3. A few days before arrival in Australia you'll need to get a slot assignment if it's a larger airport like Darwin. The slot is a place to park on the international ramp while dealing with Immigration and Customs. Contact Slots@coordaus.com.au to get a slot assignment.

4. The day before you arrive, fax an Impending Arrival Report (IAR, form B364) to Customs at Darwin. If you are not carrying passengers or cargo for commercial purposes, you can be defined as a "Light aircraft" which allows you to file the IAR manually. Otherwise, you would have to file it electronically which

only handlers can do since they have access to the system and you don't. The fax number I used to file the IAR at Darwin was +61 8 8920 2559, but reconfirm this since they said they never got it, which may have been a hotel faxing problem. Note that the IAR asks for the departure and arrival airports, and the nine previous airports, by their UN Locodes (not ICAO airport codes). You can look up the UN Locodes online.

5. The day before arrival, call the quarantine people AQIS (Australian Quarantine and Inspection Service) at +61 8 8920 7080 (at Darwin) and give them your ETA.

6. The day before arrival call to confirm your allocated parking bay (slot). At Darwin the number is: +61 4 0100 5977.

7. Once you arrive you will be greeted on the ramp by the AQIS and the airport people. Do not open your door! Before anything, they want to spray the inside of your plane with a disinfectant to destroy any killer mosquitoes you might have picked up elsewhere. I knew this thanks to other pilots who had flown in the year before, so I made an effort to buy approved disinsectant myself and spray the inside of the plane at the beginning of my descent into Darwin. Several products are approved for this; I used one by Callington called "Top of Descent". I ended up buying a case (minimum purchase) and carrying the 12 cans all the way to frigging' Darwin from the UK, only to use part of one can and enjoy the satisfaction of spraying the aircraft myself and showing the can to the AQIS people through the window so I could open the door. They were delighted I was one of the few GA pilots who came prepared. The AQIS guy even wrote down the serial number on the bottom of my Top of Descent can! Again, this was one of those things I did just to see if I could get the stuff and take it there. In retrospect, it was a waste of time and money to do it. If you fly here, don't worry about the disinsectant, just wait for their okay to open the door even if it's hot, which it will be, let them spray what they want, and move on.

8. After arrival you will need to give them an Actual Arrival Report (Form B358) along with a standard Customs Declaration for Air Crew (Form B465) - are you bringing in anything to declare? The Actual Arrival Report is the only thing I forgot to prepare but the Customs guy filled it out for me to sign.

9. As a foreign-registered aircraft I had to pay a landing fee of $35 inside the terminal building at the airport office (credit cards accepted). Parking in the general aviation ramp in Darwin is free.

Once I had paid the landing fee I was done. What I've described is the entry process without a handler. There are a lot of steps, but I can say the Australians I dealt with were very helpful and good-natured in every way, quickly responding to emails and answering all my questions. That said, the Darwin people tell me planes show up in Darwin from international airports having done NO paperwork. They scramble to get it done on the spot. If they arrived just before a weekend when government offices are closed, they could find themselves in a bureaucratic limbo for a few days – physically, but not officially, in Australia.

Brazil Entry Procedures

For foreign aircraft entering Brazil, they have a relatively new online procedure for obtaining your landing and overflight permit. It starts at the ANAC website:

> *http://www2.anac.gov.br/portal/cgi/cgilua.exe/sys/start.htm?sid=390*

Finding the right place to click brings up this website form:

> *https://sistemas.anac.gov.br/SIAVANAC/pouso_sobrevoo/SolicitacaoPP.asp*

You might encounter a "this site not trusted" as I did; just click past it. Fill out the form, and as the site warns, be prepared with pdf files containing copies of all your relevant documents before proceeding to page 2 of the form. Those documents include:

1. Aircraft registration
2. Aircraft airworthiness certificate
3. Aircraft insurance policy. Make sure the pdf file you have for the policy shows both coverage details and the geographical extent of coverage (i.e. South America). The first version of the insurance policy I sent didn't have the geographic extent of coverage (South America down to Antarctica) so I had to send them a second pdf file with the complete policy – some 25 pages.
4. Pilot (crew) passport
5. Pilot (crew) pilot certificate (both sides)
6. Pilot (crew) medical certificate (both sides)

Page 2 of the form has a place where you select the type and upload each of these documents. When you've got the form done, and have specified your intended arrival date and Airport of Entry (AOE), submit the whole thing. They provide a procedure if you want to interrupt what you're doing and return to complete it later before submitting it.

Almost immediately I had an email acknowledging my submission. Within about 24 hours I had a response telling me the insurance document was insufficient because it didn't specify South America. I fixed that and within a few hours they sent me an email informing me my permit had been issued. They gave me a permit number of the format: ANANAC00XXXXX . The X's are other letters and numbers specific to each permit. Note that apparently you must do this process yourself. You can't have a permit service or others do it for you.

OK, so now I had got permit number to enter Brazil. It's important to include this number in the remarks section (RMK/) on any filed flight plan in Brazil. It was also important to arrive when and where I said I would on the application. I don't know what happens if you don't. So far, so good. ANAC was very good about keeping me posted with emails about the status of my application and what I was supposed to do next.

After landing at your Airport of Entry (Belem in my case), the next step was to **Validate** the permit. I did this by going to Customs at the Belem airport and having them issue a document whose name I forget, but the acronym for the name is TEAT (which you don't forget). When the TEAT is issued, the permit is validated and you are authorized to fly to airports in Brazil.

This entry procedure is not just about flight permission, it is also about controlling and tracking the import and export of aircraft and probably why Customs people drive the process. The entry/exit procedures in Australia are driven in the same way. From that perspective, it's a little baffling why every country doesn't track the entry and exit of private aircraft to make sure that any plane brought in to the country actually leaves and isn't sold. What's to stop someone from bringing the plane in and selling it if Customs never knows whether it has left the country?

Appendix F – Self-Handling at Brazilian Airports

The idea of a "handler" is strange to general aviation pilots in the US, Canada and few other places where we are used to a system of Fixed Based Operators (FBO's) that provide a variety of services, usually free of charge. The reason these free services exist is simple – FBO's sell fuel and that's how they make their money. FBO's will offer a lot of services to entice you to park on their ramp and buy fuel from them. In most of the rest of the world the FBO's don't sell fuel, the local petroleum companies do. Given that, how is an FBO going to make money? Well, they have to charge for their services or there'd be reason for them to be there. These services often include charter flights but in the context of visiting aircraft, they fall under the broad description of "handling" services even if they don't actually handle the aircraft and push it around. For visiting small planes they become "facilitators" who greet the plane when it arrives, marshal it to a parking place, arrange refueling, help walk the crew and passengers through Immigration and Customs, provide plane–to-terminal transport, even book hotel rooms, file flight plans, and miscellaneous other services. The problem is that most of these services have been designed and priced for much larger visiting aircraft – jets and turboprop's, multi-million dollar airplanes with affluent clientele who are willing to pay a lot of money for handling services.

On my round-the-world flight in 2011, I selectively used handlers where I thought I'd have a struggle to get in and out of the airport, like in India, Egypt, Dubai, and few other places. They were expensive, but given the tales of other pilots who have gone through these places without the benefit of a handler, it was money well spent. However, I am always posing the question "Do I really need these handlers and are their services worth what I'm paying for them?"

As I mentioned, I've paid handlers a few hundred dollars at a few places for the convenience of them making my stop more streamlined and hassle-free. Handlers, however, can charge a lot more, so for this trip from Brazil south, I decided I would avoid using handlers and instead try to manage on my own; i.e., self-handling.

When you are self-handling, there are five basic questions you need to answer for each airport stop:

1. After landing, where do I park?

2. How do I get refueled?

3. How do I get out of the airport and into a taxi to the hotel?

4. Where do I pay my airport fees when I'm ready to leave?

5. How do I get out of the airport terminal and back on the ramp to my plane to depart?

If you are entering or leaving the country, add getting through Immigration and Customs to this list.

I stopped at six airports in Brazil, all regional airports of reasonable size with scheduled commercial service. Those airports are Belem (SBBE), Natal (SBNT), Salvador (SBSV), Vitoria (SBVT), Florianopolis (SBFL), and Foz do Iguasu (SBFI). I will discuss the details of self-handling at five of these airports, the exception being Belem where I did use a handler with somewhat negative results. I'll discuss Belem last.

Natal (SBNT)

The GA parking is at the north end of the main ramp. If you come into land on runway 16L (most commonly used), you will see it immediately to the left of the runway threshold. After landing, Ground control will direct you to park there. There may or not be an Infraero guy there to marshal you in, but if not, just pick a place and park. Infraero is the Brazilian company or government unit that runs the airports in Brazil, You will see them and their trucks with their yellow and green logo everywhere at the airport.

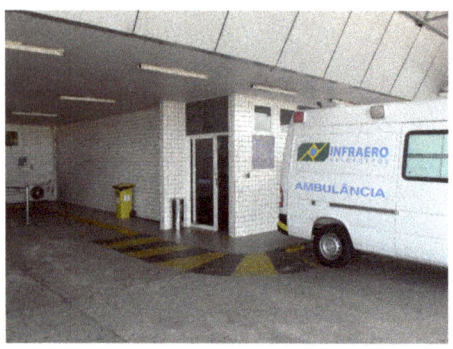

Entry door to get off the ramp and into the terminal at Natal

Before you shut down your radios, call the Ground controller and tell him you need "gasolina". This word works in both Portuguese and Spanish, and distinguishes what you want as "avgas" and not "Jet A1" fuel. Throughout the self-handling process, you'll find the people in the tower (tower and ground) are a great help for two reasons: 1) they speak English, and 2) they basically know what you need to do. If an Infraero guy is there to marshal, you can ask him for "gasolina" and he will get on his radio and call the fuelers. Both Shell and Petrobras sell fuel at airports throughout Brazil; sometimes either one or both will have avgas. At my visit to SBNT, only Petrobras had avgas. When the fueling is done they'll either want a fuel card or cash, not credit or debit cards. I always paid with cash. At Natal I made the mistake of paying most of it with US$100 bills, and then the fraction of US$100 with Brazilian Reales. This caused a lot of confusion that took 20 minutes to short out. In the end, they actually created two fuel invoices for the two different currencies, so it's best and easiest to pay with just one currency. Remember to take a lot of small bills besides US$100, like $20, $10 and $5 so change is not an issue. Once you've paid for fuel, it's a short walk to the terminal building (or an Infraero guy might give you a lift) where you enter though the ramp/crew access door shown in the photo. You'll be on the ramp side of a single bay security check point. Just walk right through the scanner

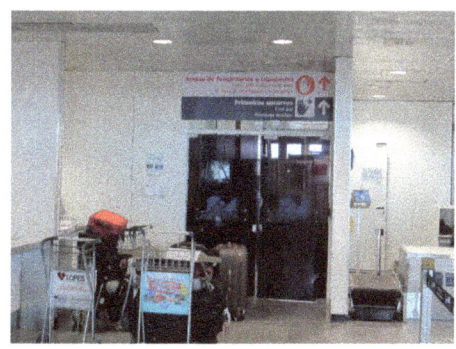

Doors to walk through at Natal to get into the terminal from the ramp security area

with your luggage – you'll set it off but no matter. Just after you pass through the scanner, look to your right and you will see a door. This is where you pay your airport fees when you depart. I didn't note the sign on the door at Natal, but it probably said "Tarifaos".

After noting the door, continue straight on through double doors and you will be in the main terminal. Turn around and note the double doors you just came through. This is where you will go when you are ready to leave. Otherwise, you are in the terminal and can get a taxi to/from your hotel or other destination.

When you return to leave, walk through the double doors and into the Tarifaos office and pay your airport fees. The person there may have very limited English or Spanish, so it is helpful to have a piece of paper with some basic information. At a few places I was presented with a form in Portuguese and English asking for the same basic information. That information is:

1. Aircraft registration. After the registration number put "aviao privado" in parenthesis. "aviao privado" means private aircraft.

2. Aircraft type (model name)

3. Aircraft MTOW (kgs or lbs)

4. Owner/Operator name and address

5. Arriving from (airport code) on (date)

6. Departing to (airport code) on (date) at (time)

They will use this information to calculate navigation charges, airport landing and parking fees, etc. This may take 10 to 15 minutes. They will then print out an invoice and present it to you. I paid the airport fees at all my stops with a credit card. At Natal the fees were about US$200 for my plane for one night. Once you've paid your fees, they'll call the tower and notify them. The tower won't let you leave unless the fees are paid. With the fees paid, go back out and go through the security checkpoint. For me there was some confusion because they didn't know any English and thought I was a tourist in the wrong place. I do wear an "Air Crew" ID badge but no pilot shirt or any of that so I basically look like another scruffy tourist. The paper I used in the fee office helped explain what I was doing, but they called an Immigration guy over anyway who spoke some English. I told him I wasn't leaving the country, I was flying on the Salvador in my private aircraft. He looked at my passport and pilot's license (keep it handy). He was OK with that, I went through security, through the door onto the ramp and I was ready to leave Natal

Salvador (SBSV)

SBSV is a much larger airport than Natal and complicated at the time because it was under construction to accommodate increased traffic for the upcoming world cup matches. They were also building a new stadium which the taxi drivers were proud to point out as we drove passed.

After landing, I was directed to park at Apron 4 which is far from the terminal and barely in sight of the tower. I was greeted by an Infraero guy who marshaled me to a parking spot. I shut down and asked him for "gasolina". He got on his radio and called the fuel truck – Petrobras got there first and filled the plane. I paid with cash – all Brazilian this time as I recall. During the fueling, the Infraero guy left so I didn't really have any way to get to the terminal. The right thing to do at this point would have been to turn on my radio and call the Ground controller to ask for transport to the terminal. However, there was a large modern building just off the parking area that looked like civilization so I wandered over there. It turned out to be a large maintenance hangar for an air taxi service. With a combination of English and broken Spanish, I communicated that I needed a ride to the terminal. One of the guys agreed to help me. We jumped in his personal vehicle and he drove out through the security gate to the access road that led to the terminal. A nice guy to do that for me. At that point I got a taxi and was off to the hotel, wondering how I would get back to my plane on Apron 4.

Entry door from the main terminal to the office to pay fees at Salvador

Returning to the airport to depart, I figured out a few things. On the lower (arrival) level, as you face the terminal from the street, the cash machines are all the way at the end of the hall to the left, around a corner where you would never see them just wandering around the terminal. Everything down that hall looks like offices of air taxi services, but that's where the machines are if you need cash. The place where you get back on the ramp and pay fees is also on that level on the left hand side near the post office ("Correio") and the emergency medical room. I can't recall if the office to pay fees is before or after security, but either way look for the door with the "Tarifaos" sign. Go through the fee-paying process as described for Natal. My fees here were about US$250, higher that Natal but I stayed two nights and it's a bigger airport. Then go through security (use the piece of paper to explain "aviao privado" if needed). After the fees are paid, the last task is to get back to the plane. Tell the people at security you need "transport". This word seems to universally work. They asked me to wait and eventually a large crew shuttle bus showed up that was making the rounds transporting airport workers of all kinds around the airport. I had added to my piece of paper "Apron 4". They understood where that was and I needed to get there. It took about 15 minutes to actually get back to Apron 4. Once there, I walked out to my plane and was ready to leave. After startup and ready to taxi, Infraero shows up with a "follow me" truck. I was departing on runway 17, the alternate runway, which in right next to Apron 4; i.e., "follow me" meant follow him about 20 meters off the apron onto the taxiway. Unnecessary, but I still appreciated that they systematically take all the steps. It showed consistency and discipline in how they run the airport and that's good.

Vitoria (SBVT)

Vitoria is a small airport with limited parking. As I mentioned in the Chapter 17, it is a PPR airport. I really don't know how you go about getting prior permission, but if you're a small plane and show up without PPR, it's probably not a tragedy unless they have no place for you to park. Again, I was marshaled into a parking place by an Infraero guy, asked him to get the "gasolina" truck, and with the plane fueled and covered, headed into the terminal after first getting an explanation of the PPR issue and promising to leave first thing in the morning. I told them they could move my plane it they needed to. I went through the normal passenger doors to get into the arrival hall and from there took a taxi to a nearby hotel for a one night stay.

Coming back the next morning I looked around for the office to pay fees and was puzzled. They had an airport information booth so I tried that. They spoke good English there but didn't really understand what I needed. I finally asked a guy at a "Skytours" office (Mario) for help. His English was great and he took the time to help me figure out where I needed to go (thanks Mario). So without Mario, I can now tell you the office to pay the fees is off the corridor leading to the arrival hall from the main part of the terminal and marked with a "Sala AIS" sign (sorry, no photo). When in doubt, look for a "Sala AIS" sign. It doesn't look like a door you should walk through, but go through anyway and look for a door on the right with the "Tarifaos" sign.

There is a large table in there and several desks in this office. I gave then my (updated) piece of paper explaining my aircraft, arrival and departure. The person that collects the fees was away from his desk so it took maybe 15-20 minutes for him to return, do the calculation, and print the invoice which I paid as before with a credit card.

Door from main terminal at Florianopolis to go through security to and from the ramp

After paying fees, getting back on the ramp was a little tricky. I asked the people in the fee office for "transport". They actually had a young guy, new to the job, who spoke reasonable English and led me to the security portal for ramp/crew personnel. I went through there and an Infraero guy with his yellow pickup truck (you'll see them all over Brazilian airports) gave me a lift back to my plane though it would not have been a long walk. From there I was good to go.

Florianopolis (SBFL)

Florianopolis is a very popular tourist destination with its famous beaches. Because of this, they are more used to having visiting private aircraft, including foreign aircraft. The parking ramp is still small, with a flight school using part of it for their collection of C152's. As before, I was marshaled in by an Infraero guy. We needed to reposition the plane to save room, so I got out the tow bar and he helped me push it into place. He called the fuel truck and I got the plane refueled. AT SBFL, the guy insisted on US cash, not Brazilian – I don't why – but he did bring me my change in US$ when I left. One common question, posed in Portuguese, had come up from the Infraero guys on the ramp which I finally understood at SBFL. They were asking me if I wanted the plane fueled now or when I left. I always fuel when I arrive for reasons I've explained before. Now that I understood the question, the right answer is "agora", similar to the Spanish "ahora", meaning "now". I have locking gas caps on N788W so I'm not too concerned about somebody stealing my fuel while the plane is sitting on the ramp. With the plane parked and fueled, Infraero showed up with the air-conditioned crew shuttle to give me a short ride to the terminal. I walked through the ramp access door, along a corridor, backward through the security scanner, and out into the terminal to get a taxi to the hotel. Along that corridor I noted the door labeled "Tarifaos" where I would pay fees on departure. Out in the terminal, turn around and note the doorway you just walked through. When returning to the airport, go through these doors, through security, pay fees, and ask for transport back to the plane. At this point it was getting to be routine.

Foz do Iguacu (SBFI)

The airport on the Brazilian side of Iguazu Falls is a single runway and ramp, but gets a fair amount of commercial traffic because the Falls is such a popular and world-famous destination. Consequently, they actually have a reasonable size ramp for parking general aviation aircraft where the tower directed me after landing. Once again, Infraero was there to marshal me to a parking spot and get the fueler on the way – Air BP this time instead of Shell or Petrobras. Unlike SBFL, this guy would only take Brazilian Reales in cash. With the plane parked and fueled, I headed for the terminal. They actually have a pedestrian pathway painted blue leading from the GA parking to the terminal. Walk passed the departure/arrival doors the regular passengers use to get to the commercial planes. You will see a sign 'Sala AIS" by a door that also says "Saida" (exit). It looks a little unlikely, but go through this door and you will get to a security check point where, as before, you can walk backward through the scanner. Just after you do this, note a stairway going up to your right. I recall it also had a sign "Sala AIS". There is an office at the top of the stairs down a corridor to the right with a big "C" sign on the door (at least when I was there). This is where you pay airports fees when you depart. After going backward through the security checkpoint, you are in the terminal and can get a taxi to your hotel.

Departing SBFI, I was also leaving Brazil for Argentina so I had a few more departure steps than usual – primarily dealing with the TEAT document and the AVANAC permission (see Appendix E). When I departed, I focused on getting these done first; that was a mistake given the way this airport is laid out. The first thing you want to do when you leave is go up the stairs and pay the airport fees (about US$250 at SBFI departing the country). After paying the fees, go back down the stairs and to the embarkation area. There, behind glass walls, is the Customs office. Present them with the TEAT and AVANAC documents. They will inform you that they also need two copies of a GenDec signed and stamped by the Federal Police to process, in effect, terminate, the TEAT and the AVANAC since you are leaving the country.

The Federal Police office, unfortunately, is located off the embarkation hall for international flights. Leave your luggage in the Customs office, take your GenDec's and passport, go around the corner like you are checking in for a flight, but don't get in line. Stay along the right hand wall where there is a roped off corridor to the International Embarkation Hall. You will be stopped and asked for your ticket. You don't have a ticket, so show them the piece of paper described above with "Aviao Privado". They will make a phone call, then say OK and let you pass. Go through the security checkpoint into the international departure hall and you'll find the Federal Police office on the right. They will stamp and sign the GenDecs. Then make your way back to the Customs office the way you've just come.

With the stamped GenDecs, Customs will process the TEAT and AVANAC in the computer system and mark them "Finished." In fact, I got an email within an hour notifying me of the change of status. I have to say, the Brazilians are on top of their process. It is important to formally get the status changed to "Finished". If you just let it expire, it creates an abnormal situation which may make it difficult to get another AVANAC permission and TEAT if you return to Brazil.

With the Customs process concluded, you are ready to leave so go back to the International Embarkation hall (like you were going to the Police office again), go through security with your luggage, but this time, ask the guy at the security check point to open the door from the embarkation hall onto the ramp. They have the keys, and with the number of private aircraft they deal with each year, are accustomed to doing this. Once on the ramp, walk along the blue pathway to your plane and you're ready to leave for Brazil.

Belem (SBBE)

I used a handler in Belem because I was uncertain of the Customs process and thought I needed help. Consequently, I can't really speak directly to the process for self-handling on entering Brazil at Belem. I got in a dispute with the handler (Lider Aviacao) over a ridiculous charge for parking on the apron in front of their hangar. I did prevail in the dispute by getting the parking charge reduced. However, the primary positive outcome of this dispute was to give me strong motivation for self-handling at the rest of my stops.

Even though I used a handler at SBBE, given what I now know about how the airports work in Brazil, I can tell you what I would have done at SBBE if I didn't have a handler. After landing, Ground control instructed me to exit the runway at A and park by the northeast corner of the main terminal building. Of course a Lider guy was there to marshal, but without Lider, I would have expected an Infraero guy to marshal me to parking like at the other airports. I then would have asked the Ground controller for the customs office which is inside the main terminal building in the northeast corner near where I parked. The doors into the terminal were opened with a key card the Lider guy had, but assuming no handler, I think the Customs guy would have met me at the door because they need to come out and inspect the plane anyway. Once inspected, I think we would have gone back into the terminal to the Customs office and done the TEAT and AVANAC documents just as we did. It took about 30 minutes. They posed a few questions, but nothing that couldn't have been figured out and answered without someone there to translate (which the Lider guy did). Once the documents were issued, I would have returned to the plane and called the Ground controller on the radio and asked for a place to park for 2 nights. I didn't notice any places specifically for GA parking because I was headed to the Lider apron, but there must be places the airport provides for GA parking. There are open apron spaces on the Jeppesen airport diagram away from the terminal. Once parked, I think the process of getting "gasolina" and transport to/from the terminal via Infraero would have worked the same as it worked at the other Brazilian airports I visited. I don't know where the Infraero Tarifaos office is to pay airport fees in the terminal, but I think I could have found it with a little leg work. In short, I think it is entirely possible to enter Brazil at SBBE and do self-handling as I did with the other airports.

Summary

Overall, I think self-handling at airports in Brazil based on my experience is quite manageable. In fact, it's rewarding and satisfying to work through the process alone rather than just being led around by a handler who essentially insulates you from what's going on. I make these long international flights in a small plane because they are engaging and challenging. Managing the process for arrival and departure at foreign airports myself is an extension of that. I will add the caveat, however, that my descriptions of specific processes and where things are located is based on my experience in January, 2013. They may have changed.

I think Brazil is really well-organized for accommodating visiting GA aircraft on pleasure flights. The AVANAC/TEAT process worked perfectly and just as described on the website. The airport fees are high, but I came to realize that part of what you're paying for is the assistance of the Infraero ramp crews along the way, and transport. When you consider that crossing the Caribbean requires no overflight or landing permits (except Cuba), and crossing Guyana, Suriname, and French Guiana also require no overflight or landing permits, it makes it pretty straightforward (in terms of paperwork) to fly all the way to Brazil from the USA. You will just need to file flight plans and do the AVANAC/TEAT online process for Brazil and you will be inside Brazil and able to fly all around this very interesting country.

Appendix G – Antarctica Permit Documents

This Appendix contains three documents which were necessary to get permission to fly to and land at King George Island (SCRM) in Antarctica. These are:

1. Initial Environmental Evaluation (IEE) prepared for the U.S. Environmental Protection Agency

2. Waste Permit Application prepared for the U.S. National Science Foundation which runs the U.S. Antarctica Program

3. Application to the Chilean Government's Direccion General de Aeronautica Civil (DGAC) for permission to land at SCRM

Two Chilean documents about flying to Antarctica must be reviewed before preparing the permit application for Chile. At the time I did my applications they could be found at:

http://www.aipchile.gob.cl/dasa/aip_chile_con_contenido/ais/2%20ENR%20Parte%202/ ENR%207%20Rutas%20Visuales/ENR%20H%20%207.17%20ENR%207.24%20 Procedimiento%20autorizacion%20hacia%20Territorio%20Antartico.pdf

and

http://www.dgac.cl/images/IMG/pdf/otros/dap/dap06_08.pdf

Initial Environmental Evaluation

Anderson Flight to Antarctica 2014

Aircraft owner/pilot, expedition leader:
Harry R. Anderson, Ph.D.
250 Eagle Place NE
Bainbridge Island, WA 98110
Email: hra@phywave.com
Home phone: +1 206-780-0344
Mobile phone: +1 541-915-5112

US contact:
Harry R. Anderson, Ph.D.
250 Eagle Place NE
Bainbridge Island, WA 98110
Email: hra@phywave.com
Home phone: +1 206-780-0344
Mobile phone: +1 541-915-5112

Summary

This IEE covers a proposed flight to King George Island on the Antarctic Peninsula by aircraft N788W planned for late January or early February, 2014. One person will fly the aircraft, a 2001 Lancair Columbia 300, from the Punta Arenas, Chile airport (SCCI) and land at the Chilean base Teniente Rodolfo Marsh Martin Aerodrome (SCRM) on King George Island. The pilot will then refuel the aircraft and takeoff to return to Punta Arenas. There will be no other landings or stops in Antarctica. There will be no passengers or other aircrew.

The flight, landing and takeoff activities are expected to have no more than minor and transitory impacts on the Antarctic environment.

All activities for this flight will be carried out in accordance with the Antarctic Treaty; the Environmental Protocol to the Antarctic Treaty on Environmental Protection and its Annexes; Antarctic Treaty Consultative Meeting (ATCM) Recommendation XVIII-1; the Antarctica Flight Information Manual (AFIM) revision 3-11, Guidelines for the Operation of Aircraft Near Concentrations of Birds in Antarctica, ATCM Resolution 2 (2004), and applicable domestic statutes and regulations.

1. Description of Purpose & Activity

The primary purposes of the expedition are: 1) conduct near real time measurements of airborne black carbon densities along the flight route to and from Antarctica, and 2) enjoy and take aerial photographs of scenery along the Antarctic Peninsula. There are no plans for wildlife viewing.

2. Aircraft Specifications

- Registration: N788W (USA)
- Owner, operator and pilot: Harry R. Anderson
- Model: Lancair Columbia 300 (ICAO flight plan type: COL3)
- Model year: 2001
- Engine: Teledyne Continental IO-550-N, fuel injected (2000 hours TBO)
- Engine power: 310 bhp at 2700 rpm
- Fixed landing gear
- Empty weight: 2354 lbs (1068 kg)
- Maximum takeoff weight (MTOW): 3400 lbs (1592 kg)
- Length: 25.2 feet (7.68 m)
- Wingspan: 35.8 feet (10.9 m)
- Cruising true airspeed (75% power): 190 kTAS (typically)
- Cruising true airspeed (63% power): 165 kTAS (typically)
- Useable fuel capacity in wing tanks: 98 gallons
- Useable fuel capacity in ferry tank: 60 gallons
- Fuel consumption (at 63% power, 10,000 feet altitude): 11.5 gph (typically)
- TKS™ de-icing system
- The aircraft will be fitted with an aethalometer for measuring airborne black carbon densities

3. Air Crew

The pilot and only crew member of the aircraft is Dr. Harry R. Anderson. Dr. Anderson is an experienced pilot with more than 1600 hours of Pilot-in-Command time in a variety of fixed-wing aircraft. He holds a Commercial Pilot certificate for single-engine and multi-engine aircraft with an Instrument rating. He also holds a Private Pilot certificate for single-engine seaplanes.

Dr. Anderson is also an experienced yachtsman. He owns *RAYTRACE*, a 37 foot Bavaria sloop he sails around the waters of the Pacific Northwest and Canada.

In 2011 Dr. Anderson completed a solo flight around the world in aircraft N788W, visiting five continents and crossing the equator twice, a total of more than

24,000 nm. That trip consisted of several long over-ocean flight segments of more than 1000 nm, with the longest more than 2000 nm from Maui, Hawaii to Monterey, California. By comparison, the over-water portion of the flight from Punta Arenas to King George Island is about 550 nm. His around-the-world route included flight segments over frigid arctic regions in Canada, Greenland, and Iceland. In additional, Dr. Anderson is based in the Pacific Northwest where he routinely encounters and deals with winter flying conditions. A blog describing his round-the-world flight can be found at:

http://blog.travelpod.com/travel-blog/harry4123/1/tpod.html

In February 2013, Dr. Anderson made an attempt to fly his aircraft to King George Island. He flew aircraft N788W to Punta Arenas where he waited nearly 3 weeks for a suitable day of weather. A suitable day did not occur so he had to abandon the attempt. However, during this period he was able to make a flight well out over the Drake Passage to a location south of 60 degrees south latitude and them return to land at Puerto Williams for re-fueling. This initial attempt and the flight over the Drake Passage gave Dr. Anderson very valuable knowledge and experience with the weather conditions in this part of the world. He has used this information to better equip aircraft N788W for the mission with more in-flight fuel capacity and with a de-icing system. With these aircraft upgrades and the knowledge from his 2013 flight experience, he is confident he can successful achieve the objectives of this expedition on 2014.

Dr. Anderson holds a BSEE degree from the University of California at Santa Barbara, a MSEE degree from Oregon State University, and a Ph.D. in Electrical Engineering from the University of Bristol in the United Kingdom. He is an expert in wireless communications network design, simulation and optimization. He has published numerous peer-reviewed technical papers and a graduate level reference text entitled *Fixed Broadband Wireless System Design* (2003, John Wiley: Chichester). He is a successful entrepreneur having founded, grown and sold high tech companies. He is currently majority owner of software company EDX Wireless, Inc. (*www.edx.com*) based in Eugene, Oregon.

In February, 2011, Dr. Anderson took a two week Quark Expeditions cruise to the Antarctica Peninsula (the "Crossing the Circle" cruise) aboard the ship Sergey Vavilov. During this cruise Dr. Anderson attended the requisite seminars on proper practices for protecting the flora and fauna of Antarctica, including maintaining appropriate distance while observing wildlife. The Quark cruise included several zodiac landings ashore where these procedures were used.

In addition to his education and practical experience with Antarctic environmental protection methods aboard the Vavilov, Dr. Anderson has read the documents listed in the References in Section 9 of this IEE which include several pertaining to minimizing environmental impact while visiting Antarctica.

4. Proposed Expedition Itinerary

The flight duration in each direction (with neutral winds) is expected to be just under 4 hours. The flight schedule will be adjusted to take into account weather conditions which cannot be predicted this far in advance. The actual date of the outbound flight may shift by several days if necessary awaiting a suitable weather window. The actual flight altitude will also be selected on the day of the flight to take advantage of the most favorable winds and avoid icing conditions. The itinerary is shown in Table 1.

Table 1: Proposed Itinerary – Anderson Flight to Antarctica 2014			
Location	Aerodrome ICAO code	Arrive	Depart
Punta Arenas, Chile	SCCI	1-20-2014	1-30-2014
King George Island, Antarctica	SCRM	1-30-2014	1-30-2014
Punta Arenas, Chile	SCCI	1-30-2014	2-10-2014

Since the flight each way takes less than 4 hours, and there are approximately 18 hours of daylight during this time of year at these latitudes, it is possible to fly to Antarctica in the morning, spend a few hours there to refuel the plane, visit a research station and take photographs, and then make the return flight to South America in the afternoon. This itinerary results in the lowest environmental impact and does not require the hospitality of the Chilean research base for overnight accommodation. It also has the advantage that a shorter weather forecast window is needed; i.e., one 12 hour daytime period of solid good weather (which Dr. Anderson is willing to wait for) is all that would be needed to accomplish the primary objectives of the expedition.

4 a. Itinerary Adjustments

It can be expected that the date of the proposed itinerary will be adjusted to take advantage of suitable weather conditions. No alternate flight routes are planned for this expedition.

4 b. Assessment of Alternatives to Proposed Activity

The identified need of the activity is the exercise of the tourism privilege acknowledged in Chapter VII of the Treaty.

Flying to Antarctica is the only way to meet the identified need. Having noted that, changing the itinerary dates in response to weather conditions is anticipated.

4 c. Alternative of Not Proceeding with the Flight

The expedition consists of one person in a small, single engine aircraft that will be in the Antarctic Treaty area for less than a day. Stores of fuel and other potential pollutants are necessarily limited. As such, the impact of this flight will be both minor and transitory. Canceling the expedition based on objective environmental risk therefore does not appear to be justified.

However, the alternative of not proceeding with the flight may also occur if permission to land at the Teniente Rodolfo Marsh Martin Aerodrome on King George Island is not granted by the government of Chile. As explained in Section 5b below, the range of aircraft N788W is such that it is technically imperative to land at this aerodrome in order to re-fuel the aircraft. Because landing at the aerodrome is essential for re-fueling the aircraft and completing the expedition, permission from the government of Chile to land at their aerodrome is likewise essential. If permission to land is not granted, it will not be possible to complete the flight and the expedition will be canceled.

5. Expedition Activities

This section describes the specific expedition activities including the potential for environmental impact and mitigation measures.

5 a. The Flight from Punta Arenas, Chile to King George Island

The flight from Punta Arenas to King George Island will be mostly over the water of Drake Passage, and take less than 4 hours. However, for aerial photography purposes and weather conditions permitting, it is planned to fly as far south as Deception Island so some overflight of land areas will occur. To mitigate the impact of such overflights, the following procedures will be used:

- Flight Operations with respect to concentrations of birds will be conducted in accordance with *Guidelines for the Operation of Aircraft Near Concentrations of Birds in Antarctica*, ATCM Resolution 2 (2004), and the *Antarctic Flight Information Manual* Revision 3-11 (2011).

- There will be no overflight or landings near or at Antarctic Specially Protected Areas (ASPA's).
- The aircraft will not approach closer than 2,000 ft (610 m) to animal concentrations nor will it hover or make repeated passes over wildlife concentrations.
- The aircraft will not fly over animal colonies, and will not fly at altitudes less than 2,000 ft (610 m) in the vicinity or limits of these concentrations. If any disturbance in animal life is observed while in flight, the flight pattern will be immediately changed.
- The aircraft will maintain a vertical separation distance of 2,000 feet (610 m) AGL and a horizontal separation of ¼ nautical mile (460 m) from the coast where possible.

The aethalometer carried on board to measure airborne black carbon is a passive device that collects air samples through a small tube, passes the air through a filter, and then optically analyzes them. It is a small battery-operated device that produces no discharge. It will remain inside the aircraft at all times.

5 b. Visit to King George Island

The time at King George Island will be spent in two activities:

1. Tourism. A brief visit to a nearby research station is planned. There are several research stations on King George Island and the small village of La Villa des Estellas with a year-round population of 80 and summer season population of over 150. Given this relatively high concentration of human activity for Antarctica, the passive presence of one additional person (Dr. Anderson) in this area of human activity for a few hours will have an incremental impact that is clearly minor and transitory.

2. Refueling the aircraft. The range of aircraft N788W is not quite adequate to make the flight to King George Island and back without refueling, especially if headwinds are encountered during the flight. Consequently it will be necessary to refuel N788W after landing at King George Island. Since no high octane aviation gasoline (avgas) is available at this base, N788W will carry 50 gallons of avgas as cargo on the flight from Punta Arenas to King George Island for refueling. Once at King George Island, this fuel will be pumped from the cargo fuel container into the wing tanks using a manual fuel pump so that N788W has full wing tanks for the return flight to Punta Arenas. A spill kit containing fuel absorption material will also be carried on board for use in case of a spill during the refueling process. The method and precautions to be taken during this fuel transfer are discussed in detail in Section 5f.

5 c. The Flight from King George Island to Punta Arenas, Chile

The flight back from King George Island to Punta Arenas will be mostly over the water of Drake Passage, and take less than 4 hours. This flight is planned to be directly north from King George Island over the Drake Passage to Punta Arenas. No overflight of land areas in the Antarctica Treaty Area south of 60 degrees south latitude will occur (other than briefly during takeoff from King George Island).

5 d. Waste Management Plan

Three types of waste may be generated during the flight:

- Air emissions from engine exhaust. These emissions are managed by proper engine maintenance. They are disposed of (dispersed) by the natural winds occurring in the flight area.
- Liquid wastes. Amount: less than 2 liters. Liquid waste will be stored inside the aircraft in a bottle designed for the purpose. This waste will be disposed of upon returning to Punta Arenas.
- Solid wastes. Amount: less than 2 kgs. Solid waste will be stored inside the aircraft in containers designed for the purpose. This waste will be disposed of upon returning to Punta Arenas.
- There will be no discharge of liquid or solid wastes, or wastes of any kind, while the aircraft is in flight.

While at King George Island, the existing facilities for human waste disposal will be utilized if possible. Any liquid or solid waste not so disposed of, or garbage, generated during the visit will be stored on the aircraft and taken back to Punta Arenas on the return flight for disposal.

5 e. Impact of Landing and Taking Off from King George Island

The aerodrome at King George Island is used by numerous aircraft for military purposes, for the support and resupply of research activities, and to ferry tourists who visit the island and who board cruise ships visiting other parts of the Antarctica Peninsula. These aircraft are typically large turboprop aircraft, much larger and heavier than aircraft N788W. As such, the impact of the repeated operation of these aircraft on the environment in terms of noise, exhaust pollution, and physical disturbance to the runway surface at the aerodrome, are vastly greater than the impact of aircraft N788W. Consequently, the incremental impact of a single landing and takeoff by a light aircraft like N788W is minor, transitory and negligible.

5 f. Refueling Procedure at King George Island

As noted above, while at Lieutenant Rodolfo Marsh Martin Aerodrome (SCRM) on King George Island, it will be necessary to refuel aircraft N788W from a fuel storage container carried aboard the aircraft. The aircraft will carry as cargo a single custom-made rectangular metal container (drum) with 50 gallons of aviation gasoline (avgas). This container will be securely strapped down during the flight. During refueling, fuel will be pumped from this drum into each of the wing tanks using a manual pump and hand nozzle to control fuel flow and shutoff. The metal fuel drum will always remain in its strapped down position in the aircraft. During the refueling, absorbent pads will be placed around the wing tank filler inlet to catch any drips that may occur from the nozzle. In addition, absorbent pads will be placed under the wing to catch any fuel that may drop off the wing toward the ground.

The main environmental hazard during the refueling operation is a minor fuel spill. A spill kit will be on board the aircraft. This commercially-assembled spill kit consists of:

10 - 18" x 24" absorbent pads

2 - 3" x 48" absorbent socks

1 – 18" x 24" x 4" plastic disposal bag

1 – pair of nitrile gloves

1 – pair of goggles

1 – instruction manual

The spill kit will be utilized to prevent, contain and clean up inadvertent spills as needed. Clean-up procedure: For spills on the aircraft wing, the absorbent pads will be placed on the spill area to absorb and pick up the spilled fuel. Similarly, for spills onto the ground, the absorbent pads will be placed on the spill area to absorb the spilled fuel. In addition, the soil where the spill occurred will be picked up and placed in plastic bags. It is not expected that snow or ice will be present at the refueling location, but should fuel spill onto snow or ice, that also will be picked up and placed in plastic bags.

All absorbent pads and other used spill kit material will be packaged in plastic disposal bags and placed inside the aircraft and returned to Punta Arenas for proper disposal. The plastic bags containing any picked-up soil, snow or ice where a spill occurred will also be placed inside the aircraft and returned to Punta Arenas for proper disposal.

The refueling will be done in an area designated for this purpose by the controlling authority at the aerodrome. While refueling, any sources of ignition, in particular, smoking, will be prohibited within 100 feet of the aircraft.

5 g. Additional Procedures to Mitigate Environment Impacts

Before leaving Punta Arenas airport, Dr. Anderson will wash and vacuum clothing to be worn at King George Island. He will vacuum the interior and wash the exterior of aircraft N788W prior to departing Punta Arenas to prevent the translocation of invasive species. The pilot will wear a pair of clean boots with open sole patterns (rubber farm boots) while at King George Island. These boots will be new, out-of-the-box, boots. They are being brought to King George Island for the singular purpose of wearing while walking around on the island. Although new, as a further precaution against contamination, the boots will be cleaned using a Virkon S solution. Virkon S is a broad spectrum disinfectant which is available in powder form so it can be easily carried aboard aircraft N788W. At Punta Arenas the Virkon S will be dissolved in water to prepare a solution of the recommended concentration. That solution, along with a stiff brush, will be used to clean the boots just prior to departing Punta Arenas for King George Island. The same cleaning procedure will be used again on the boots when returning from King George Island to ensure there is no transference from Antarctica back to South America. The used Virkon S solution will be disposed of in Punta Arenas as recommended by the manufacturer.

The expedition will not bring dogs or any other non-native animal or plant species into the Antarctic Treaty Area.

During the visit to King George Island, it is not known whether Dr. Anderson will come into the proximity of local wildlife such as penguins or other bird life, seals or other water mammals, etc. Observing wildlife is not an objective of this expedition. However, if such encounters do inadvertently occur, as noted above Dr. Anderson, during his Quark cruise in 2011, has learned and utilized appropriate techniques to avoid disturbing wildlife. In addition, he has reviewed the document entitled *Guidelines for Visitors to the Antarctic* available on the IAATO website and listed in the References section 9 of IEE.

6. Communications and Coordination Plans

Communication will be maintained via satphone and HF radio during the flight segments for the purpose of reporting position and flight status, obtaining weather forecasts and current weather reports (METAR's), and determining landing conditions at the SCCI and SCRM airports. While in Punta Arenas, communication via email and cellphone will also be used.

As an expedition of one person and one aircraft, there will be no need for a support team for this expedition or coordination with other components of the expedition. The expedition will be self-sufficient. The flight from Punta Arenas to King George Island will be coordinated with authorities in Punta Arenas before departure to avoid having too many aircraft at Lieutenant Rodolfo Marsh Martin Aerodrome at one time where there is limited parking space. Given the size of the airport at Punta Arenas, no coordination of landing permission and parking space is needed there.

With regard to coordinating this visit to the Chilean base, I have contacted Mr. Luis J. Rossi, Director of International Relations, at the Directorate General of Civil Aeronautics (DGAC) in Santiago, Chile. Mr. Rossi has provided a list of 4 items for approval of this visit to their base:

1. Request overflight and landing permission from the DGAC (Chilean CAA).
2. The flight must be related to scientific research.
3. The Antarctic Program of the USA must inform the Foreign Relations Ministry (RR.EE) of the proposed trip.
4. After all authorizations have been received, the crew must coordinate the flight with the 4th Air Brigade of the Chilean Air Force in Punta Arenas, since only one aircraft at a time can operate to/from the Chilean Antarctic base.

Item 1 is a routine procedure for flights over foreign countries and will be done in January or February, 2014, when the date of the departure flight is better known. With regard to Item 2, as noted above, the aircraft will be equipped with a portable aethalometer for measuring airborne black carbon densities along the route of flight. Airborne black carbon is a primary factor affecting global warming. With regard to Item 3, the process of obtaining authorizations from the US State Department, the EPA and the NSF (of which this IEE is part), is intended to lead to satisfying Item 3 on this list. Item 4 to coordinate space at the Chilean base will also be done after arriving in Punta Arenas and the departure flight date is being determined.

Dr. Anderson successfully obtained flight clearance to land at SCRM from the government of Chile for his flight in 2013. Since the parameters of this proposed 2014 expedition are the same as that of the 2013 expedition, it is expected that Chile will once again be willing to grant clearance for this flight. Furthermore, aircraft N788W is now equipped with a de-icing system and longer range making it a more capable aircraft for this mission than in 2013 and therefore of less safety concern to Chile. Dr. Anderson has once again contacted Mr. Rossi at the DGAC in Chile with a request for clearance for this 2014 flight. That request has been forwarded to the appropriate agencies in Chile. Addendum A are copies of their inter-agency emails in Spanish (with English translation) with the first email addressed to me. The emails indicate these agencies have no objection to approving my flight but their approval is pending the receipt of documents showing that the US government has approved the flight, including the environmental impact assessment as set forth in this IEE and the Waster Permit from the NSF. With approval of the IEE and issuance of the

Waste Permit, based on these emails it is expected that Chile with issue a clearance for my flight as they did last year. However, as noted above, if Chile does not grant flight clearance for some reason, it will not be possible to complete this expedition and it will be cancelled.

7. Emergency Contingency Plans and Insurance

All expeditions create some risk of requiring outside assistance. The aircraft N788W and pilot Dr. Anderson are reasonably prepared to reduce that risk as explained in the following sections.

7 a. Aircraft Preparation and Equipment

Aircraft N788W is maintained following the requirements set forth in the FAA Rules. It is equipped for flight in instrument conditions using both traditional radio navigation aids such as ILS, VOR and NDB, but also using TSO'd GPS-based RNAV procedures. The standard flight equipment aboard N788W includes:

- King KCS 55A HSI with slaved compass
- King KI-256 Flight Director
- Altimeter
- Air speed indicator
- Turn coordinator
- Vertical speed indicator
- S-TEC 55X two axis autopilot
- Shadin Fuel Flow meter
- EDM-701 engine monitor
- Stormscope with output displayed on Garmin GMX200 display
- Outside temperature gauge
- Flight chronometer
- Heated pitot tube
- Alternate static port
- 121.5 and 405 MHz Artex ME406 ELT
- Annunciator panel for fault conditions
- Auxiliary power cable for engine starting from a vehicle or other 12-14 VDC power source
- TKS™ "weeping wing" de-icing system

The standard navigation/communication equipment aboard N788W includes:

- Dual GPS (Garmin GNS530W primary) with moving map display
- Garmin MDX200 terrain and moving map display
- ADF
- DME
- Two NAV radios
- Two VHF COMM radios
- Two CDI's for navigation and approach procedures
- GTX330 Mode S transponder
- HF radio
- Iridium satellite phone
- Jeppesen worldwide airport, approach and terrain data cards
- iPad 2 loaded with aviation e-charts and moving map display and independent GPS receiver
- Paper maritime navigation charts for the Antarctica region

7 b. Emergency Equipment On-Board the Aircraft

The emergency equipment on-board the aircraft is primarily designed to deal with a water landing and evacuation by the pilot to a life raft with possible prolonged survival at sea until a rescue vessel can reach the raft. In the event the water landing is close to a shoreline, additional equipment for camping is also on-board the aircraft. The emergency equipment on-board the aircraft includes:

- 4-person Winslow Ultra-Light FA-AV (UL) covered life raft designed for arctic conditions
- Manual inflation pump
- Raft knife
- Raft repair kit
- Collapsible bailer bucket with handle
- Sponges
- Signal mirror
- Rescue streamer
- Whistle

- Oral inflation tube for the life raft
- Flashlight
- USGS aerial flares
- Raft retaining line (75 feet)
- NOAA-registered EPIRB with GPS reporting (personal locator beacon)
- Handheld GPS by Garmin
- Handheld aviation and marine ICOM VHF radios
- Iridium satellite phone
- Cold water immersion (survival) suit by Mustang to be worn during flight
- Inflatable life vest
- Survival knife
- Spare batteries for the radios and GPS
- First aid kit
- Water and provisions for surviving several days on the life raft
- Survivor "06" watermaker
- Backpack
- Sleeping bag
- Tent
- Propane camp stove
- Cooking pots
- Fire extinguisher

7 c. Search and Rescue (SAR) Plan

During the four hour flight, the most likely, but highly improbable, threats to the safety of the aircraft and crew are 1) an engine power failure, and 2) an inadvertent encounter with severe airframe icing conditions. Depending on where these events occur, the aircraft could be required to make an emergency landing in the water. The response to such threats to the safety of the aircraft and crew will be escalated in this order:

Prevention: This step has been taken through proper aircraft engine maintenance and assuring that uncontaminated fuel is used so that engine failure is extremely unlikely. As noted above, Dr. Anderson has already made several long over-ocean flights in this aircraft so has substantial personal experience with the aircraft's reliability. As noted above, the engine on N788W has a 2000 hour TBO (time between overhauls).

Currently the engine has about 740 hours. At the time of the Antarctica flight, it is anticipated the engine will still have less than 800 hours, well below the 2000 hours TBO and in middle of the typical engine "sweet spot" for performance and reliability.

Regarding ice, the flight will only be launched when weather conditions are suitable and conducted at flight altitudes and sky conditions where icing will not occur. Also, by design aircraft N788W is a fiberglass/composite aircraft with smooth wing, tail and fuselage surfaces. As such, it has a lower propensity for collecting structural ice than aircraft of conventional construction using multiple aluminum panels affixed to a frame with rivets and screws. As described in reference [8], in January, 2012, a Slovenian pilot successfully made the flight to King George Island in a Pipistrel, a smaller, slower, less capable aircraft than N788W. The Pipistrel is also made of similar fiberglass/composite construction with no airframe de-icing equipment. Furthermore, in prior years individual pilots in small light aircraft of conventional design and aluminum construction without airframe de-icing equipment have successfully made the flight across the Drake Passage to land in Antarctica and safely return (see References [6] and [7]). For these reasons, Dr. Anderson has every confidence this flight can also be completed safely without difficulty from airframe icing. However, for the 2014 expedition the margin of safety with regard to icing has been substantially increased with the installation of the TKS "weeping wing" de-icing system that is capable of keeping the airframe and propeller free of ice for an extended period of time.

Communication: Routine reports of position at flight route intersections, with status and weather observations, will be made via HF radio and/or satphone to appropriate the air traffic control (ATC) facilities monitoring the flight at 56-61-745474 or 56-61-745417. Such position and status reports are standard practice for aircraft in flight.

Then, in this order:

1. Alert surrounding aircraft and vessels with a PAN PAN on VHF, and alert MRCC Chile via satphone, at 011 56- 32- 2208639 / 56-32-2208637
2. Deal with the threat using means and expertise already on the aircraft following the emergency checklist kept on-board the aircraft.
3. Request assistance from aircraft and vessels via VHF (123.45 MHz inter-aircraft hailing frequency for aircraft; channel 16 on marine VHF).
4. Request assistance from MRCC 5th District via satellite phone.
5. Activate the aircraft ELT and personal EPIRB if indicated

As described above, the aircraft carries a high quality covered life raft and an extensive array of survival and signaling equipment should a water landing actually occur and the aircrew is forced to abandon the aircraft.

7 d. Emergency Training of the Air Crew

Dr. Anderson has received training from retired USCG rescue personnel in water landings, deploying and entering an inflated life raft on rough seas, and rationing and allocating resources for an extending period aboard a life raft. As noted above, Dr. Anderson is also an experienced yachtsman who sails his 37 foot Bavaria sailboat around the sometimes rough waters of Puget Sound and the Pacific Northwest. As such, he is well-versed in dealing with conditions at sea.

7 e. Insurance

Aircraft N788W and pilot Dr. Anderson are covered by a US$1,000,000 liability insurance policy with a US$10,000 rider to cover expenses for search and rescue operations. The policy is issued by insurance carrier U.S. Specialty Insurance Company. In addition to the insurance, Dr. Anderson has substantial personal financial resources to reimburse expenses for search and rescue operations.

8. Conclusion

Based on careful consideration of the activities planned for this expedition to Antarctica, and the proposed minimization and mitigation measures that will be utilized, it is the conclusion of the expedition leader and operator that this expedition will have no more than minor or transitory impact on the Antarctica environment.

Since this is a single, one-time only, expedition, there are no cumulative impacts to the Antarctica environment from this proposed expedition. With regard to cumulative impacts in light of other existing and known proposed activities, based on the minor and transitory nature of the impact from this proposed expedition, it is the conclusion of the expedition leader and operator that there will be no cumulative impact on the Antarctica environment from this expedition.

9. References

1. Antarctica Flight Information Manual (AFIM), Revision 3-11. (2011).

2. Guidelines for the Operation of Aircraft Near Concentrations of Birds in Antarctica, ATCM Resolution 2 (2004).

3. Guidelines on Contingency Planning, Insurance, and Other Matters for Tourist and Other Non-Governmental Activities in the Antarctica Treaty Area. ATCM Resolution 4 (2004).

4. Guidelines for Visitors to the Antarctic. IAATO website, 2011

5. Secretariat of the Antarctic Treaty. Status of Antarctic Specially Protected Area and Antarctic Specially Managed Area Management Plans. Hobart: ATS website, 2012.

6. *Wings Around the World*. Polly Vacher. Grub Street, London, 2008.

7. http://www.earthrounders.com/cgi/gannon_letters.php. Letters and flight route map by Bob Gannon.

8. *http://www.worldgreenflight.com*. Blog by Matevž Lenarčič, including the flight from Ushuaia to King George Island in 2012 in a light sport aircraft.

Waste Permit Application

Anderson Flight to Antarctica 2014

Aircraft owner/pilot, expedition leader:
Harry R. Anderson, Ph.D.
250 Eagle Place NE
Bainbridge Island, WA 98110
Email: hra@phywave.com
Home phone: +1 206-780-0344
Mobile phone: +1 541-915-5112

US contact:
Harry R. Anderson, Ph.D.
250 Eagle Place NE
Bainbridge Island, WA 98110
Email: hra@phywave.com
Home phone: +1 206-780-0344
Mobile phone: +1 541-915-5112

Summary

This Waste Permit Application is for a proposed flight to King George Island on the Antarctic Peninsula by aircraft N788W planned for January or February, 2014. One person will fly the aircraft, a 2001 Lancair Columbia 300, from the Punta Arenas, Chile airport (SCCI) and land at the Chilean base Lieutenant Rodolfo Marsh Martin Aerodrome (SCRM) on King George Island. The pilot will then refuel the aircraft and takeoff and return to Punta Arenas. The outbound flight to King George Island and the return flight to Punta Arenas, Chile will be carried out in the same day. There will be no other landings or stops in Antarctica. There will be no passengers or other aircrew.

The flight, landing, refueling and takeoff activities are expected to have no more than minor and transitory impacts on the Antarctic environment.

All activities for this flight will be carried out in accordance with the Antarctic Treaty; the Environmental Protocol to the Antarctic Treaty on Environmental Protection and its Annexes; Antarctic Treaty Consultative Meeting (ATCM) Recommendation XVIII-1; the Antarctica Flight Information Manual (AFIM) revision 3-11, Guidelines for the Operation of Aircraft Near Concentrations of Birds in Antarctica, ATCM Resolution 2 (2004), and applicable domestic statutes and regulations.

1. Waste Permit Effective Dates

Since the exact date of the flight will be highly dependent on weather conditions which cannot be predicted this far in advance, it is requested that the Waste Permit be issued to be valid for the time period from January 1, 2014 to March 31, 2014.

2. Aircraft Specifications

- Registration: N788W (USA)
- Owner, operator and pilot: Harry R. Anderson
- Model: Lancair Columbia 300 (ICAO flight plan type : COL3)
- Model year: 2001
- Engine: Teledyne Continental IO-550-N, fuel injected (2000 hours TBO)
- Engine power: 310 bhp at 2700 rpm
- Fixed landing gear
- Empty weight: 2354 lbs (1068 kg)
- Maximum takeoff weight (MTOW): 3400 lbs (1592 kg)
- Length: 25.2 feet (7.68 m)
- Wingspan: 35.8 feet (10.9 m)
- Cruising true airspeed (75% power): 190 kTAS (typically)
- Cruising true airspeed (63% power): 165 kTAS (typically)
- Useable fuel capacity in wing tanks: 98 gallons
- Useable fuel capacity in ferry tank: 60 gallons
- Fuel consumption (at 63% power, 10,000 feet altitude): 11.5 gph (typically)
- TKS™ de-icing system
- The aircraft will be fitted with an portable aethalometer for measuring airborne black carbon densities

3. Air Crew

The pilot and only crew member of the aircraft is Dr. Harry R. Anderson. Dr. Anderson is an experienced pilot with more than 1600 hours of Pilot-in-Command time in a variety of fixed-wing aircraft. He holds a Commercial Pilot certificate for single-engine and multi-engine aircraft with an Instrument rating. He also holds a Private Pilot certificate for single-engine seaplanes.

In 2011 Dr. Anderson completed a solo flight around the world in aircraft N788W, visiting five continents and crossing the equator twice, a total of more than 24,000 nm. A blog describing his round-the-world flight can be found at:

http://blog.travelpod.com/travel-blog/harry4123/1/tpod.html

In February, 2011, Dr. Anderson took a two week Quark Expeditions cruise to the Antarctica Peninsula (the "Crossing the Circle" cruise) aboard the ship Sergey Vavilov. During this cruise Dr. Anderson attended the requisite seminars on proper practices for protecting the flora and fauna of Antarctica, including maintaining appropriate distance while observing wildlife. The Quark cruise included several zodiac landings ashore where these procedures were used.

4. Management of Waste Products and Environmental Impact of this Flight

The flight to King George Island will be done using aircraft N788W, a single-engine piston engine aircraft that uses high octane aviation gasoline (avgas) as fuel. Given the range and fuel consumption of this aircraft, it will be necessary to refuel the plane at King George Island using avgas carried on board the aircraft during the outbound flight from Punta Arenas. The following sections address in detail how waste products that may be generated during this flight will be handled. The refueling procedure is also described in detail along with the plan to mitigate any inadvertent fuel spill that may occur during refueling.

4 a. Waste Management Plan

Three types of waste may be generated during the flight:

- Air emissions from engine exhaust. These emissions are managed by proper engine maintenance. They are disposed of (dispersed) by the natural winds occurring in the flight area.

- Liquid wastes. Amount: less than 2 liters. Liquid waste will be stored inside the aircraft in a bottle designed for the purpose. This waste will be disposed of upon returning to Punta Arenas.

- Solid wastes. Amount: less than 2 kgs. Solid waste will be stored inside the aircraft in a container designed for the purpose. This waste will be disposed of upon returning to Punta Arenas.

- There will be no discharge of liquid or solid wastes, or wastes of any kind, while the aircraft is in flight.

While at King George Island, the existing facilities for human waste disposal will be utilized if possible. Any liquid or solid waste not so disposed of, or garbage, generated during the visit will be stored on the aircraft and taken back to Punta Arenas on the return flight for disposal.

4 b. Refueling Procedure at King George Island

As noted above, while at Lieutenant Rodolfo Marsh Martin Aerodrome (SCRM) on King George Island, it will be necessary to refuel aircraft N788W from a fuel storage container carried aboard the aircraft. The aircraft will carry as cargo a single custom-made rectangular metal drum with 50 gallons of aviation gasoline (avgas). This container will be securely strapped down during the flight. During refueling, fuel will be pumped from the drum into each of the wing tanks using a manual pump and hand nozzle to control fuel flow and shutoff. The metal fuel drum will always remain in its strapped down position in the aircraft. During the refueling, absorbent pads will be placed around the wing tank filler inlet to catch any drips that may occur from the nozzle. In addition, absorbent pads will be placed under the wing to catch any fuel that may drop off the wing toward the ground.

The main environmental hazard during the refueling operation is a minor fuel spill. A spill kit will be on board the aircraft. This commercially-assembled spill kit consists of:

10 - 18" x 24" absorbent pads

2 - 3" x 48" absorbent socks

1 – 18" x 24" x 4" plastic disposal bag

1 – pair of nitrile gloves

1 – pair of goggles

1 – instruction manual

The spill kit will be utilized to prevent, contain and clean up inadvertent spills as needed. Clean-up procedure: For spills on the aircraft wing, the absorbent pads will be placed on the spill area to absorb and pick up the spilled fuel. Similarly, for spills onto the ground, the absorbent pads will be placed on the spill area to absorb the spilled fuel. In addition, the soil where the spill occurred will be picked up and placed in plastic bags. It is not expected that snow or ice will be present at the refueling location, but should fuel spill onto snow or ice, that also will be picked up and placed in plastic bags.

All absorbent pads and other used spill kit material will be packaged in plastic disposal bags and placed inside the aircraft and returned to Punta Arenas for proper disposal. The plastic bags containing any picked-up soil, snow or ice where a spill occurred will also be placed inside the aircraft and returned to Punta Arenas for proper disposal.

The refueling will be done in an area designated for this purpose by the controlling authority at the aerodrome. While refueling, any sources of ignition, in particular, smoking, will be prohibited within 100 feet of the aircraft.

4 c. Impact of Landing and Taking Off from King George Island

The aerodrome at King George Island is used by numerous aircraft for military purposes, for the support and resupply of research activities, and to ferry tourists who visit the island and who board cruise ships visiting other parts of the Antarctica Peninsula. These aircraft are typically large turboprop aircraft, much larger and heavier than aircraft N788W which weighs less than 3400 lbs (1,542 kg) when fully loaded. As such, the impact of the repeated operation of these aircraft on the environment in terms of noise, exhaust pollution, and physical disturbance to the runway surface at the aerodrome are vastly greater than the impact of aircraft N788W. Consequently, the incremental impact of a single landing and takeoff by a light aircraft like N788W is minor, transitory and negligible.

4 d. Additional Procedures to Mitigate Environment Impacts

Before leaving Punta Arenas airport, Dr. Anderson will wash and vacuum clothing to be worn at King George Island. He will vacuum the interior and wash the exterior of aircraft N788W prior to departing Punta Arenas to prevent the translocation of invasive species. The pilot will wear a pair of clean boots with open sole patterns (rubber farm boots) while at King George Island. These boots will be new, out-of-the-box, boots. They are being brought to King George Island for the singular purpose of wearing while walking around on the island. Although new, as a further precaution against contamination, the boots will be cleaned using a Virkon S solution. Virkon S is a broad spectrum disinfectant which is available in powder form so it can be easily carried aboard aircraft N788W. At Punta Arenas the Virkon S will be dissolved in water to prepare a solution of the recommended concentration. That solution, along with a stiff brush, will be used to clean the boots just prior to departing Punta Arenas for King George Island. The same cleaning procedure will be used again on the boots when returning from King George Island to ensure there is no transference from Antarctica back to South America. The used Virkon S solution will be disposed of in Punta Arenas as recommended by the manufacturer.

The expedition will not bring dogs or any other non-native animal or plant species into the Antarctic Treaty Area.

During the visit to King George Island, it is not known whether Dr. Anderson will come into the proximity of local wildlife such as penguins or other bird life, seals or other water mammals, etc. Observing wildlife is not an objective of this expedition. However, if such encounters do inadvertently occur, as noted above Dr. Anderson, during his Quark cruise in 2011, has learned and utilized appropriate techniques to avoid disturbing wildlife.

5. Certification

I certify that, to the best of my knowledge and belief, and based upon due inquiry, the information submitted in the application for a permit is complete and accurate. Any knowing or intentional false statement will subject me to the criminal penalties of 18 U.S.C. 1001.

_____   _____
    Harry R. Anderson, Ph.D., P.E.   Date
        Expedition Leader

Application for Private Aircraft Operation To Antarctic Territory

from Punta Arenas (SCCI) to Teniente R. Marsh Martin Aerodrome (SCRM)
Section 2.1

a. The application is made on September 10, 2013 at Bainbridge Island, Washington, USA

b. The name of the private aircraft owner/ operator: Harry R. Anderson

c. The address of the aircraft owner/operator is:

> Harry R. Anderson, Ph.D.,P.E.
> 250 Eagle Place NE
> Bainbridge Island, WA USA
> Fax: +1 206-780-0344
> Cellphone: +1 541-915-5112

d. The nationality of the private aircraft owner/ operator is: USA

e. The aircraft type is a Lancair Columbia 300 (ICAO type COL3)

f. Aircraft registration mark: N788W

g. Pilot. Name: Harry R. Anderson

> Nationality: USA.
> Licenses: U.S. FAA Commercial pilot license for single engine and multiengine land aircraft (ASEL and AMEL). Instrument rating. Private pilot license for single engine seaplane aircraft (ASES).
> Experience: The pilot has more than 1700 hours of pilot-in-command experience, including a solo around-the-world flight completed in 2011 in aircraft N788W and a flight over the Drake Passage in 2013.

h. Number of crew: 1 (the pilot only). Number of passengers: 0.

i. Purpose of flight: scientific research measuring concentrations of airborne black carbon (BC).

j. Date of Entry into Chile at Iquique: approximately January 27, 2014. Arriving from Guayaquil, Ecuador.
Date of Departure from Chile at Punta Arenas: approximately February 24, 2014. Departing to Rio Gallegos, Argentina

k. Length of stay in Antarctic Territory: 1 day.
Date of flight to Antarctic Territory: Approximately February 3, 2014. The flight date may vary due to weather conditions. It is currently planned to make the outbound flight to SCRM and the return flight to SCCI in the same day.

l. Base of operations in Antarctic Territory: Teniente R. Marsh Martin Aerodrome, Villa Las Estrellas, King George Island

m. Communication Systems: VHF radio, HF radio, satellite phone.

n. Survival equipment: covered life raft for arctic conditions, cold water flight survival suit, life vest, registered 406 MHz personal locator beacon with GPS, signaling equipment, survival provisions.

Aircraft N788W is now equipped with a TKS™ "weeping wing" de-icing system.

o. Insurance: This is a private aircraft operation. The aircraft and pilot carry liability insurance and insurance to pay for search and rescue operations.

p. Schedule of activities in the Antarctic Territory: measurements of black carbon concentrations and photography while airborne. Re-fueling aircraft while at King George Island. Aviation gasoline (avgas) for re-fueling will be carried as cargo on board the outbound flight.

q. Signature of Applicant:

_____   _____

Harry R. Anderson, Ph.D., P.E.   Date
Expedition Leader

www.ingramcontent.com/pod-product-compliance
Lightning Source LLC
Chambersburg PA
CBHW040327300426
44113CB00020B/2675